THE ASCENT OF GEORGE WASHINGTON

BY THE SAME AUTHOR

Almost a Miracle: The American Victory in the War of Independence

A Leap in the Dark: The Struggle to Create the American Republic

*Setting the World Ablaze: Washington, Adams, Jefferson, and
the American Revolution*

The First of Men: A Life of George Washington

Adams vs. Jefferson: The Tumultuous Election of 1800

John Adams: A Life

Struggle for a Continent: The Wars of Early America

The Loyalist Mind: Joseph Galloway and the American Revolution

THE ASCENT OF GEORGE WASHINGTON

The Hidden Political Genius
of an American Icon

JOHN FERLING

BLOOMSBURY PRESS

New York   Berlin   London

Copyright © 2009 by John Ferling

All rights reserved. No part of this book may be used or reproduced
in any manner whatsoever without written permission from the publisher
except in the case of brief quotations embodied in critical articles or reviews.
For information address Bloomsbury Press, 175 Fifth Avenue, New York, NY 10010.

Published by Bloomsbury Press, New York

All papers used by Bloomsbury Press are natural, recyclable products
made from wood grown in well-managed forests. The manufacturing processes
conform to the environmental regulations of the country of origin.

Map credits: "Washington's Virginia and Western Country" by
Gary Antonetti/Ortelius Design; all others by kind permission of
Oxford University Press.

LIBRARY OF CONGRESS CATALOGING-IN-PUBLICATION DATA

Ferling, John E.
The ascent of George Washington : the hidden political genius of an American icon /
John Ferling.—1st U.S. ed.
p.   cm.
Includes bibliographical references.
ISBN-10: 1-59691-465-3 (alk. paper hardcover)
ISBN-13: 978-1-59691-465-0 (alk. paper hardcover)
1. Washington, George, 1732–1799.   2. Presidents—United States—Biography.
3. Generals—United States—Biography.   4. United States—Army—Biography.
5. United States—Politics and government—1783–1809.   I. Title.

E312.F46   2009
973.4'1092—dc22
[B]
2008051215

First published by Bloomsbury Press in 2009
This paperback edition published in 2010

Paperback ISBN: 978-1-60819-095-9

1 3 5 7 9 10 8 6 4 2

Typeset by Westchester Book Group
Printed in the United States of America by Worldcolor Fairfield

For Carol, who has always supported and encouraged my work

CONTENTS

Maps

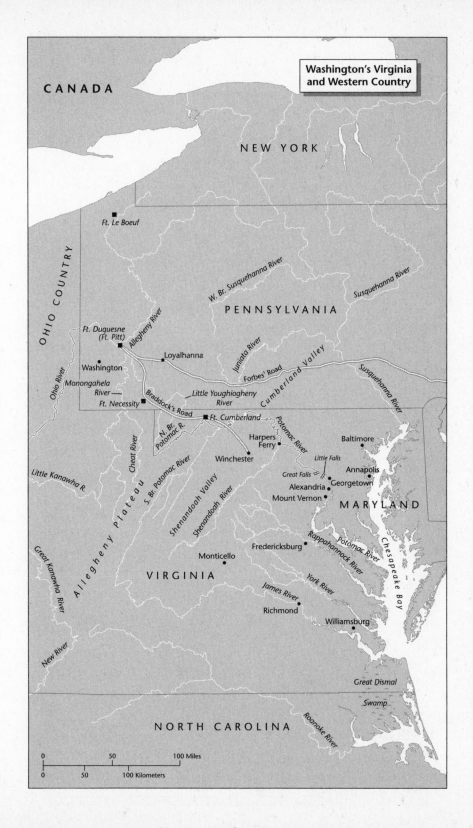

Washington's Virginia and Western Country

CANADA

NEW YORK

OHIO COUNTRY

Ft. Le Boeuf

PENNSYLVANIA

W. Br. Susquehanna River

Susquehanna River

Allegheny River

Ft. Duquesne
(Ft. Pitt)

Loyalhanna

Juniata River

Forbes' Road

Cumberland Valley

Susquehanna River

Washington

Ohio River

Monongahela
River

Little Youghiogheny
River

Braddock's Road

Ft. Necessity

N. Br.
Potomac R.

Ft. Cumberland

Cheat River

Allegheny Plateau

S. Br. Potomac River

Little Kanawha R.

Harpers
Ferry

Potomac River

Baltimore

Winchester

Little Falls

Annapolis

Great Falls

Georgetown

Alexandria

Mount Vernon

MARYLAND

Shenandoah Valley

Shenandoah River

Great Kanawha River

Fredericksburg

Rappahannock River

Potomac River

Chesapeake Bay

Monticello

VIRGINIA

York River

New River

James River

Richmond

Williamsburg

Great Dismal

Swamp

NORTH CAROLINA

Roanoke River

0   50   100 Miles

0   50   100 Kilometers

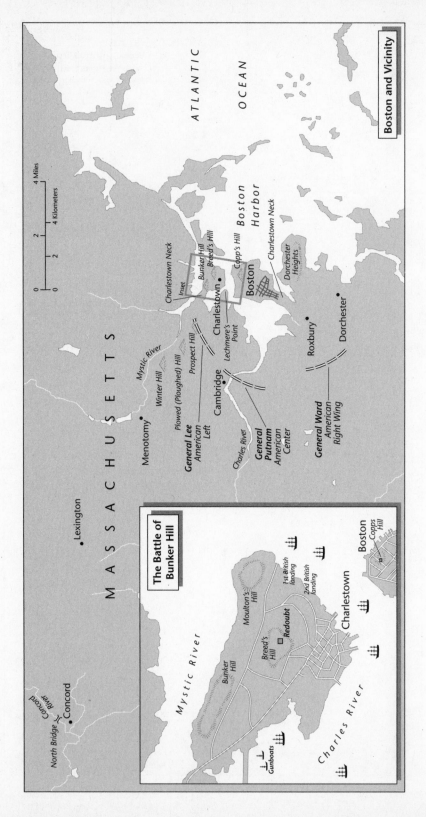

Boston and Vicinity

ATLANTIC OCEAN

MASSACHUSETTS

Lexington

Menotomy

Mystic River

Winter Hill

Plowed (Ploughed) Hill

Prospect Hill

General Lee
American Left

Cambridge

Charles River

General Putnam
American Center

General Ward
American Right Wing

Roxbury

Dorchester

Charlestown Neck

Inset

Bunker Hill

Breed's Hill

Charlestown

Lechmere's Point

Copp's Hill

Boston Harbor

Boston

Charlestown Neck

Dorchester Heights

0   2   4 Miles
0   2   4 Kilometers

The Battle of Bunker Hill

North Bridge

Concord River

Concord

Mystic River

Bunker Hill

Moulton's Hill

Breed's Hill

Redoubt

1st British landing

2nd British landing

Charlestown

Boston

Copps Hill

Charles River

Gunboats

x

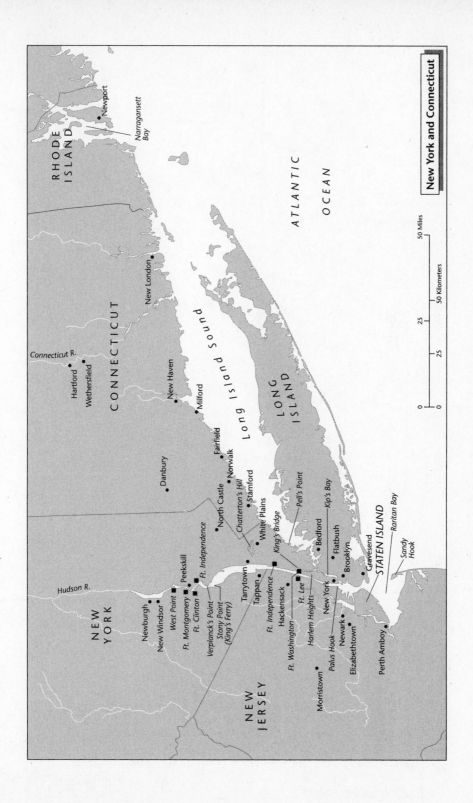

New York and Connecticut

RHODE ISLAND

Newport

Narragansett Bay

CONNECTICUT

Connecticut R.

Hartford
Wethersfield

New London

New Haven

Milford

Danbury

Fairfield

Norwalk

North Castle

Chatterton's Hill

Stamford

White Plains

Long Island Sound

LONG ISLAND

ATLANTIC OCEAN

Pell's Point

Kip's Bay

King's Bridge

Bedford

Flatbush

Brooklyn

Gravesend

STATEN ISLAND

Raritan Bay

Sandy Hook

NEW YORK

Hudson R.

Newburgh

New Windsor

West Point

Ft. Montgomery

Ft. Clinton

Peekskill

Ft. Independence

Verplanck's Point

Stony Point
(King's Ferry)

Tarrytown

Tappan

Ft. Independence

Hackensack

Ft. Lee

New York

Ft. Washington

Harlem Heights

Palus Hook

Newark

Elizabethtown

Perth Amboy

Morristown

NEW JERSEY

50 Miles

50 Kilometers

0   25   25   50

xi

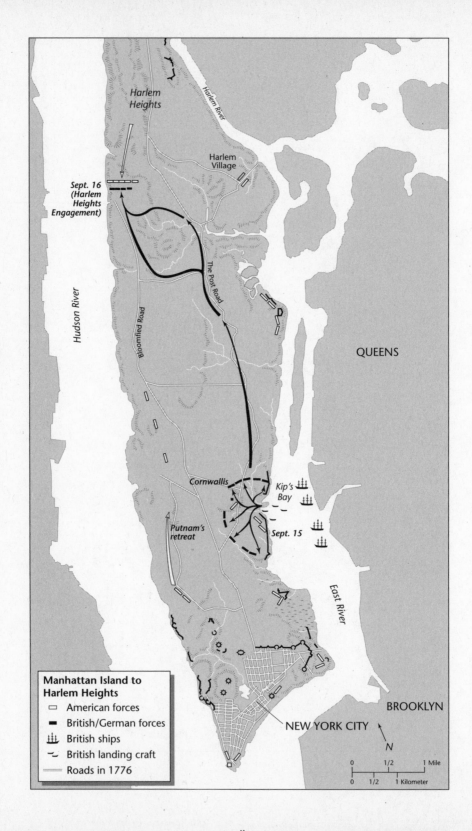

Harlem Heights

Harlem River

Harlem Village

Sept. 16 (Harlem Heights Engagement)

The Post Road

Hudson River

Bloomfied Road

QUEENS

Cornwallis

Kip's Bay

Putnam's retreat

Sept. 15

East River

BROOKLYN

NEW YORK CITY

N

Manhattan Island to Harlem Heights
- American forces
- British/German forces
- British ships
- British landing craft
- Roads in 1776

| 0 | 1/2 | 1 Mile |
| 0 | 1/2 | 1 Kilometer |

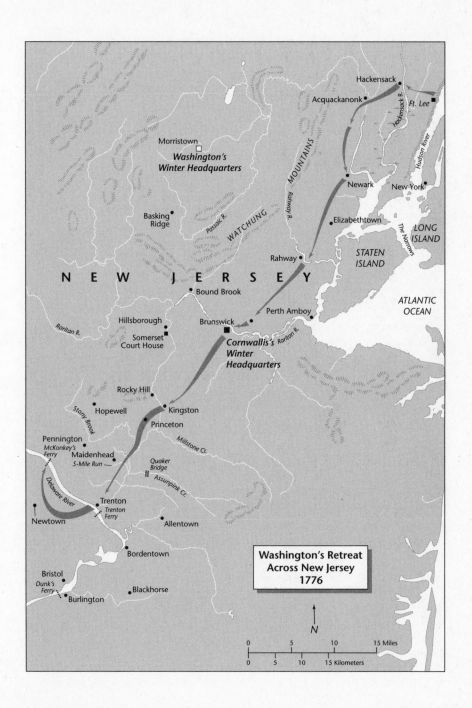

Hackensack

Acquackanonk

Hackensack R.

Ft. Lee

Morristown
**Washington's
Winter Headquarters**

Newark

New York

Rahway R.

WATCHUNG

MOUNTAINS

Elizabethtown

Passaic R.

Basking
Ridge

N E W   J E R S E Y

Rahway

STATEN
ISLAND

LONG
ISLAND

Hudson River

The Narrows

Bound Brook

Perth Amboy

ATLANTIC
OCEAN

Raritan R.

Hillsborough

Brunswick

Raritan R.

Somerset
Court House

**Cornwallis's
Winter
Headquarters**

Rocky Hill

Stony Brook

Hopewell

Kingston

Princeton

Pennington

Milstone Cr.

McKonkey's
Ferry

Maidenhead

Quaker
Bridge

5-Mile Run

Assunpink Cr.

Delaware River

Trenton
*Trenton
Ferry*

Newtown

Allentown

Bordentown

Bristol
*Dunk's
Ferry*

Blackhorse

Burlington

**Washington's Retreat
Across New Jersey
1776**

N

0		5		10		15 Miles
0	5	10		15 Kilometers		

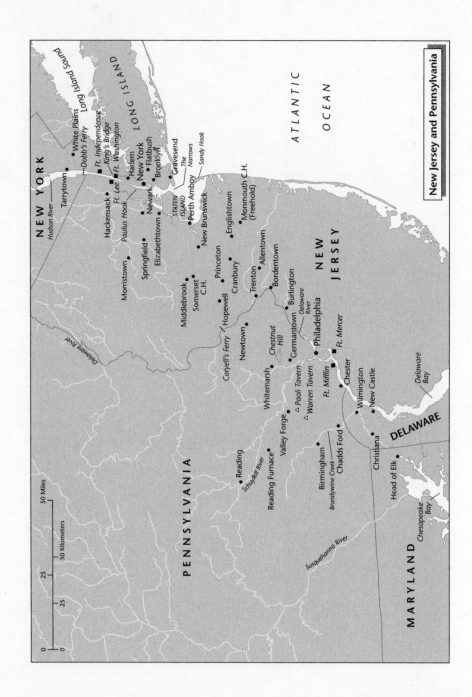

New Jersey and Pennsylvania

NEW YORK

ATLANTIC OCEAN

LONG ISLAND

Long Island Sound

Hudson River

Tarrytown
White Plains
Dobb's Ferry
Ft. Independence
King's Bridge
Ft. Washington
Harlem
New York
Flatbush
Brooklyn
Gravesend
The Narrows
Sandy Hook

Hackensack
Ft. Lee
Paullus Hook
Newark
STATEN ISLAND
Perth Amboy

Morristown
Springfield
Elizabethtown
New Brunswick
Englishtown
Monmouth C.H. (Freehold)

Delaware River

Middlebrook
Somerset C.H.
Princeton
Cranbury
Allentown
Trenton
Bordentown

Hopewell
Coryell's Ferry
Newtown
Burlington
Germantown
Delaware River

NEW JERSEY

Philadelphia
Ft. Mercer

Whitemarsh
Chestnut Hill
△ Paoli Tavern
△ Warren Tavern
Ft. Mifflin
Chester
Wilmington
New Castle
Delaware Bay

Valley Forge

Reading
Schuylkill River
Reading Furnace
Birmingham
Brandywine Creek
Chadds Ford
Christiana
DELAWARE

PENNSYLVANIA

Head of Elk
Chesapeake Bay

Susquehanna River

MARYLAND

50 Miles
50 Kilometers
25
25
0
0

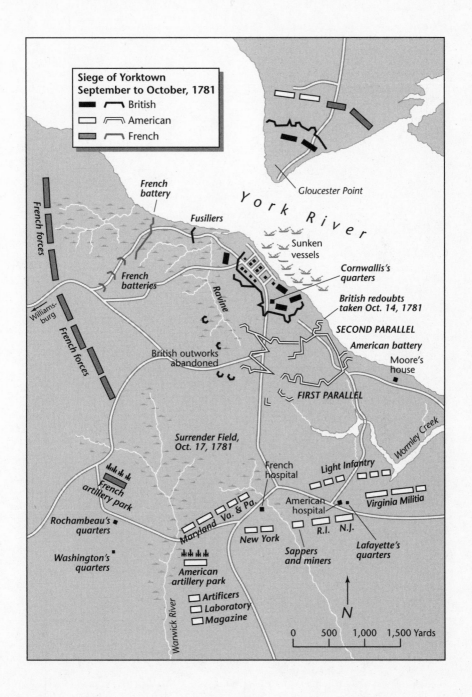

Siege of Yorktown
September to October, 1781

British
American
French

Gloucester Point

York River

French
battery

Fusiliers

Sunken
vessels

Cornwallis's
quarters

French
batteries

Ravine

British redoubts
taken Oct. 14, 1781

SECOND PARALLEL

American battery

Williams-
burg

French forces

British outworks
abandoned

Moore's
house

FIRST PARALLEL

French forces

Wormley Creek

Surrender Field,
Oct. 17, 1781

French
hospital

Light Infantry

French
artillery park

American
hospital

Virginia Militia

Rochambeau's
quarters

Maryland

Va. & Pa.

R.I.

N.J.

Lafayette's
quarters

New York

Washington's
quarters

American
artillery park

Sappers
and miners

Warwick River

Artificers
Laboratory
Magazine

N

0   500   1,000   1,500 Yards

PREFACE

There were differences in the politics of eighteenth-century America and those of today, but not as many as might be thought. Political practices were strikingly modern. Elections determined who held most offices. Candidates courted the voters much as they do today, albeit not with television or the Web. Once national politics emerged, with the Continental Congress in 1774, politicians then, as today, represented their colony, district, or state. Woe to any officeholder who betrayed the powerful interests that dominated the state that had elected him. Political parties had come into existence by the early 1790s. By then, too, politicians went after their political adversaries with a predatory gusto that was at least as savage as exists today, charging them with hypocrisy, branding them as dangerous radicals, fixating on their war record (or lack thereof), searching for hints of personal scandal—something like an extramarital affair or financial malfeasance—that might prove to be politically ruinous.

Even the broad contours of that time bore a resemblance to what has been experienced by recent generations of Americans. A great decisive war—the French and Indian War in their age, World War II in modern America—set the stage for a period of epic change and reform (the American Revolution after 1776, the civil rights revolution and the counterculture and feminist movements in the 1960s and 1970s), followed by a long, pivotal struggle between progressives and conservatives to determine how much of the earlier sweeping change would endure. In the first party battles of the new American Republic, the most conservative faction embraced a military hero—something conservatives would do from time to time with other soldiers, as well as with famous athletes and movie stars—not only claiming him as their own, but portraying him as interested only in the national welfare. In short, their hero was characterized as above politics, a slant that would often be repeated in American political history, though never again so successfully.

In our time no individual played an important role in each of the three stages, but, incredibly, in the second half of the eighteenth century, George Washington occupied a crucial post during every towering event. He led Virginia's army in the French and Indian War, commanded the Continental army in the Revolutionary War, presided over the Constitutional Convention, and served two terms as president beginning in 1789.

Most of Washington's contemporaries thought him uniquely above politics, or "disinterested," as they put it, meaning that he made decisions judiciously, letting the chips fall where they may without regard to sectional, provincial, or personal interest. Alone among the nation's public officials, Washington was thought to see things only through the prism of what was best for the United States. They additionally believed that Washington did nothing to advance his reputation.

Could this be true? Could Washington have been so different from others of his time? At the time of his death in 1799, Washington had been a public official for much of the preceding fifty years. Had he been above politics throughout his public life? Was he ever above politics? What, if anything, did Washington do to elevate his standing in the eyes of his countrymen?

During the last twenty years of his public life—from the Valley Forge winter in 1778 onward—Washington was regarded as an Olympian figure and was revered by many. Washington's contemporaries often spoke of him as godlike, a view fostered by such nineteenth-century hagiographers as Parson Weems and John Marshall. No other Founder was thought of in that manner—nor were any of Washington's successors. Even today, Washington stands apart from most of America's cherished heroes. His image adorns our currency and military medals. Upward of a million people annually visit his home, Mount Vernon, a larger number than trek to the residence of any other American leader. At Mount Vernon's gift shop and elsewhere, shoppers can find china embellished with the image of a mythical Washington praying in the snow at Valley Forge, and children's books abound that depict him as flawless. Television channel surfers occasionally come across adulatory made-for-television movies that portray Washington as heroic and his contemporary critics as menaces to civilization. Washington may not be regarded as godlike today, but his popular image remains that of a demigod.

Serious scholars have long since moved past hagiography, and for more than a century they have sought to discover the unvarnished Washington. Biographers have rummaged through the broad features of his life, while other historians have dug into his nooks and crannies, exploring Washington as a soldier, slave owner, parent and husband, entrepreneur, and president. Nothing has attracted more attention than Washington's character.

On the other hand, nothing about Washington has attracted less attention than his political activities. Though Washington served in the Virginia assembly for nearly twenty years before the War of Independence, his legislative career has been passed over with insufficient scrutiny. Save for the so-called Conway Cabal in 1778 and the Newburgh Affair in 1783, General Washington's wartime political activities have gone largely unnoticed.

As for his presidency, Washington—even in the hands of the best historians—has by and large continued to be seen as above politics, much as he was thought to have been at the time of his death. James Thomas Flexner, perhaps Washington's foremost biographer, portrayed the first president as devoid of any partisan agenda. Washington, Flexner wrote in the 1970s, consciously sought a midway point between partisan extremes, as he saw himself as "the keystone of an arch, holding all upright and in equilibrium."[1] Douglas Southall Freeman, in an encyclopedic seven-volume biography that appeared in the 1940s and 1950s, had already taken a similar stance. Freeman portrayed President Washington as the great mediator, striving to stay above politics by reducing personal animosities between the right-wing Alexander Hamilton and the left-wing Thomas Jefferson in order "to prevent damage to the new government."[2]

Freeman's and Flexner's themes of Washington's disinterestedness were echoed by their contemporary, John Miller. In an influential political history of the 1790s, Miller, a distinguished historian, wrote that Washington, believing that "Jefferson and Hamilton had the same end in view," tried "to mark out a line by which both could walk in peace and understanding" without "endanger[ing] the existence of the Federal government."[3] Stanley Elkins and Eric McKitrick, who a couple of generations later coauthored their own notable history of the politics of the Federalist-dominated 1790s, had another take. Washington, they concluded, was pre-modern in his thinking. Abhorring partisanship as "destructive," he instead "worked out for himself" a role of standing "resolutely above all party and faction."[4]

Some scholars have detected partisanship in Washington's actions but have appeared to be unwilling to acknowledge it. Joseph Charles, the author of an influential study on the origin of political parties in the United States, fancifully suggested that Washington "is to be blamed not for aligning himself with a party, but for not knowing that he had done so."[5] Richard Hofstadter, one of the most important historians of the last century, attributed Washington's partisanship to "intellectual confusion." Washington really did not want to side with either the Federalist Party or the Republican Party, Hofstadter wrote; the president wished only to restore "that spirit of happy unanimity which had been manifested in his own [unanimous] election."[6] Marcus Cunliffe, who a half century ago penned an authoritative assessment of Washington the man and leader, surmised that by the time of his presidency, Washington's private self had vanished and he had come to see himself as the real-life Cincinnatus, the "hero and emblem" who may have acted in a partisan manner but who sincerely believed that his every action was taken only in the national interest.[7] In his wonderful book on presidential courage, historian Michael Beschloss wrote that "Washington's dream" was "that America might forever be governed by natural consensus—no parties, no factions, just patriots," and that he did all within his power to make his dream a reality.[8] Peter Henriques, a friend of mine who may know more about Washington than any scholar, has written that the first president's only goals were "to bind America together" and "to secure the union."[9] Jay Winik, in a recent engaging account of the birth of the modern world, portrayed Washington as selflessly acting and thinking "in cosmic terms," making himself into "a sovereign" entity and the very "embodiment of the nation itself."[10] Joseph Ellis, in his important 2004 biography of Washington, contended that Washington forged a "Fabian presidency." Washington tried his best to remain "above the fray," but when he did lean toward the policies of the Federalist Party, he acted cautiously and wisely, seeking to restrain partisanship lest the party's actions would "push federal sovereignty further . . . than public opinion allowed.[11]

These writers are excellent historians who have written good history. This book, however, takes issue with their portrayal of Washington as nonpolitical and steadfastly seeking to stay above politics. I believe that George Washington was highly political. He was confronted with politics and politicians when, as a young man, he commanded Virginia's army in the French and Indian War. To be sure, he was political during the more than fifteen years that he sat in Virginia's House of Burgesses before the American Revolution. Some choices that he made as commander of the Continental army were political in nature. General Washington shrewdly employed his political dexterity to successfully manage relations with a fractious, meddlesome Continental Congress and irascible state officials. A master of political infighting, he outmaneuvered rival generals and defused dissent from those below him. Washington was decidedly partisan in the movement to write and ratify the Constitution. He came to the presidency with a political agenda in mind. Yes, Washington claimed—often and loudly—that he was not a politician, but not everything that he said should be taken at face value. He was a highly political individual, one of the very best politicians in American history. George Washington was so good at politics that he alone of all of America's public officials in the past two centuries succeeded in convincing others that he was not a politician.

That Washington was not disinterested does not detract from his standing. In some ways, it should enhance his reputation. Rather than being seen as someone who did not know what he was doing or who was filled with self-delusions, the Washington in this book repeatedly comes to a reasoned judgment on complex issues and forges a strategy for their realization.

One other thing. An exploration of Washington's life in politics, which heretofore has escaped penetrating scrutiny, will, I believe, open a new window through which he can be seen. It will afford a more rounded picture of Washington, a real-life person with real political interests, passions, agendas, and attachments, a man whose stature was elevated to the heights by conscious political decisions, and a man who, with unparalleled canniness, pursued politics to further his interests.

As a scholar, I first encountered Washington early in my career when writing a book about early American warfare. His name kept cropping up. Wanting to know more about him, I began a biography, and in 1988 *The First of Men: A Life of George Washington* appeared. Thereafter, I turned to other things, including a biography of John Adams and a history of America's colonial wars. But after a dozen years or so, I came back to Washington. Intrigued by books on comparative history, I decided to explore three Founders—Washington, John Adams, and Thomas Jefferson—by contrasting their behavior in the American Revolution. While writing that book, *Setting the World Ablaze* (2000), I was surprised to discover that by looking at Washington in a comparative manner, I was led to ask questions about him that I had not asked in the biography.

Now I have come back to George Washington once again, this time to examine him as a politician, and I believe, as with my earlier comparative history, that writing this book has led me to ask new questions that have resulted in fresh insights.

This book is not a biography. It has little to say about Washington's relationship with his wife and stepchildren, his amusements, or the conditions faced by his slaves, to name just a few things that a biographer would wish to explore. I have focused specifically on matters that somehow or other involved Washington in political activities. And as character is important in how public officials are seen, and in the decisions they make, this book additionally seeks to understand what shaped and drove Washington and how his character influenced his political choices.

A book entitled *The Ascent of George Washington* of course also looks into Washington's rise, what he did—and what was done for him, by whom, and for what reasons—to facilitate his ascent into America's pantheon of heroes.

A word about technique. Throughout the book I have used the spelling that appears in the primary sources, doing so from a belief that this will afford readers a better look at the author of the documents and provide some flavor of the times themselves.

I owe a debt of gratitude to many people who helped with the writing and completion of this book. I am especially indebted to two good friends, Matt deLesdernier and Jim Sefcik, who read the manuscript and offered thoughtful suggestions and helpful criticism. Robert Previdi deserves some of the credit, or blame, for the book, as he suggested back in 2005 that I consider writing a book on Washington's life in politics. Many people responded to questions that I raised as the book proceeded. Philander Chase, Edward Lengel, Jennifer Wallach, Nancy Hayward, Edith Gelles, Arthur Lefkowitz, Beth Prindle, and John Folmar dropped what they were doing to search out answers to my questions. The book would not have been possible without the assistance of Angela Mehaffy, director of interlibrary loan at the Irvine Sullivan Ingram Library at the University of West Georgia, who cheerfully ordered tons of books for me. I want to thank Sona Vogel, a wonderful copy editor; Peter Beatty, who answered many questions; my agent, Geri Thoma; and my editor, Peter Ginna, without whom this book may never have come into being.

John Ferling
November 21, 2008

INTRODUCTION

THE FOUNDING FATHER WHO WIELDED POWER WITHOUT AMBITION

I T WAS THE DAY after Christmas, but there were no signs of a holiday in
Philadelphia. December 26, 1799, had been set aside in the city as the
day for a mock funeral to honor George Washington, who had passed away
at Mount Vernon twelve days earlier. Congress had called for the funeral.
It additionally asked that all Americans wear black armbands for the next
thirty days and resolved to build a marble monument to Washington in the
Federal City on the Potomac River, a site that many Americans were already calling "Washington." On this day of mourning, the front doors at
the President's House and Congress Hall were draped in black, as were businesses and churches and even ships in Philadelphia's harbor.

Public ceremonies customarily follow the demise of the famous. Sometimes the displays of grief are more ritualistic than authentic, but Washington's death indisputably cast a mournful spell across the new American
nation. As the first lady, Abigail Adams, noted, a "universal melancholy has
pervaded all classes." When President John Adams passed on the news of
Washington's demise to the nation, he wrote in a heartfelt announcement
that the American Republic had lost its "most esteemed, beloved, admired
citizen."[1]

December 26 dawned gray and cold in Philadelphia, adding to the gloom
of the business at hand. Though Washington had been buried at Mount
Vernon on December 18, it was fitting for Philadelphia to host a grand

memorial service. Not only was it still the nation's capital, but it was where Washington had spent nearly 10 percent of his life. He had served in the Continental Congress in Philadelphia in 1774 and 1775, and on several occasions during the long War of Independence he had returned for consultation with Congress. Twice during the war, he had ridden at the head of the Continental army as it paraded through the streets of the city, first in 1777 as he prepared to defend Philadelphia against the British army and again in 1781 en route to Yorktown, Virginia, and the climactic battle of the war. Washington had returned for four months in 1787 to preside over the Constitutional Convention, and he came back in 1790 as president of the United States.

Philadelphians awakened to artillery fire on this solemn day. All through the morning, at thirty-minute intervals, sixteen cannons, one for each state, boomed out homage to Washington. By late morning, some ten thousand people, many dressed in black or festooned with sable armbands, sashes, or plumes in their hats, stood silently on the streets along the announced funeral route. At noon, as bells tolled in several churches and soldiers fired minute guns, the procession stepped off from Congress Hall. A trumpeter on horseback led the way, followed by cavalry and infantry units marching to the doleful cadence of muffled drums. Next came a spirited riderless horse, white like Washington's familiar parade mount, its hoofs reverberating loudly on Philadelphia's cobblestone streets. It sported black trimming, including black and white feathers on its head. Fabric adorned with the image of the American eagle hung round the horse's massive chest. An empty saddle was strapped to its back and reverse boots were in the stirrups. General Alexander Hamilton, the commander of the Provisional army, and his staff followed, riding on horseback ahead of the pallbearers who carried the empty, flag-draped casket. After the coffin came the cabinet, members of Congress and the Supreme Court, and several others who had served under Washington in important posts. Local officials brought up the rear. President and Mrs. Adams, who did not march, waited at the church for the procession to arrive.

The procession came south on Fifth Street, turned onto Walnut, then moved slowly north on Fourth until it reached the German Lutheran Church, chosen for this occasion not because Washington had been Lutheran—he had usually worshipped in an Episcopalian church—but because it was the largest church in the city, capable of holding up to four thousand people, as it would on this day.[2] It was dark in the cavernous nave. Small candles, the only illumination, cast faint light, causing spectral shadows to dance on the walls.

The service was not brief. It lasted more than four hours, until deep into the somber afternoon. There was music and a long sermon delivered by an Episcopalian bishop, and numerous eulogies were interspersed throughout. Whatever the bishop said was forgotten almost as soon as he finished. Save for one eulogy, the same was true of all the obsequies pronounced that day. Only the eulogy of Henry Lee was remembered. A Virginia congressman, Lee had earlier served as a cavalry officer in the Revolutionary War and had come to be widely known as "Light Horse Harry." Lee had seen an inordinate amount of combat in the late war and had won a reputation as one of America's most daring soldiers. Following the war, he had written a history of the southern campaigns, of which he had been a part. His history did not make for scintillating reading. But he was a better orator than writer; he was chosen to speak for that reason—and because, like most of the other eulogists, he was a staunch member of the Federalist Party, which controlled Congress and with which Washington, who had postured as a nonpartisan, had habitually sided.

Lee's eulogy soon appeared in nearly every newspaper in the country and was available in twenty separate pamphlets.[3] Like those of most public speakers of the day, Lee's oratory was speckled with flowery bombast. There were lines such as "Methinks I . . . hear falling from his [Washington's] venerable lips" the admonition to "Be American, in thought, word, and deed." Lee enumerated Washington's many virtues, including "his clear and penetrating mind, a strong and sound judgment, calmness and temper for deliberation, with invincible firmness and perseverance," and above all his "dignified and commanding" presence. It was as if heaven had fashioned Washington and given him to America. Without General Washington, Lee said, the war could not have been won. With President Washington, the nation had been saved from a potentially disastrous foreign war and internal discord had been quelled.

Lee's oration lasted nearly twenty-five minutes, and from it came a single line that stood out—that, in fact, would be remembered above all the thousands of ringing observations made in the tumult of eulogies. In resounding tones, Lee declared that George Washington had been "first in war—first in peace—and first in the hearts of his countrymen."

To that enduring thought, Lee added another idea, one that would appear in virtually every funeral oration given for the late Founder. Washington, Lee said, had always served and acted in a selfless manner. His intentions and his every action had sprung solely "from obedience to his country's will."[4]

THE CEREMONY IN PHILADELPHIA was not the only memorial service for Washington. Soon after the news arrived of Washington's passing, rites were observed in every major American city and in many small towns. Congress proclaimed February 22, Washington's birthday, a day of national mourning, and memorial services were conducted on that day at many sites, including halls, muster grounds where militia companies assembled, and Masonic temples, as Washington had been a member of the Masonic lodge in Alexandria, Virginia. A ceremony in New York City was held in a theater. The stage scene featured a tomb, a portrait of Washington swathed by a sword and shield, flags, an American eagle that wept tears of blood, a pyramid, and sixteen black banners, each inscribed in gold with the name of a state. Soon after the curtain rose, an actor appeared and read a long poem honoring Washington.

Normally, however, the pieties were offered by public officeholders, lawyers, soldiers, and clergymen, some of whom, realizing they were exalting a mortal, were decidedly uncomfortable, fretful that God might visit His wrath on America for such idolatry. No one will ever know how many eulogies were finally delivered for Washington, but 346 were printed and have survived.[5]

Common themes appeared in these eulogies. Washington's "first victory was over himself," as he had overcome his lack of formal education through a zeal for personal improvement. He had been endowed by nature with attributes that enabled him to "over-awe" others, even to cause educated men to "sink unnerved" and "tremble" in his presence. His exemplary qualities included what one orator labeled "masculine features": rationalism, common sense, industry, and honesty. When called on to make an important decision, Washington had listened to advice, weighed the options, and made his choice only after careful deliberation. Not even the most gifted men were the equal of Washington, countless eulogists said. "In him," one speaker asserted, "all the qualities which constitute the excellence of man . . . were almost miraculously united and reconciled." Washington, it was often said, had been prudent without being timid, cautious but lion-hearted. Fear never vanquished courage in this man. But what made Washington so imposing, and so successful, according to many eulogists, was his ability to keep his passions in check. His self-control permitted his other virtues to flourish, for naturally dangerous inclinations were always "obedient to his stronger mind." This quality, they said, had set Washington apart from all the great heroes of other times and other societies. Nearly every eulogist mentioned that Washington not only had never abused the power vested in him, he had surrendered power at the conclusion of the Revolutionary War and again after two terms as president. Washington, many said, had been "incorruptible." So extraordinary was Washington that some insisted he had been lent to America by God, and several eulogists declared him to be the American Moses—the man who saved his countrymen from foreign "bondage," leading them "thro' seas of blood" to liberty. Washington had made "a nation great, independent and happy."[6]

But once these myriad virtues had been cataloged, nearly every eulogist agreed that Washington had displayed a further quality, a trait that superseded all others, the unassailable attribute that had set him apart from all men and ultimately made him a great man. A patriot with a "truly paternal" love for his country, Washington had always acted from "disinterestedness." "This was greatness! This was patriotism indeed," one orator declared. Many proclaimed that "power . . . had no charm for him," that "personal aggrandizement" was never "his object" when he held public office. He took on authority only when his countrymen asked him to do so, and he exercised power only to secure the "happiness of mankind." Always, his service was that of a patriot answering the call to duty. Said one eulogist: "He was a MAN, the best friend of man, and everything wearing the form or feature of humanity, must feel a pride in being called his kinsman," for Washington had wielded "power without ambition."[7]

The consensus of the speakers shone with the clarity of crystal. Washington's "scattered virtues . . . shine[d] in separate stars" that "shall never be again collected in one glorious constellation."[8] Never again would there be an equal of Washington. Someday, perhaps, someone would emerge who was as wise and brave, but it was not likely that America would ever again find a leader who exhibited all the wonderful qualities that Washington had possessed and who also was, like the country's Founding Father, a patriot devoid of personal ambition.

THIS WAS NOT WHERE THE FABRICATION of the fable of George Washington began. Mythmaking about Washington had begun in the depths of despair during the Revolutionary War and had gained momentum in the tremulous years that followed, as the very existence of the young American Republic hung in the balance.

The real Washington burned with ambition: ambition for his country, to be sure, but also for renown, power, wealth, and success. That he was able to fulfill these ambitions in commanding the Continental army through a long, grueling revolutionary war, and then in steadying the new nation as it struggled to stand on its feet, was perhaps the sign of George Washington's greatness.

What can be seen in Washington with great clarity is that his overweening ambition was visible from an early age.

PART ONE

RISE FROM OBSCURITY

1

Soldier for Virginia:
An Introduction to Politics

Like Terry Malloy, the pug in the movie *On the Waterfront* who wanted to be somebody, young George Washington wanted to go places, to be known, to win acclaim. At his birth in 1732, George's prospects were poor. He was a product of his father's second marriage. The sons from the first marriage, George's half-brothers, had been provided a formal education, including study abroad. They also received a bountiful inheritance when their father, Augustine Washington, died in 1743. But Augustine's demise appeared to stop George's ascent before it began. There was no money for continuing George's formal education, much less for sending him to England to complete his schooling, and his inheritance was meager. George received ten slaves and Ferry Farm, a worn-out tract across the Rappahannock River from Fredericksburg, Virginia.[1] With that bequest he might become an important figure in King George County, though no one in the broader world would know him. But from an early age, George Washington wanted more. He wanted to stand apart from others. He wanted to be seen as a man of substance.

George said almost nothing about his father, mentioning him in only three passing references in thousands of pages of correspondence.[2] Augustine had accumulated a small fortune as a tobacco planter, land speculator, and proprietor of an iron forge, and he was a prominent figure in northern Virginia, where he held several local offices. Ambitious young males usually aspire to surpass the accomplishments of their fathers, and that appears to have been true of George. Yet it was not Augustine who was George's role model. It was Lawrence Washington, an older brother from their father's first marriage.

Fourteen years older than George, Lawrence had studied in England. After returning home, he enlisted as an officer in a colonial army raised to fight alongside British regulars in a war with Spain, the oddly named War of Jenkins' Ear that erupted in 1739. Lawrence was sent to the Caribbean, then to South America, where he experienced combat. The war was a bloodbath for the American troops, and Lawrence was fortunate to survive and return home. Worldly, educated, well-to-do, dashing in his resplendent uniform, and deferred to as a hero by the most influential men and captivating women in Virginia, Lawrence cut an impressive figure. His stature increased when he was appointed adjutant general of Virginia, a post that made him the foremost soldier in the province. Soon, he was elected to the House of Burgesses, Virginia's assembly, a feat never realized by Augustine. The crowning touch came in 1743. Lawrence married into the Fairfax family, which claimed title to six million acres in Virginia and, needless to say, was the most prominent clan in the Northern Neck, the area around the Rappahannock and Potomac rivers. Lawrence and his bride took up residence on a lush green rolling estate overlooking the Potomac River. Having inherited the property from his father, Lawrence named his country farmhouse in honor of a British officer under whom he had recently served. He called it Mount Vernon.[3]

When George was just entering adolescence, Lawrence issued him a standing invitation to visit Mount Vernon. George came as often as his mother would permit him to make the thirty-five-mile trek. At Mount Vernon, as well as at Belvoir, the Fairfaxes' neighboring estate only seven miles away, George discovered a world that he had never known. Although Mount Vernon may not have been larger than Ferry Farm, it must have been more elegantly furnished. Belvoir, on the other hand, was a grand structure, an architectural showcase gracefully adorned with exquisite molding and rich paneling and decorated tastefully with furniture and accessories from England. But it was not just the homes that excited young George. He was stirred by the people in them. People of influence visited Mount Vernon and Belvoir. Likely for the first time, George found himself in the presence of adults who were well-read and thoughtful, men who were accustomed to wielding power and hobnobbing with those who exercised even greater authority, men and women who comfortably exhibited cultivated manners. All of them, or so it must have seemed, were wealthy and enjoyed an opulent lifestyle, and all venerated Lawrence, who wore his splendid uniform on special occasions.

Adolescents have always studied the world about them and dreamed of their future. Young Washington was no exception. Early in his teenage years, Washington not only came to see Lawrence as the embodiment of the most worthy qualities, but knew that he wished to attain the exalted status of those who frequented Mount Vernon and Belvoir. Through observation and self-study, Washington set about doing what he could to put himself on an equal plane with those he admired. In adolescence, he underwent a metamorphosis from a callow youth into a more polished young man who could easily and comfortably fit into the world of the planter aristocracy and who was able to interact more easily and confidently with those who exercised considerable political power. George quietly watched and listened to others. He gained a knowledge of what to say in certain situations and, probably painfully, discovered that at times the safest course was to say nothing. He learned etiquette as well, some of it from the *Rules of Civility, and Decent Behaviour in Company and Conversation,* a century-old collection of 110 maxims of gentlemanly behavior that he found somewhere and copied in his own hand. The guidebook included useful admonitions about such things as not spitting, picking teeth, biting nails, or scratching one's private parts in public, but it also stressed the importance of controlling one's temper, exhibiting modesty, and acting with civility toward others, especially one's social inferiors.[4]

Guided in all likelihood by Lawrence, and drawn to read what he heard others mention, young Washington was shaped to some degree by his self-study. Based on works that he alluded to from time to time later in life, he appears to have been especially influenced by *Seneca's Morals,* a compilation of essays on ethical behavior by the first-century Roman philosopher, and by *Cato,* Joseph Addison's early-eighteenth-century drama about the Roman republican who had chosen suicide over submission to Caesar. *Seneca's Morals* emphasized that success in part hinged on the virtues of sacrifice, tenacity, courage, restraint, and the control of one's emotions. Addison's *Cato* not only linked success with service and devotion to one's country but taught that one must be deserving of success.[5]

Refined behavior alone would not assure Washington a place in the world of the gentry. Wealth or a formal education would open doors, but Washington possessed neither. The right marriage could lead to upward mobility, and marrying well had been a habit among George's forebears. But with neither money nor an education, the odds were long against young Washington marrying above himself. Two other avenues could facilitate upward mobility. Lawrence's example demonstrated that a man could go places quickly through military service, though in these years peace prevailed and Virginia did not trouble itself with the expense of an unnecessary army. Young Washington was in a hurry, so much so that at age fourteen he sought to enter Great Britain's Royal Navy as a commissioned officer. His mother, Mary Ball Washington, thought it a "very bad Scheme" and refused to assent, which closed that option.[6]

A slower second option was available to a man on the make. Knowledge of land surveying could be acquired through self-study. It was a respectable and often lucrative occupation in Washington's Virginia, as the population was growing and new frontiers were opening steadily. An industrious surveyor could earn twice the income of a thriving tradesman such as a weaver or tanner. Furthermore, as money was scarce, surveyors were frequently paid with land, which in time could be turned into considerable wealth. Though surveying was not a rapid means of ascent, the careers of some surveyors demonstrated how such a vocation could lead to fortune and influence.[7] Young Washington began to study surveying.

Starting around age fifteen, George learned surveying through self-help books, such as *The Young Man's Companion,* and it is probable that he was tutored by some of the surveyors employed by the Fairfaxes. At age sixteen, George first gained hands-on experience when he accompanied a Fairfax surveying team to a job in what then was the dark wilderness along the South Branch of the Potomac River. The very next year, 1749, George was appointed surveyor of Culpepper County. To become a county surveyor, one ordinarily had to endure a lengthy apprenticeship and to have accumulated considerable experience running surveys. Young Washington had neither. Obtaining this post was his introduction to politics, for he could not have gotten the position had not powerful patrons—doubtless Lawrence and the Fairfaxes—pulled the necessary strings. In the forty months that followed, George conducted dozens of surveys. Some were in the Shenandoah Valley, and many were farther west in present West Virginia, where he worked in dense forests and on the steep, slippery hills that hugged the Cacapon and Little Cacapon rivers. Many of his surveys were on land belonging to the Ohio Company. That enterprise, created by some of Virginia's wealthiest men, including the governor, many of the Fairfaxes, and two of George's older half-brothers, claimed to possess five hundred thousand acres in the West. By his twentieth birthday, George had acquired nearly twenty-five hundred acres on the Virginia frontier.[8]

By then, George had lost Lawrence, who died in 1752 of tuberculosis, a great killer of young people at the time. Through Lawrence's will, George inherited property in Fredericksburg. What is more, even as Lawrence lay on his deathbed, George, though devoid of military experience, asked Virginia's governor to appoint him adjutant for the Northern Neck. (With Lawrence's demise imminent, Virginia had abolished the position of adjutant general and broken the province into several military districts.) Once again, young Washington's powerful patrons interceded on his behalf, wielding their political influence. Although he did not receive the position he wanted, George, who was only twenty years of age and had never soldiered, was vested with the rank of major and given command of the southernmost district.[9]

In the seven years since he had first met Lawrence and visited Mount Vernon, Washington had taken giant steps to overcome the obscurity he had feared would be his destiny. His early ascent had not just happened. His diligence and industry were important, and the excellent connections that he enjoyed—and which he no doubt cultivated assiduously—were crucial. But his patrons had not gone to bat for him solely because of family ties and kindness. Young Washington was conspicuous. He was physically imposing. He literally stood out because of his height. In an age when the median height for adult males was five feet seven inches—and the median for European-born males in the colonies was five feet four—Washington soared to six feet three and weighed roughly 175 pounds. An eyewitness described the early twenty-something Washington as having a small, flat waist, broad shoulders, and long, muscular arms. Washington

exhibited the striking look of what we would expect today in a gifted
athlete, and in fact, throughout his life numerous observers remarked on
his agility, usually saying that he walked with a fluid, graceful saunter, and
many described him as without an equal as a horseman, a role that called
for athleticism.

Just as today's extraordinary athletes, for better or worse, gain attention
from their peers and often from doting adults, young Washington was set
apart from other boys and young men his age, though not just in his phys-
icality. Leaving nothing to chance, Washington had sought to cultivate
those qualities that might turn heads. He made an early habit of standing
ramrod straight, dressed well and fashionably, and learned to look others in
the eye when speaking to them. One observer described how he trained
his "blue gray penetrating eyes" on those whom he addressed. No one
ever described his eyes as soft or sensitive. Washington was not handsome,
but he was striking, formidably so. He exuded ruggedness and perhaps a
slightly intimidating air, though there was sufficient polish to his demeanor
that he struck many as at once "engaging" and "composed and dignified."
By his twenty-first birthday, Washington had also gained some experience
in leading others, having already commanded considerably older men who
constituted the surveying parties that he took to the frontier. As Washington
made the transition from adolescence to adulthood, he must have struck his
benefactors as ambitious, intelligent, eager to succeed, and willing to work
hard. All in all, he was a polite young man who displayed charm as well as
strength, tenacity, sturdiness, and vigor. He was what people sometimes refer
to as a born leader, though in reality Washington was not born this way. He
had taken what nature had given him and through observation, self-scrutiny,
thoughtfulness, perseverance, and industry reached a point that others saw
him as a potential leader.[10]

LIKE ALL PEOPLE, Washington was at the mercy of history. Had Virginia
enjoyed a long generation of peace when he came of age, Washington
would not be known today. He would have surveyed and farmed and been
regarded by contemporaries in his neighborhood as successful. But the
chances are good that he would have done nothing that subsequent generations would have remembered. Washington must have prayed that fate
would smile on him, as it had on Lawrence, giving him an opportunity to

do something extraordinary. In 1753, his opportunity arrived. Young Washington made the most of it.

War clouds were gathering for another British–French conflict. Those two great powers had fought three wars in sixty years. Their most recent encounter had ended inconclusively, prompting many to think that the belligerents had made peace in 1748 merely to catch their breath before renewing hostilities. Those bitter rivals were antagonists in Europe, but also in myriad places around the globe where their imperial interests collided. One such place was a region that Virginians called the Ohio Country—what Americans today generally refer to as the Midwest—the fertile, beckoning lands beyond the Appalachians and between the Ohio River and the Great Lakes. France and Great Britain each claimed the territory. Indeed, a portion of those frontier lands supposedly belonged to the Ohio Company, whose director after 1752 was the royal governor of Virginia, Robert Dinwiddie.

When France deployed an army in the Ohio Country in 1750, some in Virginia urged an armed response. Dinwiddie, not eager to be blamed for starting a war, preferred first to consult London. By 1753, he had received his instructions. Crown officials told him that his first step should be to inform the French of Britain's rightful claim to the region and to demand the removal of all French troops. For this, Dinwiddie needed a volunteer to carry his message. The mission would hardly be easy. The emissary would have to cross the mountains in late autumn and winter, entering a foreboding wilderness inhabited by Indians who were mostly enemies of the British. In October, George Washington came to Williamsburg, Virginia's capital, to volunteer.

Some public officials complained that Washington was too inexperienced for such a delicate mission, but Dinwiddie saw qualities that he liked in this young man.[11] Washington was one of the province's adjutants. He had run nearly two hundred surveys, many in the rugged hilly no-man's-land of western Virginia. Age, stamina, and experience in the wilds were on his side. He was closely connected with the Fairfaxes, who were among Dinwiddie's associates in the Ohio Company. Colonel William Fairfax, the owner of Belvoir and a member of the Governor's Council, must have relished the prospect of having someone trustworthy go to the region and scout around a bit, keeping an eye out for prize lands. He put in a word on Washington's behalf with the governor. On the last day of October, with a foretaste of the looming winter already apparent on frosty mornings, Washington was summoned by Dinwiddie to the expansive and elegant Governor's Palace and given the job of carrying the chief executive's letter to the French.

Nor was that all he was to do. Washington's instructions—which were written in part by Colonel Fairfax—directed him to be a diplomat and spy as well. He was to meet with the chief of the Seneca Indians, whom the English called "the Half-King." Tanacharison, as the sachem was known among his own people, was an occasional British ally. Washington was to visit his village, which lay about twenty miles above the head of the Ohio River, and prepare the way for the Seneca to join with the English against the French. Washington was also told that when he reached the headquarters of the French army, he was to gather information on the size of the enemy force and the nature of its fortifications. Off the record, Washington was additionally instructed to reconnoiter the Forks of the Ohio, where the Allegheny and Monongahela rivers met, for a site where Virginia might build a fort. This was crucially important to the Ohio Company, whose charter, issued by the British government, required that it establish such an installation in order actually to gain legal title to the hundreds of thousands of acres it coveted in the Ohio Country. That private and public interests should intersect was as old as government itself, and there is no reason to believe that Washington was surprised to find that such private pecuniary considerations were driving the policies of his colony's government.[12]

Washington was eager to carry out his mission. He departed for the Ohio Country on the very day he was commissioned. Accompanied by a party of six that included a translator, Indian traders, and a gunsmith, Washington trekked across a corner of Maryland and into southern Pennsylvania, pressing onward from one brown ridgeline to another until, three weeks out from Alexandria, Virginia, he reached the Forks of the Ohio. Traveling by foot and canoe, he explored the area carefully. It was snowing hard by the time the party pushed farther north to parley with the Seneca, and even colder when, on the final day of November, the men began the last arduous leg of their journey. Their destination was Fort Le Boeuf, near Lake Erie and almost 150 miles above the Forks of the Ohio. There, Washington hoped to meet with French officials.

A French army patrol intercepted the party of Virginians a few miles below Fort Le Boeuf. Fortunately for Washington, the soldiers were not trigger-happy. Following a brief discussion, they took the ragged band of Englishmen forward, even pausing in a driving snowstorm to permit Major Washington to change from his buckskins and moccasins—attire that he called his "Indian walking Dress"—to the fashionable clothing of an English gentleman. The French at Fort Le Boeuf were gracious hosts. They wined and dined their guests for forty-eight hours and even provided them with food and liquor for the return trip. While the French decided how to respond to Dinwiddie, they left Washington remarkably free to amble about, making mental notes of the fort and its garrison. Finally, on the evening of December 14, the French commander handed Major Washington a sealed letter for Dinwiddie. While he did not know the contents of the communiqué, Washington had heard enough during the otherwise convivial dinner conversations to know that the French regarded the Ohio Country as theirs by right of discovery and exploration. He knew, too, that the French response he was to carry back to Williamsburg almost certainly meant war.

To hasten their return home, the Virginia party divided up. Washington traveled with Christopher Gist, a veteran frontiersman. Their trek back to Virginia consumed barely a third the time of the journey out, though it proved to be infinitely more dangerous. Coming south from the ominously named hamlet of Murdering Town, a gun-toting "French Indian," as Washington later described him, fell in with the two Englishmen. After walking ahead of them for a spell, the warrior suddenly wheeled and attempted to fire his single-shot handgun, but it misfired. Washington and Gist overpowered their assailant. Subsequently, both claimed that they disarmed the would-be killer and "let him go." Gist insisted that he "would have killed him; but the Major would not suffer me to kill him."[13] The following day, Washington, gaunt and exhausted from the rigors of the punishing expedition—Gist described him as "much fatigued" and "very weary"—fell off a raft into the swollen, ice-logged Allegheny River. He might have drowned or died of hypothermia had it not been for Gist. Though suffering frostbite himself, Gist hauled Washington from the swirling water and built a fire so that the major might thaw out.[14] The remainder of the odyssey, though wearying beyond anything Washington had ever endured, was uneventful, and he reached Williamsburg early in 1754, seventy-seven days after he had departed it in October.[15]

After reading the response of the French commander—who had declared that he was not "obliged to obey" Virginia's demand that France quit the Ohio Country—Governor Dinwiddie knew he would ask the assembly to appropriate funds to ready Virginia for an inevitable showdown with the French. Washington's troubling oral report only confirmed the chief executive's belief that war was unavoidable. Major Washington brought word that a French army of fifteen hundred men encroached on Virginia's land in the Ohio Country. Furthermore, Washington told the governor that the French not only had candidly confessed that "it was their absolute Design to take Possession of the Ohio," but "were not slack in their Inventions" to lure the Seneca into an alliance or neutrality. Dinwiddie asked Washington to quickly submit a written narrative of his mission. In less than twenty-four hours, the twenty-one-year-old Washington prepared a remarkably lucid draft, a well-written report that would match in quality, if not surpass, what most college students today are capable of producing. The governor arranged to have the account published in Williamsburg, and in the ensuing months it was reprinted in numerous American newspapers and in London.[16]

Little time passed before Washington was in a position to gain even greater acclaim. Convinced that Virginia must act quickly if it was to beat the French in establishing a fort at the Forks of the Ohio, Dinwiddie summoned one hundred militiamen from two Northern Neck counties and named Major Washington their commander. He was to march the militiamen to the Ohio. It was a shaky plan at best, and it never got off the ground. Not a single militiaman turned out. Seeing the futility of his course, Dinwiddie summoned the House of Burgesses into a special session, and in February 1754, the assembly voted funding for a volunteer army of three hundred that would be called the Virginia Regiment. The lure to induce men to volunteer was the promise of bounty lands following the war.[17] Washington wasted no time contacting influential political figures in Virginia about an appointment to a higher rank than he currently held. Saying that he did not wish to head the army, he asked for the rank of lieutenant colonel, the number two post in the provincial force. His sole motive in wishing to serve, he asserted, was his "sincere love for my country."[18] Washington got what he wanted. Colonel Joshua Fry, a fifty-four-year-old mathematician and cartographer who had studied at Oxford and was no stranger to the frontier, was named colonel of the little army. Washington was promoted to the rank of lieutenant colonel.

While Fry remained in Virginia to tend to recruiting, Washington marched about half of the projected army deep in the western Pennsylvania wilderness. He had only 186 men under him, but he expected Fry to bring the remaining soldiers and all the army's artillery, though he did not know when the reinforcements would arrive. What he did know from intelligence reports was that in April, the French had deployed a one-thousand-man force at the Forks of the Ohio to construct their own fort, an installation they would call Fort Duquesne. Washington also knew that even with the full Virginia army, he would be outnumbered by more than three to one. From a military standpoint, Washington's best option would have been to retreat to Virginia and await substantial reinforcements. But there were potentially undesirable personal and political ramifications to a withdrawal. New to authority, untested, and insecure, Washington was not eager to sound retreat before the enemy had even been spotted. Besides, throughout the spring he had been entreating Tanacharison to round up his Native American allies to accompany the Virginia Regiment. Though he did not know how many Indians, if any, would join him, Washington must have feared that backing down at this point would be seen as a sign of weakness with long-term implications for Virginia's relations with the western tribes. Washington consulted with his officers, most of whom were older, more experienced soldiers, and it was agreed to press forward to Red Stone Creek, about thirty-five miles below the Forks, where a defensive position could be established and the army could await fresh orders.[19]

As the army painstakingly moved ahead, clearing a road through the hilly and rapidly greening forest, Washington engaged in diplomacy. Calling himself "Connotacucarious"—"Devourer of Villages"—a name bestowed on him the previous fall by Tanacharison, Washington continued his efforts to raise Indian allies. He also informed the governors of Pennsylvania and Maryland of the French activities, hoping that it might lead to help from those provinces. Apologizing for his brazenness in approaching them, Washington said he was doing so solely from the "glowing zeal I owe my country."[20]

It was at this point, too, that young Colonel Washington first clashed with Governor Dinwiddie. Sitting in his tent, with the forest leafing out all about him and his men "slaving dangerously . . . through woods, rocks, mountains," Washington composed an unctuous letter to the chief executive, not the sort of missive that the older, more self-assured Washington would have drafted. "I really believe" that were it "in your power, as it is your inclination," all the Virginia Regiment's problems would be solved. As it was, however, the little army was laden with troubles. There was such a dearth of noncommissioned officers in each company, Washington began, that it produced "clogs upon the expedition," causing him to "despair of success." He should have stopped there. Instead, unsure of himself, Washington permitted his veteran officers to prod him into an ill-advised remonstrance about their "trifling pay" and how they faced danger for the "shadow of pay." To make matters worse, Washington candidly acknowledged that he had gone over the chief executive's head by already raising the matter with acquaintances on the Governor's Council. Dinwiddie, a flinty Scotsman, was not amused. While he agreed with his young commander about the dearth of sergeants and corporals, Dinwiddie straightaway advised Washington that it was "ill timed" for him to have raised the question of pay. Lieutenant Colonel Washington and his officers should have considered that issue "before engaging in the Service," a bristling Dinwidde shot back.[21]

Washington soon faced a more immediate problem. Still more than twenty-five miles below Red Stone Creek, Washington learned from Seneca scouts on May 25 that a French force of indeterminate number had set out to the south from the Forks of the Ohio. He was told that they wished "to meat Miger Georg Wassiontton," but also that they had "deisind [descended] to strike the . . . Englsh."[22] Given the dearth of information, not to mention the incongruities in the written message, Washington had to be prepared for any eventuality, but especially for an attack. After all, he was leading an army toward a region that the French had unmistakably claimed as their own.

Dinwiddie's orders to his young commander, drafted weeks earlier, did not make Washington's choice any easier. Washington, the governor had instructed, was to "act on the Difensive," though he was to "kill & destroy" any enemy that sought to uproot the few Virginians who had already settled in this hostile land. But as any news that the governor received from his commander would be at least a week old, Dinwiddie gave Washington the freedom to act as circumstances required.[23]

Fearing the approach of a numerically superior force, Washington chose to follow Dinwiddie's instructions to act defensively. He began to entrench where he was, in a clearing known as the Great Meadows. His men had been digging for two days when Christopher Gist, the frontiersman who had rescued Washington six months earlier, showed up with word that the enemy party that was advancing south from the Ohio numbered no more than fifty soldiers, if that many. Although he did not know whether Gist's intelligence was accurate, Washington made a crucial decision, and one that violated Dinwiddie's instructions to keep the army within its fortifications. Washington divided his meager force, sending half his soldiers—some ninety men—ahead. It was a risky move. If the French soldiers Gist had seen were merely an advance party of a substantially larger force, both halves of the Virginia Regiment would be easy picking for the enemy.

Washington was mad for glory. He was eager to prove his courage both to his officers and to powerful figures in Virginia, and zealous for the combat that would bring the renown for which he hungered. He did not have long to wait for his first taste of battle. Only hours after detaching half his army, Washington learned from a messenger that Tanacharison had spotted signs of the French not far ahead. Colonel Washington divided those men with him, taking forty of them with him on a rainy night march through the dark, knotted forest in search of his prey. He had resolved on a surprise attack.

Several hours of tough hiking on "a Night as dark as Pitch" brought Washington to the Seneca camp, where he and Tanacharison parleyed. Washington proposed that they "go hand in hand and strike the French." The sachem agreed, and the two forces set off on a brief trek through the heavy, sodden woods. Just as day was breaking on May 28, the campfires of their prey were spotted. Creeping closer, Washington discovered that the French, who had posted no sentries, were making breakfast. He ordered his men to encircle the Frenchmen, while the Senecas formed an outer ring. The Indians were to deal with any enemy soldier who succeeded in escaping through the English line.

Washington waited for what must have seemed an eternity for the last man to get in place. When all was ready, he screamed the order to open fire. The French never had a chance. Taken by surprise, they were victims of a massacre. Some were killed instantly in the initial volley. Others were wounded, including the French commander, sieur de Jumonville. When the firing stopped, up to twelve French soldiers lay dead at his feet— Washington variously reported that ten, eleven, and twelve Frenchmen had perished—and several wounded Frenchmen were scattered about. But the killing did not end with the cessation of the gunfire. Immobilized either by bloodlust or the awful sights that he was beholding for the first time, Washington made no attempt to stop the carnage. Tanacharison cracked open Jumonville's skull, extracting his warm brain, which he squeezed through his fingers like a sponge. Frenzied by their sachem's act, other Indian warriors went on a rampage. Ignoring the enemy prisoners who had come through the ambush unscathed, the Indians scalped many of the wounded, even decapitating one and impaling his head on a pike. When there were no more wounded to slaughter and the massacre at last ended, Washington read the papers that he found on Jumonville's body. His counterpart had not been leading a war party. He had been bringing a message to the English. Jumonville had been sent on a mission precisely like that which had taken Washington to Fort Le Boeuf six months earlier.[24]

Washington had tasted combat and found it a heady experience. In one of the very few memorable lines that he wrote during his long life, Washington, in a letter written a few days later, declared that he had "heard Bullets whistle and believe me there was something charming in the sound."[25] However, in the immediate aftermath of his ambush, Washington was beset with anxiety, and with good reason. Having ordered a hostile act against a peaceful party, he had considerably stretched Dinwiddie's elastic orders. Nor was he even the commander of the Virginia Regiment. Apprehensive, young Washington turned to damage control. He wrote the governor that the French he had killed were really "Spyes of the worst sort" sent to lay the spadework for an enemy attack and cautioning Dinwiddie not to be duped by whatever "smooth Story's" were spun by the score or more prisoners he was sending back to Williamsburg. The captives "ought to be hang'd," he told the chief executive.[26]

Something else troubled Washington. As some in the French party had escaped and would notify their commander at Fort Duquesne of what had transpired, Washington knew that he was a marked man. A large French force would come after his little Virginia army. Washington did not panic, however. He recalled the men he had unwisely sent ahead a few days earlier and, at Great Meadows, continued the construction of a defensive installation. Revealingly, he christened it Fort Necessity. Knowing that he would never reach the Ohio as he had been ordered to do, Washington, at least subliminally, had begun to prepare his defense of his campaign. The name implied it was necessity, not a lack of valor, that had compelled him to stop here, almost sixty miles short of the Forks of the Ohio.

As Washington's small, circular stockade took shape, his Indian allies departed. They had no stomach for fighting from inside a fort. Besides, the disheartened Indians had concluded that the gray-faced, nervous Virginians were certain to be outnumbered and encased in a pathetic enclosure that inevitably would be a death trap. They saw what Washington could not, or would not, see. The Virginians were doomed.

Ultimately, some four hundred English crowded into and around Fort Necessity. The remainder of the Virginia Regiment arrived in June, bringing word that Colonel Fry had died in a fall from his horse three days after Washington's attack on Jumonville's party. Washington was unmistakably in command of the Virginia army, though in the next few days an independent company composed of men from South Carolina, a provincial unit attached to the British army, also marched in. Its commander, Captain James Mackay, who had been soldiering since Washington was five years old, held a commission from the Crown, which under British law meant that he outranked any colonial officer who, like Washington, did not hold such a commission.[27]

Washington, who had worked hard to achieve his position of command, had no intention of submitting to Captain Mackay. Anxious and threatened, he railed in a message to Dinwiddie about the interloper's wish to take command of his men, and he claimed that Captain Mackay's presence was impeding the operations of the Virginia Regiment. Mackay solved the problem by establishing his men in a separate camp outside Fort Necessity and by acting—as Washington acknowledged—as "a very good sort of a Gentleman."[28]

One reason Mackay handled matters in this fashion may have been that he recognized the novice Virginia commander was constructing a fatal snare. Mackay may simply have wanted room to maneuver. Fort Necessity was surrounded by hills and woods, making it easy for an enemy to surround the facility and pick off the defenders as if this were a turkey shoot. That, it turned out, was precisely what the French did. A French and Indian force of some nine hundred men—the majority were Canadians—under Louis Coulon de Villiers, Jumonville's brother, arrived on July 3 primed for battle. En route to the Great Meadows, they had discovered the bodies of Jumonville and his men, scalped and evidently left unburied by Washington. Many of the French were avid for revenge.

The battle that ensued was brief and one-sided. From high ground and thick forests on every side of the fort, the French directed a deadly triangulated fire at Washington's beleaguered men. Finding the Virginians' horses and cattle an inviting target, the French and Indians killed them at once. Soldiers in the Virginia Regiment were gunned down, too. By the time a late afternoon downpour largely ended the fray, one quarter of Washington's men were casualties. Many were grievously wounded and thirty were dead or dying. Only Villiers's fear of enemy reinforcements kept him from killing every last Englishman. Instead, he offered to permit Washington to surrender, a gesture that one of the Virginia officers later said was "no disagreeable News to us." The men were "Wet; Muddy half thigh up," and, as one acknowledged, aware that there was no escape from "this pickle." With his life hanging in the balance, Washington not only surrendered on July 4, but signed an incriminating document in which he confessed that Jumonville had been murdered. In return, the British were not taken captive—often a death sentence in eighteenth-century wars—but were permitted to march back to Virginia.[29]

In the wake of this disaster, Washington faced a monumental job of rehabilitation. His reports, penned in a triumphant tone, emphasized that the French had suffered losses exceeding three hundred—they had actually sustained nineteen casualties—and that the defeated Virginians had marched home from the beleaguered fort with "our Drums beating and our Colours flying." He stressed that his army's defeat was due to insufficient supplies and a callow soldiery. He never, then or later, admitted any errors on his part.

Most of Washington's attention was focused on his damaging admission of Jumonville's murder. Not for the last time in his career, Washington pinned the blame on someone else. This time, his translator, Jacob Van Braam, was made the scapegoat. Though Van Braam was fluent in French, had resided in Virginia for two years, and had been welcomed by the army as its translator following his effective service in that capacity during the mission to Fort Le Boeuf, Washington claimed that he "was a Dutchman, little acquainted with the English tongue." In the event that such a shaky explanation was unconvincing, Washington additionally questioned Van Braam's integrity, implying that he had deliberately skewed the translation, "whatever his motives" may have been. Van Braam was not around to provide his side of the story. One of two hostages demanded by the French, he languished in Canada for the next six years, after which he soldiered with the British army before settling in Wales. Van Braam never returned to Virginia and never gave an account of the episode.[30]

Washington was not treated as a pariah when he returned to Virginia. Many understood that he had been sent on a fool's errand, and some probably thought it best not to incur the malice of his influential patrons. Washington was also helped by the fact that none of the officers in the Virginia Regiment criticized his conduct. One, Major Adam Stephen, who had been promoted by Washington and whose brother worked for the Fairfax family, published an account in Virginia and Maryland newspapers that defended Washington for having remained in Pennsylvania to make a stand against a superior adversary.[31] Nevertheless, gossip about Washington's failure swirled, and some criticism was aired publicly. From as far away as New York, critics who thought Washington "too ambitious of acquiring all the honor" condemned him for having acted rashly. Some in London dismissed his failure as merely what was to be expected from Americans who "have no knowledge or experience" as soldiers. In Virginia, a few who dared to speak out speculated that he had mishandled the Indians, a view given sustenance by Tanacharison's postmortem remark that Washington was "good natured" but unsuited for Indian diplomacy, as he treated the Native Americans "as his slaves."[32]

Publicly, Dinwiddie and the assembly expressed their gratitude for Washington's service.[33] But in private, the governor recognized that young Washington had been an improper choice for the demanding responsibilities he had been given. Dinwiddie appeared to have come to that judgment before Fort Necessity, and following the debacle at Great Meadows, he told Washington that some of the Virginia Regiment's problems stemmed from "the want of proper Command." Dinwiddie also informed London, somewhat disingenuously, that his lieutenant colonel had violated his orders to avoid a showdown until anticipated reinforcements from New York and North Carolina arrived. Washington's orders, in fact, had been to delay his attempt to drive the French from the Forks of the Ohio until he was reinforced.[34]

In August, when the long awaited reinforcements at last reached Virginia, Dinwiddie ordered the intercolonial force—it was composed of Virginians, Carolinians, and New Yorkers—to "march over the Allegany Mountains," but he appointed Colonel James Innes, a Scottish-born North Carolina planter and veteran militia officer, to command the army. That force accomplished even less than Washington's army. It never reached Pennsylvania. The following month, Governor Horatio Sharpe of Maryland received a commission from London that made him commander in chief of all British forces tasked with securing the Forks of the Ohio, and he too set out to put together an intercolonial army, though he was stymied, in part, by the fast-approaching winter.[35]

Sharpe's appointment was bad news for Washington. Having heard on the grapevine that Sharpe had criticized his performance in leading the Virginia Regiment, Washington had earlier fired off a letter defending his actions. With that air of haughtiness that so often was characteristic of royal officials, Sharpe responded by noting with disapproval Washington's "freedom" in approaching him. An anguished, and supine, Washington was compelled to mend fences, and he doubtless learned a valuable political lesson about appearing to act impertinently.[36]

When Sharpe, like Innes before him, went nowhere, an exasperated Dinwiddie wrote London for help. While awaiting an answer, he broke up the Virginia Regiment into several companies, with no officer holding a rank above captain. His step, approved by Sharpe, smacks—at least in part—of having been taken as a means of ridding Virginia's army of Lieutenant Colonel Washington. If so, it succeeded. Rather than submit to a humiliating demotion, Washington resigned. His short-lived stab at military glory was in tatters.[37]

Washington was bitter. "My commission [was] taken from me," he raged.

He also complained, in private, that Dinwiddie had lied to him, claiming that "an order from home" had left him with no choice but to strip Washington of his authority.[38] Washington's assessment was at least half-correct. He wanted another chance, although with his stock having sunk in Dinwiddie's eyes, Washington had little reason for optimism. Even so, he tenaciously courted friends in the assembly, reminding them that he had faced "extreme danger" as a soldier because he had seen it as his "indispensable duty" to Virginia to do so. Adding that his decision to leave the army was due to "the call of Honour," not to an aversion to soldiering, Washington underscored that his "inclinations are strongly bent to arms."[39] Rumors were circulating that another stab would be made at raising an intercolonial army, even that the British might dispatch a force to the colonies, in which case the redcoats would raise provincial forces, the very sort of colonial army in which Lawrence had served. While he waited out the long, bleak winter, eager to soldier again, Washington leased from Lawrence's widow Mount Vernon, a 2,298-acre tract, and eighteen slaves. He also inherited nine of his deceased brother's slaves.[40] Only twenty-two, Washington had attained the status of a planter and the prospect of considerable wealth, but he had gained neither the renown nor the deference that Lawrence had enjoyed. Young Washington knew, too, that neither would be his until he won glory as a soldier.

WASHINGTON'S BREAK CAME WHEN THE BRITISH GOVERNMENT, without declaring war on France, dispatched two infantry regiments and a train of artillery to America under General Edward Braddock, a sixty-year-old veteran soldier. Braddock's orders were to drive the French from Fort Duquesne. He was to be assisted by a force of seven hundred provincial soldiers that Governor Sharpe was ordered to raise. Eager to get back into uniform and to obtain a royal commission, Washington ignored Sharpe and, through intermediaries, offered his services to Braddock. The British general, he learned, was empowered to offer a commission with the rank only of captain, a demotion that Washington once again was unwilling to accept. He did not give up. Washington explained to Braddock that he wished "for nothing more earnestly than to attain a small degree of knowledge in the Military Art." As Braddock realized this young Virginian who had made two journeys to the Pennsylvania frontier could be useful to him, an agreement was reached quickly. Washington was to serve on Braddock's staff as an unpaid, unranked volunteer, performing many of the duties of an aide-de-camp. With perfect candor, Washington told influential Virginians that his "sole motive" was to "claim some small share or merit" that would win the "regard & esteem" of his fellow colonists.[41]

Washington's service with Braddock lasted barely two months, and he was actually with the general only about half that time, yet the Braddock campaign was crucial for Washington. It catapulted him back into the limelight and opened doors that had slammed shut after the Fort Necessity disaster. Seeing the British army from the inside, Washington also gleaned knowledge about how a regular army was organized and run. (He even copied Braddock's orders in a notebook so that he might emulate the general's style.)[42] After weeks devoted to planning and acquiring supplies, Braddock finally put his force in motion late in April 1755. Following the route that Washington's army had blazed, Braddock's army struggled across endless hills, moving with agonizing slowness over a road that turned to fetid ooze under the weight of horses, cattle, wagons, artillery, and soldiers. Nearly fifty days passed before the army reached the Great Meadows, twice the time that had been required for Washington's army to reach this spot, and the Virginia Regiment had been slowed by its work in cutting the road. After passing the blackened and overgrown ruins of Fort Necessity, the Anglo-American force crossed the blue green Youghiogheny River and set off on the final leg of its long trek to the Ohio. From this point, its progress was even slower, as the army had to muscle its way through the dense, airless forest, creating its own road as it proceeded. Washington was not present at this juncture. Having fallen ill with a camp fever three weeks earlier, he had been left behind. Only on July 8 did the still weak and easily fatigued Washington rejoin Braddock. He caught up with the general just in time to ride into hell.

Less than twenty-four hours after Washington returned to Braddock's side, and just after the British had slowly crossed the wide and placid Monongahela River, the van of the army stumbled into a large force of French and Indians. Both sides were surprised, but Braddock's adversary recovered first. Abandoning their European way of fighting, the French rushed into the woods. Within scant minutes, they had nearly surrounded the Anglo-American soldiers. From behind trees, which served as cover, the French and Indians poured a merciless fire into the ranks of the British. All pretense of discipline and orderly resistance gave way to terror within the Anglo-American army. Braddock was gunned down, as were numerous officers. Washington alone of Braddock's aides emerged unscathed, though his hat and coat were riddled with bullet holes and two horses were shot from beneath him. Washington never ran. He stood and fought with great valor, displaying what one historian called "the soldier's knack of fatalism that permitted him to ignore the bullets."[43] Despite the danger, he even helped carry the mortally wounded Braddock from the blood-soaked battlefield. Eventually, Washington succeeded in reaching a defensive perimeter established by some of the surviving British regulars. He was one of the few who escaped. Two thirds of Braddock's army, 976 men, were killed and wounded. The least fortunate were those who fell into the hands of the Indians. They were tortured and killed in a nightlong saturnalia of ghoulish horror. In terms of the percentage of men lost, the Battle of the Monongahela was the worst defeat suffered by the British in America prior to the War of Independence.[44]

Braddock's disaster redeemed Washington in the eyes of most Virginians. If a veteran British general in command of fifteen hundred men had failed egregiously in 1755, how could young Washington with barely four hundred men have possibly escaped catastrophe in 1754? Stories of Washington's courage under fire circulated rapidly, assisted by his own numerous written accounts of the battle and his close brush with death. Washington stressed that while the British regulars had "broke & run as Sheep before the Hounds," he and several redcoat officers, who "in genl behavd with incomparable bravery," risked their lives to rally their frightened men. He also claimed to have proposed leading the Americans in a counterattack during the battle, but that permission had been denied. Although Washington did not make public any of his accounts of the tragedy, some of his correspondents—as he must have known would be the case—saw to their publication. Even influential figures in London were aware of his valorous exploits. One, the Earl of Halifax, a member of the Board of Trade, gushed that young Washington had "behaved . . . as bravely as if he really loved the whistling of Bullets." Washington was showered with praise in Virginia. Making an about-face, Dinwiddie extolled Washington's "gallant Behavr."

Within barely a month of that terrible day on the Monongahela, Din-widdie and the House of Burgesses refashioned Virginia's army into a force of twelve hundred men organized in sixteen companies, and the governor asked Washington to reassume his old role as commander with the rank of colonel. Washington never appeared in Williamsburg to lobby for the posi-tion. Supposedly recuperating at Mount Vernon, he admitted to a close ac-quaintance that he had stayed away rather than to have appeared to "sollicit the Command." He preferred that it should not be merely offered to him, but "press'd upon me by the general voice" of his fellow Virginians.[45]

WASHINGTON WAS BACK. He was a different man, more self-assured and less inclined to toady to armchair soldiers who held civil office. He had been shaped by the laurels he had won for his gallantry and by the terror and gore of combat that he had experienced. In addition, now that he possessed Mount Vernon and a score or so of slaves, Washington was independent as never before. He knew that an alternative to soldiering existed through which he might continue his ascent within Virginia's circles of power. But he wanted to soldier. He liked the feeling of power. The lionization that came with his performance under fire was heady stuff as well. More than anything, perhaps, he desperately yearned for the victory that had eluded him in two campaigns. His Virginia patriotism, always palpable, had grown as a result of his experience with Braddock. Whereas many British regulars had broken and fled during the desperate encounter with the French and Indians, the "Virginians behaved like Men, and died like Soldier's," he had said.[46] He wanted victory for Virginia, a victory that would open the West, a triumph that he could savor and bask in. He also wanted a royal commis-sion, which would provide assurance that no man of inferior grade would ever outrank him. A royal commission would additionally enhance his stature, giving him a status never attained by Lawrence. For a proud man such as Washington, the issue of rank was never far from his mind, and it reared its head once again within days after he reassumed command of the Virginia Regiment.

Before Washington could depart for the front, Major Stephen notified him that Captain John Dagworthy, a Marylander who had held a commis-sion from the king since 1746, was at Fort Cumberland in Maryland, which Dinwiddie had designated as regimental headquarters. Though

Dagworthy had only thirty Maryland soldiers with him, Stephen added, he "will look upon himself as Commanding Officer after You have joined the Troops." Almost audibly sighing at having once again to endure such an affront, Washington set off in September for Fort Cumberland, about fifty miles below the Great Meadows. Problems with Dagworthy surfaced immediately. Washington was in no mood for this. After only one week at headquarters, he left and did not return to Fort Cumberland that year or the next. He spent the duration of 1755 in Virginia recruiting his army, though he found time to travel often to Williamsburg, where he crossly told Dinwiddie that he would not serve under Dagworthy. His honor was at stake, he said, and so too was that of Virginia, which had appropriated huge sums of money and raised hundreds more men than Maryland during the past two years. Aside from losing control of his army to Dagworthy, Washington also worried that he might be personally damaged by his behavior. He did not want to be seen as having behaved in a petty manner or to have others think that he had acted solely from "Pique and Resentment." His actions, he insisted, were undertaken solely with the broader interest of finding the means to win the war in mind. He urged Dinwiddie to intervene and resolve the matter. If the governor would not do so, he threatened to resign. Dinwiddie, it turned out, shared Washington's outrage, especially when Dagworthy refused to permit the Virginia Regiment to take supplies from Fort Cumberland, an installation built and paid for by Virginians. Dinwiddie wrote both London and Governor William Shirley of Massachusetts, the commander in chief of British troops in America, requesting a royal commission for his young colonel and brevet commissions for all the Virginia officers. When weeks passed without word from Shirley, Dinwiddie, at Washington's behest, permitted his young colonel to travel to Boston and make his case personally.[47]

Just days before his twenty-fourth birthday, Washington set off for Boston on horseback. He passed through Annapolis, Philadelphia, and New York along the way, spending time in each city. He shopped, went sightseeing, and gambled away some money at cards. His losses were heavy, roughly equal to half a year's wage for a skilled tradesman. When he finally reached snow-covered Boston, Washington found Governor Shirley—who was practiced in the ways of the "Courts of Princes," as one of Washington's officers put it—to be warm and cordial. Shirley praised the young Virginian, but he gave Washington only part of what he had come to get. Washington did not get the royal commission he coveted, though Shirley ruled that Dagworthy was serving as an officer for Maryland, not as a regular. The ruling meant that Dagworthy had no jurisdiction over Virginia's army.[48] Early in April 1756, Washington arrived back to Virginia. He had been commander of the Virginia Regiment for eight months, and he had spent more than half that time away from his army.

When he was with the army, Washington worked hard. As historian Edward Lengel has observed, Washington was faced with the absence of a modern military or civil bureaucracy, compelling him to manage nearly every last detail of fielding and maintaining Virginia's army. He reconnoitered, planned military campaigns, meticulously organized his force, located supplies, allocated pay, found wagons, hired teamsters, and distributed provisions. He even designed the officers' uniforms, somewhat inverting those of the British army by conceiving of blue outer coats and red short coats. Always a perfectionist, he kept a close eye on his officers and an even more keen eye on the men, imposing a draconian code of discipline. Floggings were commonplace—two deserters were beaten " 'till they pissd themselves and the Spectators Shed tears for them," one of the officers once reported— and executions were carried out, chiefly for repeated desertion.[49]

Nonetheless, Washington found ample time for other things. He frequently left his army to visit friends and relatives and especially to call on various members of the Fairfax family. At one point, he was absent from the army while he helped George William Fairfax, the son of the Colonel Fairfax who built Belvoir, with his campaign to win election to the House of Burgesses. Some of the time, Colonel Washington took leave of his men to explore property that he might wish to acquire. He kept an eye on tobacco production at Mount Vernon, ordered tools for his workers, furniture and clothing for himself, and scarlet-and-white livery for the slaves who attended him personally. He purchased land and additional slaves.[50]

This was a crucial learning time for Washington.[51] He continued to construct his public persona, drawing on things he had learned from Braddock's behavior. Washington had studied the veteran officer intently, finding that his "good & bad qualities were intimately blended." He hoped to emulate Braddock's bravery and "generous & disinterested" way, but he wished to avoid what he regarded as the general's mistake in failing to "disguise" his weaknesses, including his prejudices, volatile temper, and "plain and blunt . . . manner even to rudeness."[52] As always, Washington sought to hide what he thought were his own shortcomings—his lack of education, a volcanic temper, and vaulting ambition—and to exhibit what others would see as virtues, including dedication, industry, and fairness. Running the army required that he deal with civilian suppliers on a regular basis, and he appears to have quickly learned the techniques best suited for getting what he wanted. Washington also came to understand that his officers who were responsible for keeping the army well supplied were not always dependable. In the feverish crucible of command, Washington learned much about the arts of politics and leadership. Sometimes he learned the hard way, from his own egregious mistakes.

Plagued by chronic shortages during the autumn of 1756, Washington fell into the habit of sending out parties of soldiers to confiscate goods from civilians. At times, he accompanied the men and seized items by brandishing "my own drawn Sword." He learned soon enough that his actions not only destroyed civilian morale, they aroused the ire of the farmers whose goods were seized. Some insolent civilians, as he called them, were willing "to blow out my brains" should he expropriate their property. One even came after Washington with a loaded musket, leading the prudent colonel to back down.[53] Washington learned to curb his high-handed methods, and it was a lesson that he remembered during the Revolutionary War.

Perhaps the hardest lesson that Washington learned came when he lost Governor Dinwiddie's support. Problems between Washington and Dinwiddie might not have festered had the war gone well. But the war went badly. During Washington's first eighteen months back in command, one third of the men in Virginia's army were lost in what the British called "bush fighting," backcountry warfare against the Indians. Washington was unable to point to the least success. On returning to the front in April 1756, following the lengthy absence occasioned by his trek to Boston, Washington acknowledged that the enemy's numbers had increased, the "Inhabitants are in a miserable situation," and much of the Shenandoah Valley was lost. He recommended the resettlement of frontier inhabitants to areas that could be secured by the presence of forts, the plan—he pointed out—utilized by seventeenth-century "New Englanders . . . when infested as we are now."[54]

Conditions had not improved a year later when he disclosed the "melancholy Circumstances" of the inhabitants in the face of a "Sculking Enemy"
that "Ravages . . . our Frontiers," an "Enemy [that] has every opportunity
to Plunder, Kill, Scalp, and Escape."[55]

WASHINGTON ALSO ASSAILED DINWIDDIE, at least indirectly. While Washington acknowledged that he admired the Indians—he spoke with wonder
of their stamina, "stealth," "dexterity," "cunning and craft," and ability to
surmount "indefatigable Sufferings"—he never wavered in his belief that
they could be beaten. That "this Hold of Barbarians" had not been sub-
dued, he said in letter after letter, was due to the military strategy imposed
on his army by the civilian authorities. He castigated the "Chimney Corner Politicians," military novices who never visited the front lines but who
meddled in matters that should be left to soldiers. As the architect of the
Virginia army's strategy was Governor Dinwiddie, Washington did not say
any of this to the governor, though he repeatedly told him and other
politicians that Williamsburg's strategy was flawed and must be altered.
Washington criticized almost every aspect of how the war was being
waged: He had too few men; his manpower was drained away in garrison-
ing several nonessential forts; the forts were situated too far apart; the army
had been improperly organized from the start; he had not been provided
with the Indian allies he had been promised; there was a dearth of equipment. "I would be a willing offering to Savage Fury: and die by inches, to
save a people," he said melodramatically. "I . . . *know* their [the frontier in-
habitants] danger, and participate [in] their *Sufferings;* without having it in
my power to give them . . . relief."[56]

   Amid his hyperbolic rhetoric, the nub of Washington's argument was
that Dinwiddie was mistaken to focus on fighting a defensive war. The only
way to win the war was by seizing the offensive and "carrying on an Expedition against the Ohio," Washington insisted. Such a campaign would "put
a stop to the incursions of the Enemy; as they would *then* be obliged to stay
at home, to defend their own possessions." He was convinced, too, that
once Fort Duquesne was taken and the French were driven away, the Indians, stripped of their ally, would have to make peace.[57] Washington was correct, but if anyone's hands were tied, they were Dinwiddie's. Great Britain
did not send another army to America until two years after Braddock's de-

feat, and it was sent to the northern colonies, not to Virginia. During two years of fighting, moreover, Maryland had barely lifted a finger to help its neighbor, and Pennsylvania had not done much, either. Already, two armies had been sent out to reach the Ohio. Neither had made it. Washington's army in 1754 and Braddock's the following year had been destroyed. No mood existed in Virginia to try again, at least not without massive assistance. Dinwiddie came up with the best possible strategy under the circumstances: Fight a holding action on the frontier until help arrived from the parent state and other colonies.

The governor simmered quietly over Washington's criticism of strategy. He grew angrier when Washington complained of a dearth of orders from Williamsburg. Dinwiddie became incensed when Washington contradictorily charged that the governor's directives were constructed so awkwardly as to leave him in "a state of uncertainty, without knowing the plan of operations, or what scheme to go upon." Washington claimed that he had to "guess at every thing."[58]

Dinwiddie could be amiable. He could also be irascible, and Washington got under his skin. The steady drumbeat of faultfinding that poured from Washington's pen would have irritated anyone. That the carping came from a young officer who had yet to achieve his first success on the battlefield was bad enough, but it was made even worse as the governor knew that he was doing all that was politically and militarily feasible. As it was next to impossible to keep secrets in tiny Williamsburg, Dinwiddie also knew that Washington was going behind his back and complaining to the Speaker of the House of Burgesses and other influential assemblymen. Such behavior was more than galling. It was inadmissible.

Furious as he was with Washington, Dinwiddie was amazingly patient with his officer, even assisting his efforts to secure a royal commission. Throughout Washington's first year back in command of Virginia's army, the governor remained cordial. When he wrote his young colonel, Dinwiddie appeared to take pains to treat him with kid gloves: "I approve of," "I am sorry for," "if you can," "I agree with You," "As Yr private Affairs require" attention, "I cannot refuse You liberty of absence," he said in letter after letter.[59] But in September 1756, an anonymous critic assailed Colonel Washington and Virginia's army—and by implication Governor Dinwiddie—in an essay that filled nearly the entire front page of the *Virginia*

Gazette, the colony's only newspaper. Calling himself "the Virginia-Centinel," Washington's detractor charged that the war was going badly because the army was in the hands of "raw Novices and R[a]kes, Spend thrifts" unaccustomed to command who had spent much of their time in "Dbauchery, Vice and I[dl]enes . . . sculking in Forts and there dissolving in Plasure." The officers, who had fashioned a "Regiment of . . . dastardly Debauchees," had habitually "brow-beat" and "abused" the soldiery and avoided clashes with the enemy as much as possible. "Nothing brave is so much as attempted," the Centinel added. "What useless Lumber" was an army under such leadership?[60]

There had been rumblings earlier about misconduct by some of the officers in the army, and during the spring the House of Burgesses had threatened to conduct an inquiry, though nothing came of it. The allegations of the Centinel brought matters into the open. Thereafter, Dinwiddie's tone toward Washington changed. He demanded information about officers who neglected to do their duty, and—now that the shoe was on the other foot—complained about the lack of clarity in Washington's reports. More disconcerting, Washington learned from various sources that Dinwiddie and some in the assembly regarded him as deceitful, which had "lesson'd . . . [their] Esteem" for him. In time, Dinwiddie flatly told Washington that he was not just "unmannerly," but an ingrate, a man who had turned on him despite all he had done to give the young colonel his chance.[61]

Dinwiddie's charges stung Washington, as they touched on his character and honor. Washington responded that "ingratitude" was a detestable "crime." "I have foibles, and perhaps many of them," he added, though if he had erred with his army or in his relationship with the governor, it was owing to inexperience, not to "wilful" behavior. "No man that ever was employed in a public capacity has endeavored to discharge the trust reposed in him with greater honesty," he declared. He also demanded that Dinwiddie not only specify his charge of ingratitude, but never again "stigmatize me behind my back."[62]

Washington's running battle with Dinwiddie was carried out in private, but he planned publicly to rebut the Centinel. Wisely, his older half-brother Augustine, whom he consulted, stayed his hand. Urging his brother to do nothing, Augustine hurried to Williamsburg to see what he could learn. After a few days in the capital, Augustine discovered that George continued to be held in "as great esteem as ever" by the great majority of burgesses. Augustine also learned that the assemblymen wanted to keep Colonel Washington in charge of Virginia's army, if only from fear that his successor would be James Innes, the North Carolinian who held a royal commission and who was beyond their control. Augustine recommended that George not engage in a public fray with his detractor and counseled against his resigning in a huff, both of which would play into the hands of "that Scandalous Centinel."[63] Colonel Washington listened. He said nothing in public, and the tempest ignited by the Centinel rapidly blew over. The episode was another learning experience for Washington.

Even so, Washington's relationship with Dinwiddie remained strained, and the young colonel—Washington was only twenty-four years old in 1756—still did not understand his place. Pressing matters, he asked permission to leave his army and come to the capital to meet with the governor. Dinwiddie exploded. "I cannot Agree to allow you Leave. . . . You have been frequently indulg'd with Leave of Absence. . . . Surely the Commanding Officer Should not be Absent when daily Alarm'd with the Enemys Intents to invade our frontiers. I think you are wrong to ask it."[64]

Since returning to command late in 1755, Washington had been obsessed with obtaining a royal commission, and his uneasy relationship with Dinwiddie only increased his yearning for preferment. When Washington learned that John Campbell, Earl of Loudoun, Shirley's successor as commander of the British army in North America, was coming to Philadelphia in March 1757 to meet with several colonial governors, the young colonel wished to call on him. Washington had two things on his mind. He wanted to make a personal plea to be commissioned in the British army. In addition, he brazenly hoped to suggest a new strategy. He wished to recommend to Loudoun that a colonial force of three thousand men "under good regulation" be sent to "make themselves Masters" of "Fort Duquisn and the [Great] Lakes." There can be little doubt that Washington envisaged an important position for himself in that army.

Early in 1757, he sent his proposal to Loudoun's aide and he wrote directly to the British commander. His letter to Loudoun was not the most graceful missive that Washington ever penned. He went on about the faults of others (clearly Dinwiddie, though he was never mentioned by name), deplored Virginia's halfhearted attempts to field a viable army, denigrated the quality of his troops, carped about the strategy with which he was saddled, and even took a swipe at officials in London for not having done more to win over the Indians. After praising Loudoun—"don't think My Lord I am going to flatter," he insisted, after which he fawned over "Your Lordship's . . . Important Services" and added a note about his "exalted Sentiments of Your Lordships Character"—Washington swore that he was serving solely because of the "Sollicitations of the Country." He made clear his hope for a royal commission, truthfully telling Loudoun that both Braddock and Shirley had said they would have bestowed such an honor on him had they possessed the authority.[65]

When a noncommittal reply came from Loudoun's aide, Washington requested Dinwiddie's permission to leave his army and travel to Philadelphia for a face-to-face meeting with the British commander. Dinwiddie, perhaps having an inkling of what awaited Washington, consented, though he advised his young colonel: "I cannot conceive what Service You can be of in going there." Washington set off anyway, making a weeklong horseback ride to Philadelphia in the fading days of winter. Once in the city, he had to cool his heels for more than two weeks before he could see Loudoun. As he waited impatiently, Washington whiled away the time gambling, attending dances, and shopping.

When at last the meeting was set, Washington was shown into Loudoun's presence. Short, muscular, handsome, and brimming with vitality, Loudoun was an experienced commander who was renowned for his administrative skills. However, Loudoun had never previously been in America, and he had come to the colonies convinced that the provincials were neither good soldiers nor willing to provide much assistance toward winning the war. His biases and his aristocratic pomposity were evident, and he treated Washington disdainfully. Before Washington could speak, Loudoun gruffly rattled off a string of orders, including commands that the young colonel adhere to Dinwiddie's strategy and rejoin his army, where, Loudoun said curtly, the commander of the army should be. Loudoun made no mention of Washington's audacious plan for a colonial army to take Fort Duquesne. Instead, the commander in chief ordered that nearly one fourth of Virginia's army be sent to South Carolina, while the remainder was to be divided among six posts along Virginia's frontier. Washington was ordered to Fort Cumberland in Maryland with some 250 men, where he was to be joined by a larger force drawn from Maryland. When Washington tried to speak, Loudoun turned his back, signaling that the meeting was over. Not a word had been said about a royal commission or Washington's proposed strategy for liberating the Ohio Country. Washington, as proud a man as ever existed, had been treated contemptuously, as a servant in Virginia might be dealt with by an uncivil master. One can only image the burning fury and humiliation in Washington's breast as he rode back to Virginia.[66]

WASHINGTON'S JOURNEY KEPT HIM AWAY from his army for two months. Not long after he returned, great changes were set in motion in London that would profoundly affect the war and Virginia's disgruntled colonel. During the summer of 1757, William Pitt was asked to form a ministry. Pitt reconfigured British strategy. A resourceful politician with many years of experience in the House of Commons, Pitt also found the means of prying abundant appropriations from Parliament. In time, he succeeded in turning around what had been a losing war for Anglo-America, in the process becoming the Winston Churchill of eighteenth-century British politics. He recalled Loudoun and found allies to help fight the French in Europe, enabling the British for the first time to commit truly large armies to the war in America. Contemplating sending nearly twenty thousand men to America, Pitt directed the colonies to furnish an equal number of soldiers. While the Royal Navy swept the enemy from the high seas and allied armies pinned down as much of the French army as possible in Europe, Anglo-American armies were to strike their adversaries in a three-pronged offensive in North America. Two armies were to advance into Canada—one coming down the Lake Champlain corridor from New York, the other via the St. Lawrence—and a third army was to wrest the head of the Ohio from the French. Brigadier General John Forbes, a fifty-year-old Scotsman with many years' military experience in Europe and still more in America, was given command of the campaign to take Fort Duquesne. Forbes was to have seventeen hundred British regulars. The remainder of his force—roughly five thousand men—were to be provincials. Virginia's army was to make up 40 percent of the provincial mix under Forbes.[67]

Washington began jockeying for prominence even before he departed Virginia to join Forbes in Pennsylvania, where the army began to gather late in the spring in 1758. Understanding that there would be "a motley herd" of officers from several colonies, and wishing to "be distinguished in some measure from the *common run* of" them, Washington wrote acquaintances in the British army—including Colonel Thomas Gage, who twenty years later would be his opponent at the outset of the Revolutionary War—asking that they "mention me in favorable terms to General Forbes." He told them that he wished to be part of the campaign from what he called "purely laudable" motives, including his "zeal for the Service." A few days later Washington wrote directly to Forbes, a liberty he took, he said, solely because of his "disinterested regard for the safety and welfare of these Colonies." Washington advised Forbes of the importance of securing Indian allies, counsel that could hardly have been news to a general with considerable experience in America.[68]

Forbes's army grew that summer, though Washington was not with it. Forbes ordered him to see to the construction of a forty-mile-long road linking Forts Frederick and Cumberland. Far from the commander's headquarters and shackled with an assignment that was unlikely to win him laurels, Washington grew dispirited. The "appearance of Glory once in view," not to mention "that laudable Ambition of Serving Our Country, and meriting its applause, is now no more," he moaned.[69] Washington was wrong. As the summer was drawing to an end, he and his two thousand Virginia soldiers were ordered to join the main army at Raystown, about eighty miles almost due east of Fort Duquesne.

Washington had hardly joined with the Anglo-American army before he clashed with Forbes. The British commander faced two choices with regard to how best to advance on Fort Duquesne. Forbes could use the road that Washington had cleared and Braddock had taken. Or he could order a new road cut straight west, an artery that would be laid out well north of what everyone referred to as "Braddock's Road." Influential Virginians hoped that Forbes would take Braddock's Road. Their choice was prompted by economic considerations. Those who owned land along the road, or who dreamed of the teeming postwar business opportunities that would materialize if the East's sole link to the West was via Braddock's Road, believed they stood to make fortunes should Forbes make the right choice. Influential Pennsylvanians favored a new, more northerly road, and for the same reasons that were driving the Virginians. A new road cut by Forbes would tie Philadelphia to the West. Forbes had to decide. The decision he reached was grounded on military considerations. He preferred a new road. Not only would there be one less major river to cross, but logistical support could flow to the army from heavily populated eastern Pennsylvania, and the supplies could be stored in a series of easily secured magazines that were to be constructed along the new road. Unencumbered by a lengthy baggage train, Forbes reckoned that his army would be able to move rapidly, avoiding one of the pitfalls that had contributed to Braddock's destruction three years earlier.[70]

While claiming that he would "most chearfully . . . pursue any Rout . . . and shall never have a Will of my own where a point of Duty is requird," Washington launched a campaign to change Forbes's mind long before he reached Raystown. He spoke with Forbes and his aide, Captain Francis Halkett, and wrote to Colonel Henry Bouquet, commander of the Royal American Regiment—the provincial force that included Virginia's army— emphasizing that winter would set in before the new road could be built. A year lost could be fatal, Washington warned. It might result in the "miscarriage of the Expedition," and at the very least it would prolong the suffering of the frontier's inhabitants.[71]

Washington stood the chance of pecuniary gain should Braddock's Road remain the only east–west road for the foreseeable future. Furthermore, by serving as the point man for powerful vested interests in Virginia, he appears to have been seeking to lay the groundwork for his own postwar political ambitions. To be sure, other factors also led him to try "to hurry things forward," as he put it.[72] He was especially eager to conclude his military career. Washington had come down with dysentery after his return from Philadelphia in April 1757, and his health deteriorated further during the summer and fall. Suffering from "Stiches & violent Pleuretick Pains," as well as a chronic cough, he eventually was too ill to walk. In November, he returned home to consult his physician and, he hoped, to recuperate. His great fear was that, like Lawrence, he had contracted tuberculosis. Two doctors, one at Mount Vernon and the other in Williamsburg, assured him that his illness was not life threatening—"your disorder hath been of long Standing, and hath corrupted the whole mass of Blood . . . yet you will in a short time get the better of it," said one physician—and by Christmas he had begun to mend.[73] But Washington, who was twenty-six years old when he joined Forbes, had now suffered two serious illnesses while soldiering, leaving him more keen than ever to put military service behind him and return to civilian pursuits.

Something else was on Washington's mind as well. During his lengthy recuperation, he had called on Martha Custis at the White House, her estate on the Pamunkey River. Reputedly the wealthiest widow in all Virginia, Martha had inherited from her late husband one hundred slaves, six thousand acres, and liquid assets in the range of £12,000, roughly the combined annual incomes of 150 skilled craftsmen. What followed was an exceptionally rapid courtship. After spending only some twenty hours together in January 1758, the couple was engaged to be married, though the ceremony would have to wait until Washington left the army, which he vowed to do once Forbes's army took Fort Duquesne.[74]

Whatever Washington's primary motivation in making such a pother over the route taken to the Forks of the Ohio, General Forbes suspected either that the young Virginia colonel had a personal financial stake in the selection of Braddock's Road or that he was fronting for leading speculators in his colony, or both. Like Dinwiddie before him, Forbes grew to question Washington's integrity, even his suitability for leading an army. Having started with the view that Washington "has the Character of a good and knowing Officer," Forbes soon concluded that Virginia's young colonel put his "attachment to [his] province" before "the good of the army." Forbes stuck to his guns, and work proceeded on the more northerly route across rugged Laurel Hill, leaving Washington in private to despair: "All is lost! All is lost by Heavens! Our Enterprise Ruin'd." Virginia's efforts to "promote . . . [its] Interests" had fallen "Victim to . . . her Crafty [Pennsylvania] Neighbours."[75]

Washington was involved in only one action in the campaign, and it was not one that did him credit. Early in November, a force of some two hundred enemy raiders struck suddenly at a supply post near Loyalhanna (present-day Ligonier), roughly the halfway point along Forbes's new road to the Ohio, attempting to kill or take the redcoats' horses and livestock, crippling and slowing the British advance. Forbes detached several hundred Virginians to pursue the attackers, but when they were not up to the task, he sent out still more Virginians as reinforcements. Contradictory contemporary accounts make it uncertain whether Washington commanded the initial detachment or the reinforcements. What is clear is that near dusk, the two Virginia forces stumbled into each other. In their surprise, and in the gloaming, each opened fire on the other, having mistaken friends for foes. Forty men were killed or wounded in the appalling friendly fire incident. Tragedies of this sort occur in war and are always mortifying events. That Washington was shamed, ever haunted, by the occurrence seems evident. He did not write a word about it for thirty years, and when he finally offered his account of the episode—in remarks intended for public consumption—he not only blamed the commander of the other Virginia detachment, but took the lion's share of the credit for having stopped the carnage before further losses were suffered. Only one other Virginia soldier involved in the affair left an account. Captain Thomas Bullitt, a five-year veteran in Virginia's army who had been commended for bravery under fire and twice recommended by Washington for promotion, held Washington responsible not just for the calamity, but for doing next to nothing to stop the bloodshed. Bullitt said that was also the view of "several of the officers."[76]

Though the provincials had blundered egregiously, their mission paid crucial dividends. While in pursuit of the French, the Virginians captured two enemy soldiers. Under interrogation, the captives said that Fort Duquesne was lightly garrisoned, most of the men having been summoned to the defense of Canada. Forbes believed them and ordered the army to push rapidly for the Ohio. Amazingly, Washington made one last attempt to persuade Forbes to make that push via Braddock's Road.[77] Wisely, the general ignored him, and within barely a week the Anglo-American force had closed to within ten miles of the Ohio. As they prepared for their final push, the sound of a huge explosion eddied through the barren hills. Forbes quickly sent out a scouting party. It discovered that the French had abandoned and scuttled Fort Duquesne.

Virginia's objective, first envisaged by the Ohio Company nearly a decade before and fought for by thousands of the colony's soldiers since 1754, had been realized. On November 25, almost five years to the day since he'd had last stood at the Forks of the Ohio, Washington returned. He did not linger. He had accomplished what he had set out to achieve, and he was anxious to marry and launch his second career, that of influential planter. Within a week of Fort Duquesne's fall, Washington was on his way home, and he was back in Virginia by the second week in December.

When he left the army at the close of the year, Washington received a long, laudatory address from his officers. The ambitious in this age were given to obsequities, as Washington himself had demonstrated in his relationships with his patrons. The officers in Virginia's army, doubtless recognizing that their colonel was going places in Virginia's public affairs, had an incentive for flattering him. (Captain Bullitt was one of the signees, for instance, and he was not enamored of Washington as a commander.)

Still, the officers' effusive declaration bears the stamp of sincerity. Many had stuck with Washington for years because they believed in him. Others were blindly loyal, having flourished under Washington, sometimes having been elevated by him. All found much to admire in their commander in chief. They noted his industry and "punctual Observance" of his responsibilities. They thought Washington had been straightforward, mentioning his "Frankness, Sincerity, and a certain Openness of Soul." Alluding to his loyalty and fairness with his officers, they spoke of the "mutual Regard that has always subsisted between you and your Officers." They lauded his impartiality and "Regard to Merit" in assessing them. He had not buckled under the considerable burdens of command. He had not shrunk from the difficult choices necessary for making men into soldiers and officers into leaders. Indeed, the address stipulated that Washington had "train'd us up in the Practice of that Discipline which alone can constitute good Troops." He had persevered for five long years. He had displayed a meticulousness— always a Washington hallmark—to make his army the best that it could be. He had exhibited undoubted courage. However, perhaps their greatest tribute was that they had been inspired by Washington's leadership. Washington's "true Honor and Passion for Glory," they wrote, "heightened our natural Emulation, and our Desire to excel." To this they added: "In you we place the most implicit Confidence."[78] George Washington had indeed become a leader of men.

ON THE CUSP OF HIS TWENTY-SEVENTH BIRTHDAY, January 6, 1759, Washington, a civilian once again, married Martha Custis at the White House. Barely a decade had passed since he'd had set out to make a living and a name for himself. He had begun as a surveyor but became a soldier, and in that brief span of time, his achievements had surpassed those of his half-brother Lawrence. Not even the Fairfaxes were as exalted as Colonel Washington. The dizzying arc of his ascent was truly astonishing. It had to have exceeded his wildest dreams. For that matter, it had to have outpaced anything that he could have imagined as recently as six weeks earlier in cold and lonely Loyalhanna.

Washington had become somebody in Virginia, and in the process of getting there he had learned a great deal about himself and the world of politics, learning from both his successes and his mistakes.

The Burgess: George Washington, Virginia Politician

GEORGE WASHINGTON did not have a crystal ball. When he came home at the end of 1758, he assumed that soldiering was in his past and, save for ceremonial occasions, he would never again wear a military uniform. Neither Washington nor anyone else could have imagined that a vast colonial rebellion, much less a war for independence, lay in the not too distant future.

Washington assumed that the greatest adventure he would ever experience was behind him. All dreams of chasing after military glory belonged to a bygone time. He anticipated marriage and starting a family, succeeding as a tobacco planter, developing Mount Vernon, and, through land speculation and assorted business endeavors, increasing his modest fortune. He also expected to remain active in Virginia politics.

Given the acclaim that Washington had achieved, he was positioned to succeed politically and eager to reap the rewards that holding political power could bring. Although he publicly declared that no one could know his "grief" and "the pangs I have felt at parting with the Regiment," Washington left the army even though the war had not ended.[1] Not only did Virginia's army continue to fight a bush war on the frontier for nearly five additional years, but the French and Indian War raged on elsewhere. In Washington's first year home, one large Anglo-American army fought for control of the Champlain Valley while another waged a six-month campaign to take Quebec. In 1760, a British and colonial army finally took

Montreal, ending the fighting in North America, though fighting dragged on in the Caribbean and elsewhere for years to come. But no one faulted Washington for having hung up his uniform. He had soldiered for nearly five years, commanding a provincial army longer than any other American in any other colony, and the army he had commanded had won for Virginia that which the colony had set out to achieve.

JUST DAYS AFTER HIS WEDDING in January 1759, Colonel Washington, accompanied by Martha, traveled to Williamsburg for a meeting of the House of Burgesses, to which he had won election before he left the army. Winning a seat in Virginia's legislature had not been easy. Washington had tried and failed once before. In 1755, George William Fairfax had relinquished his assembly seat in Frederick County and sought election instead from Fairfax County. Washington, who immediately considered running for the vacant position, told his older half-brother John Augustine that he would stand for election if he determined that "my chance [of success was] tolerably good." Washington asked his brother to "fish out" whether several influential men whom he specified seemed "inclinable to promote my Interest." Approach them with "an Air of Indifference & unconcern," Washington advised, though if it appeared that they might be willing to back his candidacy, "you then may declare my Intentions & beg their assistance." Eschewing Fort Cumberland, headquarters for the Virginia Regiment, Colonel Washington had lived in Winchester, the principal hamlet in Frederick County, during much of that autumn, and it seems likely that he personally took pains to "sound [the] pulse," as he put it, of influential local figures. Between what he and his brother learned, Colonel Washington decided that he had a chance of success. He permitted his name to be added to the ballot for the election scheduled for December 1755.[2]

Elections in eighteenth-century Virginia, while different in many ways from twenty-first-century contests, were like today's in some respects. Elections for the House of Burgesses were called by the governor. Following the practice in England, elections were never more than seven years apart and were commonly conducted every two to four years. Two burgesses were elected at large from each county—the two candidates receiving the greatest number of votes were declared winners—while three towns and the College of William and Mary each had one representative. Election day for the 106 assembly seats was set in each locality by the sheriff and usually coincided with a day when the county court was to be in session. In Washington's time, it was common for candidates to play an active role in the election campaign. Some went on house-to-house canvasses, mingled with voters where a large gathering was assured—at church or court sessions, for instance—and even provided overnight lodging in their homes to rural voters who faced a lengthy journey to the polls. Some spread rumors and tales about their rivals or had their supporters do the dirty work for them. In the days preceding the election, many footed the bill for picnics, where liquor flowed and immense amounts of barbecue were consumed by the voters. Candidates sometimes hosted breakfasts, dinners, and balls at their residence, though these were for a more select portion of the electorate. Many candidates made available vast quantities of liquor somewhere near the polls on election day itself.

Only adult white male property owners could vote. The law stipulated that those who owned twenty-five acres of developed land or one hundred acres of undeveloped land, as well as town residents who owned their homes, could vote. Legally, only members of the Anglican Church could vote, though that law was no longer enforced. Thomas Jefferson estimated that half of the free white male population could vote, while Governor Dinwiddie thought an even larger percentage possessed suffrage rights.

An individual could vote or declare himself a candidate wherever he met the property qualifications. Although one could run for only one seat in the House of Burgesses, it was legal to vote in every county where one owned sufficient property, a practice that provided Virginia's most affluent citizens with the opportunity to cast ballots in numerous county elections.

The law also mandated that qualified voters must vote. Nonvoters were subject to a fine. But casting a ballot could be intimidating. Voting was done orally, not just before the sheriff, but in the presence of influential men who backed the various candidates. Moreover, the candidates were almost always present as well and knew who did, and did not, vote for them. By custom, the candidates did not vote for themselves. They were usually the last to vote and either abstained or voted for an opponent.[3]

In 1755, when Washington sought election for the first time, he waged a curious campaign. In fact, he conducted no campaign to speak of. He expended most of his energy on George William Fairfax's successful bid to win election in Fairfax County. Colonel Washington spent most of the six weeks prior to the election in Alexandria, juggling his military responsibilities and his fervor for helping with Fairfax's election. On one occasion while working for his patron, Washington apparently lost control of his temper during a run-in with one William Payne, a supporter of one of Fairfax's foes. Little is known about the incident. Stories circulated that the two exchanged harsh words, whereupon Payne, wielding a stick or cane, knocked Washington off his feet. Other versions suggested that Payne verbally "insulted" Washington. Whichever, many expected Washington to challenge Payne to a duel in the aftermath of their encounter. Instead, Washington, exhibiting both maturity and an impressive mastery of his emotions, apologized, admitting that he had been in the wrong.[4]

No less mysterious than the Payne incident was Washington's curious indifference to his own campaign. It may have stemmed from a belief that his interests would be better served at this juncture by tending to the happiness of the Fairfaxes than by gaining a seat for himself in the assembly. Or he may have overestimated the chances of his own victory, as the election was held six months after Braddock's debacle on the Monongahela, a time when Washington's reputation had soared.

What is clear is that Washington did little politicking. He left to John Augustine the task of rounding up much of his support. Even that was of questionable value, as it consisted of help rendered by influential friends from around Alexandria, some seventy-five miles east of Winchester. Colonel Washington did return to Winchester just before election day, but there is no record that he entertained the voters. If Washington had expected to run well, he was disappointed. Having waged a fatally inept campaign, he ran third in a field of three candidates, receiving less than 10 percent of the votes cast.

WASHINGTON MADE NO EFFORT TO WIN a House seat in the next election in 1757, but in the summer of 1758, while carrying out Forbes's orders to construct a road linking Forts Frederick and Cumberland, he once again sought election in Frederick County. He made the decision during the previous winter, prior to his courtship of Martha Custis, when he was recuperating at Mount Vernon from his second serious illness. His determination to again seek elective office perhaps suggests that he believed his return to civilian life was imminent, either because of his poor health or from optimism that Pitt's new strategy would result in military success in the near future. Or he may simply have thought that the odds of his success had improved. His chief opponent was the incumbent, Thomas Swearingen, whose reputation had been sullied by the poor showing of the Frederick militia, of which he was a leading officer.[5]

Washington was at Fort Cumberland, nearly fifty miles from Winchester, when the election was called early in July and set for three weeks later. This time around, he wanted to be present to court the voters, and never more so than after one of his supporters notified him that "the people & those whom I took to be yr friends in a great measure change their sentiments. . . . If possible I hope you'l be" in Winchester to campaign. Others, who also detected an erosion in support for Washington, urged him to "come down" to Winchester and "show your face." "Your being elected absolutely depends on your presence," one advised.[6]

This created a dilemma for Washington. Having already been upbraided by Loudoun and Dinwiddie for his frequent absences from his army, Washington was hesitant to approach Colonel Bouquet, his superior, about still another leave. Yet he was passionate about gaining a seat in the House of Burgesses. He probably thought that this would be the last time he could stand for election while the aura of actually being a soldier was on him, and it might be his last opportunity to seek election for several years. Risking the ire of Bouquet, Washington applied for another leave of absence, though he claimed without conviction that he could "hardly perswade myself to think of being absent from my more immediate Duty, even for a few days."[7]

Although Bouquet generously granted his request, in the end Washington never left Fort Cumberland. However, he worked industriously at headquarters to orchestrate a more effective campaign than he had run three years earlier. Washington lined up the support of several locally influential leaders, among them Gabriel Jones, known as "the Valley Lawyer" because of his prominence throughout the Shenandoah; James Wood, the founder of Winchester; John Hite, the son of an early settler and a town builder; and William Meldrum, the leading Anglican cleric in Frederick County. Well-to-do and powerful, these men were for the most part contemptuous of ordinary farmers—in their correspondence with Washington, they referred to the yeomen as "the Vulgar" and "the common Herd"—but they courted commoners, as they recognized that their votes "goe as farr as those of men of sence."[8]

If Washington stayed on at Fort Cumberland, he saw to it that several of his officers in the Virginia Regiment were posted in Winchester, where they could work on his behalf. He also rounded up influential acquaintances from Fredericksburg and Fairfax County who owned land in or around Winchester. They inveighed their farm tenants to vote for Washington. The efforts of this array of supporters appeared to turn the tide. "There is a good Prospect of Success in the insuing Election, as your friends Push every thing with the greatest ardour," one backer informed Colonel Washington.[9] Washington took no chances. Digging deep into his pockets to slake the thirst of the voters at picnics and other gatherings, he purchased twenty-eight gallons of rum, fifty gallons of rum punch, thirty-four gallons of wine, eight quarts of hard cider, a quart of brandy, and forty-six gallons of "Strong Beer." It added up to a quart and a half per voter, and it cost Washington over £39, nearly two years' income for a skilled tradesman. The frenetic activity, and the expense, paid off. Washington ran ahead of the other three candidates, garnering roughly 40 percent of the votes, outpacing the second highest vote getter by a wide margin, and besting Swearingen by nearly a four-to-one edge.[10]

THE HOUSE OF BURGESSES CUSTOMARILY MET twice each year. It ordinarily convened in the winter or spring for roughly two to four weeks and again in the autumn for a session of more or less similar length. As Washington soldiered until nearly the end of 1758, the first assembly session that he attended was that in February 1759. His new colleagues welcomed him with a warm resolution thanking "the late Colonel of the first Virginia Regiment, for his faithful Services to his Majesty, and this Colony, and for his brave and steady Behaviour." Witnesses said that he rose silently and bowed and blushed a bright red.[11] A legislator so uneasy before his fellow assemblymen that he not only was embarrassed by the praise and attention heaped on him, but did not seize the opportunity to speak, faced an uphill battle if he was to succeed.

Washington would serve in the assembly for sixteen years, but the discomfort that he betrayed at the very outset of his legislative career never disappeared, and he seldom shone as an assemblyman. Lacking a formal education, he often felt uncomfortable in the presence of better-educated men. As was true of most colonial assemblies, the House of Burgesses was filled with college graduates who had studied rhetoric and logic, and especially with lawyers accustomed to arguing with other attorneys, men who had honed their oratorical skills while addressing judges and juries. Jefferson, who served in the assembly with Washington for nearly seven years, once said that his colleague seldom spoke and never made a lengthy speech. Lacking a "mind . . . of the very first order," Washington, in Jefferson's estimation, had difficulty making fast decisions, an impenetrable obstacle to joining in a rapidly shifting debate on the assembly floor. But Jefferson thought Washington was prudent—it was "the strongest feature in his character," he said—and when he finally made a decision, "no judgment was ever sounder." On the rare occasions when Washington addressed the assembly, he unfailingly spoke to "the main point which was to decide the question," Jefferson added.[12]

As a soldier, Washington had been accustomed to gathering intelligence, sifting through it, contemplating what it—and his response—might mean, and, prior to making a substantive decision, summoning his principal officers to assemble in a council of war and make a recommendation. Something like that might transpire in a legislative committee, but the functioning of an assembly was nothing like the operation of an army. The House was run by its Speaker and clerk. Those powerful officers selected committee chairs, and in turn, they and the chairs determined the composition of committees, set the assembly's agenda, and controlled its pace.

In 1759 five major committees functioned in the assembly—a sixth was created a decade after Washington's election—and every legislator sat on at least one of those committees. To become a key player in the House, one had to rise to an influential position on one of the major committees, in the process surpassing a dozen or more colleagues. Washington never ascended to prominence on any committee. Jefferson, on the other hand, rose quickly in the House, becoming a committee chair in only his sixth year as an assemblyman. He had some assets that Washington did not possess. While Jefferson, like Washington, disliked and was equally ineffective at public oratory, his fellow burgesses were impressed by his nimble and formidable mind. Jefferson was also convivial and an exceptional conversationalist, and he wanted to excel in the assembly. Washington was cordial and sociable, but not genial. His "heart was not warm in its affections," Jefferson said of him, and no one ever said anything to the contrary about Washington's amiability. Washington was additionally the most taciturn of individuals. "Speak . . . but seldom," he once advised a young relative—ironically, he was giving advice on how to achieve prominence in a legislative body—and air your opinion only after you "make yourself thoroughly acquainted with the subject."[13]

When Washington entered the House, he was assigned to the Committee of Propositions and Grievances, a seat coveted by many legislators. While it regulated the militia and considered how to defend the frontier in the ongoing war, it also tended to matters that did not spark much interest in Washington, such as licensing ferry operators, regulating the fur trade, incorporating new towns, controlling stray animals, and setting fee schedules for certain public offices. Much of this was excessively trivial for a young man who for the past five years had frequently had to make life-and-death decisions. Nor did the other committees deal with matters that engrossed young Washington. They watched over the courts, elections, commerce, the rules of the House of Burgesses, and public claims. On occasion, he was assigned to a specially created committee. He chaired one panel that led to the only bill that he introduced during his first two years in the House, legislation to control "Hogs . . . running at large in the Town of Winchester." Washington chaired another committee that looked into a claim for restitution by a civilian whose property had been attacked by Indians. (The appeal was denied.) Other panels that he chaired investigated compensatory claims by severely wounded soldiers, and one considered indemnification for a soldier who had been held captive by Indians for more than two years. (That committee recommended payment of £35, £3 less than a burgess was paid for a few weeks' service each year.) Like all assemblymen, Washington from time to time introduced legislation designed to benefit a town in his district. One such bill that he sponsored would have prohibited the raising of goats and geese and forbidden swine "to go at large" within the county seat. He also sponsored legislation to help influential constituents, such as a bill that would have provided tax waivers on certain luxury imports and permitted the sale of property that was forbidden under the laws of entail.[14]

That he remained a secondary figure in the House of Burgesses during most of his tenure may not have especially bothered Washington. For all his competitiveness and ambition, he left the impression that he did not care particularly about being recognized as a legislative leader. It was sufficient to be a Burgess. He must also have known in his heart of hearts that he lacked the faculties for ascending to a paramount position in the assembly, and he did not want to make a fool of himself trying to be something that he could never be. Besides, in time he added other offices to his résumé: vestryman for Truro Parish, justice of the peace for Fairfax County, and trustee for the village of Alexandria.[15] But more than anything, Washington knew that while the members of the House of Burgesses attained a measure of respect from the public, he had already won far greater plaudits and preeminence through soldiering than was enjoyed by any legislator.

Washington asked permission to leave the legislature prior to the end of its session in the winter of 1759—members who were absent without authorization were subject to fines—and hurried home with Martha and her two children from her first marriage, four-year-old John Parke (Jacky) and two-year-old Martha Parke (Patsy). This was not the last time that Washington would depart early, but this time he was more than justified. Having just returned to civilian life after nearly five years and only recently married, he wanted to become acquainted with his new family and tend to Mount Vernon, which had lacked proper attention since Lawrence's death seven years earlier.

WASHINGTON LIVED AS A CIVILIAN for more than sixteen years before the Revolutionary War drew him away from Mount Vernon. It was a time filled with despondency, joy, and—at least as far as his entrepreneurial activities were concerned—considerable success. George and Martha, who were about the same age, enjoyed generally good health during these years, as they passed from their late twenties into their early forties. But both were dismayed that no children came of their union, and they were grief-stricken when Patsy, who had fallen ill with epilepsy at age eleven, died suddenly in the summer of 1773. Jacky's health was fine, but he grew from a pampered and spoiled child into an adolescent with a propensity for disappointing his parents. Although he was provided with educational opportunities that had eluded his stepfather, he failed to take advantage of them. A mediocre student, Jacky abandoned school altogether and married when he was eighteen.

Washington succeeded as a planter and businessman, but not without hitting many bumps in the road. Yet he was successful, and, as never before and seldom afterward, his success was due to decisions and planning for which he alone was responsible.

Even before his marriage, Washington had begun to transform Mount Vernon into a seat worthy of an influential Virginia planter. The dwelling was a one-and-a-half-story country farmhouse when it first passed to him, but during his final year of soldiering, Washington had launched a major remodeling project, raising the roof and adding a full second floor. Though Mount Vernon had been expanded dramatically, the residence that George and Martha inhabited before 1775 bore little resemblance to the mansion of their latter years, what today's visitors to Mount Vernon see. Two thirds the size of today's house, it also lacked such now familiar features as the piazza, cupola, and lush landscaping. Nevertheless, it had swelled to about twenty-five hundred square feet, not including the spacious detached kitchen. His grand new house soon groaned with Martha's furniture, items that he purchased from Lawrence's widow, and china, glassware, cutlery, and objects d'art that the couple acquired from England. Washington added to the property that constituted Mount Vernon, until by the time of the War of Independence the estate was more than twice the size it had been when it belonged to Lawrence: more than six thousand acres.[16]

WASHINGTON EXPECTED TO BE A PLANTER, the term that eighteenth-century Virginians used to designate those who raised tobacco. With thousands of acres at his fingertips—some of it was leased to tenants, who were directed to plant tobacco—he anticipated becoming a planter on a great scale. He was disappointed. Tobacco was the principal crop grown at Mount Vernon for five years and it was tended by a growing army of slaves, including the forty-six he had purchased after 1759, some of Martha's chattel, and bondsmen whom he leased.[17] Washington possessed adequate labor, but the land at Mount Vernon was poor, strangely inferior to the richer grade of soil at Belvoir only a stone's throw away. After a futile first year, Washington had fallen nearly £2,000 in debt. The next four years were better, but only marginally so, and he succeeded in reducing his in-debtedness, with its worrisome interest, by merely £100.

Washington's lifestyle contributed to his economic problems. He spent immoderately, acquiring a surfeit of luxury items—clothing, paintings, books, wine, delicacies, and toys and musical instruments for the children—as well as a seemingly endless array of tools for the farming operations. Throughout his life, Washington was a consummate consumer, though in this instance he was making up for lost time, trying to get his marriage and first experience in parenting off to a good start and filling up the empty space in his cavernous residence. But there was a habitual enjoy-it-while-you-can side to him, perhaps owing to the nagging realization that males in the Washington family tended not to be long-lived. In addition to the ex-pense of starting up both Mount Vernon and a marriage, Washington faced the two costly stays each year in Williamsburg for the legislative sessions. He also entertained lavishly, as was expected of a planter aristocrat. He occa-sionally faced considerable medical costs. For instance, in 1761 Washington was felled by another serious illness that left him to wonder briefly whe-ther he was "near my last gasp" and about to lose to "the grim King." He hastened to sumptuous Berkeley Springs in western Virginia for the me-dicinal waters and within a mere twenty-four hours pronounced that his "Fevers are a good deal abated." Before five years expired, Washington not only was debt-ridden, he had spent all the money he had acquired from his marriage.[18]

Washington was hardly the only Virginia planter to fall into debt. The mysteries and vicissitudes of the tobacco market, imperial restrictions on where the colonials could sell their product, an unfree labor system, and improvident lifestyles left most planters in debt or always staring into the abyss of indebtedness. But Washington was one of the few planters to do something about it. A shrewd businessman and risk taker, he began after five years to jettison tobacco production. It was not an easy step. Planter aristocrats in Virginia took great pride not just in growing tobacco, but in producing the finest-quality crop. It was a matter of self-esteem, and for a man such as Washington, who longed for attention and adulation, it was painful to see something other than tobacco growing at Mount Vernon.

By 1764, he was producing more wheat than tobacco, and the ratio grew more lopsided in favor of the grain each year thereafter. He could not have chosen a better time to start growing wheat, as grain prices in Europe soared in the midst of a series of bad harvest years. Washington additionally grew hemp, flax, corn, alfalfa, and buckwheat, and he set some of his slaves to fishing in the Potomac. In a few years, he had two large fishing crafts plying the river. He put many of his female slaves to work spinning fabrics, much of which—like the fish—was marketed. Washington additionally derived an income from the large mill that he built at Mount Vernon. Not everything that he tried worked. He continued to purchase land but was unable to sell most of it, and his investment in the Great Dismal Swamp along the Virginia–North Carolina border—where he hoped for windfall profits in the timber industry—was disappointing. Still, Washington the planter-businessman succeeded to the point that he stanched his further descent into indebtedness after the mid-1760s, and he even slightly reduced his existing debt. It was Patsy's tragic death in 1773, however, that enabled him to largely escape indebtedness. He sold some of her property, including her stock in the Bank of England (valued at £1,650), to settle many outstanding accounts.[19]

The same industry and perfectionist tendencies that Colonel Washington had displayed as a military commander were evident in his entrepreneurial activities. Though willing to experiment and take chances, he carefully planned and managed operations at Mount Vernon, and he put in long days looking after his workers. He demanded much of them, and the evidence suggests that he was a hard taskmaster.[20] Above all else, what stands out about Washington in these years prior to the Revolutionary War was his single-minded pursuit of wealth and the respect and acclaim it would engender.

WASHINGTON'S OBSESSION WITH WEALTH and standing at times lapped over into his public activities. He was not the first, and certainly not the only, politician to use his public position to enhance his private fortune. His introduction to public affairs had involved the machinations of investors in the Ohio Company. Though he had never invested in the company, he knew what those speculators were up to and knowingly served their interests as a means of getting ahead, all the while publicly denying that Virginia had gone to war in 1754 "to promote the Interest of a private Company."[21]

Following his military service, Washington's pursuit of western lands became a driving force in his conduct as an assemblyman. He not only hoped to secure title to some of the lush land in the newly won Ohio Country, but he fixated on acquiring a share of the bounty lands that had been promised to Virginia's soldiers. Early in 1754, after the assembly authorized the creation of an army to secure the Forks of the Ohio, Governor Dinwiddie had issued a proclamation pledging land to the men who enlisted. The governor said that two hundred thousand acres would be set aside as bounty lands, half of it east of, but "contiguous to," the Forks of the Ohio, the remainder to the west of the Forks. It was no more specific than that. Dinwiddie's promise of land to those who volunteered to soldier was not uncommon. During the many seventeenth- and eighteenth-century wars, numerous colonies proffered cash—typically an additional month's pay—and land (usually one hundred acres) to entice men to serve. Invariably, the bounties were for the enlisted men only, as the officers had abundant perquisites, including better pay, superior living conditions, the chance to win glory, and the luxury of resigning and returning home at their discretion. There can be little doubt that Dinwiddie intended Virginia's bounty lands to be solely for the enlisted men. His decree was entitled "A Proclamation for Encouraging Men to enlist," and it stated that land would be "granted to such Persons, who by their voluntary Engagement & good Behaviour," as "represented to me by their Officers," completed a tour of duty. When the war stretched on beyond that first year, it appears likely that Dinwiddie took for granted that every Virginian who subsequently enlisted in the province's army would also be due bounty lands, though he never addressed the matter.[22]

However, as long as the war continued, Washington knew that it was politically inexpedient to go after bounty land. But in 1759, his first year as a civilian, he thought the time was right to seek land in the Ohio Country, as the French had been removed from that region. During that year, Washington quietly colluded with Christopher Gist's son, Nathaniel, and two of his former officers, Captain George Mercer, his former aide-de-camp, and Captain Robert Stewart, to find the best land in the Ohio Country before others explored the area. They planned to "leave no Stone unturned to secure to ourselves this Land," as Mercer put it. Mercer, who was still in Virginia's army but appeared to be more the entrepreneur than the soldier, secured a surveyor's license with the expectation of marking off choice property for himself and his collaborators. "We cant possibly lose," Mercer added, as the "Lands on the Ohio will be valuable."[23]

Washington's connivance at this early date to attain a chunk of the best land in the Ohio Country is usually portrayed as something he entered into only because other officers had begun to scramble to secure claims. In fact, even before he left the army, Washington and his confederates had sent Nathaniel Gist, a frontiersman like his father, into the Ohio wilderness to scout for good land and establish their claims. More than a year passed before other officers, whom Mercer disingenuously smeared as "mighty Schemers," entered the picture. In a panic, Mercer reported to Washington in 1760, nearly eighteen months after he and his colonel had begun their collaboration, that Adam Stephen and Thomas Bullitt, both of whom had served in Virginia's army since early 1754, had filed surveys in Williamsburg on Ohio Country lands and planned to lobby the assembly to validate their claims.[24] A few months later, Mercer feverishly advised Washington that Stephen and Bullitt might lock up "all the best Land on the Ohio," for these rivals were seeking title to land running from near present-day Morgantown, West Virginia, north to Lake Erie and west to approximately the current Indiana-Illinois border.[25]

Though Washington and Stephen had previously enjoyed a good relationship—Stephen was the only officer who had defended Washington in the press after the Fort Necessity disaster—they had become economic adversaries. To Washington's utter astonishment, they also became political foes in 1761. Stephen decided to seek election to the House of Burgesses that year, choosing to run for one of the two seats from Frederick County. If successful, Stephen could knock Washington out of the assembly or deny election to Mercer, who also was running for election from Frederick County.

Stephen had excellent credentials. Eleven years older than Washington and a native of Scotland, he held a bachelor's degree from the University of Aberdeen and a medical degree from the University of Edinburgh. After practicing medicine as a naval surgeon for three years, Stephen moved to Virginia in 1748. Six years later, he was in Virginia's army and accompanied Washington to the Great Meadows. Stephen soldiered far longer than Washington—both he and Bullitt continued to serve for four years after Washington returned to private life—and he had risen to the rank of lieutenant colonel and been named Washington's successor as commander of Virginia's army. Stephen seemed to do everything with gusto, and the race he ran for election to the House was no exception. His was not a hands-off campaign. He took "indefaticable pains" to travel the length and breadth of Frederick County, "making Interest with it's Inhabitants," Captain Stewart reported to a worried Washington. Stewart added with a sneer that Stephen broadcast "his claims to disinterestedness, Public Spirit and genuine Patriotism," putting forward a thoughtful program designed to advance commerce and overcome frontier poverty.[26]

Washington expressed "the greatest amazement" at Stephen's behavior, which he implied was unseemly and uncharacteristic of Virginia's normal political practices. But Washington's campaign activities rapidly came to resemble those of his rival. Meticulous as always, Washington had kept copies of the 1758 poll sheets, which listed those who had voted in that earlier contest and how they had voted. Always keen on knowing who was against him, he utilized the list chiefly for determining which voters would have to be wooed. Washington spent considerable time campaigning in Frederick County. Among other things, he attended a cockfight, reactivated those who had backed him in 1758, and spared no expense in plying the voters with copious amounts of food and liquor. He also painstakingly hustled the sheriff, who under the law controlled the proceedings on election day. Nothing that he did was more important to his success in this canvass. Washington asked the sheriff to "contribute your aid toward shutting [Stephen] out of the Public trust." The sheriff did what he could to oblige. On election day, he admitted Washington's backers to the polling place first, a step that created a bandwagon effect. Many voters who waited nervously to cast their voice vote likely concluded that to vote against Washington—who stood by ominously watching the proceedings—would be tantamount to voting for a loser. Washington and Mercer were victorious, the former gaining 505 of about 1,200 votes, the latter taking 399 votes. Stephen, with 294 votes, finished a distant third.[27]

Washington's electoral triumph, however, did nothing to advance his hopes with regard to securing land in the Ohio Country. In the year after his reelection, Washington and all other aspirants for frontier land were stopped in their tracks by decisions made in faraway London. In 1762, with Great Britain still at war with France and Spain, Dinwiddie's successor,

Governor Francis Fauquier—acting at London's direction—prohibited the Virginia assembly from making grants of land that were occupied, claimed, or reserved by or for Indians until hostilities ended. The next year, peace came. Great Britain was victorious. In the Treaty of Paris of 1763, France and Spain relinquished to Britain all of North America from the Atlantic coast to the Mississippi River. But whatever hope existed that peace would lead to the abrogation of Fauquier's edict, setting off a frontier land rush, was dashed when the Crown issued the Proclamation of 1763. "We do strictly forbid . . . any purchases [of] or settlements whatever" on "all the lands and territories" west of the headwaters of rivers running into the Atlantic, it decreed. The restrictions on migration west of the Appalachians were to be "for the present and until our future pleasure be known." When that day arrived, the proclamation stated, all who had soldiered in Britain's victorious war would be awarded land, ranging from fifty acres for privates up to five thousand acres for field officers.[28]

The western frontier might be off-limits for immediate speculation, but that hardly stopped the activities of those who were mad for land. The ink had not dried on the Proclamation of 1763 before Washington, together with eighteen other speculators (including Bullitt and Stephen), formed the Mississippi Company in June 1763. Their hope was to secure title to lands well beyond the Forks of the Ohio, some 2.5 million acres in a region bounded by the Wabash and Tennessee rivers on the east and the Mississippi River on the west. The stockholders—Washington purchased stock worth £27—knew that London would not grant a charter immediately, if ever, but they wanted to be in place and competitive when the land bonanza commenced.[29]

In 1768, Britain, having at last negotiated territorial treaties with the Indians in the Ohio Country, lifted the ban on western settlement established by the Proclamation of 1763. The Mississippi Company petitioned the Crown and hired Arthur Lee, a Virginia businessman who was already in London, as its agent to look after its pursuit of a charter. The stakes were high. Not only had each stockholder invested a considerable amount of money, but, if successful, each stood to get his hands on thousands of acres of choice land. Alas, Virginia's high rollers did not succeed. Others were also interested in these prize lands, among them a coterie of some of the most influential political figures in the mother country. These English speculators formed the Grand Ohio Company and petitioned for ten times as much land as the Mississippi Company had sought. Savvy in the ways of power, Washington almost instantly saw the hopelessness of his enterprise. Alluding to the futility of competing with London insiders, he spoke of the "Predicament we stand in." Learning not long thereafter that the Board of Trade in London would side with the Grand Ohio Company, Washington wrote off his investment in the Mississippi Company as a loss. The only good news for Washington came when London announced that it was considering establishing a new colony where the Grand Ohio Company's lands were situated and that the five thousand acres promised by the Proclamation of 1763 to field officers in the last war were to be within the anticipated new colony. An outsider, Washington had lost to the well-placed in the metropolis, but he derived some solace from his expectation that a colonial government would establish order, stimulating rapid settlement. In the final analysis, Washington expected the value of his other lands near the Ohio River to increase quickly.[30]

THE REVOCATION OF THE PROCLAMATION of 1763 also meant that Virginia might at last allocate the bounty lands that Dinwiddie had promised nearly fifteen years earlier. Whatever Dinwiddie might have intended, it was a foregone conclusion that the officers would also receive bounty lands. The decision could not have gone any other way. Too many former officers were too powerful, while the impecunious men who had made up the ranks of the Virginia Regiment were politically impotent. Washington understood the reality of early American politics quite well, and for some time he had been covertly active to ensure that the lands were made available at the earliest possible moment, that the officers received the lion's share of the bounty lands, that the lands went only to those who had served in the Fort Necessity campaign (which would reduce the pool of veterans, leaving more land for each man), and that he had a hand in determining the location of the lands that were ultimately allocated.

In 1762, Washington, Stephen, and Andrew Lewis—another former officer in Virginia's army—had petitioned the Crown on behalf of "the surviving Officers and Soldiers" to permit the immediate allocation of the bounty lands.[31] The Proclamation of 1763 had stopped them in their tracks, but Washington had not been especially distressed. He predicted that the royal ban on dispensing frontier lands would shortly be lifted, as it was merely "a temporary expedient to quiet the Minds of the Indians." He was correct. In 1769, as soon as he learned of the proclamation's abrogation, Washington petitioned the Governor's Council—the upper house of the Virginia legislature—and Virginia's new governor, Baron de Botetourt, asking that they implement Dinwiddie's promise by making a grant of two hundred thousand acres to those who had joined the Virginia Regiment between February and July 1754 and to no others. Washington's petition also included some self-serving suggestions under the guise of helpful hints. He urged that some bounty lands be set aside along the Monongahela River, which plunged almost due south of Fort Pitt through Pennsylvania and into Virginia, while the remainder should hug the Great Kanawha River, which flows north and west through present West Virginia until it joins the Ohio at present-day Point Pleasant. As all this vast territory was part of Augusta County in 1769, Washington advised that the county surveyor, swamped with other duties, would be "greatly retarded" in completing the surveys and making available the lands. It would be better, he went on, that another surveyor be appointed.[32]

As was so often true with Washington, there was more than met the eye in his appeal to Botetourt. Two years earlier, in 1767, he had engaged William Crawford, a surveyor from Frederick County whom he had long known, to reconnoiter the very area that he now proposed for the bounty lands and to keep a sharp lookout for "some good Tracts." He hoped to lay his hands on "some of the most valuable Lands" in that region, Washington confided, but it was imperative that no one know what he was up to. If others became aware of "the Scheme I am now proposing," Washington said, they too would become active "before we could lay a proper foundation for success." He asked Crawford to "keep this whole matter a profound Secret," suggesting that he describe his wilderness journey as a hunting trip.[33]

Thus when Washington in 1769 proposed a specific location for the bounty lands, he had long since learned from Crawford of the suitability of the region. Washington got what he wanted. One day after he petitioned Botetourt and the council, those officials announced that they were "pleased to grant 200,000 acres of land on the Great Kanhaway, &c. to the officers and soldiers" who had joined the Virginia Regiment prior to July 4, 1754, the date of the surrender of Fort Necessity. The grant's precise location on the Kanawha was to be made by a surveyor, whose appointment was to be left to the president and masters of William and Mary College, the licensing power for county agents. Washington quickly and successfully urged the appointment of Crawford as the surveyor.[34]

Washington swiftly summoned those who had served as officers in the Virginia Regiment in 1754 to a meeting at a tavern in Fredericksburg. These old comrades, who had never been together as a group since the war, enjoyed a convivial dinner lasting several hours. Afterward, they turned to business. Washington not only proposed that they send someone to explore the grant area, he volunteered to go and to take along Crawford. Ever loyal, the officers not only consented, they agreed to cover the cost of the endeavor.

Deep into the autumn of 1770, Washington and Crawford, accompanied by a physician, several servants and slaves, and a handful of Indian guides, made a long canoe trip down the Ohio to the Great Kanawha. Washington spent five chilly November days of his nine-week journey floating down the Kanawha, scouting the land. He took copious notes, recording which areas were good for planting tobacco, those that were better for pasturage or more suitable for grains, those that were especially rich, and those that were altogether useless for farming.[35]

The next year, Crawford returned to the region with a surveying team. When he had completed surveys of slightly more than a quarter of the lands, Crawford hurried not to Williamsburg and not to meet with all the officers, but to Mount Vernon. There, he and Washington redrew the surveys in accord with the notes that Washington had carefully made the year before. With Washington alone knowing which were the best bottomlands in the tract, the surveys were presented to the Governor's Council and shown to the officers of the Virginia Regiment.[36]

Neither the memorial that Washington presented to the council nor the surveys any longer exist, but it is likely that Washington proposed a plan for dividing the bounty lands, one that he and the officers had drawn up when they convened in Winchester a few months after Crawford's return from the Kanawha. As was true of the initial meeting in Fredericksburg, none of the enlisted men were invited, or were present, at the Winchester gathering. All that is known for certain is that the council, which had rubber-stamped everything that Washington and the officers had requested during the past two years, eventually decreed that the distribution be as follows:

3 field officers . . 15,000 acres each
5 captains. . . . . . 9,000 acres each
8 subalterns . . . . 6,000 acres each
2 cadets . . . . 2,500 acres each
7 sergeants . . . . . 600 acres each
4 corporals. . . . . 500 acres each
52 privates . . . . . 400 acres each[37]

Soon thereafter, Crawford returned to the frontier and surveyed another quarter of the grant. Once again, he and Washington met and prepared the final survey before it was submitted in Williamsburg, a step that was never divulged to the other officers.[38]

The council swiftly awarded specific tracts to each of the eighty-one claimants, acting, it appears, on the recommendation of the officers, who were swayed by Washington's insistence that there was no difference in quality from one tract to another. It hardly comes as a surprise that no claimant received land "in that Country [that] is so good as your Land," as Crawford told Washington. "Your Lots of Land I think [are] much the best on the hole River," the surveyor added. Not long passed before a few of the enlisted men visited the bounty lands and some discovered that their tracts were worthless. Some complained, but the officers and captains responded with a public statement that echoed what Washington had said (Washington signed the statement, too, and probably had a hand in its preparation): "there is no great inequality in the Land." The officers also assured the men and the authorities of Washington's "disinterested conduct" and his "Intention to administer Impartial Justice" in the allocation of the bounty lands. But in time, some of the officers traveled to the Kanawha to see the bounty tract for themselves. They came away "a good deal shagereend [chagrined]" at what they found, Crawford told Washington. It is difficult to feel sorry for the officers. They had jobbed the enlisted men. Eighteen officers had used their power and influence to take seven eighths of the bounty lands that Governor Dinwiddie had intended solely for the enlisted men. Now they realized that Washington, who was even more clever at manipulating the system, had secured "the cream of the Country," as Washington himself privately acknowledged was the case.[39] Virtually every acre that he took for himself was prize bottomland.

Prior to this, Washington possessed more than twelve thousand acres.[40] His bounty lands godsend more than doubled his property holdings, and he was due to receive another five thousand acres under the terms of the Proclamation of 1763. But he was not satisfied. He made overtures to some of the enlisted men about selling their bounty land, often advising them that there was a good "chance of our never getting the Land at all," as Great Britain's projected trans-Appalachian colony would include "every Inch of the Land we are expecting." One of the men that he contacted was Jacob Van Braam, the translator he had scapegoated for the surrender of Fort Necessity. Writing him for the first time in seventeen years, Washington told Van Braam—who was due to receive nine thousand acres—that it had been "absolutely impossible to make an equal distribution of the good & bad" bounty lands and that the likelihood existed that his tract consisted of inferior lands. Washington also enlisted one of the half-brothers in his enterprise, cautioning him to approach his targets "in a joking way, rather than in earnest" to "see what value they set upon their lands." Van Braam was not duped, but some were. Others simply saw an opportunity to turn land that they did not need into cash that they could use. Washington acquired an additional 5,100 acres in this fashion, most of it at give-away prices. Eleven years after the Treaty of Paris, Washington possessed some 32,000 acres, not counting the 5,000 more he expected to receive.[41]

WASHINGTON HAD PLAYED A DECISIVE but quiet part in the matter of the bounty lands. At about the same time, he also began to play his most public role as a member of the assembly. It came about as a result of his active participation in the protest against Great Britain's new colonial policy.

When the French and Indian War ended in 1763, London moved to impose parliamentary taxes on its American colonies, something never previously done in the 150-year-old imperial relationship, and to restrict customary facets of provincial autonomy. The taxes arose from the staggering debt that Britain had accumulated during the long war. The restriction of colonial autonomy had been quietly considered in ministerial offices for two decades and stemmed from a fear that the distant and lightly controlled colonies might otherwise drift gradually toward independence.[42] Taxes and laws to tighten customs regulations came first. These revenue-raising measures were designed not to find money with which to retire the debt—new and heavy taxes were levied on residents in the homeland for that purpose—but to help pay for the large British army that was to be deployed in the trans-Appalachian West for the purpose of opening the region to settlement. London additionally created admiralty courts to replace the traditional provincial courts as sites for trying those charged with violations of imperial trade laws. The ministry also sought control of the appointment of a substantial number of justices and, with the Proclamation of 1763, to restrain western migration as never before.

Washington was not troubled by every step taken by London, and he welcomed some measures. British regulars would pacify the Ohio Country—their mere presence would be a powerful inducement to the Indians to cede tribal lands—and the projected new colony in the Ohio Country could field militiamen to assist the regulars in the event that force was needed. Both were positive strides from Washington's vantage point, as they would hasten the day when he could sell at a good price the western lands that he was accumulating. And as he was an exporter, the stricter regulation of imports set off few alarm bells at Mount Vernon. Taxation was a different matter, although Washington's response to Britain's initial impost, the Stamp Act, was tepid, to say the least. He did not even linger in Williamsburg for the House debate on the tax. In the second year of his great conversion from tobacco to grains, Washington took an early leave to return home to oversee the planting of that year's wheat crop. While the major cities were afire with street protests against the tax, and Patrick Henry fanned the flames in the House of Burgesses with his passionate oratory, Washington's diary entries read: "Sowed Turneps. . . . Began to seperate the Male from the Female hemp. . . . Seperated my Ewes & Rams. . . . Finish Sowing Wheat. . . . Began to Pull the Seed Hemp. . . ." He was not in Williamsburg to vote on the Virginia Resolves, a series of resolutions adopted by the assembly that denounced the Stamp Act as unconstitutional, though in his correspondence that fall he unmistakably agreed that parliamentary taxation represented "a direful attack upon [American] liberties.[43]

The tenor of Washington's letters suggests that he believed London had blundered into the Stamp Act and that it would be repealed rapidly as British merchants discovered that the impost had a deleterious effect on colonial trade. On the latter score, he was correct. The Stamp Act was repealed in 1766. However, new parliamentary taxes, the Townshend Duties, were imposed on America the following year, making it clear that the Stamp Act had not been an errant undertaking that Parliament had stumbled into. Parliament was bent on taxing the colonists. Washington had cheered those who had attacked the Stamp Act, saying that they were "deservedly entitled to the thanks" of all Americans who saw that parliamentary taxation was an "Act of Oppression." Riled though he appeared to be, Washington did not hurry to Williamsburg for the spring 1768 session of the assembly, which was to take up the Townshend Duties. He remained at Mount Vernon, where for six days he met with Crawford, just back from his first inspection of the possible bounty lands tract.[44] By the time Washington finally arrived in the capital, the House of Burgesses had already adopted a formal remonstrance against the taxes. Several colonial assemblies joined with Virginia in denouncing the taxes and urging their repeal, but when their pleas fell on deaf ears in London, a stronger colonial opposition galvanized. Furious essays and pamphlets poured off American presses, crowds turned out in the streets to demonstrate against the taxes, and several colonies adopted boycotts of British trade. Surprisingly, it was Washington—publicly silent until now about Britain's new colonial policies and until now content to be a secondary figure in the House—who took the lead in 1769 in pushing for Virginia to add its name to the list of colonies that had closed their ports to British imports in an attempt to force the repeal of the duties.

Though guarded in what he said, Washington evinced a hostility that ran deeper than his opposition to the taxes. He questioned Parliament's mercantile policies restricting America's free trade, century-old legislation that fell especially hard on Chesapeake tobacco planters by requiring that they market their product only within the British Empire. Also a producer of textiles, Washington further worried that Parliament might attempt to restrict his freedom to manufacture, as it had previously prohibited the production of hats, finished woolen goods, and certain types of iron.[45] In 1769, for the first time, Washington exhibited a decidedly radical outlook, a profound disaffection toward the mother country, greater than was displayed at the time by any other so-called Founding Father, save for Samuel Adams. Washington raged at "our lordly Masters in Great Britain," rhetoric that pulsated with contempt toward those who fancied themselves superior to the provincials. He denounced Britain's new policies as a threat to "the liberty which we have derived from our Ancestors," and he was among the first—if not the first—to speak of going to war "in defence of so valuable a blessing." He told other influential Virginians of his willingness to soldier once again, saying that he was ready to shoulder his musket whenever his country called. Despite his bellicose talk, Washington added that "A[r]ms . . . should be the last recourse; the de[r]nier resort." Instead, he proposed that Virginia boycott imports from the British homeland, mentioning that several northern colonies had already begun to organize embargoes. He predicted that if English and Scottish merchants faced a nearly American-wide trade stoppage "till ruin stares them in the face," they would see to the repeal of the objectionable taxes. Washington did not propose a stoppage to Virginia's exports, perhaps as he was an exporter or possibly from the certainty that the House of Burgesses would never consent to nonexportation. What is clear is that Washington, like most planters, would be largely unscathed by nonimportation. It might even prove helpful in coping with his debt problems, as, denied British goods, he would for a time be forced to curtail his inordinate consumption. If it also reduced the extravagant indebtedness of Virginia's small farmers, enabling them to better make their rental payments to gentlemen landlords, such as Washington, so much the better. Because some types of British-manufactured clothing would be disallowed by nonimportation, that might lead to increased sales for the fabrics woven at Mount Vernon, and that, too, would be for the better.[46]

Washington went first to George Mason, his neighbor at nearby Gunston Hall, who was a more active and adroit legislator. Mason agreed with his suggestion, and the two collaborated to produce a plan for a boycott. When the House of Burgesses met in May, Washington took the lead, successfully steering the boycott toward enactment. After a dozen years in the assembly, it was the first major piece of legislation for which he was responsible. The next year, when alterations were thought to be needed in the structure of the boycott, Washington was named to the committee to prepare the changes, the most important special panel to which his colleagues had ever assigned him.[47]

Washington's enmity toward British policies was not new, but the fever pitch in his tone intimated a transformation in his thinking. The simplest explanation for the sea change in his outlook—and one that is not to be entirely dismissed—is that Washington truly believed British policy was unconstitutional and posed a grave threat to American liberties.

But more than constitutional issues moved Washington toward a truly radical outlook. Deep into middle age by 1769—he had just celebrated his thirty-seventh birthday—Washington had all along been shaped largely by his intertwined quests for recognition and wealth. It stretches credulity to think that his conduct at this juncture turned on a dime. Proud and ambitious, Washington resented America's subservient status in the eyes of Britain's ruling class. He had bridled at his second-class treatment when serving as a colonial military officer, and he must have been deeply and irremediably scarred by the humiliations he had suffered at the hands of the likes of Dinwiddie and Loudoun. A military veteran who had sacrificed to help Britain win a sensational victory in a grueling war, not to mention a highly successful and wealthy planter-businessman, Washington found the thought of second-class status even more intolerable. Believing that provincials were the equal of those who lived in the British homeland, he yearned for greater American autonomy, for the opportunity for him and his fellow Americans to exercise greater control over America's destiny and their own.

Colonists danced to the tune played in London. Virginia had been unable to do anything to secure the Ohio Country without London's prior approval, and during the war its military strategy had hinged on the wishes of the commanders of the British army. Americans had not been consulted about the terms of the Treaty of Paris, nor had they had the least say in the issuance, or abrogation, of the Proclamation of 1763. London was responsible for Indian diplomacy, not the colonials. Parliament, which did not include a single American representative, made all imperial trade laws. Americans had no control whatsoever over British policy. There was nothing Americans could do to establish a new colony in the Ohio Country, no matter how badly Washington and other land speculators—or land-hungry colonists—wanted it. Virginians had been powerless to set aside bounty lands until London permitted such a step. Thousands of Americans had fought, and many had died, in the French and Indian War, but it appeared certain that it would be the well-placed and well-connected who lived in the metropolis who would collect the prize booty across the mountains. At great risk and incredible effort, Washington had risen to a position of power in Virginia, but it did him little good when his interests—or those of any American—collided with rival interests in England. His experiences in public life since 1754 must have led him to the cold and unpalatable conclusion that those at the center of power in the parent state held the whip hand. Washington had plans, investments, desires, and dreams, and none could ever be more substantive than smoke in the wind as long as faraway authorities wielded the final authority over his affairs. By 1769, Washington had moved from troubled brooding to a willingness to act.

The ministry's supercilious attitude toward the provincials was never more evident than in its truculent response to the earliest colonial protest against the Townshend Duties. After a handful of provinces sent remonstrances to London insisting that the taxes were unconstitutional, the secretary of state for American affairs, Lord Hillsborough, lectured the Americans on their "flagitious attempt to disturb the peace." To deny parliamentary authority was "to subvert the true principles of the constitution," he said, and with the carelessness of one who tosses gasoline on a smoldering fire, Hillsborough threatened to dissolve any colonial assembly that subsequently attacked the taxes. It was as if Hillsborough had rubbed the colonists' noses in their servility, and to Washington it was irrefutable proof of London's "malignant disposition toward Americans."[48]

Despite Hillsborough's bluster, it was the ministry that in the end backed down in the face of the boycotts by Virginia and several other colonies. Early in 1770, the Townshend Duties were repealed, save for a lone tax on imported tea. Several colonies continued their boycott of tea from England, and Washington adhered, refusing to serve tea from England at his table at Mount Vernon. Otherwise, during the next three years life returned to normal, and there was no hint in Washington's behavior, diary, or correspondence of uneasiness with the mother country. He devoted his customary energy to his myriad agribusiness endeavors, bought land in the Ohio Country and elsewhere—he even looked into purchasing land in Florida, though nothing came of it—and for the first time in the early 1770s became an active player in a decade-old enterprise to make the Potomac River navigable from Fort Cumberland to Alexandria, the crucial step needed to link eastern Virginia to the trans-Appalachian West by river. He maintained a good relationship with Virginia's royal governors and down to 1774 socialized frequently with John Murray, fourth Earl of Dunmore, who had become

Virginia's colonial governor three years earlier. Washington also enjoyed a cordial relationship with Maryland's governor. Busy as he was, Washington found ample time for leisure. He entertained extensively at Mount Vernon, vacationed from time to time at Berkeley Springs, gambled frequently at cards and other table games at a tavern not far from Mount Vernon, frequently attended horse and boat races, enjoyed the theater while in Annapolis and Williamsburg, was an avid hunter and fisherman, and regularly attended meetings at his Masonic temple in Alexandria.[49]

Washington turned forty in 1772, prompting him to joke to his brother that the age lines in his face made him appear as if he were "very near my last gasp." The time had come, he decided, to have his portrait painted. It was the first portrait for which he had sat, and he said at the time that he thought it would be the only painting ever made of him. The artist he hired, Charles Willson Peale, would, Washington knew, "describ[e] to the World what manner of man I am," though Washington had some control over how he was presented. For the past thirteen years, he had been an assemblyman and successful planter-businessman, but Washington spurned the garb of an eminent civilian and donned the uniform he had worn in the Virginia Regiment. Not only had soldiering been the great adventure of his life, he clearly saw it as his greatest achievement. He had never again held as much power, realized such a lofty triumph, or won such grand acclaim. He wanted to be remembered as a soldier.[50]

There was a stilted quality to the painting that Peale produced, though that was perhaps true of most portraits. Peale also had a habit of depicting many of his subjects as portly, and in this portrait Washington appears to be fifteen pounds or more overweight. During the next five or six years, Peale and other artists painted Washington. In Peale's works, Washington was always shown as stout, but others subsequently delineated their subject as lithe and trim. George Washington Parke Custis, Washington's stepgrandson, subsequently said that he believed no artist was as successful as John Trumbull in capturing Washington. In Trumbull's portraits, mostly painted nearly a decade after Peale's 1772 rendering, Washington appears well-conditioned, sinewy, and hardy. His actual appearance in 1772 is not known, but Washington certainly was a more animated individual than shines through in Peale's portrait.

While posing for Peale, Washington remarked that the artist would "be put to it" to fathom his subject's inner being.[51] No one knew that better than Washington, who worked diligently all his life to hide so much of himself from the public's eye. Peale captured Washington as a proud individual, though his rugged side and hard, forceful bearing did not come through. Nor were the charismatic qualities that enabled Washington to lead men revealed in the portrait. The spark that activated Washington, that set him apart from so many others, eluded Peale.

WHEN WASHINGTON SAT FOR PEALE, the colonists' troubles with the mother country seemed to be ancient history. A year later, by the fall of 1773, the situation had changed dramatically. The cities were afire with protests, including passionate, even violent, crowd actions, and the once moribund boycotts of dutied tea had been revived. No one was more surprised than Washington at the return of the imperial crisis. The Tea Act, a new tax that Crown authorities endeavored zealously to enforce, resurrected the dormant issues of parliamentary taxation and the legitimate degree of American autonomy. The most celebrated response to the act by the colonial protesters occurred at year's end—the Boston Tea Party.

The disturbances occasioned by the Tea Act went unnoticed by Washington, at least in his diary and correspondence. Other matters weighed on his mind that fall and winter. He learned, for instance, that the British government had ruled that the land bounties promised soldiers in the Proclamation of 1763 were to be awarded only to British regulars. Washington had believed, with justification, that all officers who had served in the French and Indian War were due five thousand acres, and in fact he had already purchased the share of another Virginia officer. Now he stood to lose ten thousand acres and the money he had spent acquiring the additional share. He ranted at London's "malice" toward the colonists. "I can see no cause why Americans (who have serv'd his Majesty in the late War with as much fidelity, & without presumption, with as much Success, as his British Troops) should be stigmatiz'd," he said. To this he added: "I conceive the services of a Provincial Officer as worthy of reward as those of a regular one."[52]

More bad news for Washington followed in 1774 when news of the Quebec Act reached Mount Vernon. In that legislation, Parliament gave all land north of the Ohio River to the province of Quebec, a step described by historian Woody Holton as designed to "abolish Virginia land speculation west of the Alleghenies." As a result, not only was Washington worried about his existing claims, but he feared that his chances for further speculation within the Ohio Country would be limited. One of Washington's former officers in the Virginia Regiment, also a speculator in the Ohio Country, railed at "the present faithless and venal Ministry." Thomas Jefferson, whose claims were affected as well, insisted that the Quebec Act was unconstitutional, even though it bore the seal of George III. Washington raged that what was happening was "altogether incredible."[53]

That spring, in May, the House of Burgesses had declared a fast day to protest London's Coercive Acts, harsh measures imposed on Massachusetts in reprisal for the Boston Tea Party. The governor, Lord Dunmore, responded by proroguing the assembly, but it met anyway in defiance of the royal governor and pledged to act in concert with other colonies to aid Massachusetts. Washington supported the burgesses' defiant actions, and in August, when the assembly, calling itself the Virginia Convention, insolently defied the governor by meeting again, Washington was present. In the interim between the two meetings of the legislators, he had served on a Fairfax County committee that prepared a series of resolutions on parliamentary policies. George Mason likely drafted the county's statement of protest, but there can be no doubt that Washington endorsed it wholeheartedly. Mason spent the night prior to the adoption of the resolves at Mount Vernon, and Washington probably contributed to the editing of the document. The resolves were in step with the Stamp Act Resolves that Patrick Henry had drafted, and the House of Burgesses adopted, in 1765, but these simmered with a more inflammatory spirit. Like the remonstrance a decade earlier, the Fairfax County Resolves stipulated that Parliament lacked the constitutional authority to tax the colonists, though it conceded Britain's right to regulate imperial trade, including Virginia's imports and exports. But the Fairfax County document went further. It accused the ministry of advancing "a premeditated Design and System" to impose "arbitrary Government" on the American provinces and, in a cry for greater autonomy, asserted that Great Britain at times "may have a seperate, and . . . opposite Interest" to those of the colonies. As much as anything, Washington and his fellow signers of the Fairfax County petition desired that Virginians be "treated upon an equal Footing with our fellow subjects" in the mother country. They even appeared to hope that a comprehensible and "just, lenient, permanent, and constitutional" framework could be established to delineate the parameters of Britain's power and the rights of the colonies.[54]

Privately that summer, Washington made it clear that he was fed up with "Petitions & Remonstrances." Actually, he had reached that point years before, when he had urged Virginia to move beyond rhetorical statements and institute an economic boycott against the Townshend Duties. In 1774, he appealed yet again to his fellow colonists to embrace "vigorous measures" that would compel London to back down. As was to be expected of a Washington-Mason collaboration, the Fairfax County Resolves had urged an American-wide boycott of British imports until "our just Rights and Privileges" were recognized by London. The resolutions proposed nonimportation in 1774, followed by an embargo of exports in the fall of 1775 in the event that Britain had not repealed the Tea and Coercive Acts. Whether Washington believed that economic pressure alone would produce results is not apparent. Nor is it clear whether he was committed to American independence at this point. The Fairfax County Resolves denied that "there is an Intention in the American Colonies to set up for independent States," though it would have been impolitic, as well as extremely dangerous, for a handful of private citizens to have said anything else.[55]

In fact, Washington's actions indicated that the enveloping despair he had first exhibited in 1769 had been transformed into rebellion. He was prepared for a strident response against Britain's imperial policies, if a majority of colonists were of like mind. Washington was prepared to use force. Bitter that his pocket had been picked by the revocation of his bounty land claims and other western actions taken in faraway London, Washington yearned to exert his free will, and influence, in quest of his goals. He longed for his life and destiny to be untrammeled by those across the sea. Long since, he had come to see that as a colonial subject, he could never hope to realize the self-sufficiency that he desired. In his most private moments, Washington must have understood that his yearnings could be realized only in an independent America in which Americans controlled their own destiny. Opportunity was what the New World had always represented for the ambitious, and for Washington the colonial rebellion was largely about gaining greater freedom for Americans to chart their own course. If that meant that the greater autonomy benefited primarily the most affluent in America and those who were politically powerful, so be it.

During 1774, Washington went about his business as if he presumed there would be no war and that the imperial relationship, though perhaps modified in some way, would remain intact. In that crisis-laden summer, he socialized with Governor Dunmore while he was in Williamsburg and spent a fortune—£5,375—to acquire land in the Pumunkey River valley.[56] Even so, it was apparent that he saw this crisis as different from those of its predecessors. The Coercive Acts were not only "despotick Measures," they were part and parcel of a "regular, systematic plan" to "fix the Shackles of Slavry upon us," he said. He also said that the cause of Massachusetts was America's cause. Though he deplored "their cond[uc]t in destroyg the Tea" in the Boston Tea Party—the Fairfax County Resolves had even stated that "if the Destruction of the Tea at Boston be regarded as an Invasion of private Property, We shall be willing to contribute towards" restitution—Washington charged that Britain was playing divide and conquer. Singling out Massachusetts for victimization was London's ploy for exploiting each colony "piecemeal."[57]

By the time the Virginia Convention was gaveled into session on August 1, the notion had germinated in "our Sister Colonies to the Northwd," as Washington put it, that all the American colonies should come together in an intercolonial congress to decide on the best response to Britain's severe measures.[58] There was talk of a national boycott—the trade embargoes during the Stamp Act and Townshend Duty crises had been undertaken by only some colonies—and as that seemed to be what he and Mason had in mind when they worked up the Fairfax County Resolves, Washington welcomed the convention's endorsement of establishing a united front to confront Great Britain.

The convention voted to send a seven-member delegation to Philadelphia in September 1774 for what was being called "the Continental Congress." The delegation was a star-studded list of provincial leaders, including the Speaker of the House and a former attorney general. Washington was chosen as well. He was the third highest vote getter of the seven, finishing behind Richard Henry Lee and Patrick Henry. He received 98 of 104 possible votes.[59]

Though Washington had played a leading role in Virginia's boycott during the Townshend Duty crisis and he had supported every radical step taken in 1774, he was far and away the least active legislator of the seven who were being sent to Philadelphia. No one could have expected Washington to play a standout role in the Continental Congress. It was likely, in fact, that he would never speak in the debates. So why was he chosen? One of the best-known Americans, Washington would lend stature to the Congress in the eyes of residents of the colonies and Great Britain alike. Unlike Samuel Adams and some others who were certain to attend, Washington was no fiery rabble-rouser, and that would send a signal to London that the American protest had popular support among prudent and moderate colonists. But Washington was sent mostly because many were convinced that this time Britain would not back down and that war would come. Some saw the Continental Congress not merely as a means of arranging a unified American resistance to the Coercive Acts, but as a necessary first step in preparation for war. There was certain to be talk in the corridors and over meals, if not in the sessions themselves, of the necessary steps for taking up arms and how to wage war. It made sense to have Virginia's premier soldier present to engage in those discussions. It also was a means of showcasing Washington. Should the day come when America created an army, Virginia, like every other colony, would want one of its own in a high position in that force.

Unlike in 1769, when he had told Mason that taking up arms was a last resort, in this instance Washington remained silent about the use of force. But it is inconceivable that this man who had soldiered for five years did not give hostilities with Britain considerable thought. In one letter, his subliminal notions appeared to seep through. Writing to George William Fairfax in June, Washington declared that the "Ministry may rely on it that Americans will never be tax'd without their consent," and in the same sentence, having barely shifted gears, he allowed that "god only knows what is to become of us, . . . having a cruel & blood thirsty Enemy upon our Backs, the Indians." Here was Washington the warrior, contemplating war with Britain on one front and war with the Indians, Britain's probable allies, on another.[60]

As a blistering sun bore down on August 30, two other delegates to the Continental Congress, Patrick Henry and Edmund Pendleton, a veteran politician whom many thought the best debater in Virginia, arrived at Mount Vernon to gather Washington for the five-day trip by coach to Philadelphia. It was Washington's first visit to the city since his crushing interview with Loudoun seventeen years before. With some twenty-five thousand inhabitants, Philadelphia was America's largest city. It had a hospital, a college, and a busy port, and its tree-lined streets were paved, at least downtown. Near the City Tavern, on Second Street above Walnut, where Washington lodged during the eight weeks the Congress was in session, brick sidewalks, dotted with streetlamps, coursed alongside the wide streets.[61]

Congress met daily, except on Sundays, at Carpenter's Hall. Its sessions generally ran from midmorning until late afternoon and were preceded and followed by committee meetings. In his leisure time, Washington did a bit of sightseeing, worshipped on three of his seven Sundays in the city— he sampled a Quaker meeting and attended mass at St. Mary's Catholic Church, each a new experience for him—and almost every night he was someone's guest for dinner.[62] Washington faithfully attended the congressional sessions, though there is no record that he spoke during any of the debates, nor was he appointed to any committee.

As remains true of legislative sessions today, much of the really important action took place "out of doors," as John Adams, one of Massachusetts's delegates, put it. At meals or over wine or steaming pots of tea, the congressmen sized up one another, learning who was an ally and how far each confederate was willing to go in defiance of Great Britain. In John Adams's code, those who were "solid, firm" would definitely support a boycott and those who were "spirited" could be counted on to support the use of force, if it came to that. There could be no doubt about where Washington stood.[63]

Washington was one of the more sought-after delegates. His views on standing up to Britain were soon enough known, but his colleagues were eager to learn his views on whether the colonists could successfully wage war against the parent state. Furthermore, nothing was more troubling to eighteenth-century Americans than the prospect of entrusting any man with the awesome power that a military commander would possess. If it came to creating an army and if Washington was made a general officer in that army, the congressmen wanted to know whether he could be trusted. Silas Deane, a Connecticut congressman, came away impressed with Washington's "easy Soldierlike Air" and his "hard . . . Countenance," a view that many probably shared. The First Congress was crucial for Washington's future, and he passed inspection, striking others as reserved, solemn, modest, prudent, decent, industrious, rugged, and possessed of an iron will.[64]

Congress, meanwhile, did precisely what Virginia and Massachusetts desired: It adopted a national boycott of goods imported from Great Britain. It also took another step that Washington clearly favored. As the militia in most colonies could be called to service only by the governor, which was hardly likely, Washington had worried that the constitutional system "has left us without the means of Defence." Congress solved that problem by urging each province to activate its militia and commence training. "A Preparation for Warr is Necessary to obtain peace," was how Patrick Henry put it. Most of the congressmen, John Adams concluded, "Shudder at the Prospect of Blood" and prayed that hostilities could be avoided. But Congress appeared to be saying that it would fight if necessary, and it warned General Thomas Gage, the commander of the British army in America, that should he use force against Massachusetts, he would be resisted by "all America."[65]

When the delegates scattered for home late in October, none knew what the future held. John and Samuel Adams appear to have thought war was the next step. Virginia's Richard Henry Lee, in contrast, presumed the ship that took word of the colonial boycott to London would return home with news of the repeal of the objectionable parliamentary acts.[66] Washington did not divulge his innermost thoughts, but he proceeded as if war were unlikely, or as if hostilities would be brief should war break out. Although he drilled Alexandria's militiamen on three occasions and contributed money to raise and supply another Fairfax County company, Washington also purchased more frontier lands, and that spring he was preparing to send a work party to the Kanawha to clear a settlement on the bounty lands he still hoped to receive. But in April 1775, word arrived at Mount Vernon of a clash between British regulars and colonial militia in Massachusetts. At Lexington and Concord, and along the road that linked those villages to Boston, blood had been shed. The carnage on that crimson day had been incredible. Almost three hundred British soldiers had been killed or wounded, while nearly one hundred Americans had been cut down.[67]

Washington left few memorable utterances in his long public career, but when he learned of that bloody April 19 in Massachusetts, his response was eloquent. A "Brother's Sword has been sheathed in a Brother's breast," he said. The fighting in New England, he continued, meant that "the once happy and peaceful plains of America are either to be drenched with blood, or Inhabited by Slaves." He knew what his choice would be. No "virtuous Man" could "hesitate in his choice."[68] An Anglo-American war had begun.

When Congress adjourned in October, it agreed to convene again on May 10, 1775, unless the imperial crisis had been resolved. Lexington and Concord meant that what Washington in February had called "our critical situation" had worsened dramatically.[69]

Once again a member of Virginia's delegation to Congress, Washington left Mount Vernon for Philadelphia on May 4. When he departed he was a civilian, but his luggage contained a buff-and-blue uniform that he had recently designed for Alexandria's soldiers. He knew that he would be a soldier again, and soon. He traveled heartened by the prospect that although the people "wish for nothing, more ardently, than a happy & lasting reconciliation with the parent State," they were willing to fight rather than surrender their liberties. And he believed that "more blood will be spilt" in the coming war "than history has ever yet furnished instances of in the annals of North America."[70]

PART TWO

AMERICAN HERO

The Crucial First Year:
Boston, 1775–1776

B Y THE TIME Washington reached Philadelphia for the meeting of the Second Continental Congress, some in the Massachusetts congressional delegation had already decided to nominate him to head a national army. On the day the war began, three weeks to the day before Congress reconvened, Massachusetts militiamen had driven more than a thousand British regulars back down the Concord Road and into Boston. That night and the next day, and during the gray, cold week that followed, thousands of militiamen from throughout New England descended on Boston to join in a siege operation that at once was designed to confine the redcoats within the city and to force them, from lack of supplies, out of the city. In no time, the five thousand British soldiers in Boston were trapped by some sixteen thousand New England citizen-soldiers, men who had for the most part been farmers, artisans, and laborers until a day or two before. Some New England newspapers called the jerry-built force the Grand American Army.[1]

It was an American army in name only. That was the rub for New Englanders, and for some from outside New England as well. There were really four separate armies besieging the redcoats in Boston, one from each of the New England colonies, Massachusetts, Connecticut, Rhode Island, and New Hampshire. Each provincial army took orders from the assembly back home, although, as the operation was taking place in Massachusetts, each tacitly acknowledged that the Bay Colony was in charge. That meant the army's commander in chief was General Artemas Ward, a native of Shrewsbury, Massachusetts, who held two degrees from Harvard and had soldiered in the French and Indian War. Ward took his orders from the Massachusetts Provincial Congress, which like the Virginia Convention was an extralegal assembly.

In short order, the authorities in Massachusetts recognized manifold problems with this arrangement. They knew that New England lacked the resources to maintain the siege army for an extended period. Besides, they thought it unfair for the region to bear the brunt of struggle against Britain's malign policies when every American colonist was affected. Early on, many New Englanders concluded that it was imperative that Congress take over the Grand American Army, flesh it out with soldiers from throughout America, supply it with provisions from throughout America, and pay for it with revenue raised from throughout America.

Not a few from outside New England were just as eager to nationalize the army, including those who desperately hoped to preserve America's ties to the British Empire. Not everyone trusted the New Englanders. Some thought the Yankees were radicals, troublemakers who covertly sought independence. After all, the Boston Massacre and Boston Tea Party had occurred in Massachusetts, and the war had broken out there as well. Moreover, Congress had hardly reassembled in May before word arrived that small forces raised by Massachusetts and Connecticut—led by Benedict Arnold and Ethan Allen, respectively—had crossed, uninvited, into neighboring New York and seized British-held Fort Ticonderoga. Virtually every congressman thought it unacceptable for each province to act unilaterally. Nearly all also considered it intolerable that an army raised by one colony could, without authorization, march into another province. Some degree of centralized control was essential. A consensus rapidly developed that it would be better to have Congress make American policy and to create a truly American army to secure the interest of all the colonies.

Since the first days of the war, the popular leaders in Massachusetts had known, as one put it, that they wanted "a Continental army of which this [siege army] will be only a part." Some wrote their congressmen to urge the appointment of Colonel Washington and Charles Lee, a veteran British officer who had retired and moved to America, "at the Head of it." New

England congressmen, in turn, launched a campaign to convince Congress that the siege army was a weak link: It was too small by half and alarmingly deficient in arms, artillery, and ammunition; illness had reached epidemic proportions, and the officers did not know how to cope with the camp diseases; the lower-grade officers were, to a man, inexperienced; without a sovereign civil government in charge, the army was "[in]capable of perfect regulation." There was some exaggeration in their plea, but not much.[2]

Congress had been in session only a few days when Virginia's Richard Henry Lee proposed the creation of a national army, but a month passed before the legislators took up the matter. The most conservative members, who at this point likely constituted a narrow majority, insisted on first petitioning George III to ask that he resolve the imperial crisis by rebuking Parliament. The more radical members thought such a petition ludicrous, but they could not afford to anger their colleagues. Unanimity was essential if war was to be waged. After protracted debate, an entreaty to the Crown was adopted during the second week of June. That cleared the way for Congress to create "the American Continental army" on June 14. As soon as the vote was taken, Massachusetts's John Adams took the floor and recommended Washington as commander of the new army. Washington had known this moment would come. Indeed, he had suggestively worn his new buff-and-blue uniform as he sat listening to the wearying days of debate. He immediately excused himself so his colleagues could talk freely. They talked for a day and a half. Some may have opposed Washington's appointment, but if so, it was from fear that New England's soldiers would not follow a non–New England commander or from anxiety that dumping General Ward might cause deep political divisions within Massachusetts. Considerable time was probably spent questioning Virginia's congressmen about Washington and discussing what authority was to be vested in the commander.[3]

The issue was never in doubt, as Washington must have known. He was appointed commander of the Continental army on the second day of deliberations. Washington was chosen for numerous reasons, some military, some political. He had commanded Virginia's army for nearly five years. He exuded leadership qualities. Grave, formal, and, if not quite unapproachable, certainly exceedingly reserved, Washington conveyed a sense that he would brook no nonsense. He radiated vigor, was in good health, and at age forty-three was young enough in all likelihood to remain fit and to see a long war through to its conclusion. He was a Virginian, a son of the largest and wealthiest American province. He was also said to be a man of indomitable will. He was unassuming as well, "a compleat gentleman," said Thomas Cushing of Massachusetts, who added: "He is sinsible, amiable, virtuous, modest, & brave." One congressman lauded Washington's self-confidence. Another praised him as "Clever." Tall and brawny, Washington evinced a rugged, even hard, manner, striking everyone as the very embodiment of a soldier. A Philadelphian who met Washington while Congress was in session gushed that the Virginian "has so much martial dignity in his deportment that you would distinguish him to be a general and a soldier from among ten thousand people. There is not a king in Europe that would not look like a valet de chambre by his side." If a national army was to supplant the New England army, some congressmen thought it imperative that it be led by someone from outside New England. Their thinking, as Connecticut's Eliphalet Dyer put it, was that the appointment of a non–New Englander "removes all [sectional] jealousies," solidly "Cements" the new American union, and "takes away the fear" that a "New England Genll proving Successfull, might with his Victorious Army give law to the Southern & Western" colonies. Above all, Congress presumed that Washington could be trusted with the awesome power he was being given. Washington's colleagues had been scrutinizing his behavior, or inquiring into it, since the First Continental Congress the previous autumn, and they had concluded, as one remarked, that he was no "harum Starum ranting Swearing fellow," but a "Sober, steady, and Calm" individual whose judgment was fed by experience.[4]

Washington started in spectacular fashion, winning adherents in three separate statements made in the first days following his appointment. On the day after being named commander in chief, Washington returned to the Pennsylvania State House—known today as Independence Hall—to address Congress. It was one of the few speeches, if not the only one, that he made in the two congresses he attended. Washington rehearsed a litany that he had made familiar while commanding Virginia's army in the French and Indian War. He felt unequal to the task, but "as the Congress desire it I will enter upon the momentous duty, & give every power I possess in their service & for the Support of the glorious Cause." To that, he added a stunning and far more important announcement. Although Congress had already voted a salary of $500 per month for the army's commander, Washington said that "as no pecuniary consideration could have tempted me to have accepted this Arduous emploiment at the expence of my domestk ease & happiness," he would accept no pay. He asked only that he be reimbursed for his expenses.[5] Few, if any, decisions that Washington made during the war were more important than his determination to eschew a salary. During the previous war, he had left himself vulnerable to the charge that he lived the high life, like a rakish nabob. Those attacks stung him deeply, and he resolved to never again leave himself open to such a damaging recrimination. Now a mature middle-aged man, Washington had learned from his mistakes as a young commander in Virginia, and from the very outset in this war he sought to avoid repeating his errors of youth and inexperience. He crafted a persona as a "noble and disinterested" patriot, which was precisely how John Adams described him for having refused to accept a salary.[6]

Before June ended, Washington also sought to overcome popular fears that he might use the army to make himself a dictator. He did so in a widely heralded speech delivered to the extralegal legislature in New York City, where he paused en route to New England to take command of the army. Washington told the New Yorkers that when he again became a soldier, he "did not lay aside the Citizen."[7] It was an awkward way of saying that he was committed to the principle that soldiers were subordinate to civilian authority. This was an established canon throughout the British world, one that Washington had grown up with, heard repeated often in the Virginia assembly and Congress, and fervently embraced. But there was more to his utterance. Many who supported the American protest and the war believed that their confrontation with what they saw as British tyranny had transformed the colonies. The protest had begun against parliamentary taxation, but along the way many activists had come to see the colonial resistance as a redemptive and republican uprising. Many rebels saw their struggle not simply as an uprising to secure greater American autonomy, but as a crusade to assure that public policy would henceforth carry out the wishes of the governed. Hand in glove with this ideal was the notion that republicanism required that those who wielded public authority were obligated to sacrifice their personal interests to the greater public good.[8] That had not always been a characteristic of Washington's behavior in Williamsburg, as his bounty lands hustle demonstrated, but once he became commander of the Continental army, he firmly embraced the concept.

A few days later, shortly after his arrival outside Boston, Washington presented a written address to the Massachusetts Provincial Congress in which he announced his intention to sacrifice "all the Comforts of social and political Life, in Support of the Rights of Mankind, & the Welfare of our common Country." Washington the soldier understood better than most that Americans must show "Patriotism without Example in modern History," as he put it, or the war could not be won.[9] He knew too that it was imperative he set an example of self-sacrifice. His remarks to the New Englanders were the first in what would be an eight-year campaign on his part to urge his fellow citizens to renounce luxury and selfish pursuits and to serve a greater common good.

Washington's behavior throughout the war leaves no doubt that he meant what he told the New Yorkers and the Massachusetts assembly. Like many colonists, Washington appears to have changed by 1775, refashioned perhaps by his idealism and the demands of America's resistance against British coercion. Washington's previous public service had been driven, or at least inflected, largely by self-interest. To be sure, his chances of economic reward increased with the growth of American autonomy, but nearly every activist was driven in part by self-centered motives, whether the quest was for wealth, renown, power, revenge, or some combination of hidden passions. Most also believed in the cause, and most probably fervently embraced the notion that a better, freer world was at hand if they could distance the provinces from the heavy reach and menacing corruption of the parent state. For the first time in his life, Washington was truly committed to an ideal that transcended his self-interest. He told the Massachusetts authorities that he was fully committed to what Americans were fighting for—a better America and the salvation of human rights.

Like many of the Founders, Washington harbored a keen sense of history, and from his youth he had thought of his place in history. He wanted to be remembered. By wearing his uniform when he sat for Peale's portrait, Washington had as much as said that he hoped to be remembered as the leader of Virginia's army in the French and Indian War. This war provided him with another opportunity to win acclaim as a soldier and to garner laurels in a grander cause than the one he had fought for a generation earlier. Washington also hoped that future generations would think of him as worthy and virtuous. He knew, as did others, that the leaders of the colonial rebellion were playing on a grand stage.

Washington was changed by the realization. Gone was the pleasure-seeking, consumer-oriented planter. Gone was the man who, in an earlier war, had abandoned his men repeatedly to look after his personal interests. Gone was the man who had been too busy with private pursuits to tend to his obligations in the assembly. The times and the cause demanded that he recast himself. He became General Washington, the self-denying and unstinting warrior who was focused on the national interest and on victory.

In his first hours as commander, Washington additionally crafted the story that he had not sought the appointment. It was "an honour I neither sought after, nor desired," he claimed unconvincingly. He wanted the world to believe that "a kind of destiny" had led to his selection. Several scholars have noted Washington's utter fearlessness in combat and have speculated that he believed Providence protected him, preserving him for something greater. Here was a variant of that notion, and in Washington's own words. It was his heartfelt sense, he said, that fate had led him to this moment and that for "some good purpose" Congress had called him to lead the army.[10]

WASHINGTON KNEW THAT HE WOULD FACE immense dangers and difficulties. He was embarking on "a tempestuous Ocean" with "no safe harbour," was how he put it. Uneasy with the prospect of criticism, such as he had faced at the hands of the "Virginia Centinel" in 1756, uncertain whether he could cope with the political leaders in thirteen separate provinces as well as the Continental Congress, and above all, unsure if he could successfully defend against Britain's army of regulars—of professional soldiers and officers—Washington confessed his "inexpressable concern" to Martha. Patrick Henry subsequently recollected that on the night of his appointment, Washington, with tears in his eyes, predicted: "From the day I enter upon the command of the American armies, I date my fall, and the ruin of my reputation."[11] However well-placed his foreboding, General Washington would in fact face a task even more arduous than he imagined.

Many were convinced that disunity among the colonists would be Washington's greatest problem, perhaps the cause of his undoing. In London, Frederick Lord North, the prime minister, and his cabinet had gone to war supremely confident of victory, in some measure because they believed not only that the colonists were strangers to one another, but that they were fatally divided by competing interests.[12] Washington thought differently, and he was more nearly correct. His travels—few, if any, provincials and none of North's ministers had traveled as extensively through North America as had Washington—led him to see potentially unifying similarities among the colonists. Most hailed from British ancestry, spoke the same language, had grown up under the British political and legal systems, and, as their strikingly unanimous outrage at London's new imperial policies since 1763 demonstrated, embraced common ideals and perceived a common threat. Washington had personally emphasized that Massachusetts's problems were America's problems. He had seen his fellow Virginians rally around the faraway New Englanders. He had been part of a Congress that defied the parent state. What is more, during that warm, sunny June of 1775, Washington sensed that the American people had received him with a rich storehouse of goodwill, beholding their new general as a man of "disinterested Virtue and distinguish'd Patriotism." That testified to America's unity, but at the same time, in the words of historian Don Higginbotham, it provided Washington with the "symbolism to promote political unity." All that Washington did and said in his first days as commander was designed to solidify the colonists' newfound union into a vibrant confederation. In a very real sense, General Washington was well in front of the thinking of most Americans. He was laying the cornerstone for an American nation, "our common Country," as he was already referring to it publicly.[13]

Washington certainly understood the limits of Congress's authority, and he knew full well that the thirteen colonies were reluctant to surrender sovereignty to a national government. But Congress was not powerless. It had taken incredibly sweeping steps in its short life. In the space of nine months, it had established a national boycott of British imports, gone to war, created an American army, and issued a Continental currency. But as Washington was well aware, Congress could only request, not require, that each colony comply with its actions, and this was true with regard to furnishing men and materials for the army. Each province would adhere to congressional policy if it possessed the capability and the will to do so. One of the lessons Washington had learned in his earlier military experience was that morale was a tenuous thing. While the American public backed the war effort in the summer of 1775, its continued support hinged on how well the war went. In addition, Congress had gone to war in 1775 to achieve reconciliation with Great Britain on America's terms. The point of the war was to force the parent state to end its objectionable imperial policies. If America's war aims changed—if Congress subsequently declared independence, for example—no one knew whether popular support for the war would increase or diminish.

On June 23, in a simple, early morning ceremony conducted as the tilting orange rays of daybreak touched the chimneys of Philadelphia, Congress sent Washington off to war. Nearly every delegate stepped outside the Pennsylvania State House for the simple ceremony. It was warm and humid, as summer mornings tend to be in that city. Several local militia units had assembled. A martial band played. Nervous horses pranced, clattering noisily on the stone path. Washington's newly selected aide-de-camp, Thomas Mifflin, a successful Philadelphia businessman, and the secretary chosen by the commander, Joseph Reed, an established lawyer in the city, waited to board a carriage. No doubt brief speeches were delivered, as there were, after all, some four dozen politicians in the assemblage. At last, the good-byes were said and Washington sprang easily on his powerful white charger to ride for Boston. With drums banging and fifes resounding and the heavy thump of treading hooves, the procession set off toward the edge of the city and an uncertain future.[14]

HAVING SURRENDERED HIS SEAT in Virginia's delegation when he left for the front, Washington no longer was a member of Congress. From this point forward he could urge, even cajole, congressional action or inaction, but there were no guarantees that Congress would listen. Much of what Congress would do or not do would hinge on political considerations— and what Congress did or did not do could have life or death implications for Washington. He was Congress's servant. General Washington fully understood that, but so there could be no mistake, Congress had given him carefully crafted instructions.

General Washington was given "full power" to act as he thought necessary for "repelling every hostile invasion" of North America and "for the
defence of American Liberty." He could recruit men, but naively and my-
opically, Congress decreed that the total number of soldiers in the Continental army was not to exceed twice the number of enemy soldiers. He
could fill vacancies in the ranks of colonels and inferior officers, though
only Congress could name general officers. "Consistent with prudence,"
he was authorized to use force to subdue those Americans who bore arms
"against the good people of the United Colonies." He was given authority to act as he saw fit in emergencies, though he was expected to be "dis-
creet." He was enjoined to abide by the Articles of War, which Congress
formally adopted a week later, and to maintain "strict discipline and order" within the army. He was forbidden to reduce the size of the army
without congressional authorization. Finally, Congress mandated that
Washington seek the advice of councils of war—conclaves of his highest
officers, a standard practice in the British army and their provincial counterparts throughout the colonial wars of the eighteenth century—prior to
making substantive decisions.[15]

Washington communicated with Congress on a regular basis throughout
the war. He wrote seven letters to Congress during the first thirty days following his departure from Philadelphia, and throughout the war he sent
dozens of letters each year to its president. He also corresponded with the
Board of War and Ordnance, a five-member congressional committee that
came into being during the following summer to oversee, among other
things, strategy, logistics, fortifications, appointments, and prisoners. Washington had alienated Governor Dinwiddie by appealing over his head to influential members of the assembly. In this war, Washington carefully
refrained from bypassing or attempting to pressure Congress, though he
now and again communicated with personal acquaintances among the delegates. He corresponded with former colleagues from Williamsburg who
had moved on to Congress—especially Richard Henry Lee, a powerful figure in the body, and Joseph Jones, a longtime acquaintance who lived near
Fredericksburg—and he was in touch now and again with congressmen
with whom he established uniquely close and comfortable relationships,
especially Robert Morris of Pennsylvania and Gouverneur Morris of New
York. Washington drew on these ties to learn what was afoot in Congress, to

urge their help with local officials, and at times to object to something that Congress was doing or considering. For instance, Washington took issue with a congressional plan to defer iron workers from military service; he sometimes objected strenuously when Congress ordered the redeployment of units under his command to another theater; and he not infrequently served as a conduit through which the concerns of the officers were brought to the attention of Congress. But he never tried to use his stature or his position at the head of the army to cow the civilian authorities.[16]

Congress sent committees to camp from time to time to meet with Washington about pressing issues. From the outset, he demonstrated subtle, ingenious skills that almost always enabled him to manipulate the congressmen to his way of thinking. His talents were never better displayed than with the first committee that Congress dispatched, a three-member panel that included Benjamin Franklin, South Carolina's Thomas Lynch, and Benjamin Harrison, his former colleague in Virginia's delegation. Washington had been told in advance that the committee was being sent to discuss important matters that he had raised. He was not surprised, therefore, when the visiting congressmen, who arrived at camp outside Boston in mid-October 1775, broached matters such as the army's lack of gunpowder, inadequate winter clothing, the depleted pay chest, and a host of other issues that Washington had brought to the attention of Congress since July.[17] The talks, conducted over glasses of wine or a warm dish of tea—as the colonists were wont to put it—were cordial, even friendly, and the congressmen pledged to rectify the problems that the commander in chief had pinpointed. But a day or two into the meeting, the congressmen stunned Washington by telling him that Congress "much desired" an attack against the British army that was besieged in Boston. Some in Congress appear to have gone to war believing that peace, and reconciliation, would be achieved by Christmas, and a few had grown impatient with an army that had remained inactive throughout its four-month existence.

Washington was more than flustered. He was angry. This was unpalatable. He had already raised the issue of attacking the British in Boston with his generals more than a month earlier, and they had unanimously recommended against an assault. They feared that losses were likely to be excessive, the chances of success slim, and the "Consequences of Failure" incalculable. Washington thought it bad enough that Congress was leaning on him to do what his generals thought inexpedient. Worse still, Congress, far from the military front and composed of men with virtually no military experience, wanted to dictate strategy, just as Dinwiddie had done twenty years before. During the French and Indian War, Washington had responded to the governor with a firestorm of passion until finally, ruinously, he had told Dinwiddie that his policies were misguided and harmful. This time around, Washington handled matters differently. While the congressmen awaited his answer, he summoned another council of war. Once again, the generals unanimously agreed that an attack was "too great a Risque." Washington reported their recommendation to the committee, but he also put the burden on Congress. Was Congress, he asked with unruffled calm, willing to sanction a shuddering bombardment of Boston, a shelling that would result in the "Loss of the Town & the Property therein?" That effectively laid the issue to rest. Later in the autumn, Congress resolved that it was Washington's decision to make, but—clearly wishing to saddle the commander with responsibility should Boston be ruined in an attack—the legislators directed that he should act only if the chances of success were good.[18]

Congress ordered one military operation in 1775 to which Washington objected, but he did not make an issue of it. Before Washington left Philadelphia, Congress had forbidden an invasion of Canada. A month later, at the end of June, while Washington was en route to Boston, Congress reversed itself and ordered Major General Philip Schuyler, commander of the army's Northern Department, to lead an invasion army to Quebec. Zeal for taking Canada was strong in New England and among New Yorkers, and their passion was fired by economic and political reasons as well as military. If Quebec was taken, it might be the decisive blow that would compel Great Britain to immediately make peace on America's terms. And if independence was declared, and achieved, America could keep Canada, which would assure the new nation of secure northern frontiers, a vast supply of rich farmlands, and bountiful fishing rights.

If Congress was enthralled with the idea of invading Canada, Washington was not. He knew that many congressmen believed "the Canadians will be pleased with it, and join" with the American invaders, but he did not share their sanguine expectations. Not only did Washington think "the Canadians are very averse to engage in this unnatural Contest," he knew the operation would siphon men and supplies from his force.[19] However, he also knew that strenuous resistance to the Canadian invasion was unthinkable. An outsider about to take command of a totally New England army, Washington understood that his success depended on maintaining the support of the Yankees. He could not afford to alienate the New Yorkers and New Englanders before he took command.

Washington went along with the planned invasion, and in time, he championed it and made it his own. He conceived of sending Colonel Benedict Arnold with about one thousand men toward Quebec by way of Maine. If the British defended Quebec, Schuyler, who was to lead his invasion force down the Champlain corridor, would be free to seize Montreal. If the British went after Schuyler, Quebec might be easy pickings for Arnold. "There may be some Danger," Washington remarked laconically, but the venture was worth the risk, he said in a turnabout, for Quebec's capture would "have a decisive Effect."[20] (Washington's initial reservations about this Quebec campaign were well-founded. Some twenty-seven hundred men set off in September, but only thirteen hundred remained when the two American armies rendezvoused outside Quebec in December. A desperate attack on Quebec on December 31 failed, with the rebels suffering the loss of nearly one half of their army, killed, wounded, or captured.)[21]

WASHINGTON DID NOT HAVE AN ADVERSARIAL RELATIONSHIP with Congress. The legislators wanted him to succeed: if he failed, their heads might go into a noose. But Washington and the congressmen often saw things through a different prism. Washington's job was to win the war. Congress also wanted to win the war, but its members were constantly aware of their decisions' political, social, and economic ramifications in the provinces they represented.

Nor did Congress always understand the problems that Washington faced. Civilians seldom realized that no eighteenth-century army was ever as strong as it appeared to be on paper. Up to a quarter of the men were habitually unfit for duty, laid up as a result of poor nutrition, exacting duties, and remorseless camp diseases. No army could function without supplies, and not everyone fully understood the Continentals' logistical difficulties. Keeping an army well furnished was a formidable task under the best of circumstances, but obtaining adequate provisions from colonies that were independent of Congress, and getting those goods to camp over hundreds of miles of unpaved roads and across rivers, was at times nearly impossible. Nor did every congressman appreciate the uncertainties with which Washington coped in deciding what to do with his army or what to expect from the enemy. His knowledge of his foe hinged on military intelligence, which was an inexact science. Information poured in from a variety of sources, much of it contradictory, all of it fragmentary, and some measure of it nearly always inaccurate. Washington had to put the pieces together and pray that he did so correctly. Sometimes he failed. For instance, during the first summer and fall of the war, he concluded from intelligence reports that the British army inside Boston consisted of 11,500 men. In fact, it never exceeded 8,400 men.[22]

No congressman was more astute than John Adams, and as the head of the Board of War in 1776–1777, he acquired a good understanding of the army and its difficulties. But like his colleagues, Adams at times was short-sighted about the problems faced by the army's leaders. Adams told the generals that their "Misfortunes are owing to Misconduct." He criticized their defensive strategy, claiming in the face of abundant evidence to the contrary that the "Army that Attacks has an infinite Advantage." However, when the Continentals assumed the offensive and failed, Adams captiously responded that the army should act with "caution and circumspection. . . . It should act chiefly upon the defensive." Blind to Washington's troubles in making civilians into soldiers overnight, Adams carped at the "Dissipation, Debauchery, Gaming, Prophaneness and Blasphemy" among the soldiery, blasted "the Pride, the Vanity, the Foppery, the Knavery . . . among too many of the Officers," and complained of the "dearth of Genius" among the general officers. Adams even said that any officer who was surprised by the enemy should be executed.[23]

DESPITE THEIR DIFFERENCES and occasional misunderstandings, Congress maintained a generally good relationship with Washington, sometimes giving him a free hand, more often working cooperatively with him. Washington's first major undertaking after assuming command was to take apart the army and reassemble it. Most scholars have portrayed Washington's action as arising from his shock and dismay at what he found when he reached Cambridge, and there is something to that. But Congress had created the Continental army in part because of the cries from New Englanders that their siege army was fatally flawed. Creating a new, national army was the Yankees' way of starting over and, perhaps, getting things right with their second chance. Among other things, both Congress and the leaders in New England wanted to have another go at the appointment of general officers, as many in the Grand American Army were political appointees who were almost certainly unfit for the colossal task at hand. The Yankee congressmen appear to have let their colleagues know that whoever was selected to command the national army would have to tear down the existing army and rebuild it. Washington likely expected to face this challenge even before he left Philadelphia, and only one week after taking command he announced that "abuses in this army . . . are considerable . . . and the new modelling of it" was unavoidable.[24]

Over the next several weeks, a "great overturning in the camp" took place, as one soldier put it. Exerting a calm authority, Washington saw to the breaking of many officers and the introduction of an unsparing discipline, as he reorganized the army along the British model.[25]

With two exceptions, Congress permitted Washington to have his way. Washington appears to have been horrified at the sight of African Americans bearing arms. Black militiamen from New England had fought on the first day of the war, joined the Grand American Army, and fought again at Bunker Hill in June. But black soldiers were not part of Washington's experience, and he issued a general order forbidding their further enlistment. His outlook was an amalgam of racism, fear that the weapons carried by African American soldiers would find their way into the hands of slave insurrectionists, and concern over whether white soldiers from outside New England would serve with blacks. He was also reluctant to set a precedent for enlisting blacks, lest the British vie to recruit them as well, a competition that Washington did not believe the Americans could win. But six months after assuming command, Washington reversed himself. He may have discovered that his black soldiers could perform as ably as his white soldiers, or he may have been swayed by the pleas of free blacks who met with him and complained of "being discarded." At the end of 1775, Washington authorized the enlistment of free blacks and said that he believed Congress would concur. It did not. Congress ruled that those African Americans already in the Continental army could reenlist, but "no others" might serve.[26]

Congress balked a second time during the first great crisis that Washington faced. The men from Connecticut and Rhode Island who joined the siege army in May had agreed to serve until December 10; those from New Hampshire and Massachusetts had enlisted through the end of the year. As the first hint of autumn appeared, Washington learned that few of these men intended to reenlist. Most were yeomen who were reluctant to leave their farms untended a second consecutive year, but most, too, were fed up with soldiering, which they quickly enough discovered to be a hard and dangerous life. Washington raged in private at the New Englanders' "dirty, mercenary Spirit" and their "dearth of Publick Spirit, & want of Virtue." He did not breathe a word of this to Congress, but early in 1776 he asked that one-year enlistments be abandoned in favor of raising soldiers for at least three years of service. To make soldiers out of civilians "requires time," he said, adding that in the long run Congress would save money and "have infinitely better Troops" by converting to long-term enlistments.[27] Congress responded by offering assorted bounties to help recruiting, but it would not contemplate longer enlistments. It feared making the Continental army into a standing army, which many congressmen, including Samuel Adams, viewed as "always dangerous to the liberties of the people," while others like John Adams looked on such an army with poisonous mistrust, convinced that it could consist only of "the meanest, idlest, most intemperate and worthless" in society.[28] Having no stake in society, Adams and others feared not only that such men would be untrustworthy soldiers, but that they would pose as much danger to American liberties as that threatened by British tyranny.

WHILE WASHINGTON KEPT A WARY EYE on Congress, he also took pains during his first months on the job to court influential New Englanders. He was, after all, a stranger in a strange land and hardly the revered man he would come to be in later years. Despite the self-confidence that he radiated for public consumption, Washington wrestled with numerous insecurities. There was his lack of formal education, now magnified, perhaps, as seemingly every New England official he met was a college graduate, usually from Harvard or Yale. Though widely exalted for his triumphs in the

French and Indian War, Washington had to have been aware not only of the dearth of his attainments on the battlefield, but of how little he had contributed to Forbes's success in taking Fort Duquesne. Washington additionally arrived in Massachusetts alert to the possibility that his displacement of General Ward might have alienated some in New England. Whatever concerns he harbored about supplanting Ward could only have increased once he learned that before his departure from Philadelphia, Ward had successfully—brilliantly, some thought—drawn the British into an attack on the entrenched Grand American Army on Bunker Hill, an elevated site across the Charles River from Boston that overlooked the city and its harbor. On June 17, General Thomas Gage had sent nearly twenty-five hundred British regulars to reclaim Bunker Hill. Ward's soldiers had fought "more like Devils than Men," according to one redcoat, and although Gage retook Bunker Hill, his army paid a terrible price for its victory. More than a thousand British dead and wounded littered the battlefield, including 40 percent of all their officers in Boston.[29]

Washington began his efforts to win over the New Englanders on his first full day in Cambridge by delivering a speech to his assembled army. As most of the soldiers were descendants of New England's Puritan founders, Washington uncharacteristically played on religious themes, building his brief address around an extract from the Bible, the 101st Psalm. In the weeks that followed, his orders rang out with references to America's "righteous Cause," an unaccustomed choice of words for him. He emphasized that this was not solely New England's fight. This was America's cause. The "entire Country is in danger" from "a diabolical Ministry" that wishes "to put Shackles upon Freeman." In the same breath, Washington reassured civilians that he and the Continental army posed no danger. He portrayed himself—quite accurately, time would demonstrate—as a civilian who had temporarily abandoned the "Enjoyments of domestic Life" and who hoped to return to his farm the moment the national emergency ended. "My highest Ambition," he added, was "to see this devoted Province again restored to Peace, Liberty & Safety."[30]

He asked some who were close to him to keep their ear to the ground for any criticism of his conduct. The "Man who wishes to stand well in the opinion of others" must "hear of imputed, or real errors," he declared.[31] In no time, Reed disquietingly reported that some civil officials in

Massachusetts were annoyed by Washington's unapproachable manner. Washington was startled. He had treated the Yankees who came to camp with what he thought was "ceremonious Civility," though obviously they had taken Washington's "ceremony" for something else. "I will endeavour at a reformation," he promised, and he appears to have done just that.[32] Though extremely busy, Washington found more time for visitors, and he consciously crafted a more genial persona. He even welcomed the wives of several influential public figures and, perhaps without doing anything out of the ordinary, dazzled many of them. Mercy Warren, the sister and wife of important political figures, was accustomed to powerful men, but she found Washington to be "the most amiable and accomplished gentleman, both in person mind and manners that I have ever met." Abigail Adams, no stranger to Boston's leading citizens, gushed that Washington must have been personally crafted by God. He was cut from "Majestic fabric," she said.[33]

Washington had begun with a heaping measure of goodwill from the New Englanders, who in the face of the Coercive Acts were desperate for outside help. He not only retained the warmth of New England, but stoked it actively through actions such as endorsing the invasion of Canada. But his stature crested when he brought the siege of Boston to a bloodless and successful conclusion. Only a handful knew that the happy end to the siege operation owed more to the generals who surrounded and advised Washington than to the commander himself.

Washington had never let go of the idea of sending his army storming across the Charles River to liberate Boston, and in January and February 1776, when the river froze, he resurrected that notion in councils of war. His general officers had never wavered in their opposition to such a scheme, and led by Brigadier General Horatio Gates—the army's adjutant general, who had served in the British army for fifteen years before resigning and moving to Virginia in 1772—they counseled that it was likely to be ruinous to send an untrained army against the well-entrenched British regulars. It was more prudent, they advised Washington, to wage a defensive war, and they urged him to occupy Dorchester Heights, which, like Bunker Hill, overlooked Boston Harbor. That might draw the redcoats into another catastrophic assault.

Congress had earlier given Washington nearly a free hand in how he deployed the army, though it made clear that it wished the Continental army to attack only when the odds of success were highly favorable. Given what Congress desired and his generals had advocated, Washington agreed to try for another Bunker Hill–style engagement. He put his generals' recommendation into operation on March 4, soon after night tightened around Boston. Work parties of nearly fifteen hundred men dragged much of the army's heavy artillery up Dorchester's shaggy, rolling slopes. Other soldiers, wielding spades and picks, constructed entrenchments on the summit. A luminous, silvery moon shone on Dorchester's summit, but Washington was fortunate. It was an unusually mild March night, and a thick, low-lying fog blanketed Boston, obscuring the redcoats' view of the surrounding countryside. Not until the fog burned off in the morning were the British aware of the American infantry crouched behind formidable breastworks atop Dorchester Heights or of the rebel artillery that was trained on the royal vessels in Boston Harbor.

General William Howe, Gage's successor as commander of the British army in America, had no stomach for another Bunker Hill. Besides, more than three months earlier, Howe had decided to abandon Boston, preferring to campaign in New York. His army would have been gone by Christmas had troop transports been available to take them away. London was aware of Howe's plan, though neither Washington nor any other rebel knew of their adversary's intentions when the anxious, tight-lipped Continentals and militiamen climbed the rugged knolls of Dorchester.[34]

Seeing no reason to fight for something he planned to relinquish anyway, Howe offered Washington a deal. Two days after the rebels had occupied Dorchester Heights, Howe proposed to Washington that if his forces were permitted to sail away unmolested, the British would spare Boston. Otherwise, Howe would raze the city. Washington, who might have captured virtually the entire British army below Canada, consented. He traded an army for a city. Boston was liberated.[35]

Washington's choice, which was as much political as military, was the right one. He made his decision at a time when sentiment was growing throughout the country, and in Congress, for declaring independence. A majority in Congress favored independence by March 1776, but it knew that such a momentous act—and one undertaken in the midst of a desperate war—must have the support of all thirteen provinces. Precious unanimity remained elusive as the Dorchester operation played out. Considerable opposition to breaking with the mother country existed in the mid-Atlantic colonies and sectors of the South, especially in the merchant-dominated cities of New York, Philadelphia, and Charleston.

Washington knew that if Boston was razed, opposition to separating from the British Empire would intensify in those other cities, where fear would build that they too would someday face the torch. That would delay independence. It might even prevent Congress from ever making the break. Although he had earlier hidden his thoughts on the issue, there can be no question that by 1776 Washington yearned for Congress to declare independence. From the outset, he wanted to get his hands on foreign, chiefly French, supplies—weapons, powder, shoes, and clothing—that were unavailable in the colonies. When the army that invaded Canada was defeated in an attack on Quebec on the last day of 1775, Washington and others knew that French aid was essential for victory. He also knew that there was no incentive for France to risk being dragged into a war with Great Britain as long as America's war aim was reconciliation. But should Congress declare independence, Britain would stand to lose so heavily in this war that France might be enticed to recognize, and openly aid, the new American nation.

Like most Americans, Washington had thought this would be a short war. He had even told Martha that he expected to be home by Christmas. But by the turn of 1776, he knew this would be a protracted war, and, a veteran soldier, he knew how difficult it would be to maintain morale in a war that lasted year after year. The destruction of Boston could have immediately eviscerated the will to fight in parts of America. In New England, where sentiment for the war possibly ran highest, the devastation of the region's greatest city could well, over time, erode the ardor to fight on.

Boston was saved, and it was emancipated. New Englanders were ecstatic. Britain had sent troops to Boston in 1768 to help enforce its new colonial policies, beginning what radicals always called "the eight-year occupation" of the city. Now it was freed, and city officials lauded Washington: "You have . . . saved a large, elegant . . . City, from total Destruction." Congress was no less jubilant. Acting on a motion by John Adams, it voted to strike a medal honoring Washington, a gold medallion that displayed the general's bust on one side and, on the other, the image of Washington, on horseback, watching the British evacuation of Boston.[36]

Washington did not bother to inform Congress of the deliberations of the council of war or of the fact that he had proposed a different course to seek Boston's liberation. He took sole credit for the bloodless victory. It was his plan to occupy Dorchester Heights, he told Congress. Howe's "flight," he added, "was precipitated by the appearance of a Work which I had order'd . . . on an Eminence at Dorchester."[37]

THE WAR IN 1776–1777: IN THE DEPTHS OF DESPAIR

GENERAL WASHINGTON HAD SOARED to majestic heights with the liberation of Boston. Within eighteen months, his stature plummeted to its lowest ebb during the Revolutionary War.

When Washington assumed command of the Continental army in July 1775, the authorities in Massachusetts had told him that a British attack was probable and imminent. Washington had braced for the blow, and throughout the long weeks during which he remodeled the army and then recruited a new one, he continually looked over his shoulder, expecting the enemy to strike. The dreaded British attack never came, and after six months Washington no longer thought it likely. Instead, by early 1776 he had come to believe that General Howe would evacuate Boston and invade New York. It made sense for Howe to do so. Not only was his army bottled up in Boston, but if he captured New York City and used his naval and armed might to seize control of the Hudson River, Great Britain could—and probably would—win the war. With the Hudson in Britain's possession, New England, which was already blockaded by sea, would be cut off from all the colonies south of New York. It would be ripe for the taking by a powerful invasion. Early on, Washington divined that this would be Howe's strategy, and he was correct. Four days into 1776, Washington pledged to "keep a watchful eye to New York," for if Manhattan fell, it would "be an evil . . . almost irremediable."[1]

While Washington was heedful of New York, General Lee, the former

British officer whom the Massachusetts leaders had wanted, along with Washington, to lead the Continental army, urged his commander to do more. British success in New York would be "so terrible that I have scarcely been able to sleep from apprehensions on the subject," he told Washington. Lee counseled that direct action must be taken to "prevent this deadfull event." Like the authorities in Massachusetts, Washington thought Lee a trenchant thinker, a restless veteran soldier with an armory of ideas. Lee had served in the British army for nearly two decades, fighting in Europe and America—he had been badly wounded in action in New York during the French and Indian War—before resigning his commission and moving to Virginia not long before Lexington-Concord. Lee had a reputation for being difficult. He not only seldom met anyone he considered his equal, he made little effort to hide his feelings, sprinkling his conversations with sarcasm and acerbity. Although Washington acknowledged in private that Lee was "rather fickle & violent . . . in his temper," the two got along well enough in 1775 and early 1776. Their good relationship stemmed in large measure from Washington's belief that Lee was his most trusted adviser. Washington made no secret of his conviction that Lee was "the first Officer in Military knowledge and experience we have in the whole army," a general who "possesses an uncommon share of good Sense and Spirit."[2]

Washington felt that Lee's advice was sound, but building defenses in New York entailed political problems. Some influential residents of Manhattan feared that defensive preparations would be tantamount to inviting the Royal Navy to shell the city. Washington also suspected that Congress, which in January 1776 remained in the control of those who wished for reconciliation with the mother country, would never sanction defensive measures in and around New York City. Facing a dilemma, he sent Lee to determine whether the city could be defended against the British, but he chose not to inform Congress. By early February, Lee had concluded that New York was defensible, and he prepared a plan for Washington's consideration. Lee never envisioned that Manhattan could be held forever. But he fancied that by establishing batteries that would neutralize Britain's navy, and by erecting formidable defensive works for the Continental army, Howe's regulars could be made to pay a dreadful price for everything they took. Lee hoped that if Britain, already shocked by the toll exacted by taking Bunker Hill, met with even more staggering losses in retaking New York City, London might make peace on America's terms. Washington concurred with Lee's plan. The commander gave his subordinate the green light to prepare New York's defense, though he still did not inform Congress of what he had ordered. Washington knew that he could not keep Lee's activities quiet for long, but once work on the fortifications had begun, it would be more difficult for Congress to call a halt. Besides, Lee, who also was well connected in Congress, informed Washington that "the very best members of the Congress . . . expect that You wou'd take much upon yourself."[3]

Washington had not violated Congress's instructions—he was not compelled to obtain its prior consent before taking substantive steps—and he had acted boldly and wisely. In no time, Congress learned what was going on and sanctioned Washington's actions as "judicious and necessary." But aware of Lee's renown as a contrary sort, Congress wisely sent a committee to New York to umpire whatever differences arose between the general and the city's civil authorities. The committeemen were put right to work. Lee and the local authorities immediately clashed over the placement of artillery and redoubts, and the general was furious when he discovered a flourishing commerce between New York's merchants and the few Royal Navy vessels in the harbor. Lee proposed the arrest and incarceration in Connecticut of all those in the two metropolitan counties who refused to take the oath in support of the trade embargo, a heavy-handed measure that the congressional committee refused to sanction. After the committeemen had spent some thirty days in the city, Congress finessed the problem by appointing Lee commander of the Southern Department, which left responsibility for New York's defenses to Washington. Immediately after Howe evacuated Boston—the British commander took his army to Halifax in April to await reinforcements for the pending summer campaign for New York—Washington redeployed his Continentals to Manhattan.[4]

As Washington had worked well with the civil leaders in Massachusetts, Congress saw no need for a mediating presence. Acting with prudence, Washington got much of what he wanted from New York's authorities. He stopped the trade with Britain's sailors, a battle Lee had not won, and secured the cooperation of the New York Committee of Safety for disarming suspected Loyalists and trying them in special tribunals.[5] But Washington compromised with the local leaders on some matters, backing down as he never would have later in the war when he felt less vulnerable. Although Washington had said that Lee was the only soldier whose engineering skills he trusted, he scuttled vital parts of Lee's plan in the face of objections by the civil authorities. In particular, Washington came to put greater emphasis on erecting defenses on Long Island and less on preparing for a street-by-street defense of New York City, the strategy that Lee had believed would inflict a ghastly toll on the enemy. Whatever its tactical advantages, local leaders knew that street fighting would utterly destroy the city, and they persuaded Washington to take a different tack.[6]

Washington consented to these choices for the defense of New York on his own. No evidence exists that he was forced by Congress into actions with which he disagreed. He arrived in Manhattan eager for the showdown battle that he had been denied during the siege of Boston. Moreover, with Boston's liberation under his belt, Washington was uncharacteristically sanguine and self-assured. Radiating confidence, he crowed in private that the enemy had "Shipped themselves off" from Boston in a great hurry. He also spoke of having gained victory in the face of greater obstacles than had ever confronted any other commanding general "since the first Institution of Armys."[7]

However, after only a few weeks in New York, Washington grew more circumspect. His army had not been tested in Boston, but the other American force, the army of the Northern Department that had invaded Canada, had suffered several appalling defeats. Late in May, it had retreated in tatters back into New York, having distinguished itself as nearly the epitome of ineptitude. Washington thought his Continentals were better trained than those who had fought in Canada, but he could not be sure how they would perform until they faced the crucible of battle. Furthermore, once he thoroughly familiarized himself with New York and saw what he had to defend, Washington's apprehension increased. Long Island and Manhattan were islands. As the rebels possessed no fleet, New York was a place where the Continental army might be trapped by an enemy that boasted the world's greatest navy. Furthermore, New York, unlike Boston, was a huge place to defend. In addition to the extensive area around Brooklyn on western Long Island, Manhattan stretched for fifteen miles or more from its southern tip to King's Bridge, the exit to the mainland in the north. Washington's problems were compounded by the fact that Howe's army was more mobile than his, as the redcoats would be transported by what Washington called the "canvas wings" of the Royal Navy. Washington clung to the hope that the intricate system of earthworks, redoubts, and obstructions that he and Lee had contrived had "put us in a respectable posture for defending this City," but clouds of doubt had gathered in his mind. As the summer of 1776 approached, Washington, more often than ever, reflected that "the events of War are exceedingly doubtfull" and that "Capricious fortune often blasts our most flattering hopes." He was anxious enough that he even wrote Congress of his "want of experience to move on a large Scale" and his "limitted, and contracted knowledge . . . in Military Matters."[8] But he never suggested that New York not be defended.

For its part, Congress from the beginning had backed the idea of fighting to defend New York. As it moved toward declaring independence, it seemed even more determined that "the greatest Exertions of Vigour & Expedition are requisite to prevent our Enemies from getting Possession of that Town." Furthermore, after the Canadian debacle, Congress knew that French aid was essential to victory, possibly indispensable to the very survival of every congressman. Many in Congress appear to have believed that a resolute defense of New York was essential to impress Versailles. To be certain that Washington understood its thinking, Congress summoned him to Philadelphia for consultation late in May.[9] No record has survived of what transpired in more than a week of discussions, but when Washington departed Philadelphia, he believed that Congress expected him to stand and fight.

Washington was not disheartened by this. He was a fighter, and he hungered for renown on a grand stage. His stature had grown following the liberation of Boston, though he knew that true fame would come only through victory on the battlefield. The great wars in Washington's time were contests between the major European powers, and they were determined through set-piece battlefield encounters. That was how the principal conflict of his time, the French and Indian War, had been settled. The definitive battle had occurred on the Plains of Abraham on Quebec's doorstep in September 1759. A British army under Brigadier General James

Wolfe met and defeated a French army under the Marquis de Montcalm, in a monumental and conclusive showdown. The British prevailed. Gaining Quebec was the hinge of British victory in that war, a triumph that changed the course of history—that much was known even by contemporaries—and transformed the reputation of Wolfe, who died in the engagement, from that of an accomplished, though largely unacclaimed, soldier to that of a mythological hero. From first to last in the Revolutionary War, Washington dreamed of winning such laurels. The key to unlocking the door to the hall of heroes, he believed, was through scoring a decisive triumph in a climactic and epic battlefield confrontation. Washington had tried for this, and had failed egregiously, at Fort Necessity, and for much of the remainder of the French and Indian War he had badgered the governor of Virginia to change strategy, hoping that he might have another shot at a resounding victory. But in 1776, he did not have to pester Congress. It wanted him to make a stand in defense of New York.

HOWE'S ARMY LANDED ON Staten Island at the beginning of July, just as Congress in Philadelphia declared independence. During the next several weeks, Howe prepared for his assault on New York, gathering intelligence and reinforcements. As the tense days of July passed, Washington discovered a grave weakness in his defenses. Since January, the rebels not only had loaded the Hudson River with every imaginable marine obstacle, they had constructed Fort Washington several miles above New York City, situating it high atop a bluff overlooking the river and filling it with powerful artillery that could be trained on ships sailing on the blue green waters far below. Washington was convinced that no large British ship could possibly get past his defensive impediments, leaving him unworried about security on the west side of Manhattan and confident that in a worst-case scenario, his army could escape across the Hudson into New Jersey. All that changed in an instant on July 12. Two British frigates, the *Phoenix* and the *Rose,* successfully ran the gauntlet. From that moment forward, Washington knew full well that he was "surrounded . . . by Water & covered with Ships." Quixotically, however, he exuded confidence. Reinforced with militia, his numbers would be roughly equal to those possessed by Howe. As his army had been more than a year in the making, he also believed that he had fashioned a decent fighting machine, superior in training and equipment to the one that had fought so magnificently atop Bunker Hill a year earlier. The "Men appear to be in good Spirits," he said a week after the voyage of the two royal frigates, "and if they will stand by me," the British would pay an immense price for whatever they took.[10]

Washington was wrong. He was nearly fatally misguided, and his own mistakes of judgment were largely responsible for what should have resulted in a decisive British victory. Washington went into the campaign with most of his army on Manhattan, but he deployed nearly a quarter of his men across the East River in or near Brooklyn. He had divided his army in the face of a superior foe, a violation of the cardinal maxim of warfare. His decision assured that his army would be outnumbered no matter where Howe chose to fight. At literally the last minute, Washington changed commanders on Long Island, where Howe's initial blow fell. He reassigned Brigadier General John Sullivan and appointed Major General Israel Putnam to replace him. In addition, even as the British made their final preparations before striking, Washington permitted his commanders on Long Island to scatter their men along a line six miles long, far too extensive for an army of seven thousand to defend against a British force that was nearly four times as large. If those blunders were not bad enough, Washington failed to secure roads that led to the rear of his army on Long Island. What followed, predictably, was a rout. In late morning on the first day—the only day—of fighting, the redcoats got behind the American force. Exploding in a scarlet blur from the woodland behind the rebels' lines, the British overwhelmed their surprised adversary. The Americans suffered heavy losses. Roughly 15 percent of Washington's men were killed, wounded, or captured. The prisoners included two American generals, Sullivan and William Alexander, who called himself Lord Stirling. The engagement ended with the surviving rebel soldiers racing pell-mell from the fire-swept field in an ugly flight back to the redoubts in Brooklyn Heights, which overlooked the East River.

One fourth of the rebel army appeared to be doomed, trapped with its back to the river and facing an overwhelmingly superior adversary. Incredibly, Washington sent reinforcements to join the ill-fated rebels in Brooklyn. If only Howe had assaulted at that moment, he might have gained a great victory, one that could have destroyed the Americans' will to continue. But remembering the carnage on Bunker Hill, Howe paused

to await reinforcements and gather additional artillery and further information. His delay was fatal. A storm blew up. Washington seized advantage of the adverse weather, including a thick fog that shrouded the East
River and incapacitated the Royal Navy. Using every boat that he could
get his hands on, Washington extricated his cornered men, pulling them
back to Manhattan. Heeding the old military maxim to "cover your tail," he
made certain that Congress knew that he alone was not responsible for
the retreat. He took the unusual step of sending to Philadelphia a copy
of the minutes of the council of war that had authorized the withdrawal
from Long Island.[11]

Once he was in the temporary safety of Manhattan, Washington repeated one of his earlier mistakes: he divided his army. He posted thirty-
five hundred men in the city itself, at the southern tip of the island. He
deployed most of his army in Harlem Heights, some ten miles to the
north of the city and slightly more than a mile below Fort Washington.
He may have taken this ill-advised step because of pressure from Congress, real or imagined, to defend New York City.

By now, Washington was rethinking the strategy to which he had been
wed since taking command of the Continental army. Shaken by his soldiers' deficiencies and his officers' shortcomings, he decided that his earlier
belief in victory through a great pitched battle was fatally flawed. After ten
long days' reflection, he concluded that he must pursue "a War of posts."
What Washington had decided on was better known as "Fabian" tactics, a
way of fighting that drew on the legacy of the successful Roman general
Fabius Cunctator, who had used evasiveness and hit-and-run tactics when
confronted by a superior Carthaginian adversary. Henceforth, Washington
told Congress, that must be the manner in which the Continental army
was employed. The commander in chief vowed "on all occasions [to]
avoid a general Action," to put nothing "to the risque unless compelled by
a necessity into which we ought never to be drawn." It would henceforth
be his policy, he added, to pick when and where he would fight. No longer
did he wish to risk his entire army on one roll of the dice. He envisaged a
war of attrition: Keep the war going until France intervened or Great Britain
lost the will to continue, or both.

Pointing out that there were signs that the enemy might next land
above King's Bridge on the northern tip of Manhattan, trapping his army,

Washington hinted to Congress that it was expedient to withdraw to the mainland, where he would have space to maneuver. To "Hazard . . . a successfull defence in the City," he added, was to risk the "fate of this Army and Its stores" on one great battle.[12] Washington's new attitude was prudent, given the uncertain performance of his army. But he was still a novice commander in chief who was buffeted by pressures from every side, and he immediately ignored everything he had just proposed.

Though he had not heard from Philadelphia since the debacle on Long Island, Washington believed that at least some congressmen wanted New York City to "be maintained at every hazard." So, too, did some of his officers, fearing that a retreat would "dispirit the Troops and enfeeble our Cause." He responded by summoning a council of war, which during the first week of September voted not to abandon the city. Although he was no doubt dismayed by the vote, Washington nevertheless abided by it. As he had before, he showed patience and diplomacy. He persisted in his efforts to persuade Congress of the wisdom of pulling the army from the city, and in private discussions, he tried to bring his generals around to his way of thinking. Both efforts worked. On September 10, Congress authorized a withdrawal from the city. With Congress's blessing in hand, Washington called a second council of war on September 12. It voted to pull the army out of the city, marching those men northward to join their comrades in Harlem Heights.

But an operation of that magnitude took time, and Howe struck again before the city could be evacuated. The British landed at Kip's Bay (on the East River near present-day Thirty-fourth Street), between the two divisions of Washington's army. Landing unopposed for all practical purposes, the British army was quickly ashore. It was within the power of the redcoats to dash from the east side to the west side of Manhattan, cutting off every road and trapping the nearly one quarter of the Continental army that was still on the southern tip of the island. But the British landing force moved with incredible languor. Every man in New York City escaped along roads the British failed to secure. They came north and were reunited with the bulk of the army in Harlem. For a second time in three weeks, the British had let a certain victory of great magnitude slip through their hands.[13]

Washington had wanted to raze New York City when the army withdrew. If most of the city was destroyed, the British would face a choice of going elsewhere—perhaps back to Halifax—to find winter quarters or of enduring a cruel and potentially ruinous winter amid the charred ruins of the city. Congress, however, categorically refused to authorize the city's destruction. Washington was so outraged that he privately branded Congress's decision as "amg . . . [its] capital errors" to this point in the war. Congress's wishes notwithstanding, Washington burned the city anyway. Or so it appears. New York City was put to the torch on September 20. That evening, with the sky glowing an eerie orange caused by innumerable fires, British officials arrested fourteen arsonists armed with "combustibles under their clothes" or carrying lighted torches, and three others were apprehended by civilian residents in the act of setting blazes. It stretches credulity to believe that it was coincidental that seventeen firebugs turned out on the same night. Washington must have defied Congress by quietly ordering the city's leveling or, more likely, by expressing his feelings before enough subordinates that he could be assured one would see to organizing the conflagration. The fire that resulted destroyed a quarter of the city—a thousand houses and buildings—and would have been far more devastating had not a sudden change in wind diverted the flames.[14]

Since late August, Washington had acted with great vigor and creativity, but his behavior during the next month is perplexing. Having proclaimed a war of posts strategy, he disregarded the farsighted new course that he had supposedly taken up. Instead of exiting Manhattan Island altogether to wage an evasive fight, Washington deployed his army in Harlem Heights and prepared for a giant showdown. This was folly. Not only had Washington already outlined the absurdity of risking all in one battle, he had pointed out the danger should the British seal off the escape routes north of King's Bridge. If he was pinioned on Manhattan, the enemy would "cut this Army in peices" and capture all its stores and arms, he had said on one occasion. He also observed that if "cut off," his army would face three options, all bad: "the necessity of fighting our way out under every disadvantage— surrendering at discretion—or Starving." Although Howe had consistently displayed no stomach for another Bunker Hill—he had declined to attack the entrenched rebels at both Dorchester Heights and Brooklyn Heights— Washington somehow convinced himself that the enemy would assault his lines in Harlem Heights. The American army remained immobile in the coffin that was Manhattan Island, waiting and waiting until, during the second week in October, Howe struck. But his blow did not fall on Harlem Heights. The British landed above King's Bridge. Washington had permitted the nightmare scenario of which he had spoken to occur.[15]

Washington's defenders have maintained that congressional pressure led him to remain in his snare, and that is the notion he appears to have promoted. When General Lee returned to Manhattan Island two days after Howe's landing and found the American army still entrenched in Harlem Heights, he was led by Washington to believe that the soldiers remained in their trap because of the "absurd interference" of Congress. In fact, there is no evidence that Congress ordered Washington to defend Manhattan, and if it had ever mandated such a course, it certainly did not do so following the debacle on Long Island. Nearly thirty days before Howe landed above Manhattan, Washington had received word from Philadelphia that "it was by no means the Sense of Congress" that the army should remain in New York "a Moment longer than he [Washington] shall think it proper for the publick Service that Troops be Continued there." Nor did Washington's generals lead him astray. By a majority of more than three to one, they had sanctioned abandoning New York a full month prior to Howe's landing. Staying in Harlem Heights to await an unlikely British assault was Washington's idea, and he said as much late in September when he announced unequivocally that he would not retreat from Manhattan.[16] What explains his mystifying action?

It is probable that confidants in Philadelphia made Washington aware that some in Congress were deeply unhappy with his performance during the campaign for New York, his first test under fire. Congressmen were complaining of the "Confusion of the Army" and the "ignorance, incapacity or indolence" of its officers. The army's general officers, one congressman fulminated, consisted of a "Multitude of Creatures who are totally unworthy of the Commissions they hold." In August, some in Congress had foreseen that Washington had erred when he divided his army between Manhattan and Long Island. "They must keep their Force together. . . . The instant they divide it they are ruined," said one. In the wake of the disastrous engagement in Brooklyn, one congressman raged that there were "strong Marks of Negligence, Indolence, Presumption, and Incapacity" among the army's leaders. John Adams charged that the generals—he

meant Washington, of course—had failed to secure key roads on Long Island and to reconnoiter properly. In addition, the commander "had been
shamefully remiss in Obtaining Intelligence, of the Numbers and Motions
of the Enemy." How much of this got back to headquarters in Harlem
Heights is unknown, but some in Virginia's delegation believed there was a
"Dark design against" Washington in the halls of Congress, and it is likely
that at least one of them tipped him off to some of the damaging allegations. It is conceivable that Washington, shocked and alarmed by the presumed disaffection in Congress, may have grown reluctant to implement a
war of posts strategy and felt he needed to make a stand.[17]

Washington's potentially shocking blunder may also have arisen from
his hallmark inclination for battle, the very state of mind that had led him
to make his injudicious stand at Fort Necessity years before and repeatedly
drove him to propose assailing his heavily fortified enemy in Boston. For
fifteen long months, he had waited impatiently for a great confrontation
with the enemy. His blood was up, and he wanted to avenge the humiliation of Long Island. He hungered for the moment of truth.

A third explanation for Washington's contradictory behavior—and the
most likely—is that for weeks he had been under a terrible strain that left
him utterly fatigued, physically and emotionally. "I am bereft of every
peaceful moment," he declared in September, adding that he was "wearied
to death all day with a variety of perplexing circumstances." In a series of
letters to his brothers in Virginia, Washington radiated telltale signs of a
man in the grip of a black depression. He had, he said, lost "all comfort and
happiness." He had never been "in such an unhappy . . . state. . . . Such is
my situation that if I were to wish the bitterest curse to an enemy on this
side of the grave, I should put him in my stead with my feelings." He
thought it impossible that he would finish the war with his reputation intact. He seemed to feel betrayed by all those who surrounded him. Even
in private, he shunned responsibility for the perilous situation in which he
found himself. He blamed supposedly unworthy subordinates and Congress's ill-advised decision to rely heavily on militia troops. Weighed with
cares, he seemed confused and immobilized. After three weeks in Harlem
Heights, he concluded that Howe was not going to attack him there but
that, instead, he "intended to draw a Line round us, and cut of[f] all com-
munication between the City and Country; thereby reducing us to the

necessity of fighting our way" out of the net. He understood the lethal danger yet did not move. He confessed at one point, "I do not know what plan of conduct to pursue." In another breath he vowed, as if uttering a death wish, to go down fighting. "I am resolved not to be forced from this ground while I have life," he wrote. So overwrought was Washington that it momentarily appeared as if he welcomed the prospect of perishing as he led his men in battle. Going out in a blaze of glory would be a "credit to the justice of my character," he said.[18]

Washington was saved by two things. Led astray by poor maps and worse intelligence, Howe had landed at Throg's Neck. The site was on the mainland shore, but mercurial tides turned it into a virtual island. Howe had to withdraw his men and find another place to land. Six days passed before the British clambered ashore again, this time at Pell's Point, slightly farther north on the mainland. In the interim, General Lee—who had successfully completed his assignment in the South before being ordered back to New York by an anxious Congress—arrived at Washington's headquarters. Instantly perceiving the gravity of Washington's mistake, Lee urged an immediate retreat off Manhattan Island. Washington had always trusted Lee's advice, and as if jolted back to reality by the counsel of this professional officer, he followed his lead. Washington at last ordered a withdrawal of all his men on Manhattan, save for those posed at Fort Washington. Setting off just as Howe landed at Pell's Point, the rebels escaped to the safety of the hilly terrain above Manhattan, scurrying one step ahead of their pursuers.[19]

The bulk of the Continental army was off Manhattan, but, bafflingly, Washington had not abandoned Fort Washington. Not only had he predicted that the British would come after the installation, but after *Rose* and *Phoenix* easily sailed up the Hudson some ninety days earlier, it should have been apparent—and some officers told him as much—that the fort was essentially useless. As signs mounted in mid-November that Howe was preparing to invest the fort, a decision had to be made.

The determination might have been different had Lee still been present to provide counsel, but he was out of touch. At the outset of November, not knowing whether Howe's next move would be to strike up the Hudson River, invade New England, or go into winter quarters, Washington had tried to cover every base. Once again, he divided his army. He posted one division in the Hudson Highlands. A second, under Lee, was deployed in Connecticut to guard against a British thrust into New England. General Nathanael Greene was given responsibility for Fort Washington. Washington took what was left of the army—about two thousand men, many of whom were militiamen—and crossed into New Jersey.

Whether or not to make a stand at Fort Washington was, strictly speaking, Greene's choice, but as Washington was on the scene, it was his call. Washington could not make a decision. He waffled and vacillated for forty-eight hours until Howe made the decision for him. The British attacked just after dawn on November 16, a month after their landing at Pell's Point. The fight was savage and elemental. In the face of a relentless, deadly fire, the British and their hired German allies, the Hessians, struggled up the steep hill, through tangled underbrush and over seemingly impenetrable man-made obstacles, until they reached the summit. Before the pale autumn sun set, Fort Washington and nearly 2,900 captives were in British hands, and another 149 rebel soldiers were dead or wounded. This time, there was no blaming Congress. Washington, not for the last time, had been unable to make a rapid decision.

Nor was he able to decide what to do about Fort Lee, a huge supply depot in New Jersey almost directly across the Hudson from Fort Washington. Seventy-two hours elapsed after Fort Washington's fall before Washington ordered Fort Lee's evacuation. By then it was too late. Acting with unaccustomed speed and daring, the British struck Fort Lee on November 19, seizing 30 invaluable cannons, 8,000 cannon shot, 4,000 cannonballs, 2,800 muskets, 400,000 cartridges, 500 entrenching tools, 300 tents, and 1,000 barrels of flour.[20]

These latest calamities—both foreseeable and avoidable—plunged Washington into a desperate and forlorn state of mind, perhaps his wartime nadir. Nevertheless, in the dismal weeks of November and December, he was sustained by hopeful signs, however tenuous. The British army that had chased the rebel invaders from Canada in May, now reinforced and clearly superior to the rebel force in the Northern Department, failed to invade New York that autumn. It had been delayed by Benedict Arnold's spirited naval defense of Lake Champlain until the first snow of the season blanketed the ground. The redcoat commander in Canada, Sir Guy Carleton, postponed his plans for plunging into New York until the following spring. When Carleton's redcoats went into winter quarters, Washington redeployed many men from the Northern Department to augment his ragtag army.

Washington exerted more of a hand in bringing on the second positive turn of events. When his first army melted away in the fall of 1775, Washington had unsuccessfully inveighed Congress to move toward long-term enlistments. Within hours of extracting his army from Long Island in late August, he revisited the issue, telling Congress, with an urgency in his tone, that all would be "entirely lost" if it persisted in waging war with a small army of one-year volunteers augmented by large bodies of militiamen. It was clear, he said, that this was going to be a longer war than most Americans had previously anticipated, one that could be waged successfully only by "a permanent, standing Army." To "place any dependence upon Militia, is assuredly, resting upon a broken staff," he also cautioned. Inexperienced and unwilling to submit to "any kind of restraint," militiamen in the New York campaign had failed to perform in "a brave & manly" fashion under fire, and their bad example had corroded his Continentals. As it took considerable time to make a soldier out of a civilian, Washington told Congress, the only hope of assuring that the Continentals "would be competent almost to every exigency" was to have them enlist for "the continuance of the War." To this, Washington added that the only means of attracting men to enlist for lengthy service was through enticing bounties, including the proffer of land, or through conscription, which he recommended.[21]

Washington sometimes exaggerated his plight, but this was not one of those times. His forceful pleas helped transform the thinking of many congressmen, though not all required Washington's prompting. For instance, John Adams, who had resisted a standing army in 1775, had rethought the matter and made an about-face. He advocated long-term enlistments. The disaster on Long Island gave Adams plenty of company. Standing armies might pose a danger to liberty, but there would be no liberty—perhaps no life—if the war was lost. Before September was out, Congress not only had enacted legislation "to engage the Troops to serve" for the duration of the war, it revised the Articles of War to allow more draconian punishments of the enlisted men, nearly tripling the maximum corporal punishment (to one hundred lashes) and increasing the number of capital crimes from two to nine.[22] In the dark moments that followed the disasters at Forts Washington and Lee, General Washington knew that there was a prospect of better days ahead. But his first priorities were to survive the fallout from his repeated failures and, if possible, to do something that might persuade men to enlist in an army that since August had suffered only disasters and near catastrophes.

Washington's string of blunders was certain to lead to recriminations, perhaps even to calls for his removal. Already aware of the displeasure among some in Congress, he discovered on the last day of November that even some in the army had lost confidence in him. On that day, a letter from General Lee arrived for Joseph Reed, Washington's former secretary, now the army's adjutant general. As Reed was away from headquarters on a mission, Washington, who was desperate for information, tore open Lee's letter. What he read was lacerating. Washington's "fatal indecision," Lee had said in his customarily caustic manner, would doom the American army. From things that Lee said, it was also clear that Reed, heretofore Washington's closest confidant in the army, shared Lee's views. (Reed, with pitiless honesty, had told Lee that Washington's "indecisive Mind" had been among the army's "greatest Misfortunes," and he added that had it not been for Lee, Washington's army would never have escaped Manhattan.) One of the few men with the backbone to criticize Washington to his face, Lee had already told the commander that he was foolish to act on the advice of his generals, most of whom were "Men of inferior judgment." Though Washington was unaware of it, Lee had also urged General Horatio Gates to hurry to Washington's side to "save your army," as "a certain great Man is most damnably deficient."[23]

During the nearly three weeks that followed the disasters at Forts Washington and Lee, Washington led his army in a retreat across New Jersey. Staying just ahead of his British pursuers, he crossed into Pennsylvania, putting the Delaware River between his beleaguered army and that of his adversary. Harried as he was, Washington still found the time to practice damage control, as he had been doing since the summertime disasters. Following the debacle in Brooklyn, he had scapegoated the militia—about which he had said little during his first fourteen months in command, save for reporting that it had bailed him out during the recruiting crisis in late 1775—charging its officers with incompetence and the men with

failure to call "forth their utmost efforts." Nor did the Continental soldiery escape his criticism. "I am obliged to confess my want of confidence
in the Generality of the Troops," he said. Once Lee persuaded him to escape Manhattan Island, Washington took credit for the decision. He imag-
inatively portrayed his perilous stay in Harlem Heights, and the retreat that
followed, as a tactical move. He had "spun the Campaign out to this time,"
he told Congress, bringing Howe to the edge of winter "without coming
to any decisive Action" and short of the "completion of the business he is
come upon"—gaining control of the Hudson up to Albany. He attributed
the notorious blunder of having defended Fort Washington to General
Greene, who was "struck with the Importance of the Post." As for the Fort
Lee disaster, its "loss was inevitable," he told Congress, implying that there
had been no time after the retreat from Manhattan to remove the imperiled stores, though in fact thirty-four days elapsed between the start of the
retreat from Manhattan and the British seizure of the post.[24]

But Washington knew that gaining one victory would do more than a
thousand words to eradicate the stain of his recent mistakes. He had long
been eager to fight, and now more than ever he hungered for action, both
to rehabilitate his image and to restore morale, which was essential to recruiting the standing army in 1777. It was as if Washington were reborn
by his tribulations. Even while retreating through New Jersey, he considered wheeling about and striking his pursuers. He pieced together his
own intelligence-gathering network that reported to him alone, and as
Lee had urged, he placed less reliance on his generals' advice. On occasion, he consulted them separately rather than convening a council of war.
Acting in this fashion, he alone knew what all had recommended.

Once Washington completed his retreat into Pennsylvania, Congress
fled to Baltimore, abandoning Philadelphia, which was only a day's march
from the British army. One of Congress's last acts before its flight was to
vote Washington "full power to order and direct all things relative to . . .
the operation of the war" for the next six months. It was a vote of confidence in Washington. Buoyed by it, he asked for even more power. He
wanted the authority to appoint and remove all officers beneath the rank
of general officers, to determine promotion procedures, arrest Loyalists,
and confiscate supplies from civilians. Congress gave him everything he

asked for. "Congress has given up most of their power," a Virginia delegate remarked. Though an exaggeration, Washington understood that he was free to act as he pleased. Bolstered by Congress's vote of confidence, he acted, and boldly.[25]

Washington saw his opening when the British abandoned their pursuit and went into winter quarters, dividing and scattering their army in cantonments throughout New Jersey. The first sunbeam of hope sprang from the sudden activity of the New Jersey and Pennsylvania militias, which throughout December repeatedly harassed Hessian patrols and garrisons, unnerving and exhausting the German soldiers. In addition, augmented by Continentals who had been summoned from quiet, snowbound upper New York, Washington suddenly possessed more men than were garrisoned in any of the Hessian cantonments near the Delaware River. This was the perfect situation for employing the Fabian strategy he had embraced back in September.

On a black Christmas night of rain, sleet, and snow, all driven by a keening wind, Washington launched a surprise attack against the Hessian post at Trenton. He scored a sensational victory, his first triumph in battle in this war—in any war, for that matter. With great daring and a penchant for putting everything to the hazard, Washington took his tired, cold men back into New Jersey six days later and fought two additional battles. One was a desperate, bloody brawl on the Assunpink Creek just outside Trenton, a battle that the rebels fought with their backs against the Delaware River. The second encounter occurred the following day in Princeton, a bucolic college town. Washington rode into battle in the van of his little army, at times no farther from musket-toting enemy infantryman than the pitcher is from the batter on a baseball diamond.[26]

In those three battles, waged within a span of ten days, Washington had done what few, if any, on either side thought him capable of doing. Acting decisively, he had put his enemy through a meat grinder. British losses exceeded two thousand men. The Americans lost a tenth that number in the campaign. Unlike the aftermath of his failures in New York, when he had pointed the finger at others for what had transpired, this time Washington took credit for the victories, always emphasizing his role, as he had also done following the retaking of Boston. With unabashed self-puffery, he told

Congress of "the Success of an Enterprize, which I had formed." He went on: "I ordered . . . I well knew . . . I was certain . . . I determined . . . I formed . . . I found . . . I threw a Body of Troops in their Way." When he recrossed the Delaware for the final engagements, Washington told Congress that should he fail, he hoped "the failure will be imputed to the true cause, the . . . difficulties I have to combat, rather than to the want of . . . the closest attention" to his responsibilities. But he succeeded, and he followed those triumphs with another account that accentuated his part in compelling the "withdraw [of] Genl Howe from" the cantonments nearest to Philadelphia and in giving "some reputation to our Arms."[27]

Washington's reports to Congress, both in the dark days that followed his disastrous New York campaign and in the bright glow of his victories in New Jersey, were an assiduous strategy of self-exculpation. There was hyperbole in his claims, but it was true that he had conceived and planned the daring Christmas surprise and the brazen second crossing of the Delaware, both risk-laden forays into the lion's den. Furthermore, for this commander who feared that he was on shaky ground with Congress, Washington's self-serving exaggeration and occasional scapegoating were understandable, if unattractive. He had assumed power with the conviction that he had been called by destiny to lead the army, a belief that hardened with his successes in Boston and at Trenton-Princeton. Now, he was fighting for his survival as commander of the Continental army.

Historian Geoffrey Perret has written, "In the life of every great commander there is one battle that stands out above all the rest, the supreme test of generalship that places him among the other military immortals."[28] Washington's moment of true greatness was his daring campaign in the week that followed Christmas 1776. As a result of his audacity, the army would survive and the war would continue. It was certain, too, that General Washington would endure. His critics were silenced, and, as after the liberation of Boston, he was acclaimed. Congress congratulated him, observing that the American soldiers, though "broken by Fatigue & ill-Fortune," had been "inspired, and animated by a just Confidence in their Leader." Those ragged soldiers had "exceed[ed] Epectation [and] the Limits of Probability." The "United States are indebted" to you, Congress said, adding: "May you still proceed in the same Manner to acquire that

Glory, which by your disinterested and magnanimous Behaviour, you so highly merit."[29]

WASHINGTON HAD FACED ONE CRISIS after another in his first eighteen months as commander. He was hardly free of cares during 1777. His greatest problem—and a relatively new woe for him—was a critical supply shortage that struck the army while it was in winter quarters at Morristown, New Jersey. The men were destitute, Washington told Congress in January. They were "absolutely perishing for want" of tents, blankets, clothing, hats, and shoes. During the siege of Boston, the Continentals had fared better than the beleaguered redcoats, and Washington's men had been reasonably well supplied in New York until defeats and hurried retreats left the army devoid of critical materials. While it cannot be said that Washington solved the supply problem—a solution was beyond the capability of any one leader—he did bring to bear the administrative skills that he had learned in the French and Indian War. One of Washington's strengths as an administrator was his attention to detail. Another was the working relationship with Congress that he had patiently, respectfully forged. Early in 1777, Congress acted rapidly to do what it could to alleviate the army's deficiencies, leaving Washington to determine how "you will distribute [the supplies] among the Troops."[30]

Food, it turned out, was the least of the army's problems, as Washington organized forage parties to find comestibles. The foragers were dispatched to take food from farmers, who in turn were given bills of credit that could be used as currency. But Washington, who had learned hard lessons about seizing private property while in command of the Virginia Regiment, instructed his men about the "infamous practice of plundering the Inhabitants. . . . It is our business to give protection, and support, to the poor, distressed Inhabitants; not to multiply and increase their calamities." Finally, Washington worked well with state officials in coping with the army's problems. Finding that politicians in the North were cut more or less from the same cloth as those in Virginia, he eschewed a heavy-handed approach and tried to deal with them in a collaborative manner: "I shall cheerfully cooperate with you. . . . I beg you will give every Assistance in your power. . . . I beg you will order." He took pains to explain what he requested, not infrequently apologizing for having to ask. He sent his aides, and sometimes his highest-ranking officers, back to their home states to work with officials face-to-face. His performance earned deservedly high praise from Robert Morris, a Pennsylvania congressman who, as a civilian, had been one of colonial America's most successful businessmen. Washington, he said, was the sort who "feeds & thrives on misfortunes by finding resources to get the better of them," where lesser leaders "sink . . . under their weight, thinking it impossible" to succeed. "Heaven . . . has blessed you with a Firmness of Mind Steadiness of Countenance and patience in Suffering," he told Washington, and his example "inspirit[ed] those that look up to" him.[31]

When Washington entered winter quarters in January, only eight hundred Continentals remained with him. "How we are to rub along till the New Army is raised I know not," he confessed, and he spent many sleepless nights that winter worrying that Howe might sweep across the frozen Delaware River and march on Philadelphia. Had the British commander done so, he would have reached Philadelphia virtually unopposed. Washington remained on pins and needles for weeks, as recruitment of the new standing army lagged. The states and the army dispatched recruiting officers to inspire, often to wheedle, men to enlist. As a last resort, most states instituted conscription to meet their established manpower quota. It was slow going. Washington was sustained through this difficult period by the militia, which he had distrusted—abominated would be a more apt word—since his days as a young commander in the French and Indian War. But having no choice, he asked the civil authorities in New Jersey and Pennsylvania to furnish militiamen to see him through. As was invariably the case during the war, when Washington asked that the militia be mobilized, the governors complied. Still, late in the winter Washington knew that if Howe acted with expedition, little hope existed that he could be stopped.[32] But Howe was Howe. He had permitted Washington to wiggle out of one snare after another the previous summer, and early in 1777, when presented with another golden opportunity that any daring commander—a Washington, for instance—would have seized, Howe remained inert.

During his most anxious moments that winter and spring, Washington reflected that "Providence has heretofore saved us . . . and on this we must principally rely." Time and again throughout the war, Washington uttered similar remarks, as if he genuinely believed that it was America's inescapable destiny to win this war. Before spring was in high season, he had also concluded that it was his good fortune to have General Howe as his opponent. Having taken the measure of his counterpart, Washington had earlier expressed his "very great surprize" that Howe had not taken advantage of the rebels' weaknesses during the winter. When the British army did not act as the campaign season dawned in 1777, Washington came to believe that Howe was "unfit for the trust reposed in him." A shrewd judge of men, Washington saw that his earlier concerns about Howe taking the field had been exaggerated. He grew more optimistic than ever. "If we can once get the new Army compleat and the Congress will take care to have it properly supplied, I think we may thereafter bid Defiance to great Britain," he remarked, almost with an air of jauntiness.[33]

Washington's redemptive Trenton-Princeton campaign fostered his newfound hope and self-assurance, but it was nourished, too, by the praise lavished on him early in 1777. America's commander in chief was lauded to a degree unmatched in the halcyon atmosphere that followed the liberation of Boston. So exalted was the commander in chief that John Adams deplored the "superstitious veneration" of Washington that had seized many in Congress. Adams feared that the extravagant acclaim would turn Washington's head, with unpleasant consequences. Most congressmen who paid tribute to Washington appear to have believed that the disasters in New York had been due to the commander in chief's inexperience or that he had been let down by those around him. Some also seem to have concluded that the six-month-old United States, which unlike all other western countries was devoid of royalty, needed a figurehead around whom the citizenry could rally. General Washington could be the glue that held together the young, fragile Union, the great man who inspired loyalty and patriotism, the father image for a paternalistic people, the lonely, altruistic, and majestic preceptor of the nation who sustained morale through the long, difficult war. Already, Congress had withheld information from the public about Washington's many blunders in 1776, and to some degree it had "Sanctifyed . . . your Name"—as Robert Morris informed the commander—in the hope that his purported example "wou'd draw forth the exertions of Some good Men." Not by accident,

some patriots at banquets and rallies invoked a cry that bore royal overtones: "God save great Washington."[34]

After Washington's triumphs at year's end, Congress's tone changed in
its dealings with the commander. Not only had it recently vested him
with extraordinary powers, Congress deferred to him as never before. It
offered some suggestions for the defense of Philadelphia but was quick to
add: "Congress means not, in any manner, to interfere with the designs, or
to counteract the Judgement of your Excellency." In April 1777, Congress
adopted a resolution asking that a significant portion of the army be deployed on the Delaware River near Philadelphia, but it hastily told Washington that the "resolves of Congress . . . you may be assured, are not
intended, by any means, to obstruct your views a single moment." Should
Washington think the troops could be put to better use, "you have only
so to order it." In May, Congress thought it might be wise to summon additional militia, but it notified Washington that it wished to "leave it entirely to you to determine" the matter. (Washington, by the way, rejected
Congress's wishes regarding the deployment of his troops but sanctioned
the militia call-up, though only on the condition that Congress understood that he must have the authority to order the militiamen beyond
their state boundaries.)[35]

THE RAPTUROUS TRIBUTES that Washington enjoyed in the winter and
spring of 1777 were seldom heard by year's end. He failed to score a victory in the campaign of 1777, though another general, Horatio Gates,
gained America's most splendid and pivotal triumph to this point in the
war.

London and General Howe had agreed back in 1775 that Great
Britain's primary objective was to secure the Hudson River, the prelude
to the army's multipronged invasion of New England. As winter receded
in 1777, Britain at last was in a position to complete what might be its
war-ending strategy. A large redcoat army had gathered in Canada over
the past year. General John Burgoyne was poised to bring it south, taking
Fort Ticonderoga before advancing on Albany, while Howe was to drive
north up the Hudson from Manhattan. The two British armies were expected to fight and defeat Continental armies along the way before they
rendezvoused in Albany. But at the last minute, Howe robbed his country

of a golden opportunity to score a decisive victory. He jettisoned the plan to go north in favor of taking his army south in quest of Philadelphia.

Howe had several things in mind. He knew that the mid-Atlantic provinces were filled with Loyalists who could help him and, once the rebel army was disposed of, reestablish British rule in the region. He fancied that a crumpling blow would be dealt to American morale if the British retook Philadelphia, home to the Continental Congress since before hostilities. Howe also hoped that the rebellion might be broken if Britain could reestablish control of both New York and Philadelphia, the two most important cities in the region, if not all of America. Most important, perhaps, Howe was confident that the threat he posed to Philadelphia would compel Washington to stand and fight, and Howe believed he could beat Washington if he could just get him onto a battlefield once again. Howe's strategy was not unreasonable, but it meant that Burgoyne would have to sink or swim on his own in the wilds of upper New York. The more prudent course would have been for Howe to cooperate with Burgoyne and to target Philadelphia, if need be, another day.

Burgoyne started well enough. Fort Ticonderoga fell in a few hours, and by early July, British regulars were only seventy-five miles from Albany. Thereafter, everything that could go wrong for Burgoyne did. The outnumbered rebels did what they could to delay his progress, felling trees across his path, destroying more than forty bridges, damming some streams to make them too shallow for boats and plugging still others to create bogs where roads had once run, building interlocking timber barriers, burning crops, and driving away livestock. The frenetic rebel activity paid dividends. Burgoyne's army advanced only about forty miles in fifty days. As the redcoats toiled in the hot, airless forests, forging ahead ever so slowly, the American force grew steadily, mostly with militiamen who streamed in to save their families from the British invader and its Indian allies. By September, Burgoyne was heavily outnumbered and the Americans, under General Gates, had occupied favorable terrain along the redcoats' only route to Albany.

Burgoyne faced unpalatable choices: a retreat that might easily turn disastrous or an attempt to slug his way through a numerically superior and well-entrenched enemy army. Burgoyne chose to fight. He failed, suffering heavy losses in two engagements, Freeman's Farm and Bemis Heights.

Following the second slugfest, the rebels encircled his army. Time had run out for Burgoyne. On October 17, at Saratoga, he surrendered 5,900 men, all that was left of the 7,250 men he had set out with in May. Gates, who had spent years in the British army, had waged a by-the-book campaign, doing nothing fancy or daring and avoiding any mistakes. It was America's second victory over a British army in this war, but Gates had inflicted losses on the regulars that were several times greater than what Washington had achieved at Trenton and Princeton.[36]

HOWE IDLED IN NEW YORK until after Burgoyne had taken Fort Ticonderoga in July. When he finally moved south, Howe chose to go by sea, though Philadelphia was only some sixty-five miles from Perth Amboy, just below British-held Staten Island. The voyage was a nightmare. Thirty-two sweltering summer days were consumed in reaching land, and when the redcoats at last splashed ashore at Head of Elk, Maryland, at the top of Chesapeake Bay, they still had to cover fifty-seven miles to reach Philadelphia. The British and German soldiers, landlubbers all, were sick and exhausted when they landed. Most of Howe's horses—essential for the cavalry, the linchpin of a mobile army's intelligence-gathering apparatus, and critical for pulling artillery and baggage wagons—had perished during the dreadful journey. Howe paused for nearly two weeks to permit his battered army to mend. When he at last set off on September 7—in a night march under a sky blazing with a spectral exhibition of northern lights— Washington, just as Howe had hoped, was waiting for him along the road to Philadelphia.[37]

Since the previous September, Washington had waffled between the war of posts strategy and one of standing and fighting, though his Fabian tactics had led to his only success. That he chose to give battle, risking all once again, seems a strange choice, one so odd that a young officer under Washington thought his commander had "made a sacrifice of his own excellent judgment upon the altar of public opinion." If he felt pressured to fight, it was not because Congress overtly leaned on him to defend Philadelphia, though Washington must have feared angry recriminations, and possibly even the loss of congressional backing, should the city fall without a battle. He was also aware that some in Congress had never liked his Fabian tactics, and he probably knew—Washington's friends and allies·

in Congress kept him abreast of what was being said privately among the delegates—that some congressmen thought the Continental army should assail the debilitated British army while it lay at Head of Elk. To be sure, Washington knew that some of his general officers, too, advocated such a course, and he realized that some Pennsylvania authorities wanted him to make a stand in the hope of saving Philadelphia.[38] However, the best explanation for Washington's decision to fight was his temperament. He was never thoroughly comfortable with the war of posts strategy. Running and dodging a fight was anathema to him. A gambler by nature, he always preferred to give battle, and on this occasion he thought himself in a far better position than he had faced in New York. Although he was outnumbered by some two thousand men, the British navy—which had played a key role in his defeats in the New York campaign—would not come into play as Howe advanced on Philadelphia. Washington had also been impressed by the fight his men had waged in the Trenton-Princeton campaign nine months earlier. With a standing army under him, he must have also expected even more of his soldiers.

Washington's anxieties over his security may have been another factor in his decision to resist Howe's advance on Philadelphia. As we know the outcome of the war and the mythic status it brought Washington, it is hard to imagine his being summarily replaced at the head of the army, especially with the contest yet in doubt. But the careworn commander could not see things with such clarity. By early September, as his confrontation with Howe loomed, Washington's self-assurance may have been rattled. Early in August, Congress dumped Schuyler as commander of the Northern Department, replacing him with Gates. Although abundant evidence exists that Washington's confidence in Schuyler had also waned nearly a year earlier, it must have been unsettling for him to learn that Congress had removed such a powerful figure, something it had not done in the first two years of the war. While sound military reasons undergirded Congress's action, there were also political overtones to it. Gates, as Washington knew, had spent about as much time politicking as soldiering, in the course of which he had lobbied Congress and made himself the darling of New England. The Yankees saw in Gates not only a former British officer (he had risen to the rank of major in the British army), but an English-born commoner who had embraced radical political ideas, sharing the

New Englanders' fervor for egalitarianism and republicanism. Those same New Englanders loathed Schuyler, who in many ways was similar to Washington. He was rich, aristocratic, and a land speculator who owned thousands of acres on the frontier, and like the commander in chief, Schuyler was socially conservative. New England's delegates in Congress had long wanted to topple Schuyler, and it was clear that the Yankee congressmen had led the successful fight that finished off Schuyler as a Continental officer. Overall, Congress's action was popular. Gates was widely viewed as unrivaled as a recruiter and, especially, as an officer whom militiamen trusted and were willing to serve under.[39]

Washington never said that he was troubled by Gates's ascent, and it would be foolish to believe that he hoped for anything other than the success of the American army that defended New York against Burgoyne. However, by early September, Washington knew that Burgoyne was in trouble and that Gates might score a major triumph, and the implications of such an outcome in the campaign in upper New York—consciously or unconsciously—may have fueled Washington's zeal for seeking his own decisive battlefield victory.

Washington correctly foresaw disaster for Burgoyne. Once he learned of Howe's decision not to try to link up with Burgoyne, Washington expected the British would encounter great difficulties in their invasion of New York. With uncanny accuracy, he predicted that New England, with "nothing to fear from Genl Howe . . . will turn out their force [of] both Continl & Militia to oppose Burgoyne." Washington expected Gates, with ample manpower and time to prepare, to mount a "vigorous and successful Opposition." While the outcomes of campaigns and battles are never certain, Washington knew that Burgoyne's difficulties were mounting through August and that his force was growing steadily weaker while Gates's army was growing stronger.[40] As Washington weighed his options toward Howe, what was playing out far to the north almost certainly entered his thoughts.

The armies under Washington and Howe clashed on the rolling, jade green terrain near the Brandywine Creek, about twenty-five miles west of Philadelphia. Though autumn lay just over the horizon, September 11 was a warm summer day. Howe's strategy was to first attack across the Brandywine at the center of the rebel lines, hoping that Washington would believe it was the main British thrust. But while the assault at the center continued, Howe planned to take his main army on a long march up the Brandywine and cross above the right wing of the rebel army. If all went well, Howe would flank the rebel right and be in a position to envelop and annihilate his enemy.

Howe came perilously close to success. He crossed the Brandywine at a ford that Washington did not know existed. Washington once again had failed to adequately reconnoiter the field that he had selected for the clash, and as on Long Island, he fell for a feint by Howe. Holding inflexibly to the idea that the British assault on the American center was Howe's primary attack, Washington for several hours ignored intelligence that Howe was attempting a flanking maneuver. Once again, Washington was frozen with indecision, almost fatally so. That his army escaped before the British trap snapped shut was due in large measure to Howe's habitual languor and tardiness. Had Howe had his men in position to attack at daybreak—as Washington had done at Trenton—the British might have inflicted a mortal blow on the Americans. But Howe did not even start his march until nearly daybreak, did not get across the Brandywine until after noon, and did not launch his flanking attack until deep into the afternoon. But Washington was saved, too, because his army performed better than it had on Long Island. The men on the rebel right slowed the redcoats' progress until Washington, at last, recognized what Howe was doing and redeployed several units of Continentals accordingly. Even so, the Americans were driven to the ropes and staring into the face of a frightful defeat when twilight shrouded the battlefield, forcing a conclusion to the fray and permitting Washington to withdraw his army to safety. Washington, a disappointed British sergeant remarked, had "escaped a total overthrow, that must have been the consequence of an hours more daylight." If not a total defeat, the Americans had paid a heavy price. They suffered eleven hundred casualties, twice the losses of the British.[41]

The smoke had hardly cleared from the battlefield before some in Congress—in private conversations that got back to Washington—were complaining of the outcome at Brandywine. Carping occurred in the press as well. While Washington escaped public censure, some of the supposedly secret criticism by congressmen was directed at his generalship. Some wondered why Howe knew the lay of the land around Brandywine better than Washington, especially as the Continental army had been in the region for fifteen days prior to the engagement. Some additionally expressed astonishment that Washington had again been fooled by Howe's tactics, and not a few were disturbed by his nearly disastrous uncertainty at the height of battle.

The criticism that was aired openly was directed at General John Sullivan, not Washington. Sullivan was an easy target. After his sorry performance in Canada in 1776, Congress had relieved him of that command. He had been overwhelmed and captured on Long Island. At Brandywine, he had commanded the vital right wing of Washington's army, and his troops had come within a whisker of being flanked by Howe. Several congressmen wanted to oust him from the army, and a Maryland congressman vowed that if Sullivan remained a general officer, no soldier from Maryland would ever again be made to serve under him. The attack on Sullivan took the heat off Washington. Content for Sullivan to be the current scapegoat for his lack of success, Washington did nothing to help his subordinate, who was eventually vindicated by a court-martial. Washington took no responsibility for the many lapses that had nearly produced a crushing defeat on the Brandywine.[42]

AFTER HAVING MADE A STAND, and once again having had a close brush with disaster, Washington reverted to his Fabian tactics, retreating and maneuvering. As his army moved daily during the four days that followed Brandywine, Washington—in several messages to Congress concerning the recent engagement—took a position that had long since become customary following an unsuccessful venture. He blamed his intelligence apparatus for his having been "obliged to leave the enemy masters of the field" at Brandywine. "Notwithstanding all my pains to get the best" intelligence, Washington said, he had been provided with "uncertain & contradictory" information, though experienced soldiers knew there seldom is any other kind of intelligence in the chaos of a battle. Washington also told Congress that his losses at Brandywine were "not . . . very considerable," which, of course, was inaccurate.[43]

Whatever Washington's wishes may have been regarding another clash with Howe, he led Congress to believe that he was anxious to fight again. He reported that he was deploying his troops in the hope that he would "be able to oppose Genl Howe with success in the Feild." The closest to a battle that he came in the immediate aftermath of Brandywine occurred on September 16, when Howe discovered the location of Washington's army and marched his redcoats for a confrontation. The engagement never took place. A terrific storm blew up as the armies were assembling. Much of the rebels' ammunition was destroyed by the relentless rain, compelling Washington to retreat again. As he withdrew, Washington reported to Congress that he had been on the verge of battle, hoping "to prevent them from turning our fight flank, which they seem to have a violent inclination to effect."[44]

In the wake of what contemporaries called the "Battle of the Clouds," Washington continued to suggest that he planned an action that would visit "a reverse of fortune" on the enemy, as he put it, making the British pay a heavy price for taking Philadelphia. He had "a firm intent of giving the Enemy Battle," Washington assured Congress, and he acted as if he meant what he said. Sending officers into Philadelphia and its environs in search of materials, Washington ultimately found sufficient ammunition to permit him to take the army into battle. He told Congress that he planned to fall on the rear of Howe's army as it attempted a crossing of the Schuylkill River on the west side of Philadelphia. As he was certain that he knew where the British must try to make their crossing, and as he knew that no army could get across a river rapidly, Washington asserted that his was a plan with "a prospect of success." However, the British did not cross the Schuylkill where Washington expected. In fact, the American army was out of position, twenty miles away from the site of the British crossing, when Howe cleared the last hurdle for taking Philadelphia. Over a span of twelve days following Brandywine, Howe had marched and maneuvered over a wide area—his men had tramped at least fifty miles—and the British army had never encountered serious opposition from the Continental army.[45]

Fifteen days after Brandywine, Philadelphia fell. Washington took no responsibility for the loss of the city. Howe had gotten into Philadelphia, he reported, through a serious of "perplexing Maneuvers" that confounded those whom he had entrusted with gathering intelligence. What is more, his men had been hamstrung by a shortage of materials, due in some measure, Washington said, to the "disaffected" residents of southeast

Pennsylvania who had refused to aid the American army. The shortages, he contended, had "impeded Our Movements very considerably."[46]

On September 26, with a British army band playing "God Save Great George Our King" and a large number of cheering residents lining the streets, Howe's red-clad soldiery marched into Philadelphia. It arrived four days after Congress—"with the utmost precipitation and in the greatest confusion," according to a bemused Loyalist observer—fled the city for York, Pennsylvania, a tiny village some seventy-five miles to the west that was to be its home for the next nine months. (In his messages to Congress, Washington referred to the flight as a congressional "adjournment.")[47]

As September faded, Washington learned of Gates's steady success in seeing that Burgoyne was "in a fair way of being utterly ruined."[48] But Washington did not require word of Gates's impending triumph to drive him to accomplish something before the campaign of 1777 concluded. His pride, not to mention his commitment to the cause, led him to attempt something, and in the days after Philadelphia fell, Washington, with white-knuckled resolve, fixed on the idea of a surprise attack on an outlying redcoat post.[49] If successful, he could close the year's fighting with a bold initiative, just as he had closed 1776 with his Christmas assault on the Hessian cantonment at Trenton.

FOR LOGISTICAL REASONS, and to secure the principal road leading to Philadelphia, Howe had divided his army, posting half in the city and the remainder, roughly eight thousand men, at Germantown a few miles to the north. An assault on Germantown, Washington thought, offered a good opportunity for success, as he would possess a significant numerical superiority. Working for days on the planning of the operation, Washington ultimately envisaged another long nighttime march, as he had undertaken at Trenton, followed by a strike at dawn. He had more time to prepare the assault on Germantown than had been available to him to plan for Trenton. The additional time may have been a drawback, as it enabled Washington to contrive a dangerously intricate plan of operation. The keys to victory were surprise and simultaneous strikes by American forces that were to approach Germantown from every direction.

But after the Christmas attack at Trenton, it was unlikely that the enemy would be caught off guard again, and to Washington's disappointment, British pickets learned of the rebels' advance. Washington's scheme for the various divisions of the rebel army launching a synchronized strike also went awry. The Americans' night march was bedeviled by the thickest fog anyone could remember. Only one column reached its appointed place at the designated time, and the largest rebel division arrived more than thirty minutes late. If that was not bad enough, the sizable contingent of Pennsylvania militia, which was to assail the British in the southern sector of the hamlet, was pinned down by a ridiculously small number of Hessians.

Despite these myriad problems, the Americans came close to scoring a major victory. Several things went wrong, as almost always occurs in the tumult and confusion of combat, but one of the greatest impediments to victory arose from a misguided decision by Washington. Early in the engagement, while the Americans had some momentum, a contingent of 120 redcoats took control of the large, two-story residence owned by Benjamin Chew, the former chief justice of Pennsylvania. The small British presence in the American rear posed little danger to the Continentals, but Washington unwisely squandered an entire brigade, precious firepower, and a full hour in an unsuccessful attempt to dislodge the British defenders. (One third of the Americans lost in the battle fell at the Chew house, while the enemy lost only four men at that site.) The presence of that brigade and its artillery in a more crucial sector of the field might have turned the tide. Instead, after a battle that lasted three hours, the Americans withdrew from the field. They had lost twelve hundred men, three times the losses of their adversary, and the British still held Germantown.[50]

Some of Washington's field-grade officers—men who were less likely to be political appointees than the general officers—were furious at what had occurred, especially at their commander's unwarranted fixation on the Chew house. It destroyed the morale of the men, said one, while another remarked that victory, which had been within the grasp of the Continentals, had been "shamefully lost" through Washington's poor leadership. Even some British officers expressed amazement that the normally "Clever Washington" had blundered so badly.[51]

As usual following a failure, Washington's report to Congress was disingenuous. He never mentioned the folly at the Chew house, attributed his lack of success to environmental conditions—fog and heavy smoke caused

confusion on the battlefield, he argued, as if only the rebels had been perplexed and inhibited by such conditions—and minimized his losses. The
"day was rather unfortunate, than injurious," he said, though he had lost
10 percent of his men. Washington also attempted to cast a positive light
on the affair by asserting that "the Enemy are nothing the better by the
event, and our Troops . . . have gained what All young Troops gain [battle
experience] by being in Actions."[52] He also spread what he had to know
were false tidings in New England, where Gates had long enjoyed his
greatest popularity and was certain to be more wildly acclaimed. The
American soldiers were "in high Spirits and much pleased with the fortune of the day," he told civilian officials in New England, even claiming
that the British losses at Germantown were at least twice those of the
Continentals and possibly three times as great. In fact, British losses were
less than half those sustained by the rebels.[53]

But something more was needed. From Fort Necessity onward, every
defeat suffered by Washington required a scapegoat. Several days after
Germantown, as recriminations in Congress and elsewhere began to be
heard, Major General Adam Stephen was made responsible for the American failure.

Stephen had served loyally under Washington in the Virginia Regiment,
but he had crossed Washington in the competition for land in the Ohio
Country and by running against him for the assembly seat from Frederick
County in 1761. They were never close afterward. Stephen had entered
the Continental army with the rank of colonel in February 1776. In eighteen months he had risen three ranks, to major general, the highest rank
beneath the commander in chief. He had seen action at Trenton-Princeton
and Brandywine. In the latter engagement, his regiment was praised in the
newspapers for having "performed admirably" in the heavy fighting to
stave off Howe's flanking maneuver. Stephen had a reputation—doubtless
deserved—as a heavy drinker, and some congressmen had complained
openly of his (and others') fondness for the bottle, though none had
claimed that he had ever been impaired in battle. A week before Germantown, Charles Carroll of Maryland had urged Stephen's dismissal because
his propensity for drink set a bad example for the enlisted men. Not only
had Washington ignored that complaint, he gave Stephen command of one
of the divisions at Germantown. Nothing untoward was said of Stephen's

performance on the battlefield at Germantown in the first several days after the clash, including in Washington's official report, written about thirty-six hours following the engagement. Then, a full week after the battle, allegations against Stephen were ginned up by some of Washington's general officers. Stephen was accused of having gone into battle in a drunken stupor, a charge that was never proven. Fixing on Stephen was convenient for many officers. Fingering him as the whipping boy took the heat off others, especially those in the spotlight for the Chew house fiasco. Should Stephen be sacrificed, moreover, it would open a vacancy in the rank of major general, one that Washington and many congressmen hoped to fill with the Marquis de Lafayette.[54] Stephen was doomed.

Court-martialed on three charges, Stephen was convicted of "unofficerlike behaviour," inattention to his duties, and "want of judgement." He was dismissed from the service, the highest-ranking officer to be ousted during the war's first thirty months. Stephen appealed the verdict to Congress, asserting that he had fallen victim to "the Object of hatred of a Person of high rank [Washington]."[55] Congress took no action on his appeal.

IN THE SPACE OF THREE WEEKS, Washington had fought and lost two battles, suffering an unsustainable attrition rate in the neighborhood of 20 percent. Gates, meanwhile, had scored America's most magnificent victory in the war, losing just 5 percent of his men. Washington began to worry about whether he would be able to remain the head of the army. Gates was more popular than ever in New England, and his fame was spreading throughout the country. People everywhere were singing a popular song that celebrated his victory at Saratoga. At formal dinners and over ale in taverns, friends toasted Gates as the "Hero of Saratoga" and "Conqueror of Burgoyne."

Seeing Gates lionized must have galled Washington, and Gates's behavior after Saratoga made matters worse. Inexplicably—not to mention foolishly and undiplomatically—Gates failed to notify Washington of his victory. Gates immediately wrote Congress, though the aide he chose to deliver the message, Colonel James Wilkinson, stretched what should have been about a six-day journey into a trek nearly twice that length, as he paused en route to visit his girlfriend. By the time Congress learned of the outcome at Saratoga, Washington had already received unofficial reports of Gates's victory from state authorities in Massachusetts and Continental officers posted in the Northern Department, including one of Gates's staff officers. It was not until thirteen days after the event that Washington received confirmation from Congress of Burgoyne's surrender, and the commander in chief made no secret of the fact that he "most bitterly" resented what he called Gates's "neglect." Fairly or otherwise, Washington interpreted Gates's conduct as a personal slight and a hostile act.[56]

This, however, was only the beginning of Washington's anxiety over Gates. Soon after official word of Burgoyne's surrender reached him, Washington dispatched Alexander Hamilton, one of his aides, to request—it was a solicitation, not an order—Gates to bring most of his army from Albany to the outskirts of Philadelphia. After all, Gates no longer had an enemy army with which to contend, but Washington did. Hamilton, in fact, was directed to make clear that although Howe had occupied Philadelphia, the British army still faced the difficult job of rooting out the rebels that guarded the Delaware River south of the city, a necessary step for opening river traffic. The combined armies of Washington and Gates might not only impede those British actions, they could play havoc with the enemy's foraging activities during the coming winter, adding to Howe's woes. Whatever Washington expected, Gates balked at his commander's directive. Gates told Hamilton that he had been ordered by Congress to retake Fort Ticonderoga but that he had few remaining troops with which to act. Gates's militiamen had gone home, and he had already sent a rifle corps to Washington. Indeed, Gates had only one brigade of Continentals and virtually no militiamen under his command. Hamilton persisted, however, and Gates soon relented, agreeing to send two thirds of his force to Philadelphia. Gates had complied with Washington's wishes, but the meeting had been stormy. Gates was furious that Hamilton was Washington's messenger. (He complained privately that no European general would have sent a lowly aide on such an assignment.) Furthermore, Hamilton was a poor choice for this undertaking. Not only was he just twenty-two years old and perhaps lacking in the diplomatic skills for such a mission, but Hamilton was close to General Schuyler—he eventually married Schuyler's daughter—and he disliked Gates, who had conspired to supplant Schuyler. While Washington got what he wanted, he heard the details of the meeting from Hamilton, which may not have been an unbiased accounting of what had transpired. The incident appears to have added to Washington's resentment and further aroused his suspicions of Gates's ill will.[57]

By early November, Washington was besieged with rumors that a "Strong Faction" within Congress wished to remove him and name Gates as the new commander of the Continental army. Washington did not know precisely what was occurring behind the curtain in Congress, but he probably knew that some congressmen believed—as Pennsylvania's Dr. Benjamin Rush, a signer of the Declaration of Independence, put it—that the army "under General Gates [was] a well regulated family," while "Washington's [was but an] imitation of an Army" that bore the look of "an unformed mob." Some proclaimed that Gates had "executed with vigor and bravery," attaining "the pinnacle of military glory." Washington's command, according to the whispers, was characterized by such "negligence" that it was hardly surprising he had been "outwitted," "outgeneraled and twice beated [*sic*]."[58] It was unsettling enough to have congressmen complain about his leadership, but atop that Washington soon learned that some of his officers had lost confidence in him.

Washington did not know the full extent of the disaffection with his leadership. But he knew enough to become convinced that he was in the maw of a great crisis.

THE UNTOUCHABLE: GENERAL WASHINGTON'S GREAT CRISIS

WHILE MUCH OF THE COUNTRY celebrated Saratoga, confident that the British disaster would draw France into the war and assure America's triumph, the occupation of Philadelphia provoked consternation in Pennsylvania and Congress. Several powerful merchants had been forced to flee the city, and houses owned by leading rebels had been appropriated by the British army. Loyalists returning to the city now that the Crown was in control soon occupied civil offices previously filled by rebels. A Tory, Joseph Galloway, was named police superintendent of Philadelphia, and he disarmed known rebels, jailed some, and executed two. He also raised a Loyalist regiment that helped the British block trade between outlying rebel farmers and the city market.[1]

Many in Congress were in a black mood that autumn. As the British had closed in on Philadelphia late in September, messengers sent by the Continental army awakened the congressmen in the wee hours of a dark night and advised them to run for their lives. They ran so quickly that one delegate from New Hampshire forgot to saddle his horse. Most faced a harrowing ride on the road that ran north from Philadelphia, never knowing whether they might encounter advance parties of British soldiers in the inky blackness. Their eventual destination was York, but most took a safe circuitous route, which meant horseback rides of nearly two hundred miles. While the humiliation of having been forced to run like jackrabbits was bad enough, some resented even more that the Congress of the United

States was made to squeeze into a crowded redbrick county courthouse in a rustic village in the Pennsylvania backcountry. Having to live in York only heightened the congressmen's surliness. The town was pretty enough, but it was small and good lodgings were difficult to find. Many congressmen shared a room with several colleagues, and at least initially, all were dependent on the army's quartermaster corps for sustenance. Some were angry that the war had not ended in 1777. Like most Americans, the members of Congress had gone to war expecting a "short and speedy issue to the unhappy dispute," as General Greene once said. Not only had the conflict not ended, it had morphed into a war of attrition, a most troubling prospect, as signs were growing that the United States lacked the capability of sustaining an army or maintaining a healthy economy during a protracted struggle. John Adams found the "Prospect . . . chilling, on every Side. Gloomy, dark, melancholy, and dispiriting. When and where will the light spring up?" he asked.[2]

In their disgruntled condition, some congressmen looked for something, or someone, to blame. The Pennsylvania militia took considerable heat for its allegedly poor performances at Brandywine and Germantown and for having done little to harass Howe's army as it crept toward Philadelphia. Pennsylvania's Tories were condemned for having given "the best of Intelligence to the Enemy, & deceived" the American army. Some suspected that there were more fundamental problems with America's war effort, though they were not easy to discern. "We have as good a Cause, as ever was fought for. We have great Resources. The People are well tempered," said Adams. What, he asked, is needed to "bring order out of this Confusion and save this Country"?[3]

Adams did not answer his query, but others did, and with asperity. For many, General Washington was part of the problem. He commanded an undisciplined army, some said. Privately, Dr. Benjamin Rush charged that Washington had permitted a spirit of carelessness and torpor to pervade the Continental army. The commander in chief, Rush said, should "see everything with his own eyes, and hear everything with his own ears." Others were profoundly troubled by Washington's Fabian strategy, seeing it as the timidity of a risk-averse general. Charles Thomson, the secretary of Congress throughout the war, had concluded that Washington was "deficient" in those "marks of true greatness which so preeminently characterized" the most successful generals throughout history. Others thought Washington had surrounded himself with sycophants who filled his head with bad advice, and not a few believed that the commander's troubles had begun when he fell under the "pernicious influence" of General Greene.

At the outset of the war, Washington had turned primarily to General Lee for advice, but after early 1776 he was often posted elsewhere, and in December 1776, he had been captured by the British. In Lee's absence, Greene gained Washington's confidence, so much so that it was rumored the commander had told Congress that should something happen to him, he hoped Greene would be made commander of the Continental army. While Greene had been part of the initial batch of general officers chosen by Congress in June 1775, some appear to have looked on him as no better than a political appointee. Every New England colony had been rewarded with at least one general, and Greene happened to be Rhode Island's, though he had never served in an army until a few weeks before Lexington and Concord. Greene had struck Henry Knox, the artillery commander in the Continental army, as "the rawest, the most untutored" of all in the initial batch of general officers, a view that was doubtless shared by many outside the army. Greene's stature was not improved by the Fort Washington debacle or by how Washington chose to cope with the British advance on Philadelphia, especially as by then it was widely believed that the campaign waged by the commander had hewed to the line urged by Greene.[4]

Rush believed Washington was deeply flawed—inexperienced, confused, indecisive, thin-skinned, and inattentive to many problems. But even Rush acknowledged that the army's problems ran deeper than Washington's shortcomings. Too many officers, he charged, were incompetent, having been political choices. Rush also concluded that Washington was distracted by having had too many powers lodged in him. For all practical purposes, Rush said, "General Washington had been made quartermaster, commissary, and adjutant general of your whole army." No one could cope with so much, he said. The result was such administrative chaos that the soldiers were doomed to inordinate suffering. In Dr. Rush's opinion, the medical department was a prime example of Washington's failure to bring about needed reforms. Tongue in cheek, Rush wrote that he had discovered a "certain method of destroying Howe's whole army without powder or ball. . . . Lead them through any of the villages . . . where we have a [Continental army] hospital, and . . . in 6 weeks there shall not be man of them alive or fit for duty."

As a result of Washington's manifold failings and the flaws in the army's structure, the Continental army, at least in Rush's view, was "no better than it was two years ago." The "Spirit of our men is good," Rush said, and he believed that the lower-grade "Officers are equal nay superior" to their counterparts in the British army. Given a better commander in chief and a "few able major generals," he concluded, the army would be "a terror to the whole power of Britain." But if changes were not made, and if the war dragged on interminably, Rush predicted that the American Revolution would be lost. "New measures, and new men alone can save us," he declared, and he proposed that the army's commander and its general officers "be chosen annually."[5]

James Lovell, a member of the Massachusetts delegation, concurred. He wished that Congress would dump Washington in favor of General Gates. Lovell even told Gates that the Continental army "is to be totally lost unless you come down" and take command. John Dickinson Sergeant, a former New Jersey congressman, said privately: "We want a general." Countless lives and dollars "are yearly sacrificed to the insufficiency of our commander in chief." Sergeant added that Washington had lost at Brandywine and Germantown through "such blunders as would have disgraced a soldier of three months standing." Abraham Clark, a member of the New Jersey delegation who had signed the Declaration of Independence, joined in the unsparing attacks on Washington. Clark predicted that victory would remain elusive until "the management of our army" was changed.[6] Thomas Mifflin, Washington's first aide-de-camp and subsequently the army's quartermaster general, had seen Washington up close for two years, and he had seen enough. Washington's "unjustifiable Arrogance," he said, had driven from the army many talented officers "who would not worship the Image & pay an undeserved Tribute of Praise & Flattery to the great & powerful" commander in chief. Washington, he alleged, had opened the army to the "most just Sarcasm & Contempt of our Enemies." Mifflin, like Lovell, admired Horatio Gates.[7]

Washington has enjoyed a reputation among historians as an excellent administrator of the Continental army, but that view was not shared by all of his contemporaries. Some saw enormous waste, and especially a shameful squandering of the army's manpower. Some thought there were far too many officers, and others were furious with the army's practice of allotting vast numbers of men as personal guards and servants to the highest officers. Washington had a Life Guard of one hundred men who protected him and secured headquarters. Few quibbled over that, but each general officer had his own guard, some of which totaled nearly fifty men. When the officers' attendants were counted as well, as much as 5 percent of the soldiery was being utilized as personal guards and servants. A study made by the army itself at one point found that 50 percent of the men in two Connecticut brigades were "Employ'd as Waiters to the Staff Officers."[8]

Washington's detractors assailed his conduct of the Philadelphia campaign, not so much because he had failed to score a victory as because he had done little after Brandywine to prevent the occupation of Philadelphia. One congressman alleged that the "Enemy were astonished" when Washington stood by idly, "having Philadelphia left open." Another said he had watched with "wonder and discontent" as Washington, who possessed a considerable numerical majority, did not try to attack the British troops at Germantown a second time before Howe redeployed that garrison to Philadelphia late in October. When Washington did next to nothing in October and November to frustrate Howe's operation to clear the Delaware River approaches to Philadelphia, his critics seethed.

Howe knew that he must open the Delaware River or his army would face the same unpleasant prospects in Philadelphia that had confronted the besieged redcoats in Boston during the winter of 1775–1776. Howe's task was formidable. Congress and the state authorities in Pennsylvania had expended considerable resources since the outbreak of hostilities to construct fortifications at two strategic points along the Delaware. They installed chevaux-de-frise, wooden beams affixed with iron spikes and anchored in the river, fully capable of ripping apart any vessel whose commander was so foolhardy as to attempt to sail through. The British cleared the impediments at Billingsport on October 2 while Washington was distracted with preparations for the surprise assault at Germantown. A second barrier—a triple line of chevaux-de-frise anchored by Fort Mercer on one end and Fort Mifflin on the other, and further defended by a frigate and seventeen assorted rebel vessels—was situated between Mud

Island and Red Bank Island and was far more imposing. On October 21, more than two weeks after Germantown, Howe sent two thousand Hessians after Fort Mercer. They were repulsed, with losses totaling nearly 20 percent. In mid-November, Howe tried again, this time targeting Fort Mifflin. Six days of hard fighting were required before the installation fell, opening the river to Philadelphia.[9]

Washington had sent only some 350 Continentals to reinforce those who were defending Forts Mercer and Mifflin. After the tragedy at Fort Washington, virtually no one expected him to commit a huge force, though some thought he should have done more. He might have attacked Philadelphia while much of Howe's army was deployed in the river-clearing operation. Or he could have struck the long line of redcoats marching south from the city to assault the forts. Many of Washington's critics lamented that America's army had not been used to make the British pay a staggering cost for having taken Philadelphia. Others thought an attack, even if not terribly successful, would have sent a positive message to potential benefactors in Europe. That had been the argument of General Anthony Wayne, who respectfully but assertively told Washington: "It is not in our Power to Command success—but it is in our Power to produce a Conviction to the World that we Deserve it."[10] When a significant American response was not forthcoming, some felt like the congressman who lamented that the bright "hope for signal success" had been squandered. That congressman added angrily that Washington had left the fate of the Delaware forts "to Heaven."[11]

Washington's inactivity after Germantown was at first blush curious. He had longed to attack British-occupied Boston in 1775–1776, and his Trenton-Princeton campaign had been the very personification of the word *daring*. In September, he had cast aside his Fabian strategy in favor of the nearly catastrophic confrontation at Brandywine. Washington summoned his general officers to councils of war on October 29 and November 24 and put the option of an attack on Philadelphia on the table. Each time, the officers debated two propositions: Should the Continental army strike Howe's army in Philadelphia? Would General Washington's "Character & that of the whole Army . . . Suffer if Something is not attempted?" Each time, a majority counseled against an attack, arguing that such a move was too risky. To fail would expose "our Army . . . to a total Defeat," warned one, while another cautioned that failure would "throw the Armey away we have." But at each council of war, many officers urged some sort of action. Some insisted that the "Honor" of the army and its commander demanded action. Some contended that further ventures were imperative in order to impress France and draw it into the war. Some advised that an attack could inflict heavy losses on the enemy, particularly if it was launched before the British had time to prepare defenses, if the element of surprise could be achieved, if the blow fell simultaneously in several sectors of Philadelphia, and if it was undertaken while a considerable portion of redcoats were deployed in Delaware River operations. Two generals thought it imprudent to attack Philadelphia but proposed that the army be "placed in such a position" outside Philadelphia "as to invite or oblidge general Howe to leave his strong holds & seek us in the field."[12]

If it was unusual for Washington to spurn the opportunity to fight, it was also somewhat out of character for him to be swayed so easily by the majority opinion of a council of war. A year earlier, stung by his repeated failures and by Lee's criticism about taking the advice of incompetent generals, Washington had skirted formal votes of councils of war by consulting privately with each of his generals. He had also cobbled together his own intelligence-gathering network, a stratagem that made him the best informed among the generals and, in turn, more likely to dominate councils of war. Basing his actions more than ever on his own judgment, he had achieved his sensational victories at Trenton and Princeton.[13] But when wrestling with what to do about Philadelphia in the autumn of 1777, he listened passively to the majority of his generals.

Actually, Washington listened mostly to Greene, just as the critics charged. On the eve of the second council of war, Washington ordered Greene to attack a much larger British force under Earl Cornwallis than had been deployed against Fort Mercer. Greene responded with a remarkable letter in which he alluded candidly to his commander's insecurities. Sometimes, he said, the "excess of caution" that comes from councils of war is not a bad thing. In this instance, he went on, neither assailing Cornwallis nor going after the enemy in Philadelphia was likely to succeed. Either course would probably "terminate to the injury of the Continent and disgrace of the Army." He knew that Washington was under enormous pressure to attempt something bold in the hope of satisfying "the Expectations of an ignorant Populace." But trouble lurked "in consulting our wishes rather than our reason." When "hurried by an impatience to attempt something splendid," the result all too often was "inextricable difficulties." You have two choices: "to fight the Enemy without the least Prospect of Success . . . or remain inactive, & be subject to the Censure of an ignorant & impatient populace." Choose the former, Greene counseled, and you will fail and be condemned "by all military Gentlemen of Experience." Choose the latter and you will face the censure of some civil officials, but you will also "give your Country an opportunity" to properly supply the army for another campaign to be waged another day. Do not "make a bad matter worse," Greene concluded. "The Cause is too important to be trifled with to shew [your] Courage, & your Character [is] too deeply interested, to sport away upon unmilitary Principles."[14]

Washington accepted Greene's advice, though he knew that backing off from a fight would provoke political problems. In fact, Greene's recommendations most likely tallied with his own thinking all along. Washington had been eager to fight at Brandywine and Germantown, but he had to know that if he failed again that fall, his troubles would soar. Besides, he expected to be in a stronger position during the campaign of 1778. With the northern frontier quiet in the wake of Saratoga, he had already begun to augment his army with men who had previously served under Gates. Furthermore, if France entered the war against Great Britain—and Washington expected it to do so—London might have to shift some of Howe's army to Europe or the Caribbean to meet the new threat. The safest course would be to go into winter quarters, reconstitute the army, and hope for improved military conditions in 1778. That was the prudent course suggested by Greene and the policy favored by Washington.[15]

Howe had other plans. He wanted to fight, and under cover of darkness on December 4, he brought nearly his entire army out of Philadelphia in the hope of surprising Washington's camp at Whitemarsh, a dozen or so miles almost due north of Germantown. When he lost the element of surprise, Howe tried to lure the rebels into battle, but Washington would have none of it. Next, Howe resorted to his time-tested tactic of a feint, hoping to find an advantageous means of bringing on a fight. This time, Washington did not take the bait. When the season's first snow fell, Howe called off his final stab at battle in 1777 and marched his army back to

Philadelphia.[16] That Washington, who had not fought in the sixty-five days since Germantown, had once again failed to use his army further angered some in Congress. Congressman Lovell, for instance, raged that he was sick of "the command of our Fabius." He summed up the frustrations of many of his colleagues: "our affairs are Fabiused into a very disagreeable posture."[17]

WASHINGTON WAS AWARE OF the invective that issued from Congress, but he would have been surprised to discover the feelings harbored by some of the loyal young officers who surrounded him. Colonel Timothy Pickering, an aide-de-camp, thought Washington was weak, ignorant, and vain.[18] Alexander Hamilton confided privately that the public's positive perception of Washington's character and abilities was "unfounded." He respected Washington's honesty but felt no love or friendship for his commander, as he found him to be given to "ill-humour." Hamilton acknowledged that it was essential that Washington's leadership be held up to the public as commendable, but the young aide allegedly thought the commander's reputation as a general was overblown. One day, he said, he would publicly expose Washington's "weakness" as a strategist and battlefield commander.[19]

Washington would also have been shocked to learn what some of the highest-ranking officers were saying about his generalship. Near the beginning of the war, General Stephen, who had served under Washington in two wars, remarked that the commander would need capable advisers, as he was "*a weak man*." General Sullivan attributed much of the soldiery's sufferings to administrative ineptitude at the highest level of command. This "is not an army—it is a mob," he lamented as the winter of 1777–1778 approached. Joseph Reed, who had been at Washington's side almost constantly during the first eighteen months of the war, thought him "only fit to command a regiment." A couple of years into the war, Mifflin concluded that the commander in chief "was totally unfit for his situations"; he thought Washington might perform ably as the "head clerk" in a mercantile company.[20] General Johann Kalb, one of the French volunteers and a soldier for nearly a quarter century, called Washington the "weakest general" under whom he had served. Kalb also predicted that if Washington ever "does anything sensational he will owe it more to his good luck or to his adversary's mistakes than to his own ability."[21] Washington knew none of this, but he learned that at least one of his generals was talking behind his back. He was tipped off by Lord Stirling, a Continental army officer, that General Thomas Conway, an Irish-born French soldier who, like Kalb, was serving as a volunteer with the Continentals, had allegedly disparaged him. Stirling had recently spent a drunken evening with Colonel James Wilkinson, Gates's young aide who was en route to York with word of the victory at Saratoga. In his cups, Wilkinson had said that Conway supposedly had written General Gates: "Heaven has been determined to save your Country; or a weak General and bad Councellors would have ruined it." Washington did not see the letter—he never saw it, in fact, as it mysteriously disappeared after Gates transmitted it to Conway late in January—but he rapidly recognized that what Conway had purportedly written was a heaven-sent opportunity.[22]

When Conway, a battle-hardened, English-speaking colonel in the French army, had arrived at Morristown in April, Washington had greeted him with open arms. Washington thought Conway "infinitely better qualified to serve us, than Many" of his Continental officers, and he urged Congress to commission the foreign volunteer a brigadier general in America's army. Congress quickly did so, and Washington gave Conway command of a Pennsylvania brigade.[23] The appointment paid dividends. Conway fought well at Brandywine and Germantown, leading Washington to single him out for praise in his reports to Congress. But serious problems arose in October when Congress contemplated promoting Conway to the rank of major general.

Conway was but one of numerous French volunteers who had flocked to the United States in 1777. Some held commissions granted by Congress, though most had been commissioned by Silas Deane, an envoy sent to Paris by Congress in 1776 to elicit French aid. Deane had agreed that three of the French officers were to hold the rank of major general, and he had even backdated a commission awarded to Colonel Tronson du Coudray, making him the senior to three veteran American major generals—Sullivan, Greene, and Knox. The three Americans were so outraged that they threatened to resign, but the tempest was eventually resolved to the satisfaction of all—save for du Coudray—when the Frenchman drowned in a ferry accident. Still, other field officers who were outranked by foreign officers, or realized that their path to promotion was blocked by the volunteers from across the sea, churned with fury. Washington, with good reason, feared a mass exodus by his seasoned senior officers should Conway be promoted.[24]

Although Conway had a penchant for acerbity—he made no effort to hide his contempt for the rebel soldiers or their officers, for instance— Washington continued to look on him with favor until several American officers grew "exceedingly convulsed" at the prospect of Conway's elevation. Only when Lord Stirling, the officer who would eventually tattle about Conway's supposed criticisms of Washington, threatened to resign rather than serve under Conway did Wasington act.

To this point, Washington had remained largely aloof from Congress's deliberations concerning the promotion of general officers. But in mid-October, three weeks before he learned of Conway's alleged remarks, Washington confided in Richard Henry Lee, the most powerful member of the Virginia delegation in Congress, that he feared the consequences should Congress promote the French volunteer. Conway's elevation, Washington warned, "will give a fatal blow to the existence of this army." The "service is so difficult . . . that almost all your officers are tired out," he continued, adding that twenty officers had resigned their commissions within the past six days. Promote Conway, Washington went on, and he would be inundated with "applications for leave to resign." Washington concluded with an open threat: Should Conway be promoted, "it will be impossible for me to be of any further service."[25]

Washington learned of Conway's letter to Gates on November 4. By then, the vexation that Conway's potential appointment had posed appeared a thing of the past, for Washington had been assured by Congressman Lee that the French volunteer would not be promoted "whilst it is likely to produce the evil consequences you suggest."[26] Reassured, Washington might have let Conway's purportedly disparaging remark pass without a rejoinder, but he saw the opening to possibly rid the army of a troublesome element and himself of a personal critic. On the day after he heard from Stirling, Washington divulged to Conway that he was aware of his unflattering comments. Conway denied that he had denigrated Washington—"you are a Brave man, an honest Man, a patriot, and a Man of great sense," he told the commander—though he admitted that he believed Washington permitted himself to be swayed by inept counselors. Convinced that he had burned his bridges in America, Conway submitted his resignation.[27]

Washington presumed the episode was behind him. In any case, he had more pressing concerns. The Conway flap occurred in the midst of Howe's campaign to clear the Delaware River. The weeks that followed—down to the middle of December—were consumed with Howe's last-ditch effort to draw Washington out to fight at Whitemarsh and, simultaneously, a tense wrangle between the commander and Congress over whether to take the army into winter quarters. After the grim winter at Morristown, Washington wished to scatter his army throughout several cantonments about sixty miles west of Philadelphia, certain that the army could be more easily supplied in several camps than at a lone site. Not a few in Congress had other ideas. Many congressmen—one said the sentiment was shared by every member of Congress, though that seems unlikely—objected to shutting down the Continental army during the winter months. As Washington's army had hardly been used in 1777, they wanted it in the field so that it might either attack Philadelphia or assail every party of redcoats that sallied out from the city. On November 28, Congress directed Washington's army to carry on "a winter's campaign with vigour and success." Washington was outraged. There were good reasons to take the army into winter quarters. It was a standard practice among European armies to use the winter to rest weary soldiers, gather supplies, repair equipment, and train new recruits while honing the skills of veterans.[28]

The issue was resolved by a compromise, though not without recriminations on both sides. Congress relented on the issue of winter quarters, while Washington abandoned the idea of multiple cantonments deep in the Pennsylvania backcountry. The commander agreed instead to establish his winter camp near Philadelphia. But there was more. The committee that Congress sent to Whitemarsh to negotiate with Washington also advised him to take the winter to introduce a "proper discipline" among his soldiers and to quell the "prevalent . . . general discontent in the army and especially among the Officers." Washington fired back that if he encountered supply problems that winter, as he suspected would be the case, he would have no choice but to use a heavy hand in taking goods from Pennsylvania's farmers. He added that no army on the planet had the resources to protect every village and farm within a fifty-mile radius of Philadelphia.

All that could be done by the army, and all that should be expected of it, was to "give the most general and extensive security" to civilians against "ravage and depredation." He also told Congress that it was "time to speak plain." Too many congressmen, he said, "seem to have little feeling for the naked and distressed Soldier." His blood boiling, Washington added: It "is a much easier and less distressing thing to draw Remonstrances in a comfortable room by a good fire side" than to face a soldier's life and "to occupy a cold, bleak hill, and sleep under frost & snow with Cloaths or Blankets."[29] With that blast, Washington ordered his men down Gulph Road, tramping under barren trees and through occasional patches of old snow. Their destination was Valley Forge.

NEVER HAD WASHINGTON'S RELATIONS WITH CONGRESS sunk to such a low ebb, though it was hardly due solely to the corrosive issue of putting the army into winter quarters. Congress had made it apparent that it was disturbed by Washington's performance in the campaign of 1777. On the day before Washington penned his fury-laden missive about congressional insensitivity toward the Continental soldiery, not only had Congress declined to accept Conway's resignation, it had promoted him to major general and named him inspector general of the army, a new post that Washington had proposed, though the commander in chief never imagined that Conway would fill the position. Conway was to be responsible for improving discipline and for the tactical abilities of the army, and he was to report to the Board of War and Ordnance, a congressional panel, not to Washington. Conway's promotion was a stunning rebuke of Washington. Vesting him with an independent position was tantamount to saying that Congress had lost confidence in Washington's ability to discipline his army.

Some scholars have suggested that Congress was unaware of Washington's views about Conway, but that is a fanciful notion. Washington had written Richard Henry Lee about Conway with the expectation that Lee would broadcast his views in Congress. A veteran politician, Lee would certainly have understood the purpose of Washington's letter. Besides, Lee was hardly the only one aware of what was on Washington's mind. It is difficult to imagine that some members of Congress, who visited the nearby army from time to time, did not hear scuttlebutt from those who surrounded the commander, if not from Washington himself. What is more, civilian officials frequently paid calls on both the army and Congress, and throughout the war they were used as conduits by both. If Congress somehow did not know Washington's thinking on this matter, it had certainly gleaned it from Conway himself, who had expanded on his troubles with Washington in the eight-page letter of resignation that he penned to Congress nearly three weeks earlier.[30]

Conway's promotion was merely Congress's latest reproach. Two weeks earlier, it had made sweeping changes in the composition of the Board of War and Ordnance, the body to which Conway was now responsible. During its eighteen-month existence, the Board of War, chaired from its inception by John Adams, had worked harmoniously with Washington. But when Adams left Congress in November, his former colleagues reorganized the board, filling three of the five slots with Gates, Mifflin, and Richard Peters, a Philadelphia lawyer. All three were looked on at headquarters as enemies of General Washington. Most tellingly, it named Gates the president of the Board of War and directed him to establish his headquarters in York, where Congress was meeting. Washington's leadership was to be placed under the scrutiny of Gates—a general thought by some in Congress to be more adept than Washington.[31]

In the face of these rebukes, Washington was certain that a vast conspiracy was plotting his removal as the army's commander. A few historians have concurred, labeling the supposed intrigue "the Conway Cabal." To be sure, some public officials in and out of Congress, and some army officers, especially some foreign volunteers, were fed up with Washington's repeated blunders, cautious tactics, indecisiveness, or choice of advisers. One member of Congress reported a considerable "buz" among his colleagues about Washington's failure to institute decent supply and intelligence-gathering systems, to reduce the alarming number of desertions, or to field a better-disciplined army. "I am afraid there may be some ground for some of those remarks," Henry Laurens, the president of Congress, privately reflected shortly after Germantown. One delegate remarked that Washington's opinions had come to be "treated with . . . much indecent freedom & Levity."[32]

But those in Congress who sought Washington's immediate removal were but a tiny fraction of the members. When Connecticut's Eliphalet Dyer said that winter that "there is not the most distant thought of removing Genll Washington, nor ever an expression in Congress looking that way," he was stating a fact. Most congressmen understood the travail that Washington had faced in the past two campaigns. He "has ever been . . . inferiour to the Enemy in numbers, and his men [have been] in want of every necessary," said a Pennsylvania congressman. Most recognized, too, that in 1777 Washington had faced the cream of the British army, and Howe's force was twice the size of Burgoyne's army that had surrendered to Gates.

Washington had not always been successful in battle, but many in Congress understood that wars were not always won solely on the battlefield. Most congressmen recognized that Washington had behaved nobly as the commander in chief. He was unsullied by the least hint of scandal. He had neither abused his powers nor misused the army. The gravitas that characterized his demeanor seemed well suited to the office he held. He had lived simply and virtuously, seeking to instill the spirit of sacrifice in others. He was famous for his industry. His dedication to the cause was unquestioned. He had never been absent from his army, save for when Congress called him to Philadelphia in May 1776 for consultation.

Washington's critics assailed him as a poor administrator, and as historian Edward Lengel has observed, the Continental army "was plagued by incompetent staff, poorly defined departmental responsibilities, and intersecting chains of command." But much that troubled the army was beyond Washington's control, as Congress understood. In a newly created union—and especially in the highly decentralized structure that reserved sovereignty to each of the thirteen states—inefficiency, even administrative chaos, was inevitable. It is unlikely that any other commander could have streamlined the Continental army, and to be sure, no one else could have worked more industriously than did Washington to make the army run more smoothly. His nearly daily inspections of the army's camp resulted in untold numbers of orders to improve hygiene and rectify problems. He wrote countless letters to those responsible for supplying the army, demanding greater oversight and better organization, and he repeatedly appealed to Congress—often exaggerating the magnitude of the problem in order to stir the delegates—to do more to find food and clothing for his soldiers. If Washington did not always succeed, he deserves credit for taking some steps that proved crucial to the army's performance and America's eventual victory. He saw to the training of the enlisted men, which (especially after

1778) produced a more capable soldiery. By mandating and enforcing inoculation among his soldiers, he mitigated the impact on the army of a raging smallpox epidemic that swept America after 1775. Indeed, a smaller proportion of Continentals perished from disease than died of sickness in the Union and Confederate armies in the Civil War seventy-five years later.[33] In addition, Washington worked tirelessly, and usually successfully, to resolve innumerable wrangles over pay and promotion that, if left unresolved, might have decimated the officer corps.

Congress was largely unaware of the negative feelings that some Continental army officers harbored toward Washington. However, it knew that the commander in chief had won the loyalty of the overwhelming majority of the field-grade officers, a set of men that some civil officials feared and distrusted as madly ambitious glory seekers. For some among these aspiring young men, loyalty might simply, pragmatically, have been the price to pay for winning coveted assignments, favorable mention in the commander's reports, or promotion. After all, Washington in his reports praised certain qualities, including "attachment" and the "purest affection," and it was not long before young officers sought to exhibit the behavior that the commander in chief so obviously relished. Many among Washington's acolytes in the officer corps realized that their fortunes were tied to his, and it hardly required a leap of imagination to believe that Washington would be a substantive political force in a victorious postwar America.

But the devotion that Washington inspired in many of his officers was genuine. They thought his self-sacrifice awe-inspiring, his courage under fire stunning, his patriotism and devotion to the cause worthy of emulation. His persistence—his air of confidence, in fact—in the face of nearly ever present adversity won their admiration, even their love.

Washington was in the habit of leading men. He had been doing so since early adulthood. He had learned the mechanics of leadership through observing Great Britain's professional officers during the French and Indian War, by reading military manuals, and by trial and error once he was thrust into a leadership role as a young Virginia officer. He had obviously devoted considerable thought to what makes a good leader, and on one occasion early in the Revolutionary War he passed along his insights to a young officer from Virginia. It was advice that leaders in any field, not just the military, might take to heart. "Require nothing unreasonable" of officers and men, he advised, but demand that whatever is ordered be complied with punctually. "Reward and punish every man according to his merit, without partiality or prejudice." Listen to complaints, and if they are warranted, act to redress them; but if the complaints are unmerited, discourage them. Guard against surprises: "Be plain and precise in your orders." Be certain that the soldiery understands "the importance of the cause, and what it is they are contending for." Avoid imperious behavior with officers, but do not be "too familiar" with them, "lest you subject yourself to a want of that respect, which is necessary to support a proper command." Finally, for your own protection, keep a copy of every written order that you issue.[34]

It has been said that all great leaders excite love and fear. None ever described Washington as friendly, kindly, or generous. Just the opposite. He was cold and aloof—"stately," to use the term that those in his company perhaps used most to describe him—and not many men felt at ease in his presence. For many, at least subliminally, Washington was a gigantic figure very much like their fathers, and for many, he appears to have been a father figure. For many too in this age of monarchs, Washington radiated many of the qualities common to the royal figures the officers had so recently venerated—solemnity, an imposing dignity, a magisterial manner. Washington's manner would not have served him well in all walks of life. It would have gotten him nowhere in Congress. But it resonated with the great majority of those officers who served beneath him in the Continental army.

There were some, probably many, in Congress who thought Gates a better general than Washington, but nearly all thought that Washington was a better man for the all-inclusive responsibilities of the position of commander in chief. With hope alive that France would soon enter the war, for instance, Congress had to keep in mind that Washington had distinguished himself by working well with Congress and the state authorities. Those skills would be crucial in dealing with a European ally.

Many in Congress also simply believed it too risky to seek the removal of the commander. Some thought the situation so delicate that it was dangerous even to speak ill of Washington. To actually seek Washington's ouster would ignite a political firestorm, and it might trigger mass resignations among the army's officers, provoking a meltdown of the Continental army. Washington "is too well established to be easily injured" and "too important to be sported with," said one congressman, who understood that

Washington was still idolized by the public. Furthermore, there could not have been a worse time than the winter of 1777–1778 to attempt to remove Washington. Not only was the army suffering at Valley Forge, but France was thought to be close to entering the war. The mere appearance of chaos in the Continental army might cause the French to remain neutral. Finally, there were many like Henry Laurens who believed that no other man could bring to the position of commander in chief as many "virtues"—Laurens called them the "props of our Cause"—as could Washington. To remove Washington, cautioned Laurens, was to run the risk of being "reduced to the State of a Rudderless Ship in a boisterous Ocean."[35]

In fact, Congress never contemplated Washington's removal. It sought to reform the army. In addition, by appointing Conway inspector general and putting Gates at the head of the Board of War, it hoped to surround Washington with professional soldiers who could provide oversight and perhaps an alternative to Greene's counsel. Finally, Congress probably hoped that Conway and Gates would keep it abreast of what was occurring in the army.

WHATEVER WAS IN THE HEARTS of congressmen, and whatever Washington may have thought in early November when he first learned of Conway's criticism, by January the commander in chief believed that a powerful "malignant faction" wished to force him out. Believing that Conway was a vital part of the conspiracy, Washington dealt with him first. Washington had learned much about responding to critics since his earlier, combative days. Rather than thundering against Conway or making a frontal assault on Congress, Washington for the most part permitted Conway to self-destruct. When Conway appeared at Valley Forge on December 29 to take up his duties as inspector general, Washington greeted him with icy formality—"my feeling will not permit me to make professions of friendship to the man I deem my Enemy," he told Congress—and informed him that he had no authority until the Board of War forwarded written orders. Conway fired back with a letter dripping with sarcasm. With his tongue planted firmly in his cheek, Conway equated Washington with Frederick the Great, the most esteemed warrior of the age. Washington did not respond, but he passed Conway's sardonic missive on to Congress.[36]

Those around Washington, who already had an ax to grind against the

French officer, reacted with sulfurous resentment toward Conway. One thought his letter an "Affront" for which Conway "deserved to be kicked." Tench Tilghman, an aide to the commander in chief, believed, as did Washington himself, that Conway's letter would be a litmus test for Congress. Congress "must clip [Conway's] Wings or affront the General direct," Tilghman thought, and that was precisely how most congressmen saw it. The president of Congress thought Conway's "taunts & sarcasm . . . unpardonable," and Abraham Clark, one of Washington's more severe critics, declared that "the Authority & Credit of the Commander in Chief must be supported." Congress would have discharged Conway immediately, but it feared offending France, so it sent him to Albany instead, now a site very much in the backwater of this war. With nothing to do, Conway for a second time submitted his resignation. This time, Congress wasted no time in accepting it.[37]

For all practical purposes, Conway was gone before the end of January, though Gates was still in place and Washington saw him as a threat. There had been no serious friction between Washington and Gates before the autumn of 1777. Gates had visited Mount Vernon before the war and when Congress created the Continental army, Washington had urged his appointment as a general officer. After the siege of Boston was lifted in the spring of 1776, the two were seldom in each other's presence or even in the same theater of operations. But tension between the two appeared when Washington, in the wake of Brandywine, requested the return of a rifle corps that he had dispatched to Gates a month earlier. Gates, who was daily expecting an attempt by Burgoyne to break out of his snare above Albany, refused. Were you in my situation, he told Washington, you would not "part with the Corps the Army of General Burgoyne are most Afraid of."[38] A disagreement of this sort between officers who were literally fighting for their lives was not uncommon, and Washington should have been—and probably was—understanding. But when Gates failed to notify him of Burgoyne's surrender, then had to be pressured into sending troops to Pennsylvania, Washington grew understandably angry and suspicious. Conway's putative letter to Gates, coupled with the swelling praise for the victor at Saratoga, made Washington even more uneasy. The commander in chief's confrontation with Congress over his Philadelphia strategy, and Congress's almost simultaneous decisions to put Gates in charge of the Board of War and to make Conway inspector general, convinced Washington that a great conspiracy was closing around him. Reports from friendly congressmen appeared to confirm what he had come to suspect. They reported the plotters' "shafts of Envy and malevolence," among other things.[39] By the time his Continentals entered Valley Forge, Washington had concluded that Gates must be either a part of the cabal or the object of the intrigue. Whichever it was, Washington looked on Gates as a mortal enemy.

As time passed, evidence mounted that Gates had not colluded with Conway. Washington discovered early on that Conway had not said half of what Stirling alleged that he had said. Conway had noted the "Want of Discipline" within the army when he wrote Gates, but he had neither criticized the American generals nor said anything untoward about Washington. Washington was aware of this by January 1778. Furthermore, at the turn of the year Gates had taken pains in several missives to assure Washington of his loyalty. "I Solemnly declare that I am of no Faction," Gates assured Washington. He apologized for anything that he had done that could possibly have troubled Washington. Gates insisted that he had never had the least malevolent intent toward Washington, adding that he never meant anything "Offensive to Your Excellency" in a single sentence that he had written. He denied ever having had a "private Connection" with Conway or even having received a letter from him prior to the one in question.[40]

But neither the exculpatory evidence regarding Conway nor Gates's repeated avowals of loyalty lessened Washington's fears. The commander in chief refused to believe a word of Gates's defense. While insisting that "My temper leads me to peace and harmony with all Men," Washington, in a dense letter chocked with carefully chosen words, as much as told Gates that he believed him a liar. He said that he believed Gates had conducted improper discussions with members of Congress and that Gates had repeatedly made false statements with regard to what Conway had said. Privately, Washington told acquaintances that he possessed "undeniable facts" that proved Gates was part of a plot to elevate himself on the "ruin of my reputation and influence." Mifflin was the "*second part* in the Cabal," Washington alleged, and Conway was also involved as a "very active, and malignant partizan." Washington never revealed the evidence in his possession that demonstrated Gates's culpability, and in all likelihood such ironclad proof never existed, but by March 1778, the commander in chief had convinced himself—or so he wanted the world to believe—that Gates was the leader of a plot to change commanders of the Continental army.[41]

Washington had a long record of preemptive strikes against those he believed posed a danger to him. He had responded belligerently to Captains Mackay and Dagworthy during the French and Indian War, and after taking command of the Continental army, he had written snide letters in which he portrayed Artemas Ward, whom he had supplanted, as a slothful and indolent old man who was frightened at the prospect of "removing from the smoke of his own Chimney."[42] Washington had taken pains, as well, to see that Ward won no laurels. With the campaign of New York looming in the spring of 1776, he had sent Ward to defend already liberated Boston.

After Saratoga, Washington saw Gates as a profound threat. Since his conquest of Burgoyne, Gates's "Name . . . hath greatly [been] exalted," one congressman put it to the commander.[43] Washington had to know that Gates had a successful track record in artful politicking. Aligning himself with important New England congressmen, Gates had seen to General Schuyler's fall and gained for himself command of the Northern Department. During the Valley Forge winter, many who hovered about Washington told him that Gates was once again intriguing with some in Congress. Some saw Gates as the leader of a cabal, but others thought him merely a "puppet" in the machinations. Not a few believed that Mifflin, who was joining Gates on the Board of War, was the sorcerer who ran the cabal and who hoped to sabotage Washington for his own ends. Some close to Washington even believed that Mifflin's black art was a "Tory Maeneuver." They thought that Mifflin, once a prosperous Philadelphia merchant, was in league with other displaced businessmen who wished to sow such chaos in the army that Congress would be forced to reconcile with Great Britain, restoring peace and prosperity.[44]

There were those, too, who doubted the existence of a plot. Before the end of February, Washington had been advised by the most important congressmen from Virginia—veterans such as George Mason, Richard Henry Lee, and Benjamin Harrison—that "a Faction in Congress aganst you had never existed."[45] What Washington believed in his heart of hearts can never be known, but what is clear is that early in 1778, he wished to sow the impression among members of Congress that Gates, Mifflin, and Conway were inextricably linked as conspirators in a plot to overthrow him as commander of the Continental army.

As the destitution, illness, and appalling toll in lives of the Valley Forge winter unfolded about him, Washington spent a portion of his time painstakingly studying anonymous letters that rebuked him, comparing handwriting samples with those of known correspondents in the hope of detecting a "similitude of hands." Shaken and angry, he was burning to learn the identity of his detractors, and before long he discovered that Dr. Rush was one of them.[46] Yet Washington had learned a thing or two by not responding to the attack of the "Virginia Centinel" twenty years earlier, and he once again remained silent in public. He wished to make it appear that he was taking the high road. Seeking to impress Congress with his apparent guilelessness, he told its members that his position made it impossible for him to respond to his critics: "My Enemies take an ungenerous advantage of me—they know the delicacy of my situation and that motives of policy deprive me of the defence I might otherwise make against their insidious attacks." Even as he said that, Washington knew that the younger officers who surrounded him, those acolytes who had hitched their wagons to his star, would serve as his spear carriers.[47]

John Laurens, Washington's aide, told his father, the president of Congress, that Mifflin was given to "great mischief." Young Laurens went on to defend Washington against what he called the "loud bellowing" of his critics, and he smeared Conway with a preposterous charge that he had acted in a cowardly manner during the Battle of Germantown.[48] Hamilton might have had his doubts about Washington, but he did not want to see what he later called his "aegis" for upward mobility replaced. He labeled Conway "vermin" and said that "there does not exist a more villainous calumniator and incendiary."[49] General Greene spread the word that Mifflin was "the head" of an intrigue "to ruin his excellency and others," and he added that "Gates favours it."[50] Conflating Washington's survival with that of the American Revolution, some of his defenders in the army insisted that to criticize the commander in chief was to betray America's quest for independence.[51]

The Marquis de Lafayette was a special case. When he arrived in July

1777, Lafayette was a callow nineteen-year-old, three years younger than Washington had been when he assumed command of the Virginia Regiment in 1754. Lafayette knew nothing about commanding under fire and even less about America or bureaucratic intrigue. Personally fond of him, but also aware that Lafayette was well connected at the royal court in Versailles, Washington saw that the young Frenchman might be especially useful. Washington developed something akin to a father-son relationship with Lafayette. It was based on heartfelt sentiment, but during the Conway crisis the American commander also played the young officer like a virtuoso. Washington apprised Lafayette of the campaign of "dirty Arts and low intrigues" against him and hinted that if successful, the conspiracy might destroy the American Revolution and whatever France hoped to achieve from American independence. Lafayette, whose love for Washington was boundless, threw Conway—formerly his good friend—to the wolves. In October, after Brandywine and Germantown, Lafayette, in his fractured English, had gushed to Washington that Conway "is a so brave, intelligent, and active officer that he schall . . . justify more and more the esteem of the army." But in January, Lafayette told Congress that Conway possessed neither honor nor principles and would resort to anything to satisfy his ambition. Lafayette also belittled Gates's success. It had been "impossible to him not to conquer" at Saratoga, he told Congress, and he added that he doubted whether Gates could hold the Continental army together for longer than six months.[52]

Nor was the counteroffensive to save Washington confined to writing letters. The fifth pamphlet in Thomas Paine's *American Crisis* series appeared that spring and was intended as an attack on those who questioned Washington. Paine not only equated the character of the American Revolution with that of the commander in chief, he asserted (incorrectly) that had Gates promptly detached most of his men to Washington, Howe would have paid a heavy price to open the Delaware River.[53] General John Cadwalader challenged Conway to a duel, in the course of which he shot him through the mouth. (The wound was not fatal, but Cadwalader boasted that he had "stopped the damned rascal's lying tongue at any rate.")[54] Mifflin, too, was confronted by Cadwalader, but he wiggled out of the challenge, losing face with many for refusing to fight.[55] The threat of political ruin, and possibly physical harm, was sufficient to silence most officials. Congressmen who believed in Washington confronted colleagues whom they suspected of harboring doubts and demanded to know whether they were "haveg a Hand in" the intrigue.[56] Congressman John Jay of New York admitted that it was too risky to utter a word of criticism about Washington.[57]

Some in Congress also went after the already beleaguered Mifflin. Four months after he resigned as quartermaster general, Congress suddenly decided in February 1778 that it wished to scrutinize Mifflin's books. An audit was to be expected, but this episode bore all the earmarks of a fishing expedition to find malfeasance. While some in Congress legitimately searched for evidence of embezzlement or "neglect of Duty" that might account for the "extraordinary deficiencies" in supplies that "had brought thousands to Misery and Death," others appear to have been motivated more by the hope of discrediting a critic of Washington. With the assistance of Henry Laurens, who did everything within his power to protect Washington, Congress spun out the Mifflin inquiry for nearly fourteen months without ever bringing charges against him.[58]

Some army officers also paid visits to suspected critics. For example, the three-hundred-pound Henry Knox called on John Adams "to sound me in relation to General Washington," said the congressman. It is unclear whether Adams was unsettled by the visit, but he never forgot it, relating the story in his memoirs a quarter century later. There can be no question that Richard Peters, a member of the Board of War, was thoroughly shaken when redoubtable Colonel Daniel Morgan, a burly backwoodsman, sought him out. Morgan railed against him for having questioned Washington's abilities. When Peters denied that he had ever raised doubts about Washington, Morgan called him a liar. Morgan's visit left Peters terrified and convinced that the colonel was mentally unbalanced. Whether Morgan gave an award-winning acting performance or actually lost control of his temper is not known, but his visit palpably rattled Peters, who thereafter felt the need to tell every living soul that he wanted nothing to do with "these dirty Matters" against Washington. Peters, in fact, publicly avowed that he "love[d]" the commander in chief "to a Degree of Adoration."[59]

Washington was advised by his supporters that he stood "too high in the public opinion" to be damaged by the intrigue. Should he continue to exhibit "the same equal and disinterested Conduct, the same labour and attention, which you have manifested in the public Service from the first of the Contest," a Virginia congressman counseled, no political harm can befall him.[60] Disinterested was precisely how Washington presented himself. "Neither ambitious, nor lucrative, motives led me to accept my present appointments," he declared, adding that his "steady and uniform conduct" had focused solely on "considerations of a public nature." He spread the word in New England, where he knew that Gates was especially popular, that "neither interested nor ambitious views led me into the service. I did not solicit the command, but accepted it after much entreaty . . . and . . . pursued the great line of duty . . . as pointedly as the needle to the pole." He told Congress: "I have no other view than to promote the public good, & am unambitious of honours."[61] At the same time, stories circulated wildly that winter that Washington was contemplating resignation, and it is not inconceivable that he was behind such talk, hoping to unnerve Congress with the prospect of disarray in the army while the soldiery suffered at Valley Forge. When first notified of the rumor, Washington did not deny it but said that he would step down if the public wished, and he waxed on artfully about "the sweets of domestic life" and going home with "much satisfaction . . . retir[ing] to a private station with as much content, as ever the wearied pilgrim felt upon his safe arrival in the Holy-land."[62]

COPING WITH THE ALLEGED CONSPIRACY consumed only a portion of Washington's time. He faced many other alarming troubles at Valley Forge. Washington had feared that nearly insurmountable problems would surface if he put the army into a single cantonment during the winter, and his fears were proven in spades. The Valley Forge winter was not the worst the Continental army faced, but it was the most memorable. A recurrent supply crisis, brought on largely by bad weather, the malfeasance of teamsters and businessmen, and the army's chaotic administrative structure, sowed untold misery within the ranks. The winter of 1778 was warmer than normal in Pennsylvania, and that was the rub. While it snowed from time to time, rain was more commonplace and more irksome. Thousands of men inhabited the unwholesome mud hole that was Valley Forge, a squalid encampment pervaded with acrid smoke and reeking with the heavy stench of human waste, rotted food, and, above all, death. Few men had adequate clothing or blankets. All faced episodic food shortages, and when they did have something to eat, it seldom amounted to a nutritious diet. The men were worked, or drilled, from sunrise to sunset, after which they retreated to damp, cold, and overcrowded log cabins for the night.

Inevitably under these conditions, disease swept Valley Forge. Upward of twenty-five hundred Continentals perished that winter, nearly 15 percent of those who had marched into camp at Christmas. Scores of officers left the army. Washington responded boldly, doing what he told Congress in advance he would do. At times, he ordered his officers to act harshly, if necessary, to secure food and necessities from civilians. He also micromanaged the search for supplies, sending units through several states, each assigned with responsibility for acquiring specific vital materials. He additionally appealed to the governors in the mid-Atlantic region to find supplies for the army, telling them that if he was to have any chance of "striking a favorable and a happy stroke" against the British before they were reinforced, he must be able to hold the Continental army intact. He said much the same thing to Congress—"the success or misfortunes of [the] next Campaign will more than probably originate with our activity or Supineness this Winter"—and in the most candid language he laid bare the threat to the army and the war effort. Up to a quarter of his men were "barefoot and otherwise naked," he reported, and he added: "I much doubt the practicability of holding the Army together much longer." A great change must take place in the supply of the army or it would inevitably face one of three options: "Starve—dissolve—or disperse."[63] The army survived that terrible winter, in part because of Washington's heroic efforts, but also because of the frenetic response of civilian officials who understood that a great crisis point in the war had arrived and must be met head on.[64]

Dealing with the unrelenting woes of his soldiery was only one of Washington's concerns that winter. Congress voted in mid-January "to concert measures with the Commander in Chief for the reformation of the army." Congress had already told Washington that the army had to be better disciplined. In addition, the belief was widespread in Congress that a general overhaul of the army was long overdue. Washington and his officers wanted change as well. With experience, they better understood the needs of the army, and in all likelihood they had picked up pointers from the professional European soldiers among them. Just before Christmas, Washington advised Congress that "great and capital change" must take place in the army's supply system. Congress wanted that as well, and a great deal more. It wished to reduce the number of battalions, reorganize the cavalry and artillery, discuss the always volatile issue of promoting general officers, and get rid of incompetent officers.[65]

Many congressional committees had visited the army. Washington was accustomed to dealing with them and handling them successfully. He did so again in this instance, exhibiting remarkable political guile. Washington housed the congressmen at Moore Hall, a capacious stone residence that served as headquarters for the quartermasters, a place where he could be assured that every need of his visitors would be tended. He soon discovered that while the committee could be troublesome, it was not hostile toward him. Congress had not packed the delegation with his enemies. Like virtually every committee that Congress created, this one consisted of five members drawn from the three sections of the nation. Headquarters had never suspected the two New Englanders, Francis Dana and Nathaniel Folsom, of being part of any anti-Washington faction. The middle states were represented by Gouverneur Morris of New York, widely thought of as a friend of Washington's, and Pennsylvania's Joseph Reed, who had tried every conceivable way to get back into Washington's good graces since the commander learned of his unflattering remarks during the New York campaign. Virginia's John Harvie, virtually a Washington puppet, represented the southern states.

Washington greeted his visitors, as he often did in such situations, by taking the offensive. Prior to the congressmen's arrival, he had asked his principal officers to submit their ideas on reforming the army. Washington condensed their views into a coherent form, and Hamilton drafted the final version, a thirty-eight-page handwritten document that one historian characterized as "nothing less than America's first great state paper," while another thought it "a minor masterpiece of military administration."[66] Before the committeemen could make any demands, Washington confronted them with his plan, which included several far-reaching proposals for change.

He began with a startling proposal. Washington urged Congress to provide the officers in the Continental army with a half-pay pension for life—with benefits extended to their widows and orphans—following the war. This was customary in the British army, whose officers made it their career and served for most of their adult lives. But nearly all the American officers were likely to serve only during this war. Furthermore, to this point all Americans had been called on to make sacrifices, to serve nobly and virtuously, and most of all disinterestedly, in the great fight for independence and republicanism. Yeomen and artisans had been asked to abandon their farms and workbenches, enlist in the army, endure austerity, face great peril, and leave behind spouses and children to survive on the most meager of incomes. In the spirit of public service, thousands of ordinary colonists had done just that. Officers made sacrifices as well, but not to the degree of the enlisted men. By 1778, the lowest-ranking officer was paid five times that of a private—the disparity had already increased threefold since the war began—and all officers enjoyed more comfortable housing and usually a better diet. They were exempt from manual labor and corporal punishment, and they were free to leave the army when they wished.[67]

But officers, too, suffered danger and privation, and Washington knew they would not sacrifice indefinitely. The cause was threatened, he said, by "frequent resignations, dayly happening" among the officers, including those of the "greatest merit." Washington knew that pushing for yet more rewards for the officer corps would not be welcomed by Congress. He doubtless remembered that he had first gotten into trouble with Governor Dinwiddie when he proposed a pay raise for his officers in the Virginia Regiment. That he now took on Congress over the pension issue reflected his conviction, but it was a measure of his desperation as well. He genuinely feared that unless this step was taken, he would lose the officer corps. Of course, he also wanted the support of the officers in his fight to beat back the challenge of the alleged cabal that threatened him.

Washington might have accompanied his pension proposal with a plea for better pay and more lucrative bonuses to attract enlisted men. Instead, asserting somewhat questionably that the pool was drained "of that class of men whose tempers, attachments and circumstances, disposed them to enter . . . into the army," he asked Congress to sanction conscription. He might also have urged benefits for the wives and children of enlisted men, but he demurred. (Later, he denounced public assistance for the dependents of the enlisted men as nothing better than "robbing the public and encouraging idleness.")

Washington proposed to deal with the discipline problem in the army by creating a military police corps. He urged the remodeling of the supply service. (Among other things, he suggested that the shortage of waggoners could be solved by hiring free African Americans from the Chesapeake states.) Finally, he asked that Congress devise "some settled rule of promotion" for field-grade and general officers, a fixed policy that would be "universally known and understood and not to be deviated from."[68]

Washington had set the agenda for discussion with the committee in camp and to keep the pressure on them he attended all but two of their meetings. The camp committee hewed closely to Washington's proposals; it altered some of his suggestions, but only after extensive consultation with the commander in chief or his officers. In some instances, the committeemen strengthened and improved what Washington requested. In March, the committee recommended virtually everything that Washington had sought, and two months later Congress approved nearly all of it, including remodeling the army as Washington wished and naming General Greene as quartermaster general. Congress balked at only one thing: Although the camp committee followed Washington in recommending half-pay pensions for life for the officers, Congress agreed to a pension for only a seven-year period following the war.[69]

WASHINGTON FACED ONE LAST BATTLE that winter of 1778. In January, the reconstituted Board of War at last convened in York. In midmonth, it proposed a wintertime invasion of Canada. Congress endorsed the operation while Washington opposed it.[70] Most historians have condemned the proposed invasion of Canada, depicting it as misguided strategically, based on wishful thinking, and little more than a power grab by Gates. They have defended Washington's opposition as militarily astute. However, it is more accurate to see the planned invasion as farsighted and Washington's resistance as myopic.

The Canadian invasion in 1775–1776 had ended disastrously, but by 1778 conditions had changed dramatically. As Burgoyne had brought nearly the entire British army in Canada with him when he invaded New York, his surrender at Saratoga in October 1777 left Canada only lightly defended. If France entered the war that winter, as was expected, Great Britain would be hard-pressed to spare any reinforcements for Canada. Many congressmen also believed that French belligerency would prompt the Canadians to warmly receive Continental soldiers, who, after all, would be co-belligerents, and possibly even allies, of the French. Some were persuaded that should the Marquis de Lafayette be chosen to lead America's invasion army, an enthusiastic welcome by the French Canadians would be assured. No one was more attached to the idea than Lafayette himself. He advised the Board of War that if the invasion was led by "a man of theyr nation . . . [with] rank in France," it would inspire them with some confidence. Spies north of the border reported "a general disaffection . . . among the Canadiens" with their presence in the British Empire. (That conclusion was more than confirmed by Britain's governor in Quebec, who told London that given the "defenceless state of every post" and "the unsettled temper of the people," it was unlikely that Canada could be held in the face of an invasion.)

The idea of attempting a second invasion of Canada was extremely popular in New England and New York, but it enjoyed widespread support elsewhere as well. Henry Laurens reported that all but three members of Congress favored an invasion. Some proponents of an invasion wanted Canadian land, others believed that driving out the British would force the Indians in Canada into neutrality, pacifying the frontiers of the northern states, and still others were convinced that a military triumph in Canada would oblige Great Britain to recognize American independence and end the war. Success was not guaranteed, but then, little is foreordained in war.[71]

The "irruption . . . into Canada," as the Board of War called its plan, envisioned forming a twenty-five-hundred-man American army led by Lafayette. Major General Conway—who was still very much with the Continental army in January when the plan was put together—and Brigadier General John Stark, a hero at Bunker Hill and later at Bennington in the Saratoga campaign, were to be Lafayette's principal deputies. The army was to be quickly assembled and would set off from Albany and proceed down the Champlain corridor, crossing the frozen lake that linked New York and Canada. It would target lightly defended St. Johns and Montreal as its first objectives. If the inhabitants of Canada came forth to help, the invaders were to pause in Montreal to await reinforcements before proceeding east to take Quebec.[72]

Washington's initial response to the proposed invasion was to applaud the idea, "as it may be advancive of the public good and on account" of Lafayette's selection to lead the army.[73] He changed step only after he discovered that the plan had originated in the Board of War and that Conway was to be a key component of the invasion army. Not only was the commander agitated by Conway's leading role in the invasion force, but Washington's plans for 1778 were completely different. He was mulling over offensives to retake New York or Philadelphia. He also was considering waiting at Valley Forge until the British acted, then responding to that initiative. The latter course seemed to hold the greatest appeal for him, at least pending the arrival of French assistance. He pronounced the Board of War's plan a "child of folly" that was likely to be "productive of capital Ills." The best chance of scoring a decisive victory was to defeat Howe's army, he insisted, but all hope of achieving that end would be diminished if an invasion of Canada drew away men and supplies from his army.[74]

Whatever the motivations of Gates and Mifflin—and they were only two members of the five-member Board of War that had recommended the invasion—Washington concluded that the involvement of his nemeses raised the specter of intrigue against him. But with his hands full with the camp committee, he knew that this was not the time for waging a public fight over the issue.

Washington claimed that he did not know enough about the planned campaign "to pass any judgement" on it. In fact, believing that he was under siege from several quarters, Washington did not wish to take a public stand. Those close to him knew his true feelings, however, and they were active. Hamilton and Greene broadcast the idea that the "whole plan" was the "creation of [a] faction . . . to increase the difficulties" of Washington, while Greene additionally sought to convince New Englanders that it would drain away precious resources from the defense of their region. Once John Laurens informed his father of Washington's reservations, Henry Laurens came out in opposition to the invasion. At the end of January, the senior Laurens—who admitted that he was "almost single in" Congress in wishing that the undertaking could be scrapped—claimed that the invasion scheme had been hatched more for political than for military reasons. The "World at large," he said, would see the invasion as a congressional "insult" to Washington.[75] Lafayette, who panted after glory, was ecstatic when he learned that he had been selected to lead the invasion. His "greatest satisfaction schall be to serve the noble cause of liberty," he declared, and he told Congress that in order to secure "our fourteenth state" he would "*francise* myself, and speak much about the french blood to gain theyr [the Canadians'] hearts." But after consulting with Washington, Lafayette hurried to York and demanded that Congress remove Conway from the invasion army. He threatened to resign and go home, taking many of the French volunteers with him, if Congress did not relent. Desperate to avoid offending France and to see the invasion through, Congress caved in. It replaced Conway with Kalb.[76]

In the end, nothing came of the proposed invasion, in some measure because so much time was squandered by Lafayette's dickering with Congress to secure Conway's removal. That was probably precisely what Washington had hoped for from Lafayette. The plan's hope of success had always hinged on the idea that the army could storm down frozen Lake Champlain and into Canada. When it grew increasingly unlikely that Lafayette's army would be prepared to act before spring, Congress pulled the plug on the operation. Always the truckler, Lafayette thereafter told Washington what he believed the commander wanted to hear. He had been "schamefully deceived by the board of war," Lafayette declared, and he added bizarrely—without explaining his reasoning—that Gates's "actual scheme" had been to secure his removal from the Pennsylvania theater of war.[77] The invasion of Canada, while fraught with risk, had held the promise of decisiveness. Had Canada fallen hard on the heels of the destruction of Burgoyne's army, and with France on the precipice of entering the war, it is difficult to see how Great Britain could have continued to fight. But the venture never came to fruition. It was a casualty of the politics of this war, and especially of Washington's insecurities.

BETWEEN THE ONSET OF WINTER and the long-awaited first signs of spring, Washington had largely silenced his critics in Congress and persuaded its members to give him nearly everything he wished. If he had been almost invulnerable before Valley Forge, he was untouchable following the winter of 1778. He had waged a clever campaign of political infighting that winter, but there was more to his success than that. The miseries of Valley Forge had demonstrated Washington's wisdom in wishing to put the army into numerous cantonments. In late April, word reached Philadelphia that America's commissioners in Paris had signed an alliance with France. The French were coming into the war. That news vindicated Washington's Fabian strategy during the past eighteen months, and in particular his caution in refusing to hazard his army by attacking the entrenched British army in Philadelphia or to be drawn into battle at Whitemarsh. The Continental army had endured. In fact, it had been not only preserved, but strengthened at Valley Forge through the incessant drilling of General Friedrich Steuben, who had been named inspector general once Conway flamed out.

The winter of uncertainty and despair at Valley Forge did something else. It buttressed Washington's image as the great leader. The Continental army had survived the winter when by all rights it should have dissolved. Washington had stayed with his army, living for a few days in his tent, suffering along with his wretched men. He had worked tirelessly to solve the supply problems, keep his officers from leaving, train his soldiers, and maintain the army for a better day ahead. Washington had been lauded for his successes in Boston and in the Trenton-Princeton campaign, but Valley Forge was the time of his transfiguration. As never before, Washington came to be seen as the truly heroic figure. He was exalted by the president of Congress, among others, as the noble warrior who had battled not only a strong, resilient enemy, but infant America's economic and organizational malaise. He was saluted as the glue that held together the army and its angry officers through the winter encampment in 1778. He had endured, the army had endured, and the hope of victory and independence endured.[78]

That winter, Washington's birthday was celebrated publicly for the first time. It was planned by General Knox, who gathered an artillery band of drummers and fifers to parade and play on a snowy, windswept field outside Washington's headquarters at Valley Forge.[79] The celebration was contrived, but veneration for Washington was swelling. Almanacs, which once had documented the king's birthday, now noted Washington's. A patriot's "Catechism" circulated that pointed to General Washington as "the best man living." A "Political ABC" for youngsters published that year proclaimed, "The W stands for brave WASHINGTON / And worlds that rejoice for the honor he's won." Literary works were dedicated to Washington, the "Saviour of his Country, the Supporter of Freedom, And the Benefactor of Mankind." Toasts to the commander in chief became fashionable. In 1778, Washington was called the "Father of his Country" for the first time, and by year's end it was commonplace for him to be praised in that manner.[80] One poem after another lauded Washington. Francis Hopkinson, a Philadelphia poet, was typical. His "Toast" to Washington in 1778 began:

> 'Tis Washington's health—fill a bumper all round,
> For he is our Glory and Pride;
> Our Arms shall in battle with Conquest be crown'd,
> Whilst Virtue and He's on our Side.[81]

John Adams, who landed in France early in 1778 to begin a diplomatic mission, reported that Washington's daring attack at Germantown was no less important than Saratoga in persuading France to ally with America. Though Washington's assault had failed, the French leaders "considered it, as the most decisive Proof that America would finally succeed."[82] Lafayette tried to convince Congress that Washington was indispensable. If "you should loose that . . . man," he asked, "what would become of American liberty? who could take his place?" No other general, he added, can "bear any comparison with our general" Washington.[83] Lafayette's advocacy aside, some in Congress were coming to a greater appreciation for Washington, a view grounded in the notion that no other man could have done a better job. To some degree, the idea grew from real fears during that winter that Washington might resign. Henry Laurens, who had wrung his hands over the prospect of Washington quitting, touted the commander as a "great & virtuous Man" for not having "acted the *half patriot,* by a hasty resignation." The loss of Washington would have spelled "the ruin of our Cause," he added anxiously, and he predicted that the commander's "magnanimity, his patience will save his Country & confound his Enemies."[84]

The notion was gathering across the land that it was necessary "to heal wounds upon our fraternal connexion" by closing ranks behind Washington.[85] Washington, it was often said, was the "Center of our Union" and America was fortunate to have such an illustrious man at the head of its army. Out of the Valley Forge winter, said Benjamin Rush in a cogent and illuminating commentary, the idea coalesced that it was a "state necessity" that America must have an inculpable great man and that General Washington was to be that man. John Adams concurred, saying that wartime imperatives had led Congress to hide Washington's blunders from the public and to inflate his achievements. Congress, Adams later declared, had "agreed to blow the trumpet of panegyric in concert, to cover and dissemble all faults and errors, to represent every defeat as a victory and every retreat as an advancement, to make . . . [Washington] popular and fashionable with all parties in all places and with all persons, as a center of the union, as the central stone in the geometrical arch." This spirit was discerned a bit later by a French visitor who found that throughout America, Washington had come to be seen as "a benevolent god." The Frenchman added that the "Americans, though a cold people," had "waxed enthusiastic" about Washington, and their first nationalistic songs "have been consecrated to the glorification of Washington."[86]

While Washington's ascent to the pantheon is much easier to make out in retrospect than it was during the grim winter of 1778, he appears to have understood that he had turned a corner by the time the army broke camp at Valley Forge in June. He spoke of the days when the "cloud of darkness hung heavy over us & our affairs looked gloomy" as a bygone time, and he gave the impression that he was speaking not just of the recent travail of his army, but of his own tribulations.[87] In the aftermath of Valley Forge, he appeared to feel more secure than at any time since the liberation of Boston, and he manifested an air of confidence and resolve not previously seen in his dealings with Congress. Nevertheless, Washington had been deeply scarred by what had occurred. While he refused to accept any blame for the army's failures, he had to know that his own shortcomings had contributed heavily to his lack of battlefield success in 1776 and 1777. He knew that some in the army understood that as well, and he was undoubtedly aware that many in Congress knew of his weaknesses. Thus, his newfound assurance notwithstanding, General Washington from this point forward acted like a man who knew all too well that if he blundered badly yet again, Congress might be not only less patient, but less forgiving.

THE NEW WASHINGTON WAS VISIBLE in the spring and summer of 1778. In his last days at Valley Forge, the army negotiated the exchange of General

Lee. Having languished in captivity in New York for nearly sixteen months, Lee was set free in a prisoner swap. Though aware that Lee had criticized his indecisiveness during the fighting in New York, Washington went to considerable lengths to welcome him back to the army. He rode out from camp to meet Lee on the Philadelphia road, ordered a parade by the army, and as an army band played softly in the background, the commander in chief wined and dined this man whom he had once regarded as his most trustworthy adviser. Washington even rearranged his schedule to meet with Lee at his subordinate's convenience—a step he took for no other man—and when Lee left Valley Forge briefly to put his personal affairs in order, Washington wrote him a waggish letter, possibly the only such missive that he penned to another general in eight years of war. Clearly, Washington was happy to have Lee at his side again. He badly wanted his advice, especially as no other general, not even Gates, was more esteemed by Congress.[88]

Little time passed before Lee played a major role in a military operation. By June, Washington knew that major changes were taking place among the British. General Howe was out, replaced by Sir Henry Clinton. With France coming into the war, London had also decided to pare down its army in North America, sending nearly half the redcoats in North America to the Caribbean to defend British possessions against the French. With its army reduced, and realizing that in thirty-six months of war it had failed to suppress the rebellion in the northern states, the British government was moving to a new strategy. Henceforth, the British army would seek to reconquer the four tobacco- and rice-producing southern provinces— Georgia, South Carolina, North Carolina, and Virginia—London's most profitable American colonies. General Clinton was ordered to abandon Philadelphia and redeploy his troops to New York City, from where many would eventually be sent south. Washington did not know all of this in June 1778, but intelligence reports led him to believe that the British planned to quit Philadelphia. He hoped, too, that if the British army proceeded by land from Philadelphia to New York, he could give it battle somewhere along the way. During the third week of June, the British marched out of Philadelphia, headed for New York by land. On June 19, the Continental army said good-bye to Valley Forge. It, too, marched north. Washington's objective was to cut off and attack his adversary.

The men in both armies suffered terribly during the trek across New Jersey. An early summer heat wave had settled over the region, and temperatures daily topped the one-hundred-degree mark, but both Clinton and Washington pushed their armies. Day after day, the men trudged across the heat-blistered landscape through clouds of dust. Six days into his pursuit, Washington summoned his generals to a council of war.

It was the second time he had consulted his generals. Several days earlier, while a British march to New York was only a hypothesis, thirteen of fifteen generals had voted not to bring on a full-scale engagement. Only Cadwalader and Wayne had thought the Americans might win in a showdown, the latter memorably advising that the rejuvenated and Steuben-trained Continental army might succeed in "Burgoyning Clinton." On June 24, at the second council of war, a majority once again advised against a general engagement. Most, including Lee, thought it inadvisable to hazard everything. As word had been received that a French fleet was headed for America, they argued that the prudent course would be to safeguard the American army so that it could act in concert with its new ally. Lee went so far as to condemn a major action as a risk that would be "to the last degree criminal." The majority recommended nothing more than harassing activities by a force of fifteen hundred men from among Washington's thirteen-thousand-man army.[89]

Washington had longed to do more. He had more confidence than ever in his army, but he also saw a fight as personally redemptive. It would purge the stain of his inactivity after Germantown and silence his critics. Washington was still wrestling with his course of action when Wayne, Lafayette, and Greene passionately urged a strike by a larger force than the council of war had recommended. If such a step was not taken, they said, the public—that is, Washington's critics in and out of Congress—would conclude that "our courage failed us."[90]

Washington wrestled with his decision for two days. After twenty-four hours, apparently having decided to follow the counsel of a majority of his generals, he offered Lee the command of a force of fifteen hundred men. Lee refused the offer, saying that it was beneath someone of his rank to accept the command of such a meager detachment. Washington then passed over Greene and Stirling and offered the assignment to Lafayette, who happily accepted. Soon thereafter, about forty-eight hours after the council of war, Washington, once again exhibiting his habitual indecision, reversed himself and accepted the course recommended by Wayne, Lafayette, and Greene. He may even have been swayed by young Hamilton, who not only scorned Lee as "a driveler in the business of soldiership or something much worse"—implying that his loyalty to the American cause could not be trusted—but blasted the cautious generals who had prevailed in the council of war as more suitable for an "honorable society of midwives." Whatever the cause, Washington suddenly tripled the size of the strike force to 5,340 men. He now envisaged something more than a harassing action. Two of the divisions he was sending out were to operate on Clinton's flanks, while a third attacked the rear of the British army. If successful, he might destroy up to 2,000 redcoats, surpassing what he had achieved at Trenton eighteen months earlier.[91]

Washington's decision led Lee to rethink matters, and he asked to be given command of the operation. Washington consented. It now was deep into June 26. The British army was continuing to move, nearing the coast where it would come under the protection of the Royal Navy. Little time remained if an attack was to be made. On June 27, Clinton's army reached the vicinity of Monmouth Court House, New Jersey. Washington ordered the attack for the next morning. Although he was in the habit of preparing the most elaborate battle plans, Washington on this occasion curiously left it to Lee to plan the attack.[92]

Lee had no time to reconnoiter the terrain. When he set out the next morning in the blotchy light of daybreak, he was shocked to discover that three ravines sluiced across the battlefield. Though he expected to be successful—he believed he would possess better than a two-to-one numerical superiority—Lee, like any commander, wanted a clear line of retreat in the event that things went wrong. The three ravines bothered him. As they could be crossed only slowly, they were the sort of obstacle that might doom an army—especially an inexperienced, panicked army—that was forced into a rapid, unplanned retreat. But Lee pressed the attack nonetheless. When the fighting began his force performed adequately, though it did not roll up its adversary. In fact, as the battle raged on under the searing sun, the British recouped, pouring in more and more men to help their beleaguered comrades. Lee's numerical superiority vanished. Before long, the two sides were evenly matched. More British arrived. Now the redcoats had the advantage. Lafayette, commanding one of the American divisions, ordered a pullback, and it triggered a spontaneous retreat among other units. Seeing that all hope was lost of destroying the rear of the British army, and with those three ravines weighing heavily on his mind, Lee ordered a general retreat, one that he believed he could carefully organize. His objective was to fall back behind the last ravine and establish a defensive perimeter. If he could accomplish that feat, he would invite Clinton to attack.[93]

Distracted by the confusion and clamor of battle, Lee had neglected to keep Washington informed. Learning from others that Lee was retreating, Washington mounted his horse and hurried toward the front, seven miles away. As he got closer to the battlefield, he encountered some Continentals who were falling back. They told him that the retreat had been unnecessary. It was not true, but in his frame of mind Washington believed it.

After his successful start with Lee back in April, relations between the two men had deteriorated. Lee looked askance at many of the reforms that Washington had introduced in the army at Valley Forge, and he readily expressed his disapproval. He even told Washington that it would be best to largely scrap the Continental army and fight the war with the militia. It had succeeded at Bunker Hill, he said. Perhaps to rub it in, Lee added that Gates had done exceptionally well against Burgoyne by relying principally on militia units. Lee never heeded the maxim that silence at times is golden. He had an opinion on every subject and an urge to air his every thought. At Valley Forge, Lee unwisely spoke his mind to anyone who would listen. He bloviated about the army, other officers, and General Washington, who, he allegedly said, "was not fit to command a Sergeant's Guard."

Washington was surrounded by men who admired him, or who at least wanted to keep him in power to facilitate their own ascent, and some of them loathed the acerbic Lee. It is not difficult to imagine that some officers were all too eager to let Washington know what Lee was saying. Long before the army marched out of Valley Forge, Washington had cooled toward Lee, though not solely from personal animosity. Lee had his own followers among the officers, adherents who sided with him at the councils of war. Glib and persuasive, and an experienced professional soldier, Lee rallied others to his side with the power and logic of his arguments. Whereas Washington was eager to fight Clinton, Lee had preached caution. Twice, Lee had carried the day at councils of war. But now there was a fight, and in the most ironic of twists, Lee was in command of the rebel units on the battlefield. When Washington learned that Lee was retreating and was told that the fallback was uncalled for, he appears to have concluded that Lee had betrayed him, that he had never wished to fight and had prematurely abandoned this battle.[94]

WHEN WASHINGTON FINALLY CAUGHT UP with Lee, the commander was already beside himself with fury. He turned the full force of his rage on Lee, demanding an explanation for the retreat. Some eyewitnesses said that Washington cursed Lee, calling him a "damned poltroon." One who was present said that Washington "swore that day till the leaves shook on the trees." Another observer said simply that Washington was "in a great passion." Surprised that his judgment was questioned, and unaccustomed to being spoken to in such an uncivil manner, Lee, perhaps for the only time in his life, was speechless. He stuttered and stammered incoherently. Washington relieved him of command and took charge of the retreat himself.[95]

What Washington did once he was in control was precisely what Lee was in the process of doing. Washington stanched the retreat and took up a defensive position behind the last ravine. Throughout the afternoon, the British attacked repeatedly, but they were unable to break through. Washington, who had a history of good luck when in desperate straits, enjoyed another such moment in this engagement. General Clinton was less experienced as a battlefield commander than either Washington or Lee, and in this action the British general made such poor use of his army that many available men never got into the fight. The Battle of Monmouth continued until sunset fell over the scorched and bloody landscape. Washington expected the fight to be renewed the next day. He slept on the battlefield under the moon's silvery gleam. But in the first pink glow of dawn, Washington discovered that Clinton was gone. During the night, while the wisps of smoke from the previous day's bloodletting yet hovered over Monmouth, the British army had resumed its march. Washington was disappointed. He had hoped for further fighting. Monmouth had been a savage fray. British losses topped 500, while about 360 Americans had been lost.[96] Monmouth was not a pivotal battle in the course of the war, but it was terribly important for Washington.

Monmouth finished Lee. It need not have been fatal for him. Had he played his cards properly, he might have survived. It is likely, in fact, that had it been Lafayette, Greene, or Stirling who had run afoul of Washington on that searing battlefield, the commander in chief might have apologized—to the extent that Washington was capable of apologizing—when passions cooled in the wake of the encounter. Given the tension between Washington and Lee, an apology was out of the question, but as Lee had ample supporters in Congress and the army, and as his conduct on the battlefield was readily defensible, he and the commander in chief might well have reached an accommodation allowing both to save face. Instead, Lee self-destructed. It was almost as if Washington, with his uncanny knack for predicting the behavior of others, knew that Lee would destroy himself.

In the two days following the battle, as evidence mounted that Lee's command decisions were commendable, Washington kept silent. Lee, however, used that time to complain of Washington's intolerable action to all who would listen, then put it in writing, even asserting—as had the commander in chief's most severe critics during the past winter—that Washington had been put up to his actions by the sycophants (he called them "wicked . . . dirty earwigs") who surrounded him. Lee demanded a court-martial in order to clear his name. He got it, though it was hardly the tribunal he might have wished. The judges were officers who served under Washington. Some were Lee's rivals. The prickly general was doomed.

Gates, Mifflin, and Conway had already learned that if it came to a choice between them and Washington, they could not win. At this juncture in this long, desperate war, Washington was untouchable. Although the court-martial transcript eloquently demonstrates that Lee had probably saved a considerable portion of the American army at Monmouth, he was convicted of "breach of orders" and having ordered an "unnecessary, disorderly, and shameful retreat." Lee was suspended from command for a year. Doubtless humiliated and resentful at his shocking fall from favor, Lee dug himself in ever deeper.

He continued to protest and even published petty and vituperative essays filled with rancor toward Washington. Congress dismissed him from the Continental army. Like so many others who publicly assailed Washington, Lee nearly paid with his life. Colonel Laurens challenged him to a duel for having disparaged the character of the commander in chief. They fought just before Christmas 1779. Laurens shot him, but it was a grazing, though bloody, wound, and Lee survived. By then, Lee had learned what he should have known at the time of the Battle of Monmouth: "No attack it seems can be made on Gen. Washington, but it must recoil on the assailant." With an insight that would have served him well had it come earlier, Lee also concluded that General Washington had come to be indispensable more for political than for military reasons. The commander in chief, Lee said, had grown so powerful that he was to be "indulged in the sacrifice of any officer whom from jealousy pique or caprice He may have devoted to destruction."[97]

VICTORY AND GLORY

Washington's war changed dramatically following the Battle of Monmouth. Congress mellowed toward him to the point of deference, and public criticism virtually ceased. Monmouth was also Washington's final battle for more than three years. Though neither he nor anyone else could have imagined it in July 1778, Washington was entering a long, risky period of inactivity.

In the immediate aftermath of Monmouth, Clinton's army had hurriedly retreated to the coast after the battle, and from there, under the watchful eye of the British navy, it moved safely into New York City. Barely a week after the redcoats came ashore in Gotham, the long anticipated French squadron under Vice Admiral Count d'Estaing arrived off the New Jersey coast. D'Estaing's navy was powerful. With sixteen sail, including a dozen ships of the line—the battleships of the day—it was superior to the Royal Navy in the mid-Atlantic region, as the British fleet was scattered along the vast American coast. But fortune had not smiled on the allies. D'Estaing had faced delays in sailing from Toulon, and his ocean crossing had been slowed by unfavorable winds. Had the French squadron crossed the Atlantic speedily, not only might it have destroyed the overmatched enemy navy before it sailed from Philadelphia, but d'Estaing and Washington could have trapped and possibly destroyed Clinton's army on the barren New Jersey coast.

Washington could not hide his disappointment, but the timing of d'Estaing's arrival was only the first frustration the American commander experienced that July. Washington had earlier considered—albeit dreamily—the possibility of a campaign to retake New York City. Now that he possessed a naval arm, the reconquest of all of Manhattan appeared to be within his grasp. Washington broached the idea to d'Estaing, who was interested until he discovered that New York's channel was too shallow for France's heavy warships. One day Washington had held to the belief that the "ruin of Great Britain" was at his fingertips; the next day his dreams were shattered.[1]

Although those hopes were dashed, another opportunity loomed, a shot at gaining a decisive victory that might induce London to make peace. Nearly seven thousand redcoats were garrisoned in Newport, Rhode Island, which Britain had captured early in the war. By acting in concert with his new ally, Washington believed he could liberate the city and destroy a considerable enemy army. Seldom had Washington radiated such confidence. He spoke of the "certainty of success," words he had not been inclined to utter during the first three years of hostilities.[2] He envisaged the French fleet cutting off the exit of the British army, much as the Royal Navy had tried to do to the rebels on Manhattan back in 1776, while Continentals and New England militia waged a ground campaign to finish off the enemy. The one thing that gave Washington pause was that the force of Continentals he had posted in Rhode Island months earlier—when little possibility of an action existed—was commanded by General Sullivan, a general noted for failure. Considering the stakes, Washington should have replaced Sullivan. Never before in this long war had the Americans launched a campaign with the bright promise of gaining such a huge victory. The move would have irked some New England congressmen, though that was not why Washington shrank from making the change. If not Sullivan, Washington could hardly have escaped appointing Gates, who remained commander of the Northern Department, wanted the appointment, and was immensely popular in New England. But Washington refused to give responsibility to Gates. Washington would not "gratify . . . a doubtful friend," General Greene candidly acknowledged.[3] Washington would not give Gates the opportunity to win a second sensational victory within the span of a year.

The glowing hopes for a substantive victory in Rhode Island dissolved in the face of dreadful bungles, horrid luck, and Washington's unfortunate decision to leave Sullivan in command. The militiamen, 60 percent of the American force, were slow to gather. Nearly two weeks passed after d'Estaing's arrival before the American force was at last ready for battle, and when Sullivan acted, he acted rashly. He attacked a full day earlier than he and d'Estaing had previously set for launching what was supposed to be a coordinated assault. On that same day, as it turned out, a superior British fleet arrived, having been scraped together while the French squadron waited impatiently for the American army to assemble. A naval engagement, it appeared, would determine the issue, but as the navies maneuvered, a huge late August storm, possibly a hurricane, blew up. It shattered both fleets. D'Estaing limped to Boston for repairs while the British sailed back to New York to be patched up. The departure of the French squadron seemed understandable to almost everyone but Sullivan, who railed in an undiplomatic manner at the French commander. Washington had to intervene to mollify d'Estaing, assuring him that the "thinking part of Mankind" understood his behavior.

What had begun as a chance for decisive victory nearly ended in disaster for the allies. The rapidly overhauled British squadron returned to Rhode Island waters before d'Estaing's heavily damaged fleet could sail. Had the Royal Navy cooperated with Newport's redcoats in a counterattack, not only might it have defeated Sullivan's army, it could possibly have bottled up and crushed d'Estaing's navy while it was being overhauled in Boston Harbor. Instead, the British commander, Admiral Richard Howe, the brother of General Howe, was preoccupied with other things. Sullivan, after a tough battle, extricated his army.[4]

The fighting in the North was over for the year, and large-scale actions were a thing of the past in New England and the middle Atlantic states. Under the leaden skies of approaching winter, d'Estaing sailed for the Caribbean. Never again in this war would a powerful French navy arrive off the coast of a northern state. Washington could not know that, but as his army went into winter quarters, he was all too aware that the campaign of 1778 had been a story of lost opportunities. As he scattered his army among several cantonments, Washington's thinking had already turned to the next season of fighting. His focus was on retaking New

York. It was an idea that grew to be an obsession for nearly the duration of this war.[5]

IN MOST RESPECTS, the Continental army's winter in 1778–1779 was the diametric opposite of that at Valley Forge. Supplies were abundant. Washington's multicamp strategy was part of the reason. The retooled quartermaster system, if not the model of efficiency, functioned better than previously and was helped because General Clinton, stripped of half his army, lacked the manpower to harass the rebel supply lines and forage parties. The weather generally cooperated as well—this was the mildest winter during the war—and the French alliance paid its first dividend. America's ally shipped over prodigious amounts of shoes, coats, and clothing.[6]

However, one feature of the winter of 1779 resembled that of the previous year. Debate over Canada flared again. Lafayette and Gates pressed for a Canadian invasion, with the Frenchman speaking breezily of his country sending a four-thousand-man army to America for such a campaign.[7] A Canadian venture remained popular with many congressmen and army officers, and this time around it was also endorsed by two influential American diplomats, John Adams and Benjamin Franklin, both on assignment in France. If anything, there was greater support in 1779 for invading Canada than there had been the year before. The idea remained extremely popular in New England and New York for the same reasons it had before, plus some new ones. Tories, aided by Iroquois, both armed by the British in Canada, had launched bloody raids on frontier settlements, especially in the Mohawk Valley. Furthermore, tantalizing evidence suggested that Canada remained vulnerable. Not only had France's entrance into the war stretched Great Britain's military resources to the breaking point, Indian agents and scouts were reporting that sentiment was strong among Canada's inhabitants for escaping British control. One agent advised that "Congress can never expect a more favorable Opportunity to dispossess the Enemy of Canada than the present." Although unknown to Congress's spies and Indian agents—or any other Americans—Canada's new royal governor, General Frederick Haldimand, had recently notified London of widespread disaffection among the citizenry. He additionally disclosed that fortifications from St. Johns to Quebec were "entirely rotten," leaving Canada "in a very defenceless state." If the rebels invaded Canada, Haldimand warned, "America most probably will be lost to Great Britain." For the first time, too, support for invading Canada had swelled among southern members of Congress. They climbed aboard the bandwagon when Great Britain, late in 1778, implemented its new southern strategy. Just after Christmas, a British force landed in Georgia and captured Savannah. Southern congressmen saw a Canadian campaign as a means of compelling Britain to abandon its war in the South. Among the congressmen who favored a Canadian invasion were those who simply wanted the Continental army to do something. In the fifteen months since Germantown, Washington's army—which since Valley Forge had steadily numbered around thirty thousand men—had done little more than fight an inconsequential one-day battle at Monmouth.[8]

Washington remained intransigent in his opposition to a Canadian invasion. When the first murmurs were heard, he proposed that the invasion scheme be shelved and that a fort, garrisoned by about three hundred men, be built to deal with the Indian and Tory raiders. Once Congress took up the issue—it did not take a stand, as it had previously, but asked Washington's opinion first—the commander in chief responded with several letters.[9] Three proposals had been floated. Some adhered to the old scheme of driving down the frozen Champlain corridor, though it no longer had much support in Congress. Gates, modifying his earlier thinking, called for an invasion via the upper Connecticut River. In order to bypass British naval power on Lake Champlain, Gates now envisaged the invading army advancing northward through the Coos region of New Hampshire, entering Canada not far below Quebec.[10] The idea of a joint allied enterprise constituted the third proposal. In dispatches that every congressman would see, Washington ignored the Champlain corridor approach and took on Gates's proposal. Despite his insistence that he was interested only in promoting the public good—"No part of my conduct is influenced by personal enmity to individuals," he proclaimed—Washington seemed intent not only on destroying Gates's credibility as a military strategist, but even on tearing down his rival's reputation for decency. (Washington's renowned biographer Douglas Southall Freeman, who was anything but unfriendly toward his subject, wondered if it was really "necessary to employ 3500 words in order to demonstrate that Washington's dislike of Gates was justified.")[11] While lashing out at Gates's "want of candor . . . and . . . politeness," Washington began by claiming that the new nation's straitened financial condition would not permit such an undertaking. Most of Washington's objections, however, reflected military concerns. He thought the venture was "too extensive and . . . too complex" and hinged on "such a fortunate coincidence of circumstances, as could hardly be hoped." It "appears to me," he concluded, that the projected invasion would be "infinitely too doubtful and precarious." With "the enemy in front [in New York], we cannot undertake a serious invasion of [Canada] at all, *even with the aid of an allied fleet.*" To this he added the dubious warning that if large numbers of men were peeled away from his army outside Manhattan, Clinton would have a free hand to once again ravage the mid-Atlantic states.[12] Washington was telling Congress to choose between Gates and himself. With his newfound stature, he knew in advance the choice that Congress would make.

Washington also wrote a confidential letter to Henry Laurens, who over the past ten months had earnestly supported the general's every wish, and in it he focused on Lafayette's proposal for a Franco-American expedition. In this missive, Washington ignored military questions altogether and focused instead on troubling national security considerations. Although France had renounced "forever its possession" of Canada in the Treaty of Alliance, Washington thought it would be unwise for the United States to trust the pledge. Once it was back in Canada, he warned, France might be unwilling to relinquish it. Even if the French did not want Canada, they might keep it as a "surety for the debts due [it] from the United States." He counseled, too, that if the war did not go well for France, America's ally might make peace with Great Britain in return for its reacquisition of Canada. Washington additionally cautioned that following independence, the French Canadians might revolt and transfer Canada to French jurisdiction. "In our circumstances," he advised gravely, "we ought to be particularly cautious; for we have not yet attained our sufficient vigor and maturity to recover from the shock of any false step into which we may unwarily fall."[13]

There can be no question that it would not be in the interest of the United States to see France regain control of Canada, especially as Versailles was tied closely to Spain, which held huge chunks of the North American West and Southwest. With peace, the United States might find itself encircled by French and Spanish colonies, much as had the Anglo-American colonists before the French and Indian War. On the other hand, it was equally contrary to America's interest for Great Britain to retain Canada. If postwar Britain possessed Canada, the trans-Appalachian West, and Florida—which London had held since 1763—it, too, would surround the United States. That France might somehow gain Canada after an invasion was a possibility, though a remote one. That Britain would maintain control of Canada was assured, unless the United States wrested it away through a military action in this war. Whether right or wrong, Washington's discourse on American national interest and international realities was a smokescreen. Viewed in light of his behavior as the war wore on, Washington appears to have raised diplomatic considerations as an artful contrivance to prevail upon those who could not be persuaded by any other means to give up their desire for a Canadian invasion.

What lay behind Washington's unwavering opposition to a Canadian invasion was known only to him. If his statements are taken at face value, he doubted that such an endeavor could succeed and was loath to see precious men and materials drained off, dashing his hopes for another New York campaign, should the opportunity present itself. If these considerations encompassed Washington's outlook, his abilities as a military strategist were flawed. It would mean that he had turned a blind eye to his enemy's manifold weaknesses in Canada, patently overrated their ability to resume the offensive in the mid-Atlantic, undervalued the capabilities of the militia to maintain vital posts in the Hudson Highlands, and—given what d'Estaing had discovered regarding the ability of the French fleet to navigate New York City's harbor—lived in a dreamworld where he fancied a joint allied operation to retake Manhattan.

Rejecting the notion that Washington was severely limited as a strategist leaves few other conclusions, none very attractive. As Lafayette was in France plumping for a joint expedition, there was no question but that Gates would command any overland Canadian invasion that would be mounted in the spring. Washington had already refused to name him to command operations in Rhode Island; it is not inconceivable that the commander's personal insecurities led him to resist the Canadian venture that Gates championed. An exasperated Thomas Jefferson provided another explanation. While governor of Virginia, Jefferson cried out (in private) that Washington was so obsessed with retaking New York that he could see no other options. Jefferson, equating Washington's fixation on New York with Spain's obsession to recover Gibraltar, came close to suggesting that Washington was driven by a psychological need for redemption brought on by his incredibly poor showing in New York in 1776.[14] Nor is it inconceivable that the so-called Conway Cabal, together with the close brush with disaster at Monmouth, had cast such a spell of anxiety over Washington that it colored his thinking. Intriguingly, after Monmouth he embraced the very course that the much maligned Charles Lee had steadfastly advocated in the run-up to the clash with Clinton's army. After mid-1778, it was Washington who deflected those who urged hazardous undertakings, preferring instead to act only in concert with France. Such a course would be safer for him, as whatever action was taken would be carried out with the imprimatur of the French commander, a professional soldier.

Whatever drove Washington's thinking, he believed that time was on America's side. He was convinced there was no imperative to act, except to respond to enemy actions. If the war dragged on long enough, he thought, Britain's lack of success would erode its will to fight and constrain it to recognize American independence. As time would tell, there were grave dangers to this way of thinking.

Washington prevailed on the question of invading Canada. Not many in Congress any longer wanted to support Gates against Washington. With Washington's friends insisting that Gates's proposal "merited nothing but Silence and Neglect," it was dismissed "without a single Remark." Gates was led to believe that his plan was impractical without assistance from the French fleet, which had sailed in November and was not expected to return before late the following summer, if then.[15] As for Lafayette's plan for a joint expedition, Laurens appears to have carried Washington's mail, much as the commander had hoped he would do. Laurens spread the fabricated story among his colleagues that Lafayette and d'Estaing had colluded to advance a proposition aimed at getting a French army back on Canadian soil, "a measure big with eventual mischiefs." In January 1779, Congress set aside Lafayette's scheme, informing him that it had resolved that "Prudence . . . dictates that the arms of America should be employed in expelling the Enemy from her own shores, before the Liberation of a

Neighbouring Province is undertaken."[16] Washington had won. The invasion of Canada was dead.

LATE IN 1778, WASHINGTON ASKED to meet with Congress.[17] He arrived in Philadelphia early in January and, together with Martha, who joined her husband every winter, was a guest at the residence of Henry Laurens. Washington's monthlong stay in the city was an eye-opening experience.

While Washington had met with innumerable congressional committees and consulted with the congressional leaders when he passed through Philadelphia on his way to the showdown with Howe at Brandywine, this was the first time in nearly three years that he had sat down with the entire Congress. The composition of Congress had changed considerably over the years. Less than a quarter of those who had held seats in Congress in May 1776, when Washington had consulted with them about the looming New York campaign, were still delegates. Even fewer among those who had chosen him to command the Continental army in June 1775 remained in Congress. After a few weeks in Philadelphia, Washington concluded that most congressmen were less able than their predecessors.

In fact, although remarkable men like Franklin, Jefferson, and John Adams had moved on to other things, talented veterans such as Samuel Adams, Roger Sherman, Thomas McKean, Elbridge Gerry, James Duane, and Richard Henry Lee still sat in Congress, and they had been joined by capable newcomers like John Jay, Philip Schuyler, and Laurens. If the level of talent had diminished, it was not by much. What was notably different was that Congress had grown more fractious. A troubled Washington appears to have equated contention and disunity with a diminution of ability. Divisions had existed within Congress since the first day that the First Continental Congress assembled in 1774, although in the early going, the delegates, driven by the hope of establishing a union where none had previously existed and the need to wage war, had sought consensus. But as hostilities dragged on, the contrasting interests of New England, the mid-Atlantic states, and the South led to frequent sectional clashes. Almost everything, from military strategy to rival territorial ambitions, was politicized. Accustomed to politics in Virginia, where everything and everyone had danced to the tune of the planter slaveocracy, Washington was unprepared for what he saw in a more heterogeneous assembly.

Congress "is rent by party"—that is, by factionalism—Washington cried
out that winter. In wartime, he said, all must put aside local interests and
work to secure victory. "Unanimity in our Councils, disinterestedness in
our pursuits, and steady perseverance in our national duty" must be restored, he added, alluding to a past that had never really existed. Be that as
it may, Washington believed that the way to reestablish the supposed concord of 1775 was by getting some of the original congressmen—as well as
other talented men who had never served in Congress—to Philadelphia.
He wrote to acquaintances in Virginia and asked pointedly why Jefferson
and George Mason, among others, were not serving in Congress: "Why
do they not come forth to save their Country?" Another concern, one no
less worrisome, also troubled Washington. He had seen military crises up
close, and more frequently than he could have wished. While in Philadelphia, Washington had witnessed another kind of crisis. He had come to realize that the nation faced implacable economic woes, and at the same
moment, he glimpsed frightening signs that the republican spirit that had
sustained the war effort was waning, at least among the most privileged and
powerful civilians in Philadelphia. "Our Affairs . . . are now come to a
crisis," he judged, adding that "we seem to be verging so fast to destruction." If the civil leadership could not find the means of resolving what
plagued the new nation, he warned, "our . . . noble struggle [will] end in
ignominy."[18]

During 1777, the first unwelcome signs of inflation had been visible.
The currency collapsed the next year. Congress tried a variety of remedies,
including selling loan certificates, suspending the issues of currency, imposing heavy taxes, and borrowing every cent it could get from France. When
nothing worked, it urged the states to confiscate and sell the property of
Tories as a means of raising money.[19] Every measure that it tried came up
short, though collectively they were sufficient to keep the war going.
There was nothing Washington could do about the financial crisis. It could
be solved—if at all—only by civil authorities. There can be no doubt that
the Continental army was hampered by the economic malaise. It was difficult to wage war effectively when a "waggon load of money will scarcely
purchase a waggon load of provision," as Washington despaired when the
price of corn soared sixtyfold and when a horse sold for the unbelievable
price of $20,000 and a hat fetched $400.[20] Yet deep as was the crisis, the

army was never immobilized, as Washington tried to make Congress think. Congress and the states believed that military actions were possible—though they would have to be financed through deficit spending and French loans—and throughout this period American armies were active, especially in the southern theater. For that matter, when Washington finally was ready to act, money was no object. He had learned during the Valley Forge winter that bombarding Congress with alarming reports was an effective means of getting what he wanted for his army. Likewise, he seized on the collapse of the currency as a justification for his defensive strategy. The economic miseries "oblige me to a more defensive plan," he often said in 1779 and 1780. Owing to the financial distress, the army was unable "to pursue such measures as the public good may seem to require, and the public expectation to demand," he added with some exaggeration.[21]

While Washington made that point repeatedly, the tone of his correspondence following his stay in Philadelphia indicates that the collapse of the spirit of sacrifice concerned him almost as much as the disintegration of the currency. During his month in the city, the general and his wife were dinner guests in the homes of Philadelphia's elite nearly every night. Washington was appalled at what he saw. While his soldiers often went hungry and seldom enjoyed a nutritious diet, he watched as the cream of society dined on multicourse meals and their tables groaned with every conceivable delicacy. The commander noted that "little virtue and patriotism" was in evidence, an observation confirmed by others. Joseph Reed mentioned having attended parties at which "public Frugality, Spirits, and Patriotism [was] laugh'd at." Samuel Adams, shocked at the extravagance and luxury that he witnessed among Philadelphia's well-to-do, exclaimed that "Foppery" had become the "ruling Taste of the Great."[22]

It was not just the sumptuous lifestyles of the wealthiest Philadelphians that troubled Washington. Businessmen were more interested in profits than in helping the national cause, he complained. He believed that their hoarding and speculation was at least partially responsible for the astronomical rise in prices. He added that "to acquire a little pelf," to "make money, and get places," Philadelphia's gentry were all too willing to "involve this great continent in extricable ruin." Unless this "avarice and thirst for gain" was brought under control, it would inevitably destroy the gains realized through the "expence of . . . blood, and treasure" during four years of war. The spirit of hedonism had supplanted the spirit of 1776, threatening to "plunge every thing" into "one common Ruin." Congress and the states, he continued, must act to restore the sacrificial spirit that had prevailed at the outset of hostilities. They must "adopt some vigorous measures for the . . . punishment of speculators, forestallers and others who are preying upon the vitals of this great Country." To this he added that "nothing . . . can save us but a total reformation in our own conduct," for otherwise the self-serving spirit of the ruling elite would drag the struggle "fast to destruction."[23]

Washington had enjoyed greater comforts than the enlisted men. During the preponderance of each year, while the army was in camp, he lived in a warm and spacious headquarters and had a varied and nourishing diet. Nevertheless, he never lived ostentatiously, and once he joined the army he put aside most of the accoutrements of wealth that he had relished at Mount Vernon. From the beginning, General Washington understood that those in the lower strata of society could not be asked to risk their all when those at the top were unwilling to renounce the good life.

But troubled as he was by the unpatriotic extravagance of the merchants and the well-off, Washington vented his rage only to private citizens. He shrank from sending his thoughts and suggestions to state governors or the president of Congress. Perhaps he thought it beyond the pale for the commander of the army to comment officially on the behavior of civilians, though he had neither refrained from public denunciations of what he called the mercenary spirit of ordinary farmers nor hesitated to excoriate the socially inferior citizenry that declined to bear arms. It is possible, even likely, that Washington hesitated to present his thoughts to Congress from fear that the reverberations that ensued would only add to the anguish of the army. Possibly, too, he suspected that after he had passionately defended his officers' push for pensions for life, his calls for sacrifice would ring hollow.

PLANNING FOR THE CAMPAIGN of 1779 also accounted for Washington's visit to Philadelphia. He wanted to do what he could to lay to rest the proposals for invading Canada, which was still being discussed. Congress was no less eager to learn what the commander in chief had in mind for the coming year. With Georgia under fire, some southern delegates were growing apprehensive about the vulnerability of their states. As it turned out, Washington's worries over Canada were resolved by the time he arrived in Philadelphia, but during his talks with Congress bad news arrived from the South. Savannah had fallen, and the rest of the state was imperiled. Many thought it likely that Georgia, the youngest of the thirteen states, was lost. "Georgia will fall immediately," Henry Laurens predicted, to which a New Yorker added that Georgia "is our Weak Sister." Laurens saw little hope for his own state, which lay next door to Georgia. Without a naval arm, Charleston could not be held, he predicted, and he anticipated "little or no opposition" to the redcoats in the backcountry. Another southern congressman despaired: "The Enemy have at length discovered our weak part."[24]

South Carolina's congressional delegation launched urgent consultations with Washington about sending reinforcements to their state. They got nowhere. The commander in chief did not see the danger that was readily apparent to the congressmen. He downplayed the British campaign for Georgia. If the British succeeded in pacifying the state, it would "contribute very little" to their war effort, he said. But he did not think that Great Britain intended a campaign to subdue Georgia. Washington argued that the enemy's thrust into the state was nothing more than an effort to secure supplies. Washington responded to South Carolina's entreaties for additional troops by asserting that he could spare "no effectual aid" from the army that sat on the doorstep of New York City. Not even a move by Congress vesting Washington—for the first time during the war—with responsibility for "directing and superintending the military operations in all the departments in these States" could budge him.[25] In the event that d'Estaing returned to New York in 1779 with the French fleet, Washington wished to be sure that his army was intact for the one operation he sought.

Congress wanted something done somewhere, and New York and Pennsylvania were demanding that the army be used against the Iroquois and Loyalists, who had staged several devastating raids on the frontiers of their states. Washington could hardly ignore their calls for assistance. He had already called for action against the Indians' depredations himself. During the previous summer, in what appears to have been a tactic to deflect the calls for a Canadian invasion, Washington had suggested an expedition to bring these Indians to heel. Congress had not forgotten the commander in chief's proposal, which was popular throughout the northern states, if only as a partial substitute for the long-desired foray into Canada. Washington had barely arrived in Philadelphia for his face-to-face with Congress before the topic came up. Both parties agreed to such a campaign.

When he returned to his army, Washington offered Gates, who was head of the Northern Department, the opportunity to command the campaign. A clear-cut victory was unlikely, and even if Gates did exceptionally well, he could not be expected to win many laurels through "bush warfare." Gates, who was in his mid-fifties and had little experience in frontier fighting, never considered taking on the assignment. With a hope and a prayer, Washington next offered the job to Sullivan and found nearly twenty-four hundred men for him. The Sullivan Expedition, as it came to be called, was supposed to be wrapped up by early summer, but fall was in the air by the time the campaign was completed. Tons of crops were destroyed, along with numerous Indian villages, but in the words of a student of the expedition, it was at best "a well-executed failure" that contributed next to nothing to America's war aims.[26]

While Sullivan's force moved steadily northward under the relentless summer sun, Washington authorized raids at Stony Point and Paulus Hook, two Hudson River sites garrisoned by British troops. That was the extent of his offensive. He would not again send an army into battle for two long years after the summer of 1779. But while Washington was inactive, the war continued. Spain and France signed a formal treaty of alliance in April, bringing Madrid into the war. The urgency with which France pursued the alliance indicated that the war was not going well. Drawn into the American conflict in some measure by Washington's daring at Trenton-Princeton and Germantown, Versailles had waited in vain for further signs of audacity during the twelve months after the Franco-American alliance was consummated. By spring 1779, the French were beginning to worry. Their ledger books were bleeding red, and they had nothing to show for a full year of belligerency. With considerable reluctance, France allied with Spain and agreed to Madrid's demands that the allies attempt an invasion of England. That, and that alone, seemed to be France's best hope of getting something out of this war it had gotten itself into.[27]

Sir Henry Clinton was barely more active than Washington, though not through choice. He contemplated a Hudson River campaign to take West Point but backed off for lack of manpower. He settled for several lightninglike coastal raids in Connecticut that sowed terror and destruction; a similar, though larger, campaign along the Virginia coast; and a successful operation to regain Stony Point.[28] There was virtually nothing that Washington could do against any of these initiatives. The American commander remained with his army near New York City, waiting and hoping that d'Estaing would return with the French fleet. But Washington's yearning to retake Manhattan went unanswered.

When d'Estaing at long last returned from the Caribbean in September 1779, he sailed to Savannah, not New York. D'Estaing's destination came about because both Congress—knowingly acting contrary to Washington's hopes—and the authorities in South Carolina beseeched the French minister to the United States to direct the fleet to cooperate with rebel troops in a campaign to liberate Georgia. The situation in Georgia had grown desperate. The royal governor had been reinstated, and a Tory legislature had repealed all rebel legislation passed since 1776. Furthermore, the likelihood existed that someday Great Britain would use Georgia as a staging area for an invasion of neighboring South Carolina. D'Estaing heeded the calls of Congress, joining with the small Continental army in the Southern Department in an attempt to retake Savannah. Yet once again the allies were frustrated. A lengthy siege operation, followed by an assault on the entrenched redcoats in Savannah in October, failed with heavy losses.[29] Most of Georgia remained in British hands.

As 1779 faded, there was little reason for cheer at Washington's headquarters. Not only had the Franco-Spanish invasion of England concluded in a dismal failure, but d'Estaing's fleet had returned to the Caribbean following its bloody failure in Georgia. Washington had no option but to put his army into winter quarters. Most of the men went to the cantonment at Morristown, where they experienced a brutal winter that in many ways was worse than what they had endured at Valley Forge. Veterans subsequently spoke of this as "the hard winter" of the Revolutionary War. It began to snow in December, and it seemed never to stop. The thermometer was stuck below freezing for weeks on end as snowdrifts swelled to over twelve feet. Many men endured this winter without adequate blankets and clothing, and as the roads and rivers were choked with snow and ice, they sometimes went days without adequate food. Washington watched with despair. At no "stage of the War," he warned, had "disatisfaction . . . been so general or alarming" within the ranks. As never before, he worried about mutinies, but save for an uprising within a Connecticut brigade, he and the army managed to make it through the winter.[30]

Near Christmas of 1779, just as the harsh winter descended on Washington's men, Clinton loaded eighty-seven hundred British and Hessian soldiers onto transports and sailed from New York, dropping over the gray, stormy horizon for parts unknown. Washington guessed that his adversary's destination was the Caribbean or South Carolina, and briefly he even dared to believe that the British were leaving North America and calling an end to the war. Only when the British armada landed in February did Washington learn their plans. Clinton's massive fleet weighed anchor several miles below Charleston, and the redcoats waded ashore while lashed by a cold winter rain. At last, Washington knew beyond a shadow of a doubt that Great Britain's war aims had shifted. The reconquest of Georgia had been more than a mission to gather supplies. It was apparent that the Lower South—the soft underbelly of the United States, in light of the sizable Loyalist and slave populations in the region—was in great peril.[31]

Washington may have turned a blind eye toward the South, but Congress had long been preparing for just this eventuality. Its commander in the Southern Department was Benjamin Lincoln, a forty-seven-year-old yeoman who had once commanded Massachusetts's army. Since the failure of the operation in Georgia, Lincoln had besieged Congress with pleas for reinforcements from among the Continentals in the North. Like Washington, he had no faith in the militia, but he also had little cause to believe that South Carolina would recruit sufficient numbers of regulars for him. Shaken by d'Estaing's inability to retake Savannah, Congress listened. It ordered three frigates from America's tiny navy to sail to Charleston and stripped Washington army's of nearly three thousand Virginia and North Carolina Continentals for South Carolina's defense.[32]

As Washington's responsibilities for the past year had included the Southern Department, he might have done more to help the rebel soldiers who were awaiting Britain's blow to fall in Charleston. After the allied failure in Savannah in October, the French fleet returned to the Caribbean. There was no prospect whatsoever that it would sail north again before the summer of 1780. This freed Washington to dispatch a considerable number of his idle men southward. However, he shrank from such a step. The only men from his army who were redeployed to the Southern Department between the failure in Savannah and the opening of the siege of Charleston six months later were those men whom Congress ordered sent to augment Lincoln's beleaguered army. Even then, Washington complained that he was left with too few troops to defend his lines and that "ruinous Consequences" might be the result."[33]

General Washington might also have used his army to strike at New York while the cream of the British army was in South Carolina. When the redcoats sailed for South Carolina, Clinton had left behind about eleven thousand men to hold Manhattan, including some drawn from Newport, which the British commander abandoned in order to pursue the war in the South. But almost half of New York's defenders were inexperienced Loyalists who had enlisted in newly formed provincial units that consisted almost solely of Tories. Washington had some twelve thousand men under him, and by appealing to governors in the region, he might have doubled the size of his force, giving him nearly a two-to-one numerical superiority. Before sailing, Clinton had wrung his hands over the likelihood of this occurring. Even more, he had worried that in the dead of winter the harbor and rivers about Manhattan would freeze, immobilizing the Royal Navy and providing the rebels the opportunity to storm across the ice and strike the British defenses. The very nightmare scenario that Clinton had feared came true within only a few days of his departure. The bitter cold that tormented Washington's men at nearby Morristown brought what was left of the British fleet in New York to a standstill. When a similar situation had existed in 1776 in Boston, Washington had proposed sending his men dashing across the frozen Charles River to attack the British defenders. In early 1780, he might have ordered an assault against the enemy entrenchments, as he had wished to do four years earlier, or, more prudently, Washington might have chosen to make powerful strikes against vulnerable sectors of British-held Manhattan. While he could not have liberated Manhattan, rebel attacks might have damaged the British, materially and psychologically, and might have compelled Clinton to call off the invasion of South Carolina and return to protect New York. Instead, Washington did next to nothing while small detachments of redcoats in Manhattan emerged from their entrenchments to conduct four raids in New York and New Jersey.[34]

ONCE CLINTON'S ARMY LANDED in South Carolina in February, the rebels were clearly in desperate straits. Not only was Lincoln confronted by a formidable royal fleet, but Clinton possessed nearly a three-to-one numerical superiority. Congress asked the governors of Virginia and North Carolina to send militiamen to Charleston, but it approached Washington with kid gloves. Congress merely adopted a resolution asking that "Your Excellency will also observe the *discretionary Directions* given to make such Detachment from the Troops under your immediate Command as their Strength and Circumstances will permit." Though Congress had not forced Washington to act, he knew that it wanted him to send some of his units southward. He had also been advised by a South Carolina congressman that Lincoln "wanted nothing to render [Charleston] almost impregnable, but a larger body of men." Washington at last was fully cognizant of the dangers posed by the British in the South. The loss of Charleston and the destruction of Lincoln's army, he said, would have a horrendous impact "on the minds of the People in that quarter." Georgia was already lost; Charleston's fall could ultimately result in the loss of a second state to the United States. Even so, Washington acted slowly. On April 2—six weeks after Clinton's army had disembarked below Charleston and nearly a full month after Congress appealed to him to help South Carolina—Washington ordered nearly 2,000 men from the Maryland and Delaware lines to march to Charleston. He announced grandly that while he could hardly spare the troops, "something should be hazarded here." His act was unavailing. Long before the reinforcements that he sent set foot on the soil of South Carolina, Lincoln had surrendered Charleston and 6,700 men—2,500 of whom were Continentals—the heaviest loss that the rebels suffered in this war.[35]

Washington had faced difficult choices. He can hardly be blamed for thinking, and saying, that disaster would follow should he detach too many men to save Charleston. In February, after revising its troop quota figures, Congress had asked the states to raise 35,211 men, and it authorized a summertime call-up of 17,000 militiamen. Washington had previous experience with Congress's attempts to raise a sizable army, and to say the least, he was skeptical this time around. At the outset of 1777, Congress had announced that it would raise 75,000 men, but the army had peaked that year at 39,000, of whom Washington had only some 17,000.[36] What is more, in 1780 Washington saw little evidence that the states were complying with Congress's request for additional men. The size of the army under Washington declined by more than one third in the fifteen months after January 1779. Washington still possessed nearly 19,000 men in February 1780—they were scattered from New Jersey to West Point, and some were posted in Rhode Island and elsewhere in New England—but during the next sixty days, when he wrestled with the choice of detaching the Maryland and Delaware units to Charleston, his army once again shrank by a third. Anxious and despairing, Washington told Congress that many of his officers were bitter and exasperated with the states and filled with "resentment . . . against the confederacy" for the army's weaknesses. Only a stronger central government could overcome the daunting insufficiencies that dogged the war effort, he implied, and he categorically stated that he "wished a plan could be adopted by which every thing relating to the Army could be conducted on a general principle under the direction of Congress."[37]

The dangers that Washington faced became crystal clear within a two-week span in late May and early June. On May 25, a mutiny erupted within the Connecticut line in Morristown, churned up among men who had not been provided with meat for ten days. It was rapidly confined and suppressed, but on June 6, more than 6,000 Hessian and Loyalist troops landed in New Jersey and marched on Morristown, where Washington had only 4,540 fit and ready men. Though Washington did not know it, the German commander, Lieutenant General Wilhelm Knyphausen, had no plans to assail the encampment. Hoping for a cheap victory, he prayed that Washington would panic and withdraw, leaving behind precious artillery and provisions that could not be drawn away because of a dearth of horses. The Hessian's plan failed, in large measure because they were stopped in their tracks more than ten miles from Morristown by the New Jersey militia. The next day, Continentals sent out by Washington joined with the militiamen and compelled Knyphausen to retreat. "A very pretty

Commemoration of Washington, by John James Barralet, 1802.
Collection of Fraunces Tavern ® Museum, New York City. Gift of Stanley D. Scott, 1984.

A model constructed using forensic anthropology depicting what Washington might have looked like as a nineteen-year-old. Courtesy of Mount Vernon Ladies Association.

Lieutenant Governor Robert Dinwiddie, painting by unknown artist, circa 1760–65. © National Portrait Gallery, London.

George Washington, by Charles Willson Peale. Painted in 1772, this is the first portrait made of Washington. Washington-Custis-Lee Collection, Washington & Lee University, Lexington, Virginia.

Major General Charles Lee, engraving by Alexander Hay Ritchie, after a caricature by Barham Rushbrooke. Courtesy of Library of Congress.

A View of the Attack against Fort Washington and Rebel Redoubts near New York on the 16 of November 1776, drawing by Captain Thomas Davies, Royal Artillery. Courtesy of I. N. Phelps Stokes Collection, Miriam and Ira D. Wallach Division of Art, Prints and Photographs, New York Public Library, Astor, Lenox, and Tilden Foundations.

The Capture of the Hessians at Trenton, by John Trumbull, circa 1786–97.
Yale University Art Gallery/Art Resource, NY.

General Horatio Gates, by Charles Willson Peale, painted in 1782, the year prior to the Newburgh Affair. By permission of Independence National Historic Park.

Washington and Lafayette at Valley Forge, photomechanical print of painting by John Ward Dunsmore, circa 1909. Courtesy of Library of Congress.

General Nathanael Greene, by Charles Willson Peale, 1783.
By permission of Independence National Historic Park.

Washington Rallying the Troops at Monmouth, painting by Emanuel Leutze, 1854.
University of California, Berkeley Art Museum and Pacific Film Archive, Gift of Mrs. Mark Hopkins.

General Washington, engraving after a painting by John Trumbull, 1780.
Washington's step-grandson thought Trumbull more faithfully captured General Washington
than any other artist. National Portrait Gallery, Smithsonian Institution.

Surrender of Lord Cornwallis, painting by John Trumbull, 1817.
Courtesy of the Architect of the Capitol.

General George Washington Resigning His Commission, 23 December 1783,
by John Trumbull, 1824. Courtesy of the Architect of the Capitol.

George Washington, by James Peale, c. 1790. Based on Charles Willson Peale's 1787 museum portrait, this painting shows Washington at the Battle of Yorktown. By permission of Independence National Historic Park.

Thomas Jefferson, by Charles Willson Peale, painted in 1791, Jefferson's second year as secretary of state. By permission of Independence National Historic Park.

Alexander Hamilton, by John Trumbull, painted in 1792, Hamilton's third year as Treasury secretary. Yale University Art Gallery/Art Resource, NY.

George Washington, by Gilbert Stuart, 1796. The "Lansdowne Portrait." National Portrait Gallery, Smithsonian Institution; acquired as a gift to the nation through the generosity of the Donald W. Reynolds Foundation.

Washington Reviewing the Western Army at Fort Cumberland, Maryland, painting
attributed to Frederick Kemmelmeyer, circa 1795. Courtesy of the Metropolitan
Museum of Art, Gift of Edgar William and Bernice Chrysler Garbish, 1963 (63.201.2).
Image © The Metropolitan Museum of Art/Art Resource, NY.

expedition," a young British officer said disgustedly, "six thousand men having penetrated 12 miles into the country—burnt a village and returned." But the threat had seemed real enough for a time, and to some it appeared to underscore Washington's sagacity in not bowing to congressional pressure to send even more troops to Charleston.[38]

There was one step that Washington might have taken to dramatically increase the number of men available to the rebel army in the South without diminishing the size of his army. Two years before the British launched their campaign to take Charleston, Colonel John Laurens, Washington's young aide, undertook to have South Carolina, his home state, raise a light infantry force composed of five thousand African American slaves. Laurens's plan was that those slaves who soldiered would be freed at war's end. An abolitionist with enlightened views on race questions, Laurens had also been influenced by what had occurred during the Valley Forge winter. With the army disintegrating that winter, General James Varnum of Rhode Island had proposed to Washington that his state be allowed to recruit a regiment of African Americans, though Congress in 1775 had forbidden the recruitment of blacks. Without either endorsing or spurning the idea, Washington transmitted Varnum's plan to the governor of Rhode Island. The state assembly rapidly embraced the scheme, and in no time Rhode Island raised a regiment of 250 black soldiers. Connecticut and Massachusetts followed suit by enlisting companies composed of African Americans, some of whom were slaves who served with their owners' consent.

Colonel Laurens appealed to his father for help with his endeavor, but Henry Laurens refused to listen until Savannah fell in December 1778. The presence of the British army just across the Savannah River transformed the attitude of the elder Laurens, and through 1779 he pitched in, even urging Congress to help in raising "Battalions . . . of able bodied Negroes." Ultimately, the success of Laurens's efforts hinged on how the plan was received in South Carolina, and there the idea of arming slaves ran into immediate trouble. The only hope of success, concluded the proponents of recruiting black soldiers in the South, was to secure Washington's endorsement. Young Laurens and Alexander Hamilton, his fellow aide and close friend, together with a handful of southern congressmen, worked on Washington, but to no avail. Henry Wiencek, the historian who has most closely studied the issue of Washington and slavery, concluded that the commander balked "because he feared consequences for his own slave property," and, in fact, Washington did predict that freeing some slaves would provoke such widespread unrest and rebellion that all those in bondage would eventually have to be set free. But there are other, more charitable explanations for Washington's reluctance to endorse Laurens's plan. With considerable justification, Washington said that he feared arming slaves would trigger a race with the British army to raise African American soldiers, a contest that he believed the Americans could not hope to win. In addition, Washington saw troublesome political issues in arming slaves. If already beleaguered South Carolina was pressured from the outside to liberate and arm its chattel, the act might be the proverbial straw that would break the camel's back. Given the widespread fear of slave insurrections that haunted the South, South Carolina might withdraw from the war rather than submit to Washington's entreaties. That was a hazard Washington would not run, and wisely so. His task was to win the war, not to conduct a social revolution. Washington refused to join with the Laurens family on this issue, and the campaign to raise southern slaves for the army died. As a result, Lincoln had only white soldiers with which to defend Charleston and not enough of them to save the city.[39]

WASHINGTON'S WAR SHIFTED WITH REGULARITY, and in the summer of 1780, two months after Charleston was surrendered, it changed again. In July, a French army of sixty-five hundred men arrived in America. Washington had not known that it was coming until after he sent the reinforcements to South Carolina early in April. If surprised, he nonetheless could have guessed why the French army was being sent. With its treasury nearing bankruptcy, France was desperately anxious to bring the war to an end. As 1780 dawned, French officers in America were reporting home that America was exhausted, its morale was sagging, and Washington's army showed no signs of acting boldly.[40] The French government concluded that its best hope for turning the tide in this war was to send over its own army. Under a blue sky and a bright summer sun, the French soldiers, garbed in their form-fitting white uniforms and led by the Comte de Rochambeau, splashed ashore in Rhode Island. It was the first French army to tread on American soil since young Colonel Washington and his fellow Anglo-American soldiers had driven them away in the French and Indian War.

The French got bad news the moment they landed. They learned of the loss of Charleston with the southern Continental army. More bad tidings reached them before their first conference with Washington could take place about six weeks later. In the aftermath of Charleston's fall, they learned, Congress had rushed Horatio Gates southward to pick up the pieces. With an army that consisted of little more than the Maryland and Delaware brigades that Washington had dispatched in April, Gates imprudently hurried deep into South Carolina. At Camden, he stumbled unexpectedly into a superior British force under Earl Cornwallis. The hero of Saratoga was soundly defeated. It was the third American army to be lost in the South in twenty months. Atop these black revelations, the French learned that the naval reinforcements they had shortly expected from home had been delayed indefinitely.

The mood was somber when Washington and Rochambeau met at last at Hartford in September. Still, the two commanders got on well. Seven years older than Washington, stocky with a ruddy complexion, Rochambeau, who exhibited a considerable degree of charm and goodwill, had been in the French army since before Washington went west on his first surveying job. He was impressed with Washington, finding him gracious, sober, thoughtful, well prepared, and given to a touching earnestness. But he questioned Washington's military plans. Washington proposed an immediate operation against New York, which Rochambeau saw as an exercise in wishful thinking. With pitiless honesty, the French commander responded not only that the allies lacked an adequate navy, but that if d'Estaing had been correct that the design of French vessels precluded them from entering New York's harbor—and there was no reason to doubt his assessment—the allies would never have a naval arm in operations around Manhattan. Even a siege was unlikely to succeed, Rochambeau advised, as an army of thirty thousand men would be needed for up to two years, and raising such a joint force was out of the question. Washington was disappointed, but he offered a backup plan. In a startling shift, he proposed a joint invasion of Canada.[41]

This was the same Washington who two years before had warned against a Franco-American invasion, advancing one dreadful concern after another should a French army ever again debouch into Canada. The uneasy contradiction in Washington's about-face with regard to Canada might be explained as an act of desperation. Washington may have realized that the course he had pursued during the past two years—a strategy predicated on the assumption that time was on America's side—had been fatally flawed. It was readily apparent that American inaction since 1778 had, at a heavy cost, gained nothing. In the interim, Great Britain had rolled up victory after victory in the South. With the reconquest of South Carolina seemingly at hand, Britain appeared to be ominously close to breaking the military stalemate that had prevailed during the thirty-six months since Saratoga. Or it is possible that Washington had previously been unwilling to approve such a risky venture as a campaign for Quebec from fear of the reverberations that would follow failure. However, if a Canadian invasion was endorsed by Rochambeau, an experienced, professional European soldier, Washington would be insulated in the event the undertaking failed.

There are still other possible explanations for Washington's change of heart. One is that he may never have meant what he had said about France posing a danger to American interests by entering Canada. He may have always seen the strategic value of invading Canada but contrived his warning in order to discourage a venture that would have weakened his own army. The presence of a considerable French army afforded Washington a freedom to act that he had not previously enjoyed. Possibly, too, Washington had opposed a Canadian invasion in 1778 and 1779 simply because either would have been commanded by Horatio Gates, his archrival. In 1778, General Greene, closer to the commander in chief than any other general officer, had remarked that Washington would not run the risk that Gates might add another decisive victory to his résumé, making him an even greater hero. Washington's inner thoughts are impenetrable, but by September 1780, Gates—after his appalling defeat at Camden in August—was ruined and out of the picture.

Rochambeau's secret orders were that he was "always and in all circumstances" to remain subordinate to General Washington, but at the same time—ironically, in view of the fears raised by Washington the year before—he had been told that the government of France was opposed to a campaign for Canada. Not only had it no interest in regaining Canada, it wished for London to retain it, as a postwar United States that was surrounded by Great Britain would have no choice but to remain dependent on France.[42] Rochambeau listened stolidly as Washington dilated on a Canadian venture but responded with several excuses for not undertaking such an endeavor. In the end, the meeting in Hartford broke up with an agreement to do nothing in the near future. It was late in the season. If and when the French naval reinforcements arrived, Rochambeau promised, the allied leaders could decide what course to take.

WASHINGTON AND ROCHAMBEAU REMAINED INACTIVE during the eight months before their next formal conference to plan a move. As the gray, scudding clouds of another winter piled up over yet another set of encampments, the revolutionary cause reached its nadir. A toxic brew of torments seemed to bring the war effort to the very precipice of collapse. On New Year's Day 1781, nearly one thousand men in the Pennsylvania Line mutinied at Morristown. They killed one officer, wounded several others, seized control of the encampment, commandeered six artillery pieces, and marched on Philadelphia. These men had served three years, which is what they believed they had signed on for, and they wanted an honorable discharge from the Continental army. In the end, they got what they wanted. A frightened congressional delegation met with the mutineers outside Philadelphia and agreed not only to drop all charges against the insurrectionary soldiers, but to give them the choice of an honorable discharge or reenlistment with eligibility for another cash bounty. Half the rebellious soldiers chose to leave the army.[43]

"We are bankrupt with a mutinous army," Congressman Lovell wrote his friend John Adams at the beginning of the year. Adams, in Europe for the past year on a diplomatic mission, reported woes of his own. Though he did not know what was going on behind the closed doors of the French Foreign Ministry, Adams guessed that America's ally was searching for an honorable exit from the war. America's friends abroad "tremble[d]" at the new nation's "current abasement," he said, as news piled up of Washington's inactivity, successive defeats in the South, the ruined economy, and, perhaps worst of all, word that one of America's generals, Benedict Arnold, had turned coat in September, attempting to hand over West Point, and with it the Hudson River, to the enemy.

Adams also informed Congress that Europe's neutral nations, their

commerce suffering because of the war, hoped to arrange a European mediation conference to end hostilities. France, he cautioned, would probably
jump at such an opportunity during 1781. Adams knew full well that a conference of European monarchies would not propose attractive peace terms
for an American republic. The best that the United States could hope for
was recognition of its independence and retention of whatever territory it
possessed when the armistice that preceded the conference took effect. If an
armistice occurred in 1781, Great Britain would keep Canada and possibly
part of present-day Maine, the trans-Appalachian West, Manhattan and
Long Island, Georgia, probably South Carolina, and possibly North Carolina. The United States—a union of ten or eleven states—would be weak,
surrounded by the British, and unlikely to survive long as an independent
republic. For Adams, who had never feared military defeat, European mediation was the great nightmare. "America has been the Sport of European
Wars and Politicks" for 150 years, he exclaimed, and he believed that the
outcome of the War of Independence was about to be determined in that
fashion as well. Cowled with gloom, Adams exclaimed that European mediation was "a most insidious and Dangerous Plot . . . to . . . deprive us of our
Independency."[44]

Adams was partially correct. It was true that Charles Gravier de Vergennes, France's foreign minister, who early in the war had exhibited an optimism bred by Washington's fervor and daring, no longer placed much
hope in America's commander in chief. The "American army . . . before
the alliance had distinguished themselves by their spirit and enterprise," he
remarked, but since France's entrance, Washington had exhibited only "inactivity." Early in 1781, Vergennes added privately that he had only "feeble
confidence" in Washington. But Adams was wrong to assume that France
was prepared just yet to leave the war. Vergennes was not ready for mediation. He had sent Rochambeau to America in 1780 with a sizable army, and
a French fleet had been there for nearly three years, albeit mostly in the Caribbean. Vergennes wanted one more shot at victory, but he conceded that
"if the Americans do not put more vigor into their conduct" in 1781, he
would turn to mediation. Against great opposition in the ministry, he even
persuaded Louis XVI to give the United States twenty million livres to be
used exclusively "for the Supply of the Army." He also sent over a massive
stockpile of military hardware and, in the utmost secrecy, ordered the

French fleet in the West Indies to sail for North America toward the end of the summer. When all that was done, Vergennes instructed Lafayette "to make General Washington fully" understand what lay behind the king's "exorbitant expenditures of war . . . for the sake of the Americans."[45]

Like Vergennes and Adams, Washington knew that 1781 almost certainly would be the allies' last chance at gaining a decisive victory. Given that, the army had to be readied for the coming campaign. When the successful mutiny in the Pennsylvania Line was followed almost immediately by an uprising within the New Jersey Line, Washington suppressed it ruthlessly. Two ringleaders were shot by a firing squad composed of their fellow mutineers.[46] Washington had quelled those internal spasms, but he knew that the "patience of the army . . . is nearly exhausted." No less worrisome to Washington was the realization that the "people are discontented" and eager for peace.[47]

WHAT NEITHER WASHINGTON NOR ROCHAMBEAU KNEW when they met first in September 1780 was that a breathtaking shift in the war was on the verge of occurring in the South. A month after Charleston's fall, the British high command, with a carefree air, had pronounced that rebel resistance in South Carolina had been broken, save for that of "a few scattering militia."[48] There seemed to be little reason to question its declaration. As the summer of 1780 drew to a close, there was no Continental army below North Carolina and not much of one there. Nor were any Continentals being sent south by Washington. Some southern leaders had long since lost patience with Washington. Despite all their entreaties, he had done little to save Charleston. After Charleston's fall, Colonel Laurens had begged Washington to come south and personally take command in this vital theater, but the commander in chief refused. Unconvincingly, Washington had responded that he could not leave the North because "the departments of the Army are now in total confusion."[49] When Gates had taken command in the South, in the summer of 1780, he had written every conceivable official asking for men, weapons, and supplies. Washington responded that the military situation in the northern states precluded him from offering any assistance.[50]

Washington's seeming indifference prompted criticism. The governor of South Carolina, John Rutledge, complained to Congress of Washington's "scarcely credible" behavior toward the war in the South. Thomas Bee, the state's lieutenant governor, protested that people in South Carolina had begun "to think that the Southern States are meant to be sacrificed." If that was the case, he added, South Carolina should negotiate favorable terms of surrender and drop out of the war.[51] Governor Jefferson also privately complained that the southern theater was being ignored. "The Northern States are safe: their independence has been established" since Saratoga, he said, adding that the British "have transferred every expectation from that Quarter" to the South.[52]

While Washington was preoccupied with affairs in the North, the war in the South slowly turned. In midsummer 1780, partisan resistance to the British army's occupation mushroomed in South Carolina's backcountry. Ordinary farmers, roused by the heavy-handed conduct of the redcoats, and awash with hatred for Anglicanism and Great Britain's social and political systems, took up arms against the invaders. With next to no help from the Continentals, the partisans surprised British patrols, ambushed enemy supply trains, and sowed terror among the Loyalist inhabitants who wished to aid the Crown. As that scorching summer waned, General Cornwallis, the British commander in the state, lamented that the "whole country" was "in an absolute state of rebellion."[53] Things only worsened for Cornwallis. In October, he lost more than one thousand men in the Battle of King's Mountain, fought near the North Carolina–South Carolina border. By December he faced not only guerrillas, but a new Continental army under the command of General Greene.

During that autumn, criticism of General Gates had mounted to a crescendo. Following his defeat at Camden in August, officers and politicians around Washington had heaped opprobrium on him, prompting Dr. Rush to remark that Gates "is now suffering not for his defeat at Camden, but for *taking General Burgoyne*" at Saratoga. Ultimately, Congress suspended Gates and, given the string of failures in the South, asked Washington to name his successor. Washington had steadfastly remained aloof from such appointments, seeing the practice as a political minefield. This time, the increasingly desperate Washington relented and recommended the appointment of Greene. Throughout the war, Greene had performed ably, but not spectacularly, though from almost the first Washington had seen qualities of wisdom, cleverness, and circumspection in the Rhode Islander.

Over the years, Washington had seen something else as well. Greene possessed a facility that had been lacking in others who had been sent to command in the South. Greene not only possessed an unusual ability to cope with civilian leaders, he thoroughly understood, and was committed to, Fabian tactics.

In the course of roughly seventy days between Christmas and March 1781, Greene, though dogged with a dearth of supplies and leading a small ragtag band of Continentals and militia, conducted the most masterful sustained campaign waged by any commander in the War of Independence, and the war turned as a result. Cornwallis's army suffered heavy losses in two battles—Cowpens in January and Guilford Courthouse in March—and additional staggering attrition during a punishing and futile chase after Greene across North Carolina in the cold and rain of a backcountry winter. By April, nearly 40 percent of the men Cornwallis had led to confront Greene had been lost. This toll led Cornwallis to a momentous decision. Though he had been ordered by Clinton not to depart South Carolina until the state was pacified, Cornwallis marched his army to Virginia. His plan was to link up with redcoats who had been engaged in that state since January and to shut down the supply routes that coursed southward through Virginia and sustained the partisan fighters in the Carolinas. If Cornwallis succeeded, the rebels would be starved into submission, and both Carolinas, as well as Georgia, would again be royal provinces. In choosing this course, Cornwallis may have been influenced by the likelihood of European mediation, but when he marched northward he left behind a theater of dark menace for one cloaked in uncertainty. He had made a bold decision and, as time would demonstrate, a monumental error.[54]

WHEN WASHINGTON AND ROCHAMBEAU MET in May 1781 in Weathersfield, Connecticut, to plan that year's last-ditch campaign, they knew few details of Greene's activities and nothing of Cornwallis's decision to march his army into Virginia. Once the pleasantries—a military parade and formal dinner—were out of the way, the two generals and their staffs sat down to talk. The discussions were frank and at times heated. After revealing the financial gift that his country was making to its allies, Rochambeau asked Washington what operations he envisioned for the coming summer. To no one's surprise, Washington urged a campaign to take New York, claiming

that Clinton was weaker than ever, having sent raiders to Virginia and reinforcements to the Carolinas. Losing his patience—a French observer later
said that Rochambeau treated Washington with "all the ungraciousness and
all the unpleasantness possible"—the French commander earnestly reiterated his objections to focusing on New York. He then proposed a campaign in Virginia. Though unaware of Cornwallis's epic decision,
Rochambeau knew there was a British army of roughly thirty-five hundred men in Virginia. The allies would have numerical superiority. If they
could trap the enemy force, the long-awaited victory that could break
Great Britain's will to continue might be achieved. But Washington was
intransigent. The allies must focus on New York. Washington "did not
conceive the affairs of the south to be such urgency," the French general
subsequently recalled. Given that Rochambeau remained under orders to
defer to the wishes of the American commander, he consented to march
his army from Rhode Island to the periphery of Manhattan, where the allies would prepare for a joint operation to retake New York.

Washington was delighted. He had prevailed, or so it seemed. The campaign for New York of which he had dreamed for three long years was
imminent. After three days of talks, Washington bade farewell and rode
back to the Hudson to await the arrival of the French army. But there was
something that Rochambeau had not divulged. He had neglected to inform Washington that the French fleet in the Caribbean had been ordered
to sail to North America that summer. Immediately following Washington's departure from Weathersfield, Rochambeau sat down at his desk and
drafted a crucial letter to the Comte de Grasse, commander of the French
fleet. He did not ask him to sail to New York. Instead, Rochambeau urged
de Grasse to bring the fleet to the Chesapeake. Unbeknownst to Washington, and in defiance of his wishes, Rochambeau was secretly planning
what he believed would be a campaign that was more likely than an attack
on New York to produce a decisive outcome. His object was to confront
General Washington with a fait accompli.[55]

As the lush days of spring faded into high summer in 1781, three army
commanders ruminated over strategy. Only Washington believed the allies could succeed in a campaign to take New York. Rochambeau and
Clinton—both lifelong professional officers—were convinced that the redcoats, having had five long years to prepare for the defense of Manhattan

and Long Island, could repulse anything the allies threw at them, even a joint land-sea siege and assault. Indeed, Clinton prayed that the allies would attack New York. If their campaign failed, as he was certain it would, the will to continue hostilities would surely evaporate in France and America. Great Britain would do very well at the peace conference that followed. In his wildest dreams, Clinton even imagined that Britain might win this war in the event of a failed allied campaign to take New York.

A MONTH AFTER WASHINGTON'S DEPARTURE from Weathersfield, Rochambeau at last informed him that de Grasse was coming north, though the French general did not disclose the fleet's destination. Instead, Rochambeau solicited Washington's opinion on where de Grasse should be asked to sail. By then, Washington knew that Cornwallis had entered Virginia and that Great Britain's army there had swelled to some five thousand men and was still growing. Washington's response revealed a flexibility seldom displayed in recent years. Perhaps the Chesapeake would be a "more practicable" area for operations that summer, he said, though he advised that it was best to leave the choice to de Grasse.[56]

In July, the French army joined the Continentals outside New York. For six weeks, the allies thoroughly reconnoitered the area and gathered every possible scrap of information about Clinton's defenses. Should something prevent de Grasse's arrival—hardly an unthinkable possibility, given the abundance of disappointments in this war—the Franco-American armies would have little choice but to attempt to take New York. As the hot summer sun scorched the region, Clinton made several key decisions. British naval intelligence had reported de Grasse's departure from the Caribbean. He and the Royal Navy commander in North America, Admiral Thomas Graves, guessed that de Grasse's destination was New York, and with their own naval reinforcements expected from the Caribbean, they also believed the British fleet would be superior. Receiving reinforcements for his army, Clinton made one other momentous decision: He opted to leave Cornwallis's army in Virginia rather than recalling it to New York. Not only did Cornwallis appear to be safe in Virginia, he might even accomplish something there. After all, his army had swelled to eighty-five hundred men since the spring. Washington seemed likely to summon every available man to New York, and Cornwallis had entrenched his army in what appeared to be an invulnerable position. He occupied a place up the York River, a tiny village named Yorktown on the peninsula below Richmond.[57]

August 14, 1781, began as an inauspicious day. But as the sun climbed into a high, blue sky, a dispatch rider arrived first at French headquarters, then at Washington's, with word that de Grasse had reached the Chesapeake. With great haste, the operation to ensnare the redcoats in Virginia—the plan that Rochambeau had furtively envisaged in May—was set in motion. The French and American armies moved out, marching away from New York.

In the course of several steamy days, the immaculately clad French and the threadbare Americans marched down some of the same heat-choked roads that Washington's army had taken in its desperate flight late in 1776. Spectators turned out to watch and cheer, as if this were grand theater—which it was. Late in August the armies crossed the Delaware, and on September 2 they paraded through Philadelphia, churning up so much dust that some residents said the city turned as white as if it had been hit by a snowstorm. When the armies reached Wilmington, Washington was notified not only that de Grasse's fleet had arrived at the entrance to Chesapeake Bay, but that Continentals and militia under Lafayette were on Virginia's peninsula and prepared to fight to prevent Cornwallis's escape. Normally the most reserved of men, Washington hugged Rochambeau when he brought the glad tidings to him. By the end of the first week in September, the allied armies were at Head of Elk, Maryland, where Howe's army had disembarked when he invaded Pennsylvania four years earlier. This time, the allies boarded transports in that harbor for the final leg of their journey. They were sailing to Yorktown.

Neither Washington nor Rochambeau was aware of it, but a seminal battle had already occurred in this venture, a showdown that has been called the most important naval engagement in the eighteenth century.[58] On September 5, while the allied soldiers were approaching Head of Elk, de Grasse's squadron and a British fleet fought the Battle of the Virginia Capes. At stake was naval supremacy on the Chesapeake. It was bloody and decisive. The French fleet had superior numbers and it thrashed its longtime adversary. The Chesapeake was in French hands. Cornwallis's escape by sea was closed.

The allied soldiery began reaching the peninsula in mid-September. At first, Cornwallis did not realize the mortal danger that was gathering all about him. He knew nothing of the great naval showdown until days after it was fought, and it was even later before he discovered that Washington and Rochambeau were coming after him. He did not move from Yorktown. By month's end, all the allied soldiers, together with Washington and Rochambeau, were present near Yorktown. There were nineteen thousand of them. The British numbered fewer than nine thousand. Cornwallis's escape by land was closed as well. Cornwallis's fate was sealed. Rochambeau, an experienced hand at siege operations, told Washington that the outcome was "reducible to calculation."

On the night of October 5, as sappers from the Continental army gathered to begin digging the first parallel that would house the artillery trained on Yorktown, a "stranger" appeared and "talked familiarly with us for a few minutes," a Connecticut soldier later recalled. Only when some French officers approached and addressed the man did Private Joseph Plumb Martin, who had served in the Continental army since 1776, realize that the stranger was General Washington. The commander in chief "struck a few blows with a pickax," a ceremony undertaken, Martin believed, so that it could subsequently be said that Washington "with his own hands first broke ground at the siege of Yorktown." Work proceeded quickly. In a few days, the first American parallel was ten feet wide and four feet deep and extended more than two miles. Once it was completed, the soldiers struggled to bring up the heavy artillery, and when the last siege gun was in place, Washington reappeared "and put the match to the first gun . . . and Earl Cornwallis . . . received his first salutation," as Private Martin put it.[59] It was followed by a shuddering bombardment, as every cannon in the French parallel on the southwest side of Yorktown and all the artillery pieces in the American parallel south and southeast of the rustic hamlet opened up on the beleaguered British army.

The fusillade continued nearly around the clock, with close to a hundred heavy guns pouring a deadly fire on the enemy. Some thirty-six hundred rounds pounded Yorktown day after day, reducing the village to rubble and rendering the air heavy with suffocating dust. The fetid corpses of horses and sometimes men littered the landscape. By October 11, the second parallels were completed and the allied siege guns advanced to within 350 yards of the nearest British post. Frightened, never knowing if they would live through the next minute, the redcoats crouched in terror in entrenchments or in damp, debris-strewn basements, and even beneath the natural overhangs at the river's edge. Cornwallis was driven to a troglodytic life. He lived in a gloomy underground bunker.

Washington and Rochambeau lived more comfortably, each pitching his tent on the flat, barren landscape about five hundred yards below the parallel farthest from the village. They conferred daily and dined together each afternoon. On the soft southern nights of early autumn, Washington often slept outside his tent, bathed by the silvery moonlight.

The final act of what Rochambeau had promised would be a calculated operation to compel the British to surrender occurred during the second week of October. Two final British redoubts—Number 9 and Number 10—had to be taken to complete the second parallel. The French were given responsibility for seizing Number 9, the Americans the other. Washington put twenty-four-year-old Colonel Alexander Hamilton, who had been with the Continental army for six years, mostly pulling duty at a desk, in charge of taking Number 10. Hamilton had begged for the assignment. He knew this was likely to be the last great act of the war and his final chance of gaining lasting fame and glory. He led four hundred men against forty-five British defenders. Despite the odds, the ten-minute fight was bloody and feral, hand-to-hand combat waged with the expectation that the losers would not survive the engagement. Hamilton's force carried the objective. Ten percent of his men were lost in the assault.

Cornwallis knew there was little hope. Perhaps a hurricane—as at Newport in 1778—might strike the Chesapeake and destroy de Grasse's fleet. Maybe an epidemic would sweep through the allied ranks. Possibly Clinton would cobble together another fleet and send it south to take on de Grasse yet again. Cornwallis made his army endure a bit longer, hoping against hope for a miracle. By October 17, he was out of hope. Under a white flag, he indicated that he was ready to negotiate a settlement.

Rochambeau and Washington were willing to parley, though unwilling to let the negotiations drag on. Given time, things could go wrong, as Cornwallis prayed might be the case. The settlement was reached in less than twenty-four hours. The guns fell silent. Under a cerulean fall sky on October 19, Cornwallis, in the shambles that remained of Yorktown, signed the Articles of Capitulation. A few minutes later, Washington,

Rochambeau, and de Grasse, who had come ashore for this grand moment, signed the document while standing on the blood-soaked soil in one of the recently captured redoubts. That afternoon, six and one half years to the day since the first shot of the war had been fired in Lexington, Massachusetts, the armies gathered for the surrender ceremony on an open plain about two thousand yards north of the tents where Rochambeau and Washington had lived for the past few weeks.

With muffled British drums adding solemnity to the occasion, the British and German soldiers marched out and laid down their arms. Though throngs of spectators from Jamestown and Williamsburg, and nearby farms and plantations, had gathered to watch history in the making, the mood was somber.

Cornwallis pleaded illness and did not attend. He vested Brigadier General Charles O'Hara, a veteran of twenty years, with the sad duty of surrendering. Washington, presiding over his first negotiated surrender in more than a decade of soldiering, refused to accept the capitulation from a subordinate of his adversary. O'Hara was made to surrender to General Lincoln, second in command of the Continental army.

Weeks would pass before word of Yorktown crossed the Atlantic, but every man on the field of surrender believed the Revolutionary War was as good as over. This was the long-awaited decisive victory. The stalemate that had lasted since Saratoga was broken. It was inconceivable that the British could continue to fight in the face of the loss of still another army, one slightly larger than that Burgoyne had surrendered four years earlier.[60]

Washington's contribution to the resplendent allied triumph at Yorktown had been nominal. Greene's brilliant campaign in the Carolinas had put Cornwallis on the road to Virginia's peninsula, and to perdition. Rochambeau had been the first to conceive the possibility of securing a great victory in the South. Behind Washington's back, and against the heartfelt wishes of the American commander in chief, he had summoned the French fleet to the Chesapeake. De Grasse had vanquished the royal squadron, which sealed the doom of the trapped enemy. Every step in the systematic reduction of Cornwallis's army through siegecraft had been planned and directed by the French professionals.

When it was over, Washington publicly thanked Rochambeau for his "cheerfull and able Assistance," an understated expression of gratitude to the real architect of the allied success.[61] Amazingly, Rochambeau graciously permitted Washington to take credit for the triumph, though doubtless he did so because France, with its vested interest in the preservation of the United States, thought the exaltation of Washington would facilitate its goal. (Much later, when Rochambeau wrote his memoirs, he tried to set the record straight.)[62]

Congress was not told what had transpired behind the scenes at Hartford and Weathersfield in the making of allied strategy. Nor were the congressmen interested in finding out. They were simply ebullient, certain that this "most decisive and important Blow" would at last convince London "of a great truth . . . that is, that America is not to be conquered."[63] Congress gushed to General Washington its "*Thanks* . . . for the distinguished services you have rendered to your Country, and particularly for the conquest of Lord Cornwallis." To that, the president of Congress added that Washington was "no less the Favorite of Heaven than of his Country," a man and a general who was held "with a peculiar veneration" by Congress for having steadfastly manifested a "Character so eminent for wisdom, courage, and patriotism."[64]

Some saw Yorktown in a different light. The immediate reaction of John Adams, in Amsterdam, was that Greene's campaign had been "quite as glorious for the American Arms," and Adams even hinted that he understood how Greene's spadework had made possible the "masterly Measure" on the Virginia peninsula. Throughout France, where the major cities were "brilliantly illuminated" over several successive nights to celebrate the allied victory, the emphasis was not on the attributes of any general, but on the "American Character," which had endured until victory was at last grasped. Wise old Benjamin Franklin in Passy, a tree-covered suburb of Paris, pondered the "glorious News" and saw a string of "rare Circumstances" almost unheard of in history: that "an Expedition so complex . . . should with such perfect Concord be assembled from different Places by Land & Water . . . without the least Retard by cross Accidents of Wind or Weather, or Interruption from the Enemy; and that the Army [of Cornwallis] which was their Object should have the Goodness to quit a Situation from whence it might have escaped [North Carolina], and place itself in another [Yorktown] from whence an Escape was impossible."[65]

Two years later, in a rare revealing moment, Washington similarly acknowledged that the American triumph in this war was "little short of a standing miracle."[66]

No one knew the miraculous nature of America's triumph better than Washington. His strategic vision had been flawed, nearly fatally so, given his obsession with retaking New York. His refusal to consider an invasion of Canada, his personal insecurities that led to defective choices in field commanders, his disregard for the southern theater, his gamble that time was on America's side and the enemy of Great Britain, all had nearly resulted in an outcome that would have been far less advantageous to America. Had this war ended in something short of a total American victory—as had appeared likely when 1781 dawned and the haunting fear of a European-imposed settlement had seemed all too real—history would see General Washington in a far different light, and one far less commendatory. But in the end, as Washington knew full well and Franklin understood, the miracle of Yorktown gained for Americans a great victory, a majestic triumph that was seen across the new nation as Washington's victory, won with some help from the French.

PART THREE

FIRST IN THE HEARTS OF HIS COUNTRYMEN

WASHINGTON AND THE POLITICS OF INTRIGUE: TO THE END OF THE WAR

Yorktown was the decisive engagement in the Revolutionary War, though considerable time passed before all knew with certainty that Cornwallis's defeat led to peace. Yorktown brought down the government of Lord North, which had taken Great Britain to war and managed the war effort throughout. The new British government appeared to be committed to peace, though a wary Franklin advised Washington that "we cannot be safe while they keep Armies in our Country."[1] Washington concurred, especially as Britain and France continued to fight on the high seas. When the Royal Navy thrashed the French fleet in the Caribbean, taking de Grasse prisoner in the spring of 1782, Washington was nearly overcome with despair. For a time, he feared the drubbing might induce France and Spain to conclude a separate peace with Britain, leaving London free once again to train its full energies on America, as it had done in the desperate days of 1776–1777.[2] Washington's uneasiness only increased when, near the first anniversary of Yorktown, a Franco-Spanish attempt to take Gibraltar failed disastrously.

Convinced that the "haughty Pride" of Great Britain would keep it at war with America, Washington, in the months following Yorktown, preached the necessity of maintaining a war footing, and he urged the states to fill their manpower quotas so that the United States would be able "to meet their [London's] hostile intentions." He kept the army in a defensive stance, arguing prudently that it was unwise to try anything risky. However, when he met with Rochambeau in July, their first get-together since Yorktown, Washington—no longer worried about a French takeover of Quebec, if indeed he had ever been troubled by such a prospect—urged a joint invasion of Canada. It was the second time that Washington had proposed an allied incursion into Canada, the very step he had denounced in 1779 at a far more grave time during the war. His sudden interest in driving the British from Canada in 1782 had little to do with the military situation. It grew from an amalgam of national security and pecuniary considerations. Depicting the "annexation" of several Canadian provinces as "matters of great moment," Washington left little doubt that he saw the acquisition of this vast region as important for those who wished to speculate in, or settle on, the frontier lands of New England, New York, and the trans-Appalachian West. Taking Canada would pacify the Indians who were dependent on Great Britain for modern armaments, he said. It would forestall "British . . . intrieguing after Peace," giving Americans access to the fur trade and to the alluring lands in trans-Appalachia and those that splayed to the west of Quebec. But as there was nothing in it for France, Rochambeau demurred. Washington never considered a unilateral American invasion of Canada.[3]

By the time Washington suggested a joint invasion, peace talks had been under way in Paris for nearly three months. At first, he was doubtful of progress, but as the leaves showed their rich autumn hues in 1782, Washington and most members of Congress had grown cautiously optimistic. They knew that Great Britain had recently sent a full team of diplomats to Paris, a most hopeful sign. Early the next year, news reached America that Britain had acknowledged that the American envoys were the representatives of the United States, in essence the long-awaited recognition of American independence. "Every day almost brings some fresh rumour . . . on the side of peace," said a joyous congressman soon thereafter.[4]

No one was happier than Washington, who was increasingly eager to return to Mount Vernon. "I am spending another Winter (I hope it will be the last that I shall be kept from returning to domestic life) amongst the dreary Mountains," he wrote from the army's snowy cantonment in Newburgh, New York, in February 1783. At least the army was in better shape than during recent winters. It had not fought a major battle or conducted a campaign in fifteen months, and in midwinter, Washington reported his satisfaction at "seeing the Troops better covered, better Clothed and better fed than they have ever been in any former Winter Quarters."[5]

THOUGH A BUOYANT MOOD SWEPT THE LAND, not everyone shared in the rapture, especially as the United States was still plagued by formidable economic problems. Even as Washington expressed jubilation that peace seemingly was near at hand, Congress sent to the states a proposed amendment to the Articles of Confederation that was meant to be a remedy for the nation's financial maladies. The Articles, the first constitution of the United States, had been drafted by Congress in 1776–1777 and finally ratified by all the states during the desperate winter of 1781. The Articles created—or, more accurately, preserved—a decentralized confederation of states. The states were autonomous and Congress nearly powerless, as it lacked the authority to regulate commerce and levy taxes. The amendment proposed in 1783 would empower Congress to levy a federal impost, a 5 percent duty on all imports. All knew that it faced an uphill battle. An earlier impost amendment, sent out for ratification in 1781, had failed in December 1782, coming up one state short of winning the needed approval of all thirteen states.

There were many players in the campaign in 1783 to vest the national government with revenue-raising powers, but among the key figures in Congress were James Madison, a shy Virginian who had been sent to Philadelphia in 1780, and Colonel Alexander Hamilton, who after six years of soldiering had left the army, passed the bar examination in New York after a few months' study, and was added to the state's congressional delegation in the fall of 1782. Madison had been twenty-eight when he came to Philadelphia, but he looked so young that several veteran congressmen mistook him for a student clerk. Hamilton entered Congress at age twenty-seven, though his hard life as a soldier likely left him looking his age, if not older. Each young man possessed a lively, fertile mind, and each had received a college education, Madison at what now is Princeton, Hamilton at today's Columbia. Otherwise, the two young men could not have been more different.

Madison, who had been born to wealth—his father was the largest slave owner in Orange County, Virginia—was sickly and introverted into early adulthood. Still an unanchored young man even after he graduated college,

Madison had returned home to a purposeless and troubled life. The American Revolution may have saved him. Jolted and stimulated by the epic events swirling about him, Madison entered politics and within five years rose from a seat on the local Committee of Public Safety to a seat in Congress.

Hamilton had grown up in humble circumstances on the hilly, green Caribbean island of St. Croix, the illegitimate child of a wayward mother and a father who was an improvident drifter. Reared in penury, Hamilton had his formal education cut short in early adolescence and was forced to take a job with a New York mercantile firm that operated on the island. Deprivation did not beat him down. Instead, it stoked the raging fire of ambition within him. He was obsessed with escaping the poverty of his youth and, like Washington, gaining renown. When he was twelve, he "contemn[ed] the grov'ling and condition of a Clerk or the like, to which my Fortune &c. condemns me." He also longed for a war, seeing soldiering, as had Washington, as a means of rapid ascent.[6] Hamilton impressed both his employer and his pastor with his nimble intellect and aggressive striving, and they found the money to send him to New York for college. The Revolutionary War erupted during his junior year. Given the war that he had prayed for, Hamilton made the most of it. He dropped out of Columbia and joined a New York artillery company created by the Provincial Congress for the defense of Manhattan.[7] Within a year, he was serving with the Continental army. With his flair for impressing older, powerful men—which had also been Washington's forte—Hamilton caught the eye of General Knox, who doubtless was instrumental in securing his appointment as an aide to Washington during the winter of 1777.

Madison entered Congress eighteen months before Yorktown and literally worked his way to the top. He never went home during his initial thirty-six months in Congress, probably the only delegate with such a record. Diligent and persistent, polite and approachable, if not overly friendly, Madison also displayed astounding energy and a fecund mind. By the time Hamilton joined the New York delegation, Madison was completing his third year in Congress and was among its leaders. Hamilton, bold and assertive, and not given to taking a backseat, rapidly rose to a leadership position himself. In no time, too, he and Madison became political allies. In a classic case of politics making strange bedfellows, the

New Yorker and the Virginian forged a bond. More than anything, what united them was their belief that if the Union was to survive in the looming postwar years, the national government must have greater powers.

Madison had only slowly come to see the need for a stronger national government. Not until Charleston fell in May 1780—leaving the Carolinas and Virginia vulnerable—did Madison understand that his state might not survive without help from a robust United States government. Madison was also a pragmatic politician who represented the interests of Virginians eager to open the trans-Appalachian West following the war. His constituents knew that a powerful national government would be helpful in prying open the West, much as Great Britain had been crucial in securing the Ohio Country in the 1750s. Hamilton's nationalism had burgeoned in his frustration and anger at observing the army's almost daily privation and experiencing its humiliating impotence. Four months before the siege of Yorktown commenced, Hamilton began publishing a series of essays entitled *The Continentalist*. Unless the "WANT OF POWER IN CONGRESS" was corrected, he had written back in 1781, the war could not be vigorously prosecuted, the nation's economic woes could not be repaired, and the Union could not be preserved. Though he said that he did not want a national government that was independent of the states, Hamilton deeply believed that the central government must have sufficient powers to override the "prejudices in the particular states."[8]

Hamilton had served at Washington's headquarters for nearly five years, but Madison had never met the commander in chief until the Continental army passed through Philadelphia en route to Yorktown. Washington had remained in the city for several days, and on at least two occasions, he and Madison attended the same dinner party. Following Cornwallis's surrender, Washington returned to Philadelphia, where he remained apart from his army for nearly four months, a time that Washington characterized as "divided between parties of pleasure and parties of business." Madison met Washington on several occasions, though the two Virginians hardly formed a close relationship. Washington was twenty years older and the most powerful man in America. Madison may have been among the most competent men in Congress, but he was not widely known outside Philadelphia; he was merely one member in Virginia's delegation, and not necessarily the most influential.[9]

Hamilton's relationship with Washington had been strikingly different. He had seen Washington almost daily from the winter of 1777 at Morristown through the siege at Yorktown. Throughout the war Washington had put in long workdays, often not leaving his desk until after sunset. When Martha was with him, which she was every year when the army was in winter quarters, the general spent most evenings with her. During the several months she was not present, Washington customarily spent a portion of his evenings with three or four aides.[10] Those were relaxing times for Washington, who unequivocally trusted his aides' loyalty. Over a glass of wine and a bowl of nuts, Washington felt free to air his thoughts, and the young men who served him did not hesitate to discuss at least some things on their minds. Given Washington's taciturn nature, it is likely that his aides did most of the talking. One can easily imagine conversations about congressional politics, the new state constitutions, African American slavery, and, after 1779, the woebegone economy. Given his nature, Hamilton probably dominated many of the discussions, and it is certain that he did so when finance was the topic. No one in the army, and few outside it, rivaled Hamilton when it came to understanding economic issues. Indeed, in 1781 Hamilton, who was all of twenty-six years of age, was the favorite of some to be the nation's first superintendent of finance, though in the end the post went to Robert Morris, who had been Philadelphia's leading merchant before the war and a member of Congress since 1775.[11]

For all his frenetic energy, Hamilton was a thoughtful sort who treasured the opportunity to read, and in his spare moments at headquarters he plunged into treatises on public finance. His position on Washington's staff also afforded him the opportunity to meet an array of veteran politicians and powerful businessmen, from whom he learned many and varied things about the realities of finance, politics, and America's political structure. Hamilton's genius was to draw all this information into a coherent understanding of the tribulations that afflicted the revolutionary effort and what might be done to restore the economy. Not coincidentally, the therapies that Hamilton came to embrace tallied with the interests of the mercantile community in important northern port cities. Hamilton was never reticent about speaking out. Ever articulate, not to say glib, he brought himself to the attention of important officials who visited headquarters, many of whom doubtless were swept up by his dazzling intellect. It is no less likely

that on many evenings in the warmth of Washington's residence at headquarters, Hamilton spoke at length on finance, politics, and the relationship
of the states and Congress. Washington was no babe in the woods when it
came to understanding the nation's ills, though Hamilton's reflections may
have helped to shape the commander's disparate ideas and observations
into a lucid outlook.

It would be wrong to think that Hamilton alone understood what
plagued the war effort. As far back as April 1780, several army officers had
met in the New Tavern in Philadelphia and adopted a manifesto deploring
Congress's lack of power and urging that it be given revenue-raising powers. Financiers who had loaned money to Congress, or bought up the securities of those who did, also wanted a central government that was both
sovereign and armed with adequate powers to secure these debts. Some of
those had a hand in the Hartford Convention, a gathering of representatives sent by the New England states and New York late in 1780 that urged
a federal impost and even recommended that General Washington be authorized to coerce the states into providing supplies to the army. The following year, Superintendent of Finance Morris urged that the national
government be granted revenue-raising authority. In private, he spoke of
the need to "open the purses of the people." Publicly, he advocated the creation of a national bank and proposed that Congress be endowed with the
power to raise revenue through head, land, and excise taxes. Unwilling to
go that far, Congress in 1781 opted for raising revenue through a tariff—
popularly called an impost—and sent to the states for ratification an
amendment to the Articles of Confederation empowering it to levy such a
duty. Before Yorktown, the proposed amendment stood a good chance of
passing. But with the war widely thought to be all but over following
Cornwallis's surrender, the sense of urgency that had gripped the land vanished like snow under a warm sun. By Christmas 1782, fourteen months
after Cornwallis was vanquished, Congress knew that the impost amendment was dead.[12]

Within a week of learning of the failure to secure ratification of the impost, some in Congress, and especially Hamilton, glimpsed an opportunity
to resurrect the revenue tariff. In the last days of 1782, General Alexander
McDougall, with two colonels in tow, arrived in Philadelphia from Newburgh with a petition from the Continental army's disgruntled officers.

The officers, together with their men, had not been paid for months. Robert Morris—"the Financier," as virtually everyone in Congress called him—had stopped paying the army earlier that year, a move that he calculated would save the hard-pressed national government some $3.5 million annually. If the army was housed and fed, Morris reasoned, that should be sufficient until the war ended, when all outstanding arrears would be settled. Besides, Morris decreed (he was sometimes privately called "the Dictator" as well as the Financier) that compensation for the officers and men in the army should come from state requisitions, not the national treasury. Washington in all likelihood very quietly concurred with Morris's scheme during his lengthy stay in Philadelphia in the months that followed Yorktown. However distasteful Washington found it to see his soldiers go without pay, he believed that Morris's solution alone offered hope of keeping the army intact until the peace treaty could be negotiated. From early in 1782 onward, the commander in chief put in long hours placating his officers over the issue of pay, repeatedly reassuring them that Congress understood their plight and, in time, would find a solution.[13]

By December 1782, however, the officers' patience was nearly exhausted. Worried not only about their back pay, the officers also feared that the half-pay pensions they had been promised earlier in the war would not be forthcoming. During the Valley Forge winter, Congress had approved a half-pay pension for seven years. In 1780, however, just after the surrender of the large Continental army at Charleston, officers who remained in the army had threatened to resign unless their half-pay pension was extended for life. Washington had gone to bat for them. Sheepishly telling Congress that whether their demands were "reasonable I pretend not to decide," he warned that "the temper of the Army . . . requires great caution" and that "the Officers are held by the feeblest ties." Congress buckled in October, acting just after Benedict Arnold's treason came to light. It agreed to award the officers half-pay pensions for life.[14]

But in 1783, with the economy still in shambles, peace on the horizon, and the army certain to be demobilized once the war officially ended, the officers were apprehensive that they would soon lose their clout and never be compensated. Driven by a sense of urgency, they decided to act. Their first step was to send General McDougall and the two colonels to Philadelphia with a memorial indicating a willingness to accept what came to be known as "commutation"—their lifetime half-pay pension would be converted into a five-year full-pay pension. Their petition emphasized that they had "borne all that men can bear," having forfeited their youth, health, and fortunes in the service of the country.[15]

Though composed in a bristly style, the message was not especially strident, but an air of menace lurked between the lines. Furthermore, when McDougall and the colonels spoke privately with many congressmen, they were more candid, and more threatening, offering "very highly colored expressions," in Madison's phrase. Behind closed doors, these officers depicted an officer corps that was a vat of discontent verging on mutiny, sufficient, they warned, to "make a wise man mad." The army's officers were impatient with Congress's waffle. Any "disappointment might throw them into extremities," McDougall divulged. If that was not alarming enough, McDougall cautioned too that many officers had lost patience with Washington, whom they saw as unwilling to do what was necessary to persuade Congress to act.[16] Some in Congress were outraged by the thinly veiled threats. Others were unhappy at the prospect of trying to find the $5 million that commutation would cost. Not a few raged that as the average officer had not served five years, commutation would provide a great many officers with a pension that exceeded what they had earned during their military service.[17] But there were congressmen who wanted to use the threat posed by the army as a vehicle for vesting Congress with the power to tax, for revenue would have to be found with which to pay for commutation. These congressmen worked hard to provoke anxiety among their colleagues. Gouverneur Morris, for instance, cautioned that the "army have swords in their hands." Others in this cagey business spread dark rumors about "a most violent political storm" that was brewing in Newburgh, that the army was "ripe for annihilating" Congress, even that a coup to dump Washington was in the works, an event that would leave the army in the hands of a commander who might be a "less scrupulous guardian of [Congress's] interests."[18]

Shaken by the sulky and resentful mutterings they had heard, some in Congress feared that archconservative officers in the Continental army harbored "tory designs"—the destruction of the American Revolution and the establishment of a military dictatorship.[19] Most congressmen did not go that far, but enough feared trouble from the army that they voted to create a grand committee composed of one member from each state to find a solution. Madison was the dominant force on the committee, which late in January recommended commutation financed by revenue garnered from an impost. But to increase the chances that the impost would be rati-fied, the committee agreed to a watered-down amendment: Some states that were especially hard hit by the war would share in the revenue, and all states could use a portion of the funds raised to help with their war debts.[20]

The Grand Committee's recommendations fell far short of the mark in the eyes of the most extreme Nationalists, including Hamilton. In the gloom of January, some who saw this as possibly their final hope for strengthening the powers of the national government formed a conspiracy. Initially, the collaborators appear to have consisted of Nationalists in Con-gress and politically connected merchants and financiers, all of whom saw unrest in the army as a golden opportunity for gaining what they had long sought. In time, some officers in the Continental army allied with them or were used by them. These officers were persuaded by Hamilton, Gou-verneur Morris, and Superintendent Morris, among others, to couple their interests with those of the investor class by demanding that the five-year pension for the army's officers be paid in federal interest-bearing bonds.[21]

Those in on the intrigue were driven by disparate aspirations. Some, like Superintendent Morris, hoped to use the army as leverage for fund-ing America's debt, a step that would be enormously profitable for the speculators who had bought up staggering amounts of the IOUs awarded by Congress throughout the war to those who had supplied the army.[22] Others were driven more by the hope of safeguarding national security in the postwar world. They believed that only a strong central government could assure America's westward expansion, protect its commerce, and provide for the national defense against Europe's rapacious superpowers. Many of the most conservative revolutionaries feared that postwar Amer-ica would witness radical social and political changes spawned by the re-publican and egalitarian philosophy of the American Revolution. Already, substantive changes were evident in some states, where men who had been unable to vote or hold office before the war were ascendant. Many conservatives believed that far-reaching changes were less likely if a truly sovereign national government could be fashioned. In a new nation characterized by such great disparities as existed within the broad American Union, it would be exceedingly difficult for a faction committed to radical change to gain control of a national government.

No one did more than Hamilton to think through this plot or to bring together the plotters. He had ties to the army and links to high rollers in the countinghouses in Philadelphia and New York, and he sat in Congress. Hamilton pulsated with intrigue. It was a way of life with him. He had become a revolutionary bent on overthrowing British rule. At Valley Forge, he had plotted to elevate Washington and to destroy the commander's rivals. In the officers' pressing wish for compensation, Hamilton saw the opportunity for introducing the fundamental changes in America's constitutional system of which he had long dreamed.

One of Hamilton's first steps was to bring Washington's old nemesis, General Gates, into the picture, partly in the hope of discrediting a despised enemy and partly in order to convince his brethren in Congress that there was a move afoot in the army to supplant Washington. Through his contacts in the army, Hamilton knew that many of the younger dissident officers were hotheads, men who were willing to use their military status to get what they wanted. As McDougall and the colonels had said, many of these men were frustrated with Washington. Some had long held Gates in higher esteem than the commander in chief, and some believed that Gates sympathized with their notion of using extralegal means to win their back pay and pension. This intrigue was hatched under such deep cover that Gates never knew who was pulling the strings—if he even knew that his strings were being pulled. Hamilton and his fellow schemers maneuvered Gates into believing that by stoutly championing the interests of the officers, while simultaneously helping powerful congressmen and merchants secure what they wanted, he would enhance his standing—and political fortunes—as the new nation entered the postwar period. Gates evidently swallowed the bait, for early in March, Major John Armstrong Jr., his aide-de-camp, wrote and distributed an unsigned manifesto to the officers at Newburgh. Attacking the "soft, unsuccessful epithet of memorial" that McDougall had carried to Congress some seventy-five days earlier, it proposed confronting Congress with an ultimatum: If the officers' back pay and commutation were not guaranteed, the army would disband if the peace talks failed and the war continued, but if peace broke out, the army would refuse to dissolve.[23] In a single breath, Armstrong's Newburgh Address—as it came to be known—had proposed treason and tyranny.

As he manipulated Gates, Hamilton alerted Washington to what was coming. Hamilton had not written Washington in a year and had sent him only one letter in the eighteen months since Yorktown. Hamilton was a man given to using others, and he had no use for Washington in 1782. Besides, Hamilton in 1781 had confessed his dislike of Washington in a heartsore letter to a confidant. The commander's character was not at all what the public believed it to be, Hamilton had confided without elaboration. But now Washington was essential for seeing that Hamilton's intrigue did not go awry and for assuring that the army was not misused—or used in any manner—by the zealots. Writing to Washington nearly three weeks before Armstrong's anonymous address appeared, Hamilton said much that was cryptic. Even so, he was certain that Washington would divine what he was telling him. Washington had always kept his ears open; little stirred in the army without his knowledge. However, on the off chance that Washington did not grasp the meaning of his letter, Hamilton advised him to speak with General Knox, an indication that the artillery chief was up to his neck in the conspiracy.

Hamilton told Washington that he was losing popularity with his officers as a result of his reluctance to espouse their "interests with sufficient warmth." He mentioned "the temper and situation of the army" and the "stat[e] of our finances," including the need to "restore public credit and supply the future wants of government." He also lamented the lack of "foresight" in Congress. Hamilton ruminated on what the army might do should the peace negotiations collapse, suggesting that it might be difficult "to keep a *complaining* and *suffering* army within the bounds of moderation." It was Washington's responsibility to see that moderation prevailed, he went on. You must *"take the direction"* of the army, he said. You must "guide the torrent, and bring order perhaps even good out of confusion." By doing so, Hamilton closed, Washington would win the respect of most officers in the army and the hearts of his countrymen. Retaining, even enhancing, the public's love of Washington was a principal component of Hamilton's intrigue. Even in the 1781 letter in which he deprecated Washington, Hamilton had said it was imperative that Americans continue "offering incense" to the commander in chief, whose "popularity has often been essential to the safety of America, and is still of great importance to it."[24] With postwar America in mind, Hamilton, as he had at Valley Forge, sought the further ennobling of Washington.

If Washington had not fathomed Hamilton's warning and stage-managing, everything must have fallen in place the minute he read the Newburgh Address. Armstrong's handiwork was posted, and the officers were asked to attend a meeting four days later, on March 15, to discuss the address and decide on a course of action. The meeting was scheduled for the Temple, a twenty-one-hundred-square-foot hall in the Newburgh cantonment so newly built that it still reeked of fresh-cut green wood. It was cold that day in the Highlands, and several inches of new, still-white snow covered the ground; but it was stuffy inside the Temple, where fires roared in several large fireplaces. Near noon, the officers stood in clusters, talking anxiously, a frisson of suspense gripping the hall. Many sensed that both the army and the Revolution had reached a precipice. No one knew what to expect, save that the orders of the day designated that Gates was to preside at the meeting.

Precisely at noon, Gates stood up to convene the meeting. As he did so, a side door opened and Washington stepped into the warm room. The commander walked directly to the rustic podium at a head table filled with field officers. Conversations ceased. Men, including Gates, hurriedly took their seats. When a breathless hush fell over the room, Washington took a sheaf of papers from his pocket, unfolded them slowly, and began to read a prepared address. Visibly dismayed by the talk of mutiny, he reminded the officers that he had been with the army from its inception. He loved the army and knew that his reputation was linked to its conduct. How, he asked, could anyone think that "at this late stage of the War . . . I am indifferent to its interest?" Still, he insisted that the army must respect "the sovereign power of the United States." The course that had been proposed in the Newburgh Address was "so shocking . . . that humanity revolts at the idea." Its author must be "an insidious Foe" of the American Revolution. If the army approved the "blackest designs" proposed contained within the address, the new nation likely would collapse. But if the officers rejected the address, they would be viewed by their countrymen as "the last stage of perfection." Washington added that he believed Congress would do "compleat justice" to the army. It had been "unwearied" in its efforts to find the revenue with which to pay the officers, but it was a representative body composed of "a variety of different Interests." Time was required for it to act. In closing, he pledged to "exert whatever ability I am possessed of, in your favor."[25]

For those whose first concern was the survival of the American Republic, it had been a magnificent statement—historian Joseph Ellis has written that it was "the most impressive speech" Washington ever wrote—but the commander had again urged patience, and that was not what the militant officers wanted to hear.[26] Besides, Washington was not a great orator. As was his habit, he had read the address in a low, soft voice that listeners strained to hear. As he paused following his final line, he was greeted by empty, sullen silence. No one knew better than Washington, a devotee of the theater and admirer of actors, that his speech had turned few heads. Washington, a polished actor himself—the best he had ever observed in his quarter century in public life, John Adams once noted—seized the moment in the playhouse that was the Temple with his final gesture.[27] He may have acted intuitively, or, given Hamilton's forewarning, he may have rehearsed the scene during the preceding days. Saying that he wanted to read something to the officers (it was a letter from a Virginia congressman filled with unadorned promises, the sort of thing the officers had heard repeatedly from Philadelphia), Washington gave the performance of his life. Once again, he reached inside his buff-and-blue coat and with deliberation extracted the missive. After slowly, meticulously unfolding the letter, he began to read from it. He stumbled over the first sentence, then faltered again on the second. He seemed to be having trouble seeing. Washington paused and purposefully reached once more into his pocket. This time he pulled out a pair of glasses and with care put them on. These men had never seen Washington wearing glasses, though he had been using reading glasses at his desk for a couple of years. As he adjusted his wire-rimmed spectacles, Washington apologized and, in a soft voice that resonated despair and fatigue, told his audience: "Gentlemen, you must pardon me. I have grown gray in your service and now find myself growing blind."[28]

It was the perfect touch, and in an instant the mood of the room was transformed. Men in the audience, tough men who had lived on the hard side for the past several years, wept openly. The audience was in the palm of his hand. All fire and zeal, and all defiance, evaporated in a flash. Washington finished the letter and without another word left the room. Knox took charge, leaving Gates to sit idly, quietly, on the dais, perhaps grasping at last how he had been set up by Washington's adherents. Knox and other men from headquarters who were true to Washington pushed through a statement of loyalty to Congress. The Newburgh Address was swept aside, never to be heard of again.

Washington had followed the script that Hamilton had prepared for him, and in a dazzling performance he had snuffed out the officers' conspiracy at Newburgh, reinforced the principle that in America the military remained subservient to civil rule, and solidified his reputation. Many would now see him as the leader who had saved the American Revolution from the menace of a standing army and treacherous officers. Even some who had never been sold on Washington's merits as a general now saw him in a different light. More than ever, he was seen as a leader to be cleaved to.

WHILE WASHINGTON SPOKE AT NEWBURGH, word of the preliminary peace treaty with Great Britain at last reached Philadelphia. The treaty was a magnificent success for the United States. America was independent. Its western boundary was to extend to the Mississippi River. Great Britain was to remove its troops from the United States. The war was nearly over, and the crisis that had grown from the many-layered conspiracy in the winter of 1783 had been dodged. But the battle to satisfy the officers continued, and Washington—as he had promised in his remarks at Newburgh, and as Hamilton and his fellow conspirators had planned all along—was part of it. Washington quickly and candidly told Congress that the officers could no longer be mollified "upon the string of forbearance." Congress must act, he added. The officers will not "grow old in poverty wretchedness and contempt."[29] It was *"indispensable,"* he added, that every soldier, enlisted men and officers, be fully paid prior to demobilization.[30] Within the month, Congress acted. It sent to the states another impost amendment that, as Hamilton had wanted, was identical to the unsuccessful emendation of 1781. Congress, badly frightened by the show staged at Newburgh, also approved the commutation plan advocated by the officers.

Washington pitched in further by dispatching a circular letter to the states as they considered the proposed amendment. While the war had been won, he said, the question of whether the Union would be preserved remained undecided. The survival of the Union hinged on giving "a tone to our Federal Government." The national government must have greater power, he insisted for the first time to a national audience, nothing less than the "Supreme Power" to overcome "local prejudices and policies" when the national well-being was at stake. Congress must have the means through which it could pay the "Soldier . . . his Stipend, and the Public Creditor his due." Unless the states ratified the impost, he warned obliquely, the Union might not survive and in its place the states would "become the sport of European politics, which may play one State against another to prevent their growing importance, and to serve their own interested purposes." The American Revolution hung in the balance, he asserted. It remained to be determined whether it would be "a blessing . . . not to the present age alone," but to "unborn Millions" in succeeding generations.[31]

Washington's stirring appeal was unavailing. With peace assured, the impost amendment narrowly failed once again. The army simmered, and in Pennsylvania a mutiny flared among troops who demanded their back pay, leading Congress to flee Philadelphia for the greater security offered by bucolic Princeton. Once there, Congress ordered the virtual dissolution of the army. Almost overnight in the early summer of 1783, the army was reduced from about eleven thousand men to some two thousand. Those still in the army, moreover, were scattered about to reduce the likelihood of a grand mutiny. In lieu of their commuted pension, the officers were given certificates that could be redeemed whenever they chose to do so. The men who were mustered out were paid with what Congress knew to be worthless certificates that the soldiers called "Morris notes," as each was signed by Superintendent Morris. These "final settlement certificates," as they were officially called, could not be redeemed for six months. As the certificates had no immediate value, and few believed they would be worth the paper they were printed on in six months, most of the soldiers sold their Morris notes to speculators for a fraction of their supposed value. Many soldiers had to do this to find the money necessary to pay for their journey home. Others took jobs, working for weeks or months before they had sufficient cash to make the trip home (some enlisted men drifted to New York City and found work in businesses that served the British army, which was awaiting Parliament's ratification of the peace accord prior to evacuating

America). One of the soldiers, left in what he described as a "pitiful, for-lorn condition," raged that the government that had been "rigorous in ex-acting my compliance to *my* engagements" had been "careless in performing her contracts with me." Most of the officers fared no better. They had been given their five years' full-pay pension in the form of interest-bearing bonds, but when the second stab at an impost amendment failed, they believed the bonds were worthless, at least for the foreseeable future. Within three years, according to Rufus King, a Massachusetts con-gressman, most of the officers had sold their bonds to speculators.[32]

Unlike Virginia's officers in the French and Indian War, the Continental army officers who were suddenly furloughed in June 1783 did not write a flattering address to their commander in chief. These Revolutionary War officers had not only asked Washington to suspend their furloughs, they had appealed to him to demand of Congress that they not be sent home until they had been fully compensated—including their commuted pension—and that the soldiers not be discharged until each had been paid $80. Wash-ington said there was nothing he could do. As summer settled in, scores of officers—roughly 375 in all—left the army.[33] They were in a sullen mood, their pockets empty, their hearts filled with rancor toward Congress and something less than adoration for Washington. So bitter were the fur-loughed field officers that they canceled a dinner they had planned for the purpose of honoring Washington.[34]

THE JARRING EPISODES THAT OCCURRED in the first half of 1783 were crit-ical for Washington. He had long been committed to American unity in order to resist British colonial policies and, after 1775, to properly wage the war. He believed the American people had united to achieve indepen-dence, and near the end of hostilities he said with little exaggeration that the soldiery "from the different parts of the Continent [though once] strongly disposed, by the habits of education, to despise and quarrel with each other" had become "one patriotic band of brothers."[35] But before 1783, Washington had been so consumed with the manifold problems of winning the war that he had not given much thought to the postwar pe-riod, or if he had, he had not written about it. Talk of a coup d'état by the army and the failed battle for the impost awakened him to a plethora of dangers, not least of which was that the wealthiest and strongest would not long tolerate an ineffectual national government that could not serve their economic interests. Washington knew that the most substantial interests in America—the financial and commercial interests in the North, the slave-owning interest in the South—would ultimately have their way. The question was whether they would realize their ends through the existing Union or in another confederation—or confederations—of their making. Not for nothing did Washington in March 1783 warn of "the forebodings of evil" to American unity that would ensue from Congress's inability to solve the economic muddle.[36]

Washington's very identity was inextricably tied to the existing Union. Not only had he fought for eight bitter years to bring it into being, but the remembrance of his service and achievements was inseparable from the survival of the Union. Alongside that reality, Washington understood that the Union and a strong central government were essential both for opening the West in his lifetime and for securing America from the many predators that stalked the international landscape. The crisis of the Union that he glimpsed in the Newburgh Affair led him to write two important documents within the space of six weeks in 1783, two of "the three great state papers issued in his years in public life," according to historian Don Higginbotham.[37]

The first, "Sentiments on a Peace Establishment," amplified America's need to maintain a standing army in the postwar world and to fashion state militias that were organized and trained in a uniform manner set out by national law.[38] The second, his aforementioned "Circular to the States," was issued in the hope of winning ratification of the impost amendment, but in it Washington argued the necessity of what in time would be called "consolidation," the need to strengthen the powers of the national government, vesting it with sovereign authority over the states. In this time of "political probation," he began cogently, Americans would have to choose between an ineffectual national government and a strapping and vibrant Union. Their choice would determine whether the United States was "respectable and prosperous, or contemptable and miserable as a Nation." There must be "a Supreme Power to regulate and govern the general concerns of the Confederated Republic," he wrote. Unless "the States . . . delegate a larger proportion of Power to Congress . . . the Union cannot be of long duration" and "every thing must tend to Anarchy and confusion." The choice facing the American people was simple, for "without an entire conformity to the Spirit of Union, we cannot exist as an Independent Power."[39]

The Newburgh crisis was important for Washington in another fashion. He divined Hamilton's ingenuous—or craven—handiwork in the conspiracy. He knew that his former aide had endeavored to "maugre the justice" of the army's cause and to "use as mere Puppets" both the army and certain officers as a means "to establish Continental funds." Hamilton, he knew, had been willing even to "make a sacrifice of the Army and all its interests" to serve his own ends.[40] Whatever Washington had thought of Hamilton before this, he now knew the frightening and menacing lengths to which his former aide would go. Some men would have found the revelation so disquieting that they would have cut their ties to an individual given to intrigue and potentially risky machinations. It brought Washington closer to Hamilton. With his unsurpassed intellect, deft feel for politics, raw ambition, combativeness, and close ties to the mercantile and moneyed interests certain to dominate the middle Atlantic states, Hamilton was a force to be reckoned with. Aware of the lengths to which Hamilton had been willing to go to destroy Lee and Gates, among others, Washington did not wish to incur his enmity. Even more, should the need arise, Washington wanted to be able to draw on the benefits that Hamilton might provide.

Finally, Washington's actions, as Hamilton had promised, had enhanced his reputation. At Princeton, General Washington became the toast of choice at meals, a congressman reported. In that same spirit, David Howell, a Rhode Island congressman, gushed: "I admire [Washington] almost to a pitch of Idolatry," adding that the commander in chief was widely seen as "the Sheat anchor of the cause." That many in Congress shared Howell's reverence seems apparent, as the delegates in September ordered an equestrian statue of Washington erected at whatever locale was eventually designated as the capital of the United States.[41]

FOUR DAYS AFTER HIS THEATRICS in the Temple, Washington learned that a preliminary peace treaty with Great Britain had been signed (it would become official once Britain reached an accord with France). He must have been overjoyed, but habituated to shielding every emotion from the outside world, he offered a characteristically pedestrian response in public: "we have abundant reason to be pleased at the event." There was another reason for his low-key response. Washington was not given to looking backward. He dwelled in the present, with his eyes trained on the future. The war was as good as over, and it was rapidly being subsumed by another issue. As he remarked to a correspondent only ten days after learning of the peace accord, independence would be meaningless unless "local politics, and unreasonable jealousies . . . yield to such a constitution as will embrace the whole and make our Union respectable."[42] Washington knew in March 1783 what would be the next great political battlefield in America, and he had chosen the side with which he would ally.

Shortly after learning of the treaty, Washington and his British counterpart, Sir Guy Carleton, issued orders that hostilities were to cease, though the Continental army would remain intact until all prisoners of war were released and the British army abandoned New York City and sailed from America. Three months passed before every captive was freed, and it was not until late November that the redcoats finally departed. In the interim, Washington undertook an arduous three-week vacation in the tangled rural regions of northern New York, a jaunt on which he searched for, and purchased, attractive real estate in the region that had been the scene of the Sullivan Expedition. Washington also spent an additional ten weeks in Princeton discussing with Congress its plans for the postwar army. Though he urged that only a modest army be maintained—merely 2,631 men—Congress took no action. In fact, save for commutation, none of Washington's celebrated recommendations in 1783 were realized for several years.[43]

When Washington learned that the British army was packing for its departure, he said farewell to the army in a lengthy, formal address in which he focused as much on the future as on the past. His greatest achievement, he appeared to say, had been to successfully create "a disciplined Army . . . from such raw materials." He said nothing of the contributions made by Gates or Greene to America's victory, but he elaborated yet again on the need to see that the powers of the national government be enhanced, lest the "honour, dignity, and justice of the nation . . . be lost forever."[44]

The handful of officers who remained in the army sent Washington an address of their own. They were bitter over how the country had treated them—their "sufferings & services seem already to be forgotten by multitudes," Timothy Pickering, the quartermaster general, had raged in private—and many were still rankled by what they felt had been Washington's halfhearted assistance on their behalf.[45] Making no attempt to hide their sour feelings, the officers literally sent their address to the commander in chief, mailing their composition rather than hand-delivering it. Lavish praise was not to be found in the two-page disquisition. The officers never mentioned Washington's role in gaining the American victory, though they lauded his "patriotism and disinterested virtue." Virtually the entire document dwelled on the injustices done to the army by Congress.[46]

Two weeks after he bade farewell, Washington led what remained of the army—merely a few hundred men from Massachusetts and New York—on its final march. Setting off as dawn spilled over the landscape, the soldiers came down out of the highlands above Manhattan, marching for New York City. At the beginning of the last week in November, the Continental army set foot on Manhattan Island for the first time since November 1776. On November 23, the day appointed for the British army's departure, Washington brought his army to the periphery of New York City. Fittingly for an army that had so often been slow to act during the war, the British were running behind schedule. Two days passed before their last soldier left Manhattan. When the final redcoat exited the city, Washington ordered his men to march in. Under a flawless blue sky, with a chill November wind blowing briskly off the Hudson River, the army set off on the last leg of this trek and of the war. Knox, with a select corps, rode at the head of the army. A martial band, with drums beating and fifes playing, followed. Soldiers carrying flags and banners that stood straight out in the strong breeze came next, followed on foot by civilian authorities, eight abreast. Washington, immaculate in his uniform and majestic astride his powerful white charger, was next, heading up a line of the highest-ranking officers and their staffs. The soldiers, many in threadbare, makeshift uniforms, brought up the rear. The army proceeded down Broadway, lined this day with cheering residents who were anxious for a glimpse of Washington, hailed far and wide as the conqueror of the vaunted British and

Hessians.[47] Washington spent nearly a week in town, attending an array of formal dinners. In his final ceremony, Washington took leave of his officers at a noon repast at Fraunces Tavern.

Tables were set with cold meats and fruit, bottles of wine and brandy. But little was consumed, and no speeches were given. After all these years and all the tensions of this year, there was not much to be said. Washington did not know many of the men who were present. Most of those who had served the longest with him had been furloughed against their will six months earlier. Only Generals Knox, Steuben, McDougall, and Timothy Pickering—who once had been Washington's aide—had been with the commander in chief over the long haul. Not every officer still in the army bothered to attend, nor did any who were out of the army but living nearby. Colonel Hamilton, for instance, who now practiced law in Manhattan and lived just a couple of blocks from Fraunces Tavern, chose not to attend. As the good-byes were said and Washington embraced each man, tears were shed as men were moved both by affection for one another and by the realization that an epoch in their lives—perhaps the most exciting and meaningful period they would ever experience—was ending this day. When all the farewells were said, Washington hurried out the door and rode for Annapolis, where the footloose Congress had moved.[48]

Two items remained on Washington's agenda as commander in chief. One was to submit the final installment of his wartime expense account. When appointed commander of the Continental army in 1775, Washington had agreed to serve without a salary, asking only that he be compensated for his expenses. Anticipating a brief war, he had initially paid his expenses out of pocket, but beginning in 1777, having realized that this would be an extremely long conflict, he turned to borrowing and filing regularly for reimbursement. When he arrived in Annapolis, Washington submitted his final expense statement covering the previous two weeks. (In January, he received the balance owed him—$857 and 52/90 of a dollar. That final installment brought his total expenses for the entire war to $64,355.)[49]

Washington's second wish was to resign his commission and return to Mount Vernon. Although his surrender of power amazed his contemporaries, and continues to astonish some, Washington's act was hardly startling. He was a civilian first—he spent only about 15 percent of his adult life soldiering—and he longed to return to the charms of home and to put Mount Vernon and his finances in good order. Even more, perhaps, no position existed that could possibly have been fulfilling for Washington. After eight years in command of a wartime army, he had no desire to remain the head of a tiny peacetime army that could not be adequately funded. A chief executive did not exist under the Articles of Confederation, and Washington had no wish to be part of Virginia's delegation to Congress, where he would do little more than listen to endless speeches and wearying debates. The two most important positions were the diplomatic posts in Versailles and London, but neither a life in diplomacy nor the protracted absence from Mount Vernon that it would entail appealed to him. Washington's reputation was made. He wanted to go home and bask in the acclaim he had yearned for since his youth. And he longed to turn his attention, as he had before the war, to increasing his fortune.

Washington spent four days in Annapolis. On his last night there, Congress gave a dinner in his honor that was attended by up to three hundred persons. "Every man seemed to be in Heaven" at the opportunity to be near America's paladin, said one congressman, who added that the occasion was so solemn that "not a soul got drunk." Thirteen toasts were offered. Washington gave the last one: "Competent powers to congress for general purposes." The next morning, he resigned his commission, offering up a muted little speech to Congress and galleries packed, as one congressman noted, with "people of the first fashion" who had come to pay "their affectionate attachment to our illustrious Hero . . . by a most copious shedding of tears."

Washington's speech took no more than three or four minutes to deliver. Speaking in a barely audible voice, he took no credit for America's victory, instead attributing it to the steadfastness and adeptness of his officers, the unfaltering will of the American people, and the hand of God. (He failed to acknowledge French assistance, the one hundred thousand men who had served in the Continental army, or the two hundred thousand or so who had soldiered, and often fought, in the state militias.) The United States had emerged an independent and sovereign nation, he said, and he concluded with a simple announcement: "I retire from the great theater of Action."[50] After a final bow to all, Washington departed, hurrying out the door to his waiting horse. He sped away for Mount Vernon, which he reached on Christmas Eve 1783 as the last tilting rays of light crept over the estate that he loved so much.

8

SOARING TO THE PINNACLE

WASHINGTON WAS A STRANGER to Mount Vernon. During his eight and a half years as commander in chief, he had spent but three days at his estate while en route to Yorktown and another week there following Cornwallis's surrender—ten days out of some three thousand wartime days. The Washington who returned from the war was an Olympian figure, and he seemed to construct, if not a new identity, one that was more suitable to his exalted standing. The prewar indulgences that he had enjoyed, including frequent mirthful nights with companions at the gaming table and clusters of days given over to foxhunting, were largely abandoned, and so too were long vacations at spas in the leafy western mountains. He received visitors to Mount Vernon cordially but formally, and his correspondence, never lighthearted, not only turned especially sober, but was restricted almost solely to business concerns or matters of state. Though Washington held no office between 1784 and early 1789, he hardly acted like a private citizen, and certainly not like a carefree man. His habits were stately. Already looked on reverentially as "the deliverer of his Country," Washington also wished to be seen—as a Georgia public official said of him in 1787—as a "politician and States-man" who was ever "virtuous and useful."[1]

When he came home at Christmas 1783, Washington thought his public career was over. Business ventures might pull him away from home and hearth temporarily—he in fact, traveled to Fredericksburg on business only six weeks after returning home—but he anticipated living out his days at

Mount Vernon. With "heartfelt satisfaction," he said, he was delighted to be "free of the bustle of a camp & the busy scenes of public life," not to mention his endless "watchful days & sleepless Nights" as commander in chief.[2]

Washington's joy at escaping public responsibilities was tempered somewhat by the melancholy realization that much of his life was behind him. On the cusp of his fifty-second birthday when he came home, he did not think much time was left to him. Few in the eighteenth century lived more than sixty-five or seventy years, and he did not expect to be the exception, especially as it was distressingly commonplace for men in the Washington family to die young. Washington's father and three half-brothers had perished without having reached a fiftieth birthday. While he did not dwell on it, Washington knew that he was "descending the hill" he "had been . . . climbing," as he put it. All that he wanted, he said, was to spend his remaining time quietly and peacefully, reaping, as he remarked in a rare candid moment, "a rich harvest" of acclaim, his reward for eight difficult years at war.[3]

He never put public affairs out of his mind, but other matters preoccupied him in the early years of his retirement. Shortly before the war broke out, Washington had begun to expand Mount Vernon, contemplating large additions to the house, as well as a piazza on the back and a cupola on top of the dwelling. He envisaged transforming his dignified country farmhouse into an elegant mansion suitable for a great planter aristocrat. Work had been under way for a decade, and much remained to be done when he came home. Washington assumed supervision of the final stages of the massive remodeling project—it was finally completed in 1786, and thereafter looked more or less as it does today—while devoting just as much time and thought to the grounds of his estate. From wartime acquaintances throughout the United States and abroad, he acquired and planted an enormous variety of trees, shrubs, and flowers, searched out grass seed suitable for his climate, and found an array of exotic animals for Mount Vernon.

Washington had retained his cousin Lund Washington to manage the estate during his wartime absence, and following hostilities he continued to employ a farm manager. Yet Washington was too much the micromanager to surrender matters to someone else. He planned work schedules and task assignments for his labor force, which in 1786 included 216 slaves scattered over the five separate farms that constituted Mount Vernon, and closely supervised their toil. Washington was also one of the first American farmers to embark on the new scientific agriculture that had blossomed in England. He acquired a considerable library of agrarian tracts, which he used in his experimentation with varieties of crops, fertilizers, and farm animals. Washington's work habits had not changed over the years, but directly after the war he was especially driven, remarking that his "wants are pressing." Not only had Mount Vernon failed to produce a penny of profit during the war, but Washington estimated that he had lost £10,000 when debtors paid him in depreciated paper money worth about one fourth the face value of the prewar cash and merchandise that he had loaned them. Moreover, he owed taxes, which had skyrocketed in Virginia during the war, as they had everywhere else, and years of back wages had to be paid to Lund and the craftsmen who were working on his mansion. Washington got along by calling in some £4,000 in loans, selling at below face value some of the public securities he received from Congress for his wartime expenses, and parting with some of his lands in Pennsylvania and Virginia. Although he was in alarming financial straits when he came home, Washington's prospects were always good. His income from the Custis properties routinely exceeded his earnings from Mount Vernon, and within two years Mount Vernon itself was profusely productive once again. During the fifteen years following the war, its operations alone grossed between $4,500 and $15,000 annually, this at a time when a skilled craftsman was fortunate to earn a few hundred dollars working fifty-two weeks a year. For years, too, Washington was permitted to pay his taxes with commodities—as were all Virginians—and throughout the 1780s his "creditors let their claims sleep," as he put it, while awaiting the return of sound money.[4]

Even as Washington coped with his finances—and wrote letter after letter lamenting his plight, missives in which he sought to convey the impression that he lived "in a small villa" and hovered on the precipice of ruin—he took great economic risks.[5] He once again became active in the Dismal Swamp Company, which he and nine other merchants and planters had founded in 1763 in a venture to find wealth through lumbering and the construction of a canal to link Albemarle Sound to the Elizabeth River. The company had made little headway before the war, and it got off to a rocky start following hostilities. In 1784, with Washington serving as a manager, the Dismal Swamp Company sought without success to procure a Dutch loan that might have set its operations moving smoothly. Ever after, this venture was largely a matter of chasing after rainbows. In 1795, Washington finally sold his interest in the company to Light Horse Harry Lee for $20,000. When Lee could not meet his payments, the stock reverted to Washington's estate. Some of the general's heirs eventually realized something from his investment when the company at last paid dividends, eleven years after Washington's death.[6]

Nine months after returning home, Washington journeyed west to look after his vast property holdings near Fort Pitt and beyond. Today, many dreaded business trips involve a brief flight and a couple of nights away from home. Washington's 1784 trek consumed thirty-four days and spanned 680 miles, all of it made on horseback and much of it through a cold, seemingly incessant September rain. Washington slept some nights in his tent and others in private residences, which he thought ranged in quality from "pitiful" to "tolerable good." He was accompanied by three other men, who, like Washington, brought along a slave or two. Ten days into the trip, the travelers crossed into Pennsylvania, and four days later, they reached the site of Fort Necessity, where Washington owned 234 acres and a house. Never given to reliving the past, and most assuredly not wishing to be reminded of his military failure at this spot, Washington never alluded in his diary to the desperate battle he had fought in his doomed circular fort; instead, he ruminated on the commercial possibilities of the area (it would be an excellent site for a tavern, he thought). From there, the party rode deeper into Appalachia, day after day advancing from one green ridge to another, endlessly climbing forbiddingly steep, craggy inclines and descending into the gloomy and entangling—and unremittingly wet—forest undergrowth. They came first to Washington's Bottom, a 1,644-acre tract on the Youghiogheny River. Washington had purchased this land and constructed a grist mill on it before the War of Independence. From there the sodden party rode farther west, crossing the Youghiogheny and the Monongahela before they reached Millers Run at Chartiers Creek, 2,818 acres of lush meadow land a few miles southwest of the head of the Ohio. Washington had acquired this parcel of land in 1770.[7]

Thirteen farms dotted the landscape at Millers Run, each inhabited by a family of squatters, people who had simply dropped anchor on Washington's property, clearing the land, putting in crops of corn and wheat, building houses and barns, and fencing their pastures. They had never paid Washington a cent. He was not happy. These people who had "pretensions" to his property, as he put it, must purchase his land or pay him to lease their farms, including what was owed for the entire time they had squatted. He summoned the settlers to a meeting. When every family had arrived, Washington announced in unequivocal terms that they were trespassers. They had to pay up or get out. It was a rancorous meeting. These people—for the most part hard-nosed, fiercely independent Scotch-Irish—cared little that America's most famous citizen was standing before them making demands. They were not awed by General Washington. Some of them had also fought Indians or borne arms in the War of Independence, helping to win this land for America. They also looked askance at Washington's title to this Pennsylvania property, as it bore the seals of colonial Virginia and of the hated British government. From their vantage point, they had as much right, and probably more, to this land as did George Washington. General Washington may have been accustomed to deference, but the way these farmers saw things, they had secured the land, breaking it with the sweat of their brows and living among potentially hostile Indians while they were at it. They had made the land their own, and they had no intention of kowtowing to this Johnny-come-lately, even if he was the most revered American. They refused to budge or to pay. Washington was furious. His volcanic temper erupting, he departed, threatening to take them to court. He hurried to the office of a backwoods lawyer in present-day Uniontown, Pennsylvania, who agreed to take the case. The attorney advised Washington not to seek back payment, lest the squatters burn down everything they had constructed and generally pillage the land while they were at it. Two years later, Washington's lawyer won his client's case, somehow persuading a jury in western Pennsylvania to affirm Washington's title to the land in dispute. But the squatters refused to rent from Washington. They wanted nothing to do with him or his land, and they moved away in search of farmland elsewhere. Time passed before the general found tenants for Millers Run, and he did not succeed in selling this tract until 1796, more than a quarter century after he acquired it.[8]

Washington had planned to go farther west, taking another look at much of the remainder of his forty thousand frontier acres in what today is West Virginia, Kentucky, and Ohio, land that he had garnered through surveying, soldiering, and, in one instance, purchasing bounty lands awarded to another soldier under the Proclamation of 1763.[9] He was especially interested in heading back down the Great Kanawha River for another visit to his bounty lands, which Virginia had officially awarded him once it was independent of royal authority. But shortly after his unpleasant meeting with the squatters, Washington learned that the Indians along the Ohio were restless. He cut his journey short.

Washington chose a different route for his homeward trek. He came straight south from Millers Run to the confluence of the Cheat and Monongahela rivers, near present-day Morgantown, West Virginia, after which he angled in a southeasterly direction to the North Branch of the Potomac. From there, proceeding along ridges ablaze with autumn's color, he rode to the South Branch of that river.[10] He had another project in mind and was scouting the dark hinterland to see whether it was viable. Since before the war, Washington had been involved in an undertaking of potentially grandiose proportions. He nurtured the hope of a Potomac canal, an idea that had first been hatched by the initial investors in the Ohio Company in 1747. Like Lawrence and others before him, Washington dreamed of linking the Atlantic to the Ohio Country. Doing so, he knew, would be a monumental challenge. The Potomac River would have to be coupled by canal and roads for portage to western waterways and ultimately to the Ohio. In addition, the rugged Great and Little Falls near the present District of Columbia would somehow have to be surmounted, as would three major rapids near present-day Harpers Ferry, West Virginia. Nearly 175 miles of the Potomac River between the tidewater and the western rivers would also have to be cleared. It was an endeavor that only a supreme risk taker and visionary would contemplate. If the company succeeded, the East would be linked to the trans-Appalachian West, an essential step in Washington's dream—and the reveries of all nationalists—of holding together a United States that stretched all the way to the Mississippi River. But that was only one of Washington's objectives. Confessing that he was "not . . . disinterested" economically, he knew that if his project succeeded, the lush bottomlands that he owned out west would soar in value. Nor was that all. The sky would be the limit on the value of much of the real estate that he owned in the East, some seven thousand acres in seven Virginia and Maryland counties, as well as property in Alexandria, which was likely to become the great American metropolis if a Potomac canal became operational.[11] Washington's activities on behalf of his ambition for the Potomac River were textbook examples of a savvy political operator at work.

Before the war, Washington had joined with entrepreneurs from Maryland to launch his project. Operating in Williamsburg, he secured the House of Burgesses' authorization for a private company to open the Potomac, though he failed to pry loose public funding for his private initiative. Washington was thwarted not because the assesmblymen were averse to having taxpayers facilitate the high rollers, but when Virginians who dreamed of a James River canal blocked the Potomac venture. They wanted funding for their pet endeavor. Washington's partners in Maryland were even less successful. Their initiative in the Maryland assembly foundered when businessmen in Baltimore, anticipating that the canal would redirect much of the city's commerce to Alexandria, killed the undertaking.

After the war, Washington, an American hero who was also considerably better attuned to political realities, rapidly resurrected his pet project. He renewed his activism after Jefferson, who owned considerable property on the James River, wrote him in March 1784. Jefferson advanced the idea of seeking help from the Virginia assembly for canal projects on both the James—which might be tied to the Ohio via the Kanawha River, the site of much of Washington's bounty lands—and the Potomac. It was urgent that Virginia move quickly, Jefferson said, lest New York beat it to the punch by opening a canal via the Mohawk River that would couple the Hudson River to Lake Erie. Virginia's two rivers, said Jefferson, were "the true door to the Western commerce," and he also mentioned that once those rivers were tied to the Ohio, Virginia could take on other canal projects that would link the Ohio Valley to Detroit, which, according to his calculations, was closer to Alexandria and Richmond than to New York City. Washington responded that his thinking "coincides perfectly with yours." Jefferson told others that he wished to use the "popularity of [Washington's] name" to get what he wanted from the Virginia legislature. Misjudging the depth of his correspondent's passion for the Potomac River endeavor, Jefferson added that he believed by bringing Washington into his scheme, he would be providing the old soldier with "a noble amusement in his retirement." If

Jefferson wished to use Washington, the general saw that Jefferson could be useful to him. As Jefferson was a member of Congress, which continued to meet in Annapolis, Washington saw him as a conduit for convincing Maryland's leadership that a canal to the West would be opened in the near future.[12]

Washington also turned to Madison, who had left Congress for the Virginia assembly early in 1784. During the last year of the war, Washington had struck up a correspondence with Madison after being told that the young Virginian had become a power in Congress. Though he had met Madison on several occasions, Washington was so unfamiliar with him that he misspelled his name in his earliest letters. Once the Potomac canal initiative took shape in 1784, Washington renewed his correspondence with Madison. Though Madison was cool to the idea of a Potomac canal, thinking it unlikely to succeed, he rapidly allied with Washington. Like Washington, Madison feared losing the West, and he thought that making a stab at completing the canal would soothe the settlers beyond the mountains. He also was eager to put himself in Washington's orbit.

In the fall of 1784, Washington moved into high gear. He wrote Congress, urging that the Ohio River and its tributaries be surveyed, asked the governor of Virginia to sanction companies to open the Potomac and James, and traveled to Richmond, the new state capital, to lobby personally for public funding and to line up support among businessmen and municipal officials. In the weeks that followed, Madison acted as Washington's floor manager in the legislature. Things went well enough in Richmond, though from the outset Washington knew that Virginia would not unilaterally finance a Potomac undertaking. Maryland would have to provide its share of funds. Jefferson had done the spadework, but he had departed to take Franklin's place as minister to France. Understanding that he would have to do the work himself, Washington asked Madison to have the Virginia assembly appoint a committee to meet with Maryland's officials. The legislators wasted no time in naming Washington, General Gates, and Thomas Blackburn to the committee that was to journey to Annapolis for the meeting.[13]

Gates—"my bosom friend," Washington remarked sarcastically—was ill throughout the weeklong conference, and Blackburn did not attend, leaving Washington to "fix matters" by himself, as he put it, with a ten-member delegation from Maryland. The meeting was held during the Christmas season, and if it was not bad enough to be away from home at that time of the year, Washington found that days of sitting and haggling resulted in "Heavy, & painful oppressions of the head, and other disagreeable sensations." Nevertheless, he managed, and both Washington and Maryland's delegates eventually made significant recommendations to their respective legislatures. While Madison shepherded their proposals through the Virginia assembly, Washington remained in Annapolis to lobby until the Maryland legislature also approved an identical bill. Each state authorized the Potomac Company, capitalized it at $222,222— consisting of five hundred shares worth $444 apiece—and purchased fifty shares. Virginia not only simultaneously created the James River Company, it awarded Washington fifty shares in the Potomac Company and one hundred in the other, so that altogether the two states provided more than $66,000, or nearly one quarter, of the start-up capital for the Potomac River undertaking.[14]

IN MARCH 1785, JUST BEFORE THE COMPANY began operations, Washington hosted a conference of commissioners from the two states to settle jurisdictional matters and make preparations for clearing the portage roads. The meeting had ramifications beyond the issue of navigating the Potomac. At its conclusion, the commissioners urged further meetings among the states to provide for uniform trade policies throughout the Union.[15]

By May, the company was up and running. Washington, who purchased five shares in each company, an investment of $4,400, was elected its president, an office he held for four years, all the while declining a salary. He also refused to accept the 150 shares that Virginia had given him in the two companies, insisting for all to hear (his remarks were read in the Virginia assembly, as he knew would be the case) that he would not break his longstanding vow "to shut my hand against every pecuniary recompense" while in the public service. In the end, Washington accepted a compromise solution. He would keep the shares, but all dividends would go to charity. The arrangement kept the public investment in the Potomac River project intact, and it enabled Washington, who for a year had sought public assistance for a private business venture from which he stood to realize a fortune, to adhere to his lofty oath. He worried a bit that some might see his act as "an ostentatious display of disinterestedness," though he doubt-less expected, as Jefferson assured him was the case, that his countrymen would find his "motive . . . pure and without any alloy." If any did not see his actions in that light, none dared say so.[16]

For eighteen months before the Potomac Company commenced busi-ness, Washington had been convinced that, if properly capitalized, work to link east and west via the Potomac River would be immensely rewarding, both personally and for the United States. When he started what he once called his "great political work" on behalf of this project, Washington had "despair[ed] of any aid from the public." But the company had what he described as "a favourable beginning," and to Washington, its future ap-peared rosy. He and his managers rapidly hired workers and specialists. Three years later, on the eve of his presidency, while telling potential in-vestors that navigation was "in a fair way of being opened in as short a time . . . as could have been expected," Washington reported privately to the board of directors that operations had been "retarded" and that for the foreseeable future the best that could be expected was "a partial though not a perfect Navigation" in the region above the falls and below Fort Cumberland. In short, linkage to the Ohio and commerce from one end of the Potomac to the other was years away, if it could ever be attained.[17]

The harsh reality that he divulged in private was a foretaste of lingering woes. Though Washington remained hopeful of eventual success, the company's engineers were overmatched and the enterprise was chroni-cally underfunded. Often lacking the needed technical competence, the company's so-called experts were reduced to trial and error when con-fronted by rapids on the approach to Harpers Ferry and by the Little Falls and the Great Falls near Georgetown. Their floundering experimentation burned the company's capital and squandered the lives of innumerable workers. After 10 percent of the free labor force died within two years, the company turned to slave labor. The company eventually constructed five canals and managed to endure for forty-three years, though it never turned a profit in Washington's lifetime. It paid its first dividend three years after his demise, yet soon thereafter it was losing money again. In the nineteenth century, it had to compete first with the National Road, which reached Wheeling on the Ohio River in 1818, and later with the railroad, which dealt a crippling blow to most canal projects, including the Potomac River enterprise.[18]

DESPITE ECONOMIC ADVERSITY AND BUSINESS disappointments, Washington was happy. He was with Martha, and his stepgrandchildren, the children of Jacky Custis, frequently visited or even lived at Mount Vernon. Washington was surprised that it took him nearly two months to acclimate to retirement, but once he made the adjustment, he told correspondents of his "great delight" in the "pursuits . . . of a rural nature," living with the "implements of Husbandry & Lambkins around me." His correspondence reflected the dramatic changes in his day-to-day existence. During his second year at home, Washington wrote almost as much about the difficulty of growing tobacco or the proper method of manuring his fields as he did of public affairs.[19]

He basked in the adulation of his countrymen, and foreigners heaped praise on him as well. Benjamin Franklin wrote that "your long and painful Labours . . . have laid us all under eternal Obligations." A former Continental army officer told him that he would "ever esteem it one of the greatest Honors of my life that I served my Country . . . under the Direction of Genl. Washington." Frenchmen called Washington "the Great Hero of the Western World" and the "Saviour of His Country, the Benefactor of Mankind, the Protecting Angel of liberty, the pride of America." One Frenchman compared him to Caesar but added that because Washington had not abused his powers, the American people "shall be happier" than were the Romans. Acquaintances in the French army informed Washington that "tributes of praise" were offered to him from throughout Europe, where he was seen as a "Great Man." Even some in England thanked Washington for having defeated Great Britain, as it might save liberty there as Washington and the Continentals had saved it in America. The common theme in the tributes that poured in was that Washington had displayed "consummate abilities and unparalleled virtue" and that he was the "Commanding Character" of his age.[20]

Before the war, a guest dropped in occasionally at Mount Vernon. After the war, hardly a day passed that several visitors did not knock on the front door of Washington's mansion. They were sightseers and opportunists, former army officers and public officials from every state. For youth of the time, a visit to Mount Vernon became a part of one's finishing school, much as traveling abroad would be for the affluent in succeeding generations. For adults the trip was made to pay homage, and for some it was nearly a religious experience. "No pilgrim ever approached mecca with deeper enthusiasm," one visitor noted. So many came that Washington at times lost track of his guests' names or their calling in life. Now and again, he noted in his diary that he had dined with "a Mr. Clare," "a Mr. Stephens," "a Doctr Graham," "two reverend Gentlemen," or "a Mr. Noah Webster."[21] Painters and sculptors descended on Mount Vernon in profusion as well. Fifteen years after Washington hired Charles Willson Peale in 1772 to paint what he had believed would be the only portrait ever made of him, copies of numerous wartime and retirement renderings of Washington spread through the land, making him uniquely recognizable in that era before photography.

On occasion, someone wrote him about the war. He had not been home long when a correspondent asked about his relationship with General Charles Lee, but Washington responded that he wished to neither rehash the war nor defend himself against his critics. He longed for his remaining days to be "undisturbed and tranquil," he said.[22] But Washington was not as disinterested as he wished others to believe. He took pains to address both his greatest defeat and his most important triumph, eager to be absolved of the former and to gain full credit for the latter. He wrote to William Gordon, a Roxbury, Massachusetts, clergyman who was writing a history of the winning of independence, that his decision to defend Fort Washington was in response to Congress's order that the post be "pertinaciously held," a claim he knew was patently untrue. He also distorted history when, writing to a New Englander whom he thought likely to publish the letter, Washington claimed not only that he and Rochambeau had agreed to try to trap Cornwallis in Virginia before de Grasse was asked to bring his fleet to the Chesapeake, but that he had abandoned all thoughts of attacking New York more than a year prior to Yorktown.[23]

Washington knew that his Revolutionary War papers would be a key element in assuring his lasting fame, and six months before Yorktown he somehow persuaded the penniless Congress to fund the transcription of his papers. A host of secretaries, headed by Lieutenant Colonel Richard Varick, worked on the project in Poughkeepsie for more than two years,

eventually completing twenty-eight volumes of papers. Washington carefully planned their shipment to Mount Vernon in the last weeks of the
war. In one of the last duties assigned any of his soldiers, the papers were
transported under guard in six large wagons, and all had safely reached his
mansion by the time Washington arrived home.[24]

Washington also retained David Humphreys, one of his former aides, to
write his official biography. Humphreys had earlier urged his former
commander to write his memoirs, but Washington declined, saying that he
lacked the time, and besides, his "defective education" left him ill-
equipped for such an undertaking. In reality, Washington had always shied
away from obvious self-promotion. "I consider it . . . pitiful vanity to court
applause," he said. He preferred that others sow the approbation that he
would harvest. Engaging Humphreys not only assured Washington that
his first biographer would be a blindly loyal follower, it gave the general
the opportunity to manage the endeavor.[25]

At Washington's invitation, Humphreys moved in 1787 to Mount Vernon, where during a residence of some eighteen months he was given access to the general's correspondence and permitted to interview his subject.
Washington also read through and corrected Humphreys's first draft.
Washington ordinarily had a nearly unerring facility for picking the right
person for the job, but he erred in retaining Humphreys, who managed to
crank out only a brief biography. His life history of Washington consisted
of a few pages on the French and Indian War in which he whitewashed his
subject's failures, a brief section on Washington's postwar years, and, incredibly, merely two paragraphs on the Revolutionary War. Meager as it
was, only about 10 percent of what Humphreys had written—merely five
pages—was published in Washington's lifetime.[26]

One reason Washington may have been eager to retain Humphreys was
that he feared his reputation had been sullied through his association with
and support of the Society of the Cincinnati. Only some thirty days after
the sinister activities at Newburgh, steps were taken by officers in the
Continental army to create the organization. They claimed the Cincinnati
was to be merely a fraternal order that might also provide beneficence to
those who fell on hard times. It sounded harmless, even noble, and it
may have been, but many Americans who had never fully trusted the officer corps were deeply suspicious of the Cincinnati. Remembering the

threats made at Newburgh, not a few Americans anticipated that in time the organization would become politically intrusive. As membership in the Cincinnati was to be hereditary, the paramount fear aroused by the new organization was that it would pave the way for the establishment of a hereditary aristocracy. Initially, Washington dismissed the objections of the critics as due to "ignorance, envy & perhaps worse motives." He grew wary after the Massachusetts assembly denounced the organization, and he changed step entirely following Jefferson's warning that he might be tarnished through his association with the Cincinnati. Thereafter, while protesting that his motives in being part of the Cincinnati were "immaculate," Washington asked not to be reelected as president of the society (he had been chosen as the Cincinnati's first president just prior to the army's demobilization), and he attempted to persuade the organization to rethink its hereditary membership policies. Washington even had Humphreys carry his message to the Cincinnati and lobby for change. When he failed on all counts—the members of the Cincinnati repeatedly reelected him as their president—Washington tried to disassociate himself as much as possible by simply not attending the society's meetings.[27]

WASHINGTON NEVER SOUGHT HELP from Congress for his Potomac canal venture. With Congress dependent on the states for its revenue, he knew that the rival interests of the states—what he habitually referred to as provincial "jealousies"—would defeat the measure. Besides, he added, it was nearly impossible to overcome the "inertitude which prevails in Congress" against enacting "great, & truly wise" policies that were in the national interest. He had not been home a month before he lamented that the states' unwillingness to yield powers to Congress might mean that the recent struggle for "peace & independency" was "to very little purpose." Washington's trip to western Pennsylvania led him to another unsettling conclusion: "The Western settlers . . . stand as it were upon a pivot—the touch of a feather, would turn them any way," including into the arms of Spain, which controlled the Mississippi River, the trans-Appalachian farmers' highway to the markets in the outer world.[28]

The realization only strengthened Washington's conviction that until a canal linked east and west, the United States could not be assured that it would retain the domain beyond the mountains that it had won in the

Treaty of Paris. This reinforced his belief that it was necessary to have a national government that could assist endeavors that were vital to the national interest. During the war, Washington had come to believe that it was essential to increase the power of the central government. Before he had been home a year, he had concluded that merely giving Congress greater powers would not be sufficient. He had moved toward the view that the Articles of Confederation had to be drastically overhauled. As structured, the Articles assured that the states would be "inattentive to every thing which is not local & self interestg." History, he said, demonstrated that the states would oppose "each other upon all occasions" and "counteract . . . the plans of the United States." The "foederal Government is a name without substance," he complained in 1784, for the states were not "bound by its edicts."[29]

Washington's wartime experiences had given him a national perspective. Perhaps no other American was any longer so impatient with provincial interests. Or, better, maybe no one else was more understanding of the necessity to secure the national interest, even if that meant subordinating local concerns. Washington was not a political theorist, and he never attempted to lay out a well-conceived framework of state versus national powers, but he was a realist who saw nations as predators. Nation-states sought wealth and power, and for the most part they were in the business of serving the most wealthy and powerful interests within their realms. Washington knew that North America, filled as it was with potential wealth, had attracted and would continue to draw Europe's great powers like a magnet. America's best hope for security was to be strong enough to protect itself. To achieve that end, he knew that the American people must remain united in a national union, and the central government must have the authority that would enable it to increase the nation's power. To accomplish these ends, the government of the United States had to be capable of satisfying the innumerable interests of its own people, and it especially had to have the power to help its most powerful citizens achieve their goals.

Washington knew that the war could not have been won except as a national endeavor, and he also understood that defending the frontiers, opening the West, safeguarding and expanding America's foreign commerce, and facilitating interstate trade could best be accomplished by a potent United States government. If the United States was not made strong enough to achieve these ends, it would cease to exist, broken up by having become "the sport of European politics" or, perhaps, by having failed to satisfy its most ambitious and acquisitive citizens. In either case, he said, the demise of the United States would have come about because the American people had been "the victim of [their] own folly." One week after return-ing home from the war, he already saw that because of the weakness of the national government, "important advantages are lost." He was thinking of the inability of the national government to secure western posts and force the British army out of its installations in trans-Appalachia, but he knew that other advantages would be lost if "the Sovereign has not suffi-cient power to act."[30]

It cannot be denied that the changes Washington urged would advance his personal interests. That does not mean he recommended these politi-cal changes for his own advantage. By soldiering for eight difficult years, he had demonstrated his willingness to make enormous personal sacrifices for a greater public good, and one would like to think that following his return to his civilian pursuits as a planter and businessman, nothing super-seded the national interest in Washington's mind. Before the war, how-ever, Washington had often used his power and influence in the House of Burgesses for his own ends, and it would be more creditable had he, on oc-casion, stood for something after 1783 that would have been to his detri-ment. Most people, including those in public life, are self-serving. It goes against human nature not to be. Washington was still vigorous when he returned home from the war. He may not have anticipated a long life, but he knew that he might live another quarter century or more. That possi-bility made it especially important that he be able to sell or lease his west-ern lands, successfully market what was produced at Mount Vernon and on his dower lands, and realize the full face value of all money owed him. Every reform he advocated would enhance the likelihood that he would achieve these ends, and in the near term. It is a habit of the human condi-tion to see an affinity between one's personal interests and the greater gen-eral good, and a habit, too, to exaggerate the perils that accompany a course that is not in one's interests. Washington was no exception to this rule.

While America faced very real problems in the aftermath of the war, Washington overstated the imminent threat arising from these difficulties. The optimism that he radiated with regard to the purportedly fast-approaching success of his Potomac canal project—and his awareness that similar endeavors were in the works in other parts of the country—suggests that he believed the United States was in no immediate danger of losing its western territories. There was much talk in the 1780s, some of it by Washington, of the plight of the nation's farmers. Though it was true that yeomen had lost their old imperial markets, they had found new ones through their escape from the British Empire. The new nation was weak, to be sure, but a long period of peace seemed in the offing. Not only did the United States remain an ally of France, all signs indicated that Great Britain was in no mood to become embroiled in another major North American war. America faced severe economic problems, but every American war in the eighteenth century had been followed by something akin to a depression, and the one that had come in the wake of the War of Independence was showing signs of improvement within eighteen months. No secessionist movements existed within the United States. Nor was there much of a groundswell for constitutional reform from among the mass of the citizenry. The calls for substantive constitutional remodeling came almost exclusively from major speculators, the urban financial and commercial centers in the North, and southern planters and slave owners whose states were a sectional minority in the Articles of Confederation and whose slave-owning properties lacked adequate safeguards under the existing framework.

In short, interests of entrenched wealth and power were at the forefront, alleging that a great crisis had beset the United States and that immediate change was imperative. Washington made their cause his own, whether because his interests were in sync with theirs or because he feared that these powerful interests would, if necessary, break up the Union to get what they wanted. More than anything, Washington was a fervent nationalist. But he also knew that the survival of the Union offered the best promise that his name and exploits would live on.

WASHINGTON HAD EXPANDED ON THE WEAKNESSES of the national government in his principal state papers during the last months of the war, though once he retired he addressed his concerns to only a handful of trusted acquaintances. With a wary eye on Europe's rapacious princes, Washington said nothing in public about America's problems, and when corresponding with foreigners he extolled the nation's promise. "This is an abounding Country" that will "become equally populous & happy. Some of the States . . . ran riot for a while, but they are recovering a proper tone again," he remarked more than once in 1784. To Lafayette, who knew America firsthand, Washington was more honest, but still upbeat: "It is one of the evils of democratical governments that people, not always seeing & frequently mislead, must often feel before they can act right—but then evils . . . seldom fail to work their own cure."[31]

Washington had plenty of company with regard to the need to make the national government truly sovereign, but probably no other Nationalist—as those who favored consolidation were coming to be called—would have concurred with his remark to Lafayette that a democratic consensus would form to effect that change. For that matter, it is doubtful that Washington believed what he wrote. Although he knew that for most Americans the core meaning of the American Revolution had been, and remained, an abhorrence of strong governments, he and the Nationalists were bent on vesting the central government with significantly greater authority.

The Nationalists saw many problems, but like Washington, they believed the root of America's woes lay in a state sovereignty that had emasculated the Continental Congress and, after 1781, the Congress under the Articles of Confederation. Even two years before Yorktown, it was apparent to many that the menace of runaway inflation and collapsing public credit imperiled the war effort and threatened both independence and great fortunes. By then, too, some had awakened to the belief that bringing the tottering economy under control exceeded the reach of the states and was beyond the means of an enervated national government. Somehow the war was won, though victory had seemed so unlikely at the outset of 1781 that Yorktown was widely viewed as little short of miraculous. For some, that was reason enough to establish a vigorous national government that would be better able to wage the next war. Peace only brought other afflictions. Trade among the states was snarled by a mishmash of local duties. Great Britain closed its ports to American exports—including entrée to the Caribbean sugar islands, from which American merchants had carried goods to markets outside the British Empire in colonial days—and the impotent United States government could do nothing to force

London to lift its restrictions. But for the average American, nothing was as unpalatable as the taxation brought on by the war.[32]

Though peace had come by 1784, the effects of the late hostilities lingered on in the form of a crushing war debt. Foreign loans had to be repaid by the United States, but most of the indebtedness was domestic, some incurred by the states, some by the national government. Governments had borrowed from the people, in return giving them promissory notes not unlike today's savings bonds. Furthermore, army contractors and farmers who had sold their commodities to the army had been paid with certificates that were to be subsequently redeemed. Similarly, Continental soldiers had been given certificates when they were furloughed or discharged near the end of hostilities.

It was this indebtedness that had led Superintendent Morris to embrace the second impost amendment in 1783, but when it failed to be ratified, public securities had seemed worthless. Most had been sold to speculators—dubbed "stockjobbers" by a great many Americans—for a fraction of their face value. By the late 1780s, the public creditors to whom the government debt was owed were a tiny percentage of the American public, and for the most part they were the wealthiest Americans, men who had never soldiered and rarely sacrificed during the war. But whoever owned the bonds and securities, the debt was legal, and under the law it had to be serviced. Congress asked the states for revenue to enable it to meet its obligations—40 percent of the national budget in 1785 was earmarked for debt retirement—and the states complied by levying taxes atop the already burdensome duties they had long since imposed on their citizens to cope with their own debts.

No one likes to pay taxes, and the weight of paying these taxes was made all the more onerous for many Americans by the realization that much of the revenue that was raised would go to paying speculators, not the original holders of the bonds and securities. In 1786, for instance, half of Rhode Island's wartime debt was owned by sixteen people; three years later, two thirds of the revenue brought in by taxes in Pennsylvania for its war debts went to twelve creditors. The tax burden was so great that movements aimed at tax relief blossomed in many states. It also turned some people into Nationalists, as they came to see vesting the national government with the power to raise revenue as a form of tax relief. After all, they reasoned, the burden could be shifted from states to the national government, which in turn could find its revenue relatively painlessly by levying an impost on imports or by selling western lands won in the war.[33]

Not all of the discontent among the Nationalists arose from economic maladies. Many were disturbed by the social and political changes ushered in by the American Revolution. Change had been the very meaning of the Revolution for many Americans. They had put their lives on the line to see that a "new era for politics is struck," as Thomas Paine had written in *Common Sense*. Paine had fleshed out what the struggle was about: "We have it in our power to begin the world over again. . . . The birthday of a new world is at hand," he had boldly asserted.[34] By the time Washington returned home from the war, nearly eight years to the day after *Common Sense* was published, some states had expanded suffrage rights, and here and there men who before 1775 had been denied office held important positions, including even seats in Congress. Under some of the state constitutions many more offices were filled by election, and elections were held more frequently than under the prewar colonial charters. Many men who had risked their lives soldiering to give birth to the United States, or who welcomed the ringing manifesto of human rights in the Declaration of Independence, were unwilling to accept the socially stratified society that had existed before the war. They regarded themselves as the equal of the wealthiest in society. To the Nationalists, who were for the most part social conservatives, the changes that seemed to be gaining momentum at the state level were alarming. Not a few believed that alongside its economic ills, the new United States was endangered by what they saw as an excess of democracy. Washington, who by 1786 spoke of "anarchy & confusion" unleashed by "selfinterested designing disaffected & desperate characters," shared that view.[35]

Every Nationalist was also troubled by the United States' disquieting weakness. Having supported independence in the hope of creating an illustrious new nation, they were mortified not only by what Washington called the "scurge" of national impotence, but by an itinerant Congress allegedly filled with mediocrities and so plagued by absenteeism that it often could not meet for lack of a quorum. "Our character as a nation is dwindling," Washington complained less than three years after the war.

"No Morn ever dawned more favourable than ours did—and no day was ever more clouded than the present."[36]

By 1786, Washington no longer thought—if he ever had—that the people, in their wisdom, would find a suitable constitutional solution. He had come to the conclusion that "mankind left to themselves are unfit for their own government." The "wise and the good"—the elite—would have to lead the people to the solution of putting more "energy in our governments," he said.[37] Washington's sentiments were echoed by like-minded Nationalists who had been plotting for substantive constitutional change at least since the Newburgh conspiracy. By 1786, their intrigue was building to a crescendo, and Madison and Hamilton, who had been involved to varying degrees in the machinations for an impost three years earlier, were once again active in the conniving. Both desperately wanted the United States to survive, and both were alarmed by America's gathering egalitarianism and democratization. Otherwise, they saw the crisis from different perspectives. Hamilton's prism was that of the interests of the New York financial and commercial community to which he was tied. Madison, a slave owner himself, saw things through the eyes of the Virginia planter class.

During the first two years of peace, the Nationalists publicly attacked what they believed were the defects in the existing government and urged Congress to take the initiative in proposing reforms. In the spring of 1786, Congressman Charles Pinckney of South Carolina moved that Congress either call a constitutional convention or recommend amendments to the Articles of Confederation. When Congress took neither step, Madison had an idea. Drawing on the successful meeting at Mount Vernon in 1785 between commissioners from Virginia and Maryland—which had concluded by urging conversations with other states—he induced the Virginia assembly to propose that every state send delegates to a conference in Annapolis in September 1786 to consider recommendations leading to a "uniform System" of trade for the United States.[38]

The conference was a bust. Only five states sent delegates. Even Madison, its instigator, had been warned that the meeting might be premature, as "affairs are not arrived at such a crisis" to lead to success. Furthermore, he erred egregiously in not at least trying to add Washington to Virginia's delegation, as the general's attendance would have added to the credibility of the convention. Nevertheless, Hamilton and Madison and their fellow delegates made the most of the abortive gathering. They concluded their brief stay in Annapolis by calling for a national convention to meet in Philadelphia in May 1787. It was to consider far more than commerce. Their appeal said that the Philadelphia Convention was to be for "digesting a plan" for amending the Articles of Confederation in such a manner as to "render the constitution of the Foederal Government adequate to the exigencies of the Union."[39]

During the intervening eight months, the Nationalists worked hard to make the Philadelphia Convention a success. In some ways, their greatest labor was expended on persuading Washington to attend. His presence, they knew, might induce holdout states to send delegates, and given his revered status and the trust placed in him by the public, Washington's attendance might smooth the way for ratification of whatever amendments were proposed. No one thought it would be easy to get Washington to Philadelphia. There was no question that he shared the sentiments of the Nationalists—he called the proposed convention "an object of the first magnitude," for if the articles were not amended, "there is an end put to Foederal Government"—but Washington would do nothing that might sully his celebrated reputation, including attending a meeting that might be a fiasco if several states refused to send representatives.

Washington knew, too, that many people harbored deep reservations, even suspicions, about the Philadelphia Convention, fearing that it would lead to the destruction of the states and the erosion of the breathtaking changes already unleashed by the American Revolution. Patrick Henry, whom Washington admired, refused to attend, allegedly saying that he "smelt a rat." Nor was Washington convinced that the Philadelphia meeting was legal, inasmuch as the Articles of Confederation stipulated that amendments were to originate in "a congress of the United States."[40] It is conceivable, too, that Washington was bothered by one other possibility. If the convention, as expected, proposed sweeping constitutional reforms, those almost certainly would include the creation of an office of chief executive, a step taken by nearly every state that had adopted a constitution since 1776. Washington had to know that he would be asked to accept the post. If that was the case, Washington—given his obsession with not being seen as grasping for power—might have been reluctant to be part of a convention that would create the office he would occupy.

But Washington's appearance in Philadelphia would be a great prize for the Nationalists, and many appealed to him to attend. None played a more substantive role in winning his consent than Madison and General Knox. Madison, who had visited Mount Vernon only once previously, hurried there in February 1787. In a full day's discussion, Madison doubtless was upbeat about the convention—"the appointments for the Convention go on very successfully," he is known to have told Washington—and he must have assured the general that he would see to it that Congress sanctioned the meeting (which, in time, it did). Whatever else Madison said, he departed confident in Washington's presence in Philadelphia.[41] One reason Madison was so optimistic was that Knox had paved his way. In the fall of 1786, debt-ridden and exorbitantly taxed farmers in western Massachusetts had taken up arms to impede court proceedings leading to property foreclosures. Many of the yeomen, including their leader, Daniel Shays, had soldiered extensively in the Revolutionary War, but they were no match for a huge army sent west by Massachusetts. As Shays' Rebellion unfolded, Knox kept Washington abreast of events with a series of lurid reports filled with half-truths and outright lies. He wrote that many of the insurgents had "never paid any . . . taxes" and that the Shaysites advocated legislation to "annihilate all debts," both of which were untrue. Washington, a creditor himself, believed Knox's prejudicial accounts. "Good God!" Washington exclaimed. "Who besides a tory," he asked, "could have foreseen" that Americans would be so "far gone in every thing ignoble & bad" in such a short period after independence? Massachusetts had been able to suppress the Shaysites, but Washington worried about the "combustibles in every State." Could they be extinguished if "a spark . . . set fire to" them? More than ever, Washington now believed it was essential to give "energy & respectability to the Government" of the United States.[42] But he wanted more than that. Like many of his brethren among the Nationalists, Washington had come to the conclusion that the time had come to rein in the American Revolution, check the radical impulses unleashed by the great upheaval, and establish a national government that would be a safeguard against both popular disorder and precipitous change.

WASHINGTON CAME TO PHILADELPHIA in May 1787 expecting to play only a negligible role in the convention's debates. In his heart of hearts, he must have known that he was to be a figurehead, that he was being used, as Congress had used him after 1778 to provide the glue for the Union and as Hamilton and his fellow plotters had used him in 1783 in their earlier grab for greater national powers. Those who got Washington to Philadelphia knew early on that they had acted wisely. As he traveled from Mount Vernon, Washington was acclaimed all along the way, and he received a stupendous welcome in Philadelphia. As historian Walter McDougall has written, many in the adoring crowds believed that Washington had "come north again to win the peace as he had won the war."[43]

Every state but Rhode Island was represented at the convention, and nearly every delegate was from the top rung socially and economically. In its first session, the convention chose Washington to be its president, and at the same moment it opted to keep its proceedings secret, allowing no spectators and even sealing shut the windows of Independence Hall despite Philadelphia's customary steamy summers. For four sweltering months, Washington sat daily on the dais and said nothing, save to maintain order when passions flared. He wearied of the proceedings long before the convention ended but was happy with what it did. From the outset, the delegates agreed to go beyond their stated intention of amending the Articles of Confederation, the basis upon which Congress had sanctioned the gathering. The delegates set out instead to write a new constitution, and in so doing they adhered closely to a plan conceived by Madison. The national government was to be augmented at the expense of the states. This was a convention that intended national law to be "the supreme law of the land." It was also bent on taking power from those state assemblies that both facilitated social change and embraced economic policies that alarmed the creditor class and powerful commercial interests.

The proposed national government would have the power to levy and collect taxes, regulate commerce, and protect property, including slave properties. It could intervene in the states to prevent "domestic violence" by "suppress[ing] insurrections." Most delegates apparently agreed with Roger Sherman of Connecticut, who proposed that the "people . . . should have as little to do as may be about the Government." Under the finished product, as historian Woody Holton observed, the national government was to be "less responsive to the popular will than [in] any of its state-level counterparts." Through a layered system of checks and balances, the proposed constitution was designed to make change difficult, to "check . . . changeableness," as Gouverneur Morris put it, to prevent "a majority of the whole" from acting in "concert and execut[ing] their plans," as Madison said. By proposing the creation of huge legislative districts, the delegates consciously sought to screen out what many at that time called the "lower sort" and assure that both houses of Congress would be bastions of the most successful, and most conservative, Americans. The Framers cleaved to the belief that large districts would minimize the chances of domination by a single faction, and especially mastery by a faction driven by "sinister designs" such as egalitarianism and redistribution of wealth. The proposed constitution additionally created a chief executive that was to be, as Holton added, "more powerful and more independent of his legislative branch than any of the [state] governors."[44]

The Framers were committed to overturning the American tradition of local autonomy in order to slow, if not stymie, social change. But above all, they were driven by economic motives. They wished to restore public credit and enhance economic growth, protect property, and prevent the states from enacting debt and tax relief schemes that they saw as inimical to their interests. They proposed instead a new national government that would be nearly as powerful as the British government they had only recently overthrown. They might have gone further and attempted to vest the central government with even more colossal authority. Madison, for instance, wanted the national government to have dominion over the states "in all cases whatsoever," the precise wording that Parliament had chosen when it spelled out its jurisdiction over the colonies in 1766. The Framers stopped where they did only because they feared that going further would make ratification impossible. But what they had proposed—and what it soon would facilitate—was astounding. As historian Gordon Wood has pointed out, it "violated for many Americans everything the Revolution had been about." Moreover, the consequence today of their handiwork, Wood added, is that "compared to many federal governments that now exist" in the Western world, the "United States is one of the strongest and most centralized." Whereas most of today's democracies are in the mold of the British parliamentary system of ministerial responsibility, the United

States, nearly alone, adheres to the system of separation of powers that the Framers found such an attractive vehicle for inhibiting further radical change.[45]

Washington was happy with "the momentous wk. which had been executed," he wrote in his diary on the evening the convention ended.[46] There is no reason to suspect his sincerity. During the war and its immediate aftermath, America changed dramatically as a result of the inspiring rhetoric of the American Revolution and the meaning that many citizens attached to the great struggle to break from dependency on a faraway parent state. During those years, Washington wrote millions of words. Time and again he fretted over the powers of the nation and the survival of the United States, but never did he advocate profound social or political reform. He was silent on expanding suffrage rights, lessening or eliminating property qualifications for holding office, making state assemblies or Congress more representative, eliminating slavery or indentured servitude, or reducing social stratification.

From the outset, Washington had supported defiance of Great Britain in the hope that the most influential Americans would have the autonomy to control their own destiny and that the ambitious would not be thwarted from realizing their dreams by the restraints imposed by an overseas monarchy and aristocracy. Washington came to abhor a formal aristocracy as a result of his experiences in the French and Indian War, and like Paine, he loathed monarchy long before the first shot was fired in the Revolutionary War. Nothing that he said following the war suggests that the American Revolution substantively changed his social and political outlook. He was obsessed with conserving, rather than reforming, American society, and he was happy to see those who had traditionally held sway in America continue to exercise dominion over it.

WHEN THE CONVENTION CLOSED, Washington remarked that the proposed constitution was "a Child of Fortune" facing a difficult road to ratification. The "political concerns of this Country are . . . suspended by a thread," he added. In the first public statement made by anyone in the ratification battle, Washington told Congress that the convention had produced a document containing reforms long "desired" by the "Friends of our Country," and he added that the preservation of "our national Existence" hinged on ratification. Within a month, he predicted that the foes of the document would be driven by "sinester and self important considerations," by which he meant self-serving motives. His implication was that the Framers had somehow been purely disinterested. At the same moment, he conceived and sent to a number of correspondents a strategic plan for defending the constitution that no other Federalist (as the proponents of ratification were called) improved on. He urged that Federalists stress that however flawed the proposed constitution might be, it was superior to that which existed; that criticism be countered by stressing that the constitution could be amended; and that the Union hung in the balance. Above all, Washington implored those like Hamilton and Madison, who possessed great "literary abilities," to utilize their "good pens" on behalf of ratification.[47]

The new plan of government would have to be ratified by three fourths of the states. This would not be easy. Majorities opposed the new constitution in at least four states, and perhaps five, and these included the three largest states—Virginia, New York, and Massachusetts. Elsewhere, support ranged from minimal to overwhelming, though almost everywhere considerable opposition existed in the western backcountry. Washington watched the proceedings closely, eagerly awaiting delivery of the many newspapers that he read. From time to time, he played a covert role in the ratification battle. He remained silent when Federalists fabricated and published a copy of a speech he had supposedly given at the Constitutional Convention. (He was quoted as having warned that blood would run in the streets if the constitution was not ratified.) Otherwise, he persuaded a reluctant Madison to attend the Virginia ratifying convention; gently tried to bring Patrick Henry to the Federalist side; wrote General Lincoln, who was a delegate in the touch-and-go Massachusetts Convention, probably with the expectation that his missive expressing his hope of ratification would be published; sent letters to key officials in Pennsylvania and New York; passed along political gossip to Madison; and "meddled"—his term—in Maryland's ratification process by counseling Federalists on procedural matters. When he was criticized publicly for intervening in Maryland's proceedings, Washington, with a straight face, claimed that he had never said anything about the constitution that "was not forced upon me in a manner not to be avoided."[48]

With his political antennae well-adjusted, Washington remained optimistic throughout the nine-month struggle for ratification. At last, during
the final torrid days of summer in 1788, he learned that eleven states, including all the largest provinces, had ratified the Constitution of the
United States. Only North Carolina and Rhode Island had withheld approval. Ratification won out for several reasons, including the Federalists'
adherence to Washington's strategic recommendations. Above all, they used
their pens, as he had advised. As the campaign unfolded, Madison, Hamilton, and John Jay authored eighty-five newspaper essays in defense of the
proposed constitution—what today is known collectively as *The Federalist*—
that helped secure ratification. However, nothing was more important to
the Federalists' success than having Washington on their side. Faced with
defending a new constitution that would take the country into uncharted
waters, the Federalists repeatedly invoked Washington's name, urging
Americans to once again pin their hopes on him. Federalists often played
on the theme that America's leap in the dark in 1776 had turned out successfully because Washington had shepherded the new nation to victory.
The new charter must be safe, they reasoned, or Washington would never
have been a party to its drafting. They republished his 1783 "Circular to
the States" calling for a stronger central government, and innumerable Federalists asked in newspaper essays whether it was possible that "the deliverer
of our country would have recommended an unsafe form of government
for [our] liberty." Others pointed out that the "disinterested . . . WASH-
INGTON" favored ratification. Some Federalists predicted that Washington would be called from retirement to become the first president of the
United States. As chief executive, they asserted, Washington could be
trusted to lead the new nation through the difficult shoals that lay ahead,
and they asked: "Can Europe boast of such a man? or can the history of
the world show an instance of such voluntary compact between the deliverer and the delivered of any country as will soon possibly take place in the
United States?"[49]

The foes of ratification, the Anti-Federalists, waged a spirited battle that
now and then included the rarest of phenomena, published attacks on Washington. He was reviled as a "fool from nature" who had consented to play
the dupe for the Federalists, and he was assailed as a slave owner "living
upon the labours of several hundreds of miserable Africans, as free born as

himself." But most Anti-Federalists understood that to have at Washington was to play with fire. Most took the safer course of gingerly raising questions. For example, one conceded that the general was beyond reproach but asked whether the country would be safe when such a powerful presidential office fell into the hands of Washington's successors. Another acknowledged that Washington was usually correct but wondered if he might be "fallible on a [constitutional] subject that must be . . . novel to him." One even dared to question whether *"great men are not always wise."*[50]

PRECISELY BECAUSE OF HIS EXALTED STANDING, ratification meant that Washington would inevitably be asked to serve as president. In fact, even while the ratification battle raged, he was musing privately over whether to accept the office of chief executive. Only Washington ever knew whether he really desired to become president of the United States. His public remarks were akin to his utterances on taking command of the Virginia Regiment and the Continental army. Returning to public life held "no enticing charms" for him, he said, adding repeatedly that he preferred to live out his days "an honest man on my own farm."[51]

There was a measure of truth to his remarks. Not only would he be fifty-seven when inaugurated, he was inexperienced in coping with the challenges of high elective office. There was a real possibility that his grand reputation would be shattered. On the other hand, he was desperately anxious for the new nation to survive, and he had to have believed that his presence as president might help see it through its difficult formative period. After five years of relative seclusion at Mount Vernon, moreover, Washington may have missed the electrifying throb that went with being at the very center of things, and especially so at this moment of epic importance. He had to know, too, that if the new government was established successfully under someone else's presidency, that individual would win the accolades. Basking in another's glow was not something Washington ever relished.

Once ratification was achieved, letters poured into Mount Vernon pleading with Washington to accept the presidency. Months passed before he gave a final answer. The "Future is all a scene of darkness and uncertainty to me," he insisted six months after ratification, though at Christmas 1788, he preposterously allowed that he would accept the presidency should he be convinced that Congress was filled with "disinterested characters."[52] It is difficult to believe that it took Washington all this time to make his decision, though decision making was not his strong suit. He probably saw things in the same light as Hamilton, who in September counseled that should Washington refuse to heed the "unanimous wish of your country," he ran the risk of losing his fame, which "must be . . . dear to you."[53] That Washington delayed his acceptance for so long was largely theater by the consummate actor, but not entirely self-serving. Part of his authority—his political capital—came from his image as one who did not seek power for himself, but who acted only to answer his country's call. His show of reluctance served to reinforce this.

In January 1789, Washington at last declared his willingness to be president, but he had to await his election, which was never in doubt. Under the Constitution, the president was to be elected by the electoral college, whose members were to be chosen in each state "in such manner" as its legislature decided. Each elector was "to vote by ballot for two Persons." The ballots in each state were then to be sent to the United States Senate, where they would be counted. The individual receiving the largest number of votes, if a majority, was to be the president; the person receiving the second largest number of votes was to be the vice president.

The electors in each state met and voted on the first Wednesday of February, although Washington was not notified of his election for nearly ten weeks, as the Senate had not obtained a quorum until the first week of April. When the Senate could finally meet and tabulate the electoral votes, it was found that every elector had cast one of his two votes for Washington. The second votes were scattered among several individuals, including national figures such as John Adams, John Hancock, and John Jay, but also among state leaders including John Rutledge, John Milton, and Edward Telfair. Adams finished in second place, having received thirty-four votes to Washington's sixty-nine.

Although all knew that Washington would be the winner, he remained at Mount Vernon until official word was brought to him on April 14 by the secretary of Congress. Washington's bags were already packed, and almost immediately he departed for New York City, home to the new government. Just prior to climbing into his carriage, Washington noted in his diary the "anxious and painful sensations" that he felt at saying farewell "to domestic felicity."[54]

Huge crowds turned out to see and cheer him in every dusty little hamlet through which he passed. Virtually all feted him with some sort of ceremony. Given what General Washington meant to Trenton, that little New Jersey village went all out. He entered the town by passing under an arch supported by thirteen pillars and festooned with bright green garlands. Atop the arch, in gilt lettering, was the simple inscription TO YOU ALONE. He alighted from horseback—he switched from his carriage and mounted Prescott, his great white parade horse, as he entered each village—and listened as a chorus of white-clad young girls serenaded him ("Welcome, mighty Chief! once more . . ."). Huge throngs turned out in the two cities through which he passed, Baltimore and Philadelphia. More than twenty thousand people, half the city's residents, lined Philadelphia's streets as Washington rode through.[55]

One last ceremony awaited him. Congress set April 30 as Inauguration Day. At a bit past noon on that crisp, clear spring day, Washington emerged from the President's House, where he had been staying since arriving in town six days earlier. Wearing a dark brown broadcloth suit that sported metal buttons, each adorned with an eagle, as well as white stockings and white gloves, he walked to his carriage, acknowledging the large, festive crowd. At precisely 12:30, the cavalcade set off for Federal Hall, Congress's home, a ninety-year-old white masonry structure at the intersection of Broad and Wall streets. Five military companies, including a martial band made up of drummers and bagpipers, escorted him, some units marching before the presidential carriage, others in its wake. New York's mayor and sheriff, the only participants on horseback, were in the parade as well. As the procession neared Federal Hall, Washington may have noticed that the banner fluttering above the building was the flag of the "Federal Ship *Hamilton*," an omen, perhaps, of what was to come. John Adams, who had been sworn in a few days earlier as vice president, led Washington into Federal Hall. The two men walked upstairs and out onto a second-story porticoed balcony that overlooked cobblestoned Wall Street. Washington bowed formally to the cheering crowd below and listened briefly to the artillery salutes fired from both the Battery and vessels in New York Harbor. He would not have been human had he not stolen a glance at the city that sprawled out before him, relishing this moment of having at last captured New York, the city he had been obsessed with re-taking during the war.

When all was ready, Washington, standing under a red-and-white-striped canopy and before a small table draped with red velvet, took the oath of office. After bowing once again to the crowd below, President Washington stepped back inside. In the Senate chamber now, he looked out at a forty-by-thirty-foot room that featured portraits of Christopher Columbus and assorted revolutionary heroes, including himself. The chamber was lavishly carpeted, crimson damask curtains framed the tall windows, and marble mantels handsomely embellished each of the room's fireplaces. High above the chamber stood an arched ceiling painted with a rising sun that shone among thirteen stars. The senators sat before the podium in a semicircle; members of the House of Representatives occupied temporary seats behind them or stood along the walls. There was no spectators' gallery. When all was quiet, Washington delivered his inaugural address. A Pennsylvania senator thought the speech "heavy, dull, stupid," and in fact, it was memorable only for containing nothing memorable.[56]

Following the speech, the president and the members of Congress walked together to worship at St. Paul's on Broadway, a twenty-five-year-old Anglican chapel some eight blocks away. During the evening, many residents of the city burned candles in their windows and others emerged into the chilly spring night to observe the "illuminations," backlit transparent paintings of American heroes and events that were displayed near Federal Hall. One portrayed Washington as Fortitude, the Senate as Justice, and the House of Representatives as Wisdom. Another showed Fame, an angel, descending on Washington to make him immortal.[57]

Washington had divulged no plans that he may have harbored for his presidency in his inaugural address, though in his private correspondence he had recently remarked that he did "not believe that Providence has done so much for nothing," suggesting his conviction that destiny had conducted America to victory in the war and made possible this opportunity to save the United States.[58] What is more, for years Washington, both privately and publicly, had made clear what he regarded as America's greatest problems and what he hoped to see accomplished. His ideas tallied with

those of the consolidationists—the so-called Nationalists before 1787—
who now stood on the cusp of realizing what they had been seeking since
before they sent the first impost amendment to the states nine years earlier.
With President Washington running interference for them, many consolidationists were poised to bring on the counterrevolution of which they had
so long dreamed.

PRESIDENT OF THE UNITED STATES: THE FIRST TERM, 1789–1792

PRESIDENT WASHINGTON TOOK OFFICE with a general idea of what he wanted to do, though he had only the haziest notion of the specifics of his program and no idea how to attack the daunting economic malaise. Like almost everyone, he wised to reestablish a sound currency, raise revenue, and retire the national debt. He also wished to open the West to settlement, and that meant dealing with the Indians and the British, who, in defiance of the Treaty of Paris, had not withdrawn their troops from their military posts beyond the mountains. It was imperative, too, that he should seek to normalize relations with London, both for national security needs and to restore prewar trade. Then there was the matter of style. Style was extremely important to Washington. He had fashioned a persona for himself as a young man—quiet, sober, thoughtful, and grave. He had hardly taken command during the Revolutionary War before he designed handsome uniforms for the officers, including distinctive insignias that distinguished ranks and regiments. Panache had been crucial for getting the army off on the right foot, and he thought it no less important to set the proper tone for the presidency.

Washington discussed the "business & etiquette" of the new presidency with several officials, asking for their thoughts in writing.[1] He received the longest and most important recommendations from Hamilton and Vice President Adams. Some of their suggestions overlapped, but there were crucial differences. Adams, despite having spent the past decade at the courts of European monarchs, envisaged a presidency given less to pomp than did Hamilton. Adams started with the commonsense premise that the tenor of each administration would be set by the personality of the president. Hamilton stressed that Washington should establish the "dignity" of the office, shooting "for a pretty high tone." Hamilton encouraged Washington to meet the public each week in a thirty-minute levee, while Adams advocated less stately meetings twice weekly. Hamilton advised Washington to host four state dinners and up to eight less pretentious dinners annually, though the "President [was] never to remain long at table." State dinners aside, Adams told Washington to entertain as often as he pleased and that these occasions should be "without formality." Hamilton recommended against the president ever accepting a dinner invitation at someone's home; Adams thought it would be acceptable for Washington to attend private tea parties, though public business should not be discussed on those occasions. Hamilton encouraged Washington to permit only heads of departments, foreign diplomats, and members of the Senate (but not members of the House of Representatives, the only elected officials among the bunch) to his office. Adams said the president should see whomever he "judges . . . worthy."[2]

Washington leaned toward Hamilton's counsel, and his presidency took on a monarchical air. With disgust, William Maclay, a senator from Pennsylvania, described Washington's lavish dinners and stately levees—both attended by footmen in livery and wigs—as "a feature of Royalty," and Great Britain's minister to the United States, who knew royalty when he saw it, characterized the spirit of the Washington administration as a "very kingly style."[3] Washington's habits as president were a matter of conscious choice and drew on Hamilton's recommendations, accepted practices in aristocratic Virginia, and his ingrained habits of gravitas. Washington was also influenced by his military experience. Eighteenth-century armies, like most today, were given to considerable pomp and circumstance— uniforms, parades, marching music, drumrolls—and the soldiery was expected to exhibit marked formality and deference toward those who held higher rank.

Washington wished to emphasize the power, energy, and authority of his office. To master every encounter, he assured that no official who called on him ever thought he was in the presence of an equal. Each week on

Tuesday, he hosted a formal levee. Every Thursday, he invited guests to a stuffy dinner. He greeted those who attended with a stiff bow, never a handshake. When he traveled, even on rides about the city for relaxation, Washington rode in his cream-colored carriage adorned with his family coat of arms—a griffin (a winged lion, the symbol in ancient heraldry of a guardian of treasure) atop a large stylized "GW." The carriage was usually drawn by a team of six horses and attended by coachmen and slaves in livery. Deploring the "notions of equality" that haunted the land, Hamilton had advised him to be proper and imperious, but to "steer clear of extremes."[4] Washington's conduct leaned toward pomposity, and his definition of stopping short of the extremes of which Hamilton had warned was to fashion a presidency that was a blend of royalty and republicanism. He did not sit on a throne or wear robes and capes. He dressed like any successful private citizen; a guest at one of the levees remembered that Washington had powdered his hair and wore a black velvet suit with yellow gloves. Whatever he did to tone down his monarchical bent, some of the most conservative Americans rejoiced that a sufficient royal air was retained. "You are now a king, under a different name," James McHenry, one of Washington's wartime aides, rapturously told the president. But not everyone was enthralled with his royal trappings, and when Congress decided on a title for the new executive office—the Constitution was silent on the matter of designations for federal officials—it decided on the exquisitely simple "the President of the United States." It was an act that some saw as a counterweight to what Washington was seeking to mold.[5]

Washington understood that mystique was power, but some thought he went too far in his attempts to fashion an enhanced aura about himself and his office. Theodorick Bland, a friendly Virginian, was dismayed by Washington's habits, which he thought were "more distant and stiff" than those of a monarch. Bland also worried that Washington's practices would set a precedent for his successor. Given levees of this sort for a few years, the new nation would "have all the paraphernalia . . . to give the superb finish to the grandeur of our AMERICAN COURT," he said. Not a few found Washington's incessantly cold and magisterial bearing to be repulsive. Hamilton's wife, Elizabeth, who hailed from the aristocratic Schuyler family, was put off by Washington's excessive formality and unreachable manner, which she thought he was unable to lay aside. But it was all in the eye of the beholder. Abigail Adams, an egalitarian Yankee, found Washington to be "polite with dignity, affable without formality, distant without haughtiness, grave without austerity, modest, wise, and good."[6]

On balance, the style that Washington set for the presidency bore a closer resemblance to the courts of the royal governors in pre-revolutionary America than to the republican manner that would prevail across the land within only fifteen or twenty years of his inauguration. It was no accident that he fashioned the office in this manner. He wished to set a standard for others who held power, and especially for the state governors, who could be influential at the level where problems were occurring, at least from the vantage point of the Nationalists.

FRANKLIN ROOSEVELT'S NEW DEAL in the Depression-racked 1930s was famous for its frenetic First Hundred Days, but its frenzied pace paled in contrast with the breathtakingly substantive steps taken by Congress in the weeks following Washington's inauguration. Before the heat and languor of summer vanished, Congress had passed and sent to the states for ratification the Bill of Rights—imagine Congress today passing ten constitutional amendments in one year, much less one summer—adopted a 5 percent impost on all imports and a special tax on a few enumerated articles entering the United States, and established the nation's system of courts. It even rejected one oblique hint and one direct proposal made by the new president. Though he did not fight for it, Washington let it be known that he preferred that the laws of the states and those of the federal government be uniform, but even the most zealous of the consolidationists shrank from the battle that such a move would touch off with the proponents of state sovereignty. Washington lost out on another matter, too. In his inaugural address, he had declined a salary and asked only that he be compensated for his expenses. The Continental Congress had agreed to a similar offer by General Washington in 1775, but many congressmen and Vice President Adams were put off by the idea for the presidency. They feared that the precedent it would set—and everyone understood that whatever was done by the first president would be difficult to shake—would assure that the presidency would be the exclusive province of the extremely wealthy. Congress voted Washington an annual salary of $25,000.[7]

During that busy summer of 1789, Congress also created several executive departments. It decided as well that the president could appoint department heads with the advice and consent of the Senate, and he could remove them unilaterally. Three departments had existed under the Articles of Confederation. Congress left the Department of War intact but changed the names of the other two. The Ministry of Foreign Affairs became the Department of State and the Finance Office was transformed into the Department of the Treasury. Washington kept General Knox at War and might have retained John Jay at State had the New Yorker not wished to become a Supreme Court justice. Once he accommodated Jay, Washington asked Jefferson to be the secretary of state. The Judiciary Act passed that year established the office of Attorney-General, though the Department of Justice did not come into being for another eighty years. Washington named his fellow Virginian Edmund Randolph to that post.

For many who had pushed to supplant the Articles of Confederation with a stronger national government, Treasury was the key post. The secretary of the Treasury would face the task of resolving the nearly fifteen-year-old economic troubles that had been largely responsible for bringing on the new Constitution in the first place. Furthermore, more than any other official save for the chief executive, the Treasury secretary would give shape to the new nation and to the relationship that existed between the states and the federal government. To no one's surprise, Washington urged Hamilton's appointment as Treasury secretary. His three selections followed a pattern that had prevailed since the First Continental Congress in 1775: The three appointees were to be drawn from the three sections of the nation—New England (Knox), mid-Atlantic (Hamilton), and South (Jefferson).

Though he had received warnings about Hamilton—the New Yorker was given to "artful designs and machinations" and would betray anyone to fulfill his "boundless Ambition," an anonymous writer told the incoming president, perhaps thinking that he was passing on a startling revelation—Washington informed Hamilton of his intention to name him to the Treasury post even before the office was created.[8] Hamilton could not have been happier. Given his distaste for Washington, and perhaps his belief that the general would never return to public life, Hamilton had largely ignored his former commander during Washington's first three years of retirement, not even bothering to visit Mount Vernon in 1786 when he attended the unsuccessful convention at Annapolis, merely a day's journey away. Once the Philadelphia Convention loomed, however, Hamilton realized that Washington could once again be useful. He courted him to come to Philadelphia, and after the Constitution was ratified, Hamilton did everything in his power to persuade Washington to accept the presidency. The Treasury post would be the plum of plums in the Washington administration, and Hamilton wanted the position.

Hamilton knew that the Treasury Department would be the cockpit of the new national government. The decisions made in that department would determine much about the shape of America, the lives of Americans, and the nature of American politics. By holding the post, moreover, Hamilton would be catapulted to the top rung of power in New York City, which was dominated by financial and mercantile interests. He also expected to have a free hand at Treasury. Washington was not an economist. He had, in fact, recently confessed that he was "so little conversant in publick securities of every kind as not to know the use or value of them, and hardly the difference of one species from another."[9]

If President Washington, like most Americans, had only the foggiest idea about what might be done to restore a sound currency, he knew that he wanted Hamilton in charge of the Treasury Department. He had heard Hamilton discourse on economic matters at least as far back as 1780, and during his weeks in Philadelphia for the Constitutional Convention, Washington must have heard him once again offer economic remedies. But Washington was attracted by more than Hamilton's storehouse of ideas. Given the narrow margin of ratification, Washington knew that the new government might not survive if it failed to solve the nation's economic troubles. It was imperative to get the right man into this vital position, and Washington had absolutely no doubts that Hamilton was the right man.

Hamilton was blessed with every quality Washington wanted in his Treasury secretary. Fluent and persuasive, unequaled in guile and political dexterity, Hamilton was renowned for his heroic capacity for work. But Washington was drawn to Hamilton for still other reasons. No one was ever a better judge of others than Washington, and he had sufficient experience with Hamilton to fathom his character to its very core. Daily at headquarters during the war, as well as when the Newburgh Affair played out, Washington had witnessed every side there was to Hamilton. He had beheld

Hamilton the dreamer, menacing intriguer, creative polemicist, insightful statesman, brilliant economist, and relentless avenger. Time and again, Washington had watched Hamilton bring to bear both his rich assortment of talents and his arsenal of malice. Some were aghast at what they glimpsed in Hamilton. Washington was drawn closer to Hamilton by what he saw, as if he were observing a mirror image of himself, or perhaps as if he were looking at the man he wished he could have been. Washington knew that Hamilton was a good bet to get his recommendations approved, even if he had to resort to Machiavellian schemes.

Washington nominated Hamilton in September. The Senate rapidly consented, after which Congress directed the Treasury secretary to present a plan for solving the nation's economic ills within one hundred days. Congress then recessed until Hamilton completed his task, although before the congressmen went home they left no doubt that they regarded economic matters as the nation's first priority. Congress gave the Treasury Department more money and eight times the number of clerks that it allotted to the two other departments. Hamilton, now only thirty-two, plunged into his work, toiling at the carved mahogany desk in his spare office day after day, and often deep into the night, as summer gave way to fall and autumn faded into the raw cold of a New York winter.

During the new government's first months, Washington's command style as president became evident, and it evinced both striking similarities and differences with his habits as a military commander. During the war, he had been in the habit of issuing precise and detailed orders to his principal subordinates, the brigade commanders and various department heads, such as the commissary of prisoners and supply officers. As president, he met often with his secretaries of war and state to discuss matters, issue orders, receive updates, and hear their recommendations. But as Hamilton had expected would be true, Washington rarely intruded in the Treasury Department. Hamilton never met with Washington while he prepared his recommendations. Indeed, during the nearly six years that he served under the president, the Treasury secretary never asked his advice. Jefferson subsequently spoke of President Washington as the "hub of the wheel," but that is not likely how Hamilton viewed him, at least with regard to shaping economic policy for the infant nation.[10]

Washington's unequaled influence afforded him the opportunity to be the hub with respect to fighting for wondrous changes and unpopular causes. During his first year in office, he was in a position to employ his matchless standing to conceivably bring on a profound transformation in one area that would have given all of American history a different, and more salubrious, contour.

African slavery had never been much of a political issue prior to the American Revolution. Slavery had been legal in every colony, and some five hundred thousand blacks—20 percent of the inhabitants of the United States—were enslaved in 1776. But the doctrine of natural rights proclaimed by the Declaration of Independence, and the Revolution's stirring rhetoric of liberty and equality, caused many Americans to question the legitimacy of slavery. Nevertheless, the new Constitution had left slavery intact, though it stipulated that in 1808, Congress would be free, if it wished, to abolish the foreign slave trade. No one expected slavery to be a divisive issue until 1808, if then, but nine months after Washington's inauguration, two Quaker petitions to Congress stirred the pot. One called for an immediate end to the slave trade; the other, sent by the Pennsylvania Abolition Society, urged the gradual end of slavery itself. Normally, neither petition would have received much attention. However, Benjamin Franklin, in his final public act, had endorsed the abolitionist appeal. Suddenly, slavery was front and center on the American stage.[11]

Washington was no stranger to the slavery question or to being asked to help with its eradication. He had heard Lafayette and Colonels Laurens and Hamilton dilate on the immorality of slavery during the war. Just before the war ended, Lafayette offered to buy land in the West Indies—he eventually purchased an estate in French Guiana—if Washington agreed to move some of his chattel there to be prepared for freedom, a grand experiment designed to demonstrate that freedmen could become productive citizens.[12] Washington called the idea commendable but never joined with his young protégé. Not even Lafayette's eventual declaration that he "would never have drawn my sword in the cause of America if I could have conceived thereby that I was founding a land of slavery" was sufficient to move Washington to action.[13] In May 1785, Methodist leaders urged Washington's support for their petition to the Virginia assembly on behalf of gradual emancipation. He declined.[14]

Late that same year, Washington received a letter from Robert Pleasants, a Quaker who owned a large plantation on the James River. Pleasants, who had freed his eighty slaves and hired them back as free laborers, beseeched Washington to become the fulcrum in a national campaign to wipe the scourge of slavery from the land. Not only is "the Right of freedom . . . the natural & unalienable Right of all mankind," Pleasants began, but the American Revolution had been waged for "the cause of Liberty." Pleasants therefore found it odd that those "men . . . who were warm advocates" for freedom during the Revolution "are now sitting down in a state of ease, dissipation and extravagance on the labour of slaves." It was even more inexplicable that Washington, who had been "call'd to command the American Army" in the struggle to secure "the Rights of Mankind," continued to own slaves. Pleasants asked Washington to denounce slavery and emancipate his bondsmen. In the long run, slavery was doomed, he told the general. If Washington did nothing about slavery, Pleasants warned, his reputation in history would suffer with subsequent generations that lived in a free America. But if Washington helped eradicate this curse, his selfless act would be one of the "Crowning . . . Actions of thy Life."[15] Washington, who answered nearly every letter that he received in a long public career, never responded to Pleasants.

After the war, Washington spoke often of abandoning slavery at Mount Vernon. It appears that the Revolution had changed his attitudes enough to make him ill at ease owning slaves—an outlook he had never displayed before the war. But after eight hard years of wartime sacrifices, Washington wanted to live out the years left to him in material comfort, and he fully understood that the sustainability of Mount Vernon and his planter way of life were dependent on slave labor.

When the Quaker petitions were introduced in Congress early in 1790, President Washington never considered intruding. In addition to his self-interest, Washington thought it politically wise to let the issue of slavery's abolition die rather than to sow potentially fatal discord between the sections. He felt so strongly about some divisive matters—strengthening the central government, for instance—that he was willing to become involved. Slavery was not such an issue for Washington, and after a spirited fight in the House of Representatives, the Quaker petitions died.[16]

———————

WHILE CONGRESS WAS IN RECESS awaiting Hamilton's economic report, Washington, who had considerable time on his hands, drifted back in his thinking to one of Adams's recommendations for presidential behavior. The vice president had suggested in May that Washington make a tour of the country, and he pointed out that the office was portable, as arrangements could be made to have the diplomatic communiqués delivered to the president wherever he happened to be. Washington liked the idea, but, ever mindful of the troubles he had brought on himself for his protracted absences while a young Virginia soldier, he first brought up the matter with his cabinet. He told his department heads that his absence would be brief, as he planned to tour only New England. He added that his purpose was to gain knowledge of the state of the country and its attitude toward the new national government. Washington did not mention another motive, which actually superseded the two that he divulged. Employing all the pomp and ostentation that he dared muster, Washington hoped to demonstrate to New England—the land of the Boston Tea Party and Shays' Rebellion and a region in which two of the four states either had refused to ratify the Constitution or had barely done so—the energy, dignity, and potential power of the presidency. The cabinet unanimously endorsed the proposed journey.[17]

Aside from three brief meetings with Rochambeau in 1780 and 1781, Washington had not set foot in New England since his triumphant departure from Boston in 1776. His excursion in 1789 was arduous, consuming a month. On the outbound leg, he rode from Manhattan through Connecticut, Massachusetts, New Hampshire, and even farther north to the present sites of Portsmouth, New Hampshire, and Kittery, Maine. At village after village, as artillery boomed a welcome, the president departed his carriage to climb aboard his great white parade horse for the ride into town. He was always escorted by the militia, sometimes the local company, at times even a brigade of a couple of hundred men, and now and then they were joined by a martial band. Stirring up great swirls of dust, the marchers invariably proceeded to the village green, or commons, where nearly every resident had gathered. For these people who rarely had a dignitary pass in their midst, it was a heady experience, and a tumult of celebration ensued. The most notable figure of their age was in their town, astride his horse, surrounded by soldiers and important-looking

aides and attendants. The residents jostled for a better look. In many villages, Washington spoke for a minute or two, causing a breathless hush to
fall over the crowd. In the town chosen for his evening stopover, a leading
denizen sometimes hosted a social event, a tea, a dinner, even a dance,
though on most nights the exhausted president simply went to his lodging, usually a public tavern. (He sometimes privately rated both the enter-
tainment and his accommodations in his diary—"pretty good," "very
indifferent," "not a good house," "not very inviting.") In one instance, the
presidential party got lost, which caused Washington to rant gruffly about
the "blind & ignorant" Yankees who were his escorts, though on the
whole he enjoyed himself, never wearying of basking in the acclaim of
the friendly citizenry. He visited Lexington, where the war had begun,
saw numerous old acquaintances from the war years, and as the trip commenced in October, he drank in New England's fabled autumn splendor.

The trip was especially important in two respects. In villages such as
Lynn and Newburyport, Washington for the first time observed textile and
shoe manufacturing. One factory that he visited was the Hartford Manu-
factory, which had made the suit he had worn on Inauguration Day. (Its
workmanship was "not of the first quality," he noted in his diary, "but they
are good," and certainly their broadcloth was acceptable for his servants, he
added.)[18] Washington seemed to sense that he was witnessing a preview
of a new world of manufacturing, a thought that jelled once he grasped
the economic plan that Hamilton was putting together. Washington additionally managed to demonstrate the sovereignty of the central government, though in Boston it took a comic opera occurrence to make the
point. When the president arrived in the city, John Hancock, the governor
of Massachusetts and an advocate of state supremacy, neither welcomed
him nor called on him. Washington, who was lodging at the Widow Ingersoll's boardinghouse at the intersection of Court and Tremont streets,
adamantly refused to cross town and visit the governor. Protocol, he believed, demanded that a state official defer to a national official. Ultimately,
Hancock was the first to blink. Claiming that illness had sidelined him,
Hancock wrote that he would visit Washington at the president's residence.
Tongue in cheek, Washington responded: "The President of the United
States need not express the pleasure it will give him to see the Governor—
but, at the same time, he most earnestly begs that the Governor will not

hazard his health on this occasion." Hoping to save face, Hancock had himself wrapped in bandages and carried on a stretcher to Mrs. Ingersoll's abode. Indeed, the supposedly afflicted Hancock was conveyed into a ground-floor parlor, where Washington received him. Because he lacked the thespian skills of Washington, Hancock's theatrics were not only unconvincing, they were ridiculous. President Washington had made his point.[19]

HAMILTON MET HIS DEADLINE, tendering his grand plan on January 14, 1790, a date that might be considered the moment the cornerstone was laid for the superstructure of the modern United States. Hamilton's report did something else as well. What the Treasury secretary proposed turned out to be the launching pad for the incendiary partisanship that swept the nation during the supervening decade.

Although Hamilton had spent his youth fighting for America's separation from Great Britain, he admired the British political and economic systems. As for Washington, the Revolutionary War for Hamilton had been about enabling America and Americans to pursue their destiny. He was neither bothered by Britain's conspicuous class distinctions nor put off by its system of government. He made little effort to hide his belief that "the British Govt was the best in the world." In a six-hour speech at the Constitutional Convention, Hamilton had urged that Britain's system of governance be the template for the American government, even recommending a Senate whose members served for life and an executive that would be an "elective monarchy." The beauty of monarchy, he had said, was not merely that the king was "above corruption," but that in the conduct of foreign policy, a monarch was the best bet for attending to "the true interest and glory" of the nation. (According to his notes, Hamilton had planned to recommend a hereditary monarchy for the United States, but in the end he stopped short of such apostasy.)[20]

Not surprisingly, Secretary Hamilton's report recommended an American economic system modeled on that of Great Britain. He bolstered his proposals with the ruminations of well-known thinkers, including David Hume, Montesquieu, and Thomas Hobbes—and some who are no longer so well remembered, like Malachy Postlewayt—but for the most part it was as if his blueprint had been traced from the economic framework that had existed in Britain for nearly a century. Two generations before Washington's birth, the British had established the Bank of England and funded its public debt, which is to say the government guaranteed the repayment of its debt through revenues that were raised by borrowing and taxation, chiefly an excise on liquor. Under this system, the government always had money and the most affluent Britons, from whom the government borrowed, could grow steadily more affluent through their investments in government bonds and securities. In addition, given the availability of revenue, the military could be strengthened, wars without end could be waged, the colossal growth of the British Empire could proceed. Wealth generated by overseas colonies could be pumped back into the home islands. Much of it was to be for the benefit of the most affluent citizens, though a portion of the prosperity could trickle down to tradesmen and a rising middle class. One of this system's most attractive qualities was that the wealthiest and most powerful citizens were tied inextricably to the national government, a bond that seemingly ensured the government's survival. The system produced wealth, power, and security for Great Britain. This was Hamilton's dream for America, and it had been for some time. The Revolutionary War had barely started in 1775 when he published an essay that looked toward the "higher pitch of grandeur, opulence, and power" that would accompany an American victory. Fifteen years after Lexington and Concord, Hamilton was in a position to push for the creation of this very system and to dream that, if implemented, his plans would see to the fiscal stability, independence, and durability of the new American Republic. Though unaware of all that lurked in the crannies of Hamilton's thinking and planning, Washington dreamed the same dream of a grand American future.[21]

What Hamilton produced in January was, it turned out, only the first of several reports. The *Report Relative to a Provision for the Support of Public Credit* ran forty thousand words. It was complex and not easily digested. With clarity, however, the report revealed for the first time the scope of America's indebtedness. The new nation's debt totaled $79 million. State debts constituted nearly a third of this amount, and about 20 percent of the $54 million national debt stemmed from loans made by foreign governments. Hamilton proposed that the debts be consolidated, with the national government assuming the state debt. He also recommended that the existing bonds, certificates, and securities that had been issued by the states and Congress be exchanged for new ones that were to be funded, with the government pledging to pay interest on the debt from revenues raised by taxation. The new securities were to have no fixed date of maturity and were to pay a lower interest rate. Fearing that the existing rate of 6 percent would necessitate higher taxes than the public would tolerate, Hamilton proposed a 4 percent interest rate rising to 6 percent in 1801.

Hamilton was convinced that his plan would restore faith among creditors in the ability of the United States government to service its debt. He was certain, too, that his plan would increase the money stock, bringing to an end the habitual scarcity of money that had plagued Americans throughout the colonial era. Furthermore, by establishing the new nation's credit, Hamilton believed that his plan would make it possible for the United States to borrow in times of emergency. Although he hardly trumpeted the point, Hamilton understood funding to be "an instrument of war," for by assuring the ability to borrow money, Hamilton sought the means by which the new nation could secure its interests.[22] In this sense, Hamilton and those who understood his plan—and Washington certainly understood the feature about borrowing in times of peril—saw the enactment of Hamilton's report as essential for the realization of actual American independence.

Most people in the eighteenth century believed that indebtedness was deplorable, whether it involved individual or governmental debts. Quite aware of this, Hamilton declared in his report that debts invite "prodigality," but, thinking of the English system that he so admired, he also told his fellow countrymen that the "proper funding of the present debt, will render it a national blessing."[23] Over and above the question of creating an ongoing debt, Hamilton knew that two of his recommendations were likely to create a firestorm. It did not take clairvoyance to foresee that there would be opposition to the national government's assumption of state debts. The core of the Anti-Federalists' resistance to the Constitution had been an apprehension of an excessively strong national government. Debt assumption would not just strengthen the new central government, it would, at least in the minds of some, fatally weaken the states. Nor was it difficult to predict that some would object that stockjobbers, a literal handful of the fattest of the fat cats in the land, almost all of whom lived in northern cities, would be the first great beneficiaries of funding.

Washington, in his inaugural address, had prayed that "party animosities" might be avoided, and he may even have believed that his presence at the head of the administration would subdue political fracases.[24] That was not to be. Yet while it was hardly surprising that the Treasury secretary's plan sparked a fight, what amazed nearly everyone, and most especially Washington and Hamilton, was that the opposition was led by Madison. Washington was furious that Madison "stirred" up "long and laboured debates" over such a "delicate" subject, and it ushered in a chill, if not a break, between the two. In the run-up to Inauguration Day, and during Washington's first nine months in office, Madison had been what one historian has called the president's "prime minister."[25] He had stayed at Mount Vernon for a time, advised the president on numerous matters, and even helped draft his inaugural address. But following Madison's opposition to Hamilton's plan, his relationship with Washington would never be the same.

Although Washington remained silent in public, he privately endorsed Hamilton's plan, and for a variety of reasons. One was political. He knew that what Hamilton had proposed was vital to those who dominated the northern cities and, hence, the states above the Potomac. This, in large measure, was why the northern mercantile and financial interests had wanted to overthrow the Articles of Confederation, and Washington knew that if the new government was to succeed and the Union was to survive, those powerful interests had to have their way. But there was more. Washington shared Hamilton's dreams. As a businessman who had struggled unsuccessfully with the Potomac canal and Dismal Swamp projects—owing to a shortage of capital, he believed—Washington welcomed the advent of finance capitalism, which is what Hamilton was seeking to hatch. As a frontier land speculator, Washington saw the growth of national power that Hamilton promised as essential for the rapid pacification of the West. As a Nationalist eager to achieve the maximum strength and security of the United States, Washington saw no competing vision that offered the promise contained in Hamilton's program.

If Washington was startled by Madison's sudden flip-flop from Nationalist to the leading foe of greater power for the national government, he was not alone. Most contemporaries were perplexed by Madison's changed outlook, as historians have been ever since. But if Madison is seen as a politician and not as an idealized paragon of statesmanship, his behavior comes into focus. Madison had badly wanted to be a senator, but the Virginia assembly, unhappy with his fervor for a strong central government, had passed him over in favor of two Anti-Federalists. Madison had won election to the House, but only after a tough battle in which, for the first time in his life, he had been compelled to go on the hustings and court voters. If that was not a sufficient wake-up call, Madison knew that Hamilton's plan to assume the debts of the states was not popular in Virginia, which, like many southern states, had made considerable strides in reducing its debt. Madison knew that he could no longer afford to be heedless of what those at home wanted.

Like the thoroughgoing politician he was, Madison structured his opposition to Hamilton's plan in such a manner that Virginia might realize something from it. He additionally took a strong stance as a negotiating ploy, planning to fall back in time to a more acceptable position. Madison first—and largely for show—proposed that the original owners of certificates be cut in on funding. It was a fight that he had to know was hopeless from the beginning. (He would lose by a three-to-one margin in the House.) But Madison had a hidden agenda. He entered the battle hoping for a compromise that would net something for his state. (Madison won the nickname "the Big Knife" from his colleagues for his adroitness at cutting compromise bargains.)[26] With the help of Jefferson, Madison succeeded.

Jefferson, who had lived in Paris for the past five years—he had succeeded Franklin as the American minister in France—had returned to Virginia in December 1789 to tend to private business. When he disembarked in Norfolk, Jefferson discovered Washington's offer to become secretary of state. Unlike Hamilton, who had lusted to be part of Washington's administration, Jefferson wanted no part of it. He preferred to return to his diplomatic duties in France, but Jefferson had an inability to say no to Washington. After much soul-searching, he consented to join the administration.[27]

When Jefferson finally arrived in New York in the spring of 1790, Hamilton's funding proposal was center stage. Jefferson, for reasons that were more ideological than those that had aroused Madison, objected to Hamilton's plan, but he had been away so long that he felt out of touch. Jefferson was unfamiliar with the players, uncertain about the political factions that had coalesced over Hamilton's scheme, unclear even where bluffing stopped and hard-nosed, deadly reality began. Jefferson followed Madison's lead, pitching in only to help his young fellow Virginian, and friend, land a compromise.

The hottest issue of the day, aside from funding, was the location of the site of the national capital. Since the end of the war, numerous places had been suggested, but five predominated: New York City, Philadelphia, Baltimore, somewhere on the Susquehanna River in Pennsylvania's backcountry, and somewhere on the Potomac. Madison badly wanted to establish the capital on the Potomac, partly because he owned land along the river, but mostly because he knew that it was coveted by many speculators and entrepreneurs in Virginia. Jefferson, whose interest in linking east and west via the Potomac went back at least to 1784, was also avid for placing the capital on that river. Jefferson and Madison found Hamilton surprisingly amenable to a deal, even to betraying the interests of his allies in his hometown, New York. Hamilton wanted funding for the central government more than he wanted to locate the capital in Manhattan. He knew that New York would flourish with or without the national capital. Funding was the great prize that he had chased for nearly a decade, and in June 1790, he easily struck a deal with the two Virginians. Funding was enacted, and the capital was to be moved to Philadelphia—it was transferred from New York in the autumn of 1790—while work proceeded on the Federal City that was to exist on the Potomac.

According to the Residence Act, the capital was to be situated in a ten-mile-square District of Columbia that was to be located anywhere between where the Conococheague Creek and the Anacostia River flowed into the Potomac, a space of some one hundred miles. The act left it to President Washington to select the precise location. The legislation additionally stipulated that the Federal City must be ready for occupancy by the national government in ten years—by the summer of 1800—or the capital would remain permanently in Philadelphia. Washington rarely intruded in Congress's work and seldom requested specific authority, but he wanted, and received, a largely free hand in planning for the architecture and construction of the Federal City. He knew that if Congress became involved, things would be so ensnared in never-ending controversy that the city would not be ready to receive the federal government within a decade.[28]

Washington had played a role neither in arranging the compromise nor in securing passage of the Residence Act. His involvement with the Potomac was too well-known to pretend disinterest; besides, given the separation of powers, he steadfastly remained aloof from congressional deliberations. But his search for the best site of the capital was so transparently dictated by his self-interest that it aroused whispers at the time, though no one dared speak out. The president made a public display of conducting a supposedly dispassionate exploration for the most advantageous location. He traveled the one-hundred-mile Potomac route and spoke with local officials in numerous towns. Many offered up land and money in the hope of influencing his decision. (Shepherdstown, in present-day West Virginia, for instance, raised $20,000.) It was all for naught. As many suspected, Washington had made his decision before he undertook the trek. He wanted the capital located where the Anacostia and Potomac rivers met, though once he investigated closely, he realized that the site was a nudge too far north to serve his interests. He swiftly asked Congress to authorize moving the southern end of the District of Columbia a tad lower so that it would include Falls Church and Alexandria, towns in which he owned property.[29]

THE RESIDENCE ACT HAD HARDLY BEEN APPROVED—though Washington's entreaty to move the District of Columbia to include Alexandria had not been acted on—before the next installment of Hamilton's economic program was delivered to Congress in December 1790. Hamilton made his recommendations on successive days.

Maintaining that the impost could not be raised without causing deleterious effects to commerce, and asserting that additional revenue was required to cover the cost of assuming the state debts, Hamilton first urged a tax on distilled spirits. Such a step meant a duty on whiskey distilled by backcountry farmers, the very people who had been the bedrock of Anti-Federalism. Overhead costs negated all profits for a trans-Appalachian farmer who transported his corn across the mountains to sell in the East, but that same yeoman could earn $16 from the sale of the kegs of corn whiskey that a single mule could carry to eastern markets. Hamilton's tax would threaten that farmer with the loss of most, if not all, of his profits. Something was hidden within the legislation's verbiage. Hamilton's plan favored large distillers in the East, as they would pay a per-gallon tax while the small farmer-distiller paid according to the gallon capacity of his still. Hamilton's plan was not only to transfer wealth from the least affluent to the most prosperous, but to foster industry consolidation, creating a big business with considerable capital for investment. Within the interstices of Hamilton's plan lay a scheme for the further transference of economic and political power to northern and eastern cities. The backcountry would now pay a price—quite literally—for having lost the ratification battle.[30]

On the day after he urged the whiskey tax, Hamilton proposed a Bank of the United States capitalized at $10 million.[31] Drawing on the English experience, Hamilton believed that a national bank could do wonders for early America. It would provide the new nation with one currency—at the time, old Continental dollars, state-issued money, and even foreign currency were in circulation—increase the supply of money, provide credit for business and government, collect revenues, serve as a depository for government funds, and become a site for debt liquidation. The Treasury secretary was not trying to start capitalism in the United States. It already existed. Capitalism, one scholar has written, arrived "locked in the holds" of Christopher Columbus's vessels and the ships that brought the first English settlers to Virginia and New England, and it had been "germinating, spreading, and transforming the western world" ever since.[32] Instead, Hamilton—according to his biographer Ron Chernow—wished to "foster the cultural and legal setting in which [capitalism] flourished" and, in the process, launch in America the Industrial Revolution that, he recognized, was gathering in England.[33]

Many who lived in the eighteenth century looked on banks with suspicion. Not untypical was the Virginia planter who reacted to the Treasury secretary's proposal with the acid comment that he would no more walk into a bank than he would enter a bawdy house. Jefferson and Madison, who had not been unduly alarmed by Hamilton's plan for national debt funding, shared the consternation of their fellow Virginian. Not only would southern planters have little use for a bank, its stockholders—who, they knew, would be almost exclusively northern merchants and financiers, including some of the very men who had tenaciously resisted the break with England all the way down to July 4, 1776—would be in a position to exert incredible influence and power on Congress and even the states.

The two Virginians saw control of the new national government tipping ever more into the hands of northerners. But those were not their only objections to the Hamiltonian program that just now was coming into sharp focus. Jefferson had been startled by the transformation that had occurred in the United States during his five-year absence after 1784. When he arrived in Manhattan, Jefferson had heard well-heeled residents of New York speak openly and longingly about America's return to monarchy, and he beheld Washington comporting himself in a disconcertingly royal manner. Hamilton's vision was clearly that of an Anglophile. Jefferson feared that if Hamilton's program was enacted, the new United States Republic would take a long stride toward remodeling itself on the British prototype.

Jefferson was one of many Americans who saw the Bank of England as a prop of monarchy and an impediment to progressive change. He feared that the creation of a Bank of America would aid those in the United States who were least committed to republicanism and many other promises embodied in the American Revolution. As was true of many in his time, Jefferson also saw banks not only as the means through which capitalists exploited and suppressed the poor, but as institutions that fostered greed and whetted the appetite of many for sumptuosity, the great enemy, he thought, of the simplicity that allegedly sustained republicanism. That spirit—what today would be called market values—had, he believed, corrupted England, and it would destroy the rural virtues that had characterized colonial America. If Hamilton's vision prevailed, Jefferson was convinced, the rural way of life would in time be subsumed by all things urban, as farms disappeared and smokestacks sprang up.[34]

Something else gnawed at Jefferson. He had lived in Paris and visited London, and in both cities he had seen the squalor in which the lion's share of the inhabitants lived. Some Americans were deprived as well—those in bondage, to be sure, including the residents of Mulberry Row at Monticello—but most free inhabitants of the United States lived relatively prosperously in rural enclaves. Jefferson dreamed of America's preservation as a land of property-owning farmers, people who lived comfortably, were well provisioned, and had a stake in society. It was a formula for ensuring the success of America's republican experiment. Only 5 percent of Americans lived in cities at the time, but Jefferson knew that as cities grew in size and wealth, they would become more powerful politically. Even if cities constituted merely 15 or 20 percent of America's population, they would dominate the nation's political system and, he feared, vitiate the spirit of republicanism.[35]

In the gloom of winter, Congress passed the bank bill. The only hope left to Jefferson and Madison lay in a presidential veto. The Virginians were optimistic that Washington would see things their way. After all, the president was a rural Virginian, and he would consult Attorney General Randolph, also a Virginia planter. Furthermore, the governor of Virginia had written Washington asking that he do something to prevent the creation of the bank. Jefferson had deferred to Madison during the funding battle, but now, and for the duration of Washington's presidency, Jefferson took charge of the opposition to Hamiltonianism. Madison became Jefferson's satellite, and in the process he recanted the positions he had taken at the Constitutional Convention concerning a strong central government. Early in 1791, Jefferson approached Washington with a lengthy treatise arguing against the constitutionality of the bank. Jefferson appended to his tract a speech that Madison had delivered on the floor of the House, which also questioned the constitutionality of the bank bill. Washington read their opinions and, as expected, that of Randolph as well, which also concluded that Congress lacked the constitutional authority to create a national bank. Washington next asked Hamilton for his opinion.[36] One day after reading the massive report that Hamilton prepared—it exceeded twenty thousand words—Washington signed the bank bill into law.

Two things had dictated Washington's action. Circumstantial evidence suggests that he had been in conversation with senators who wanted a quid pro quo from him: If he would sign the bank bill into law, they would adjust the boundaries of the District of Columbia along the lines that Washington desired. The day after he signed the bill, the Senate approved the boundaries that Washington desired for the Federal District.[37] Second, although Washington had probably not thought in terms of a Bank of the United States during the most desperate days of the war, he had come to see Hamilton's plan as representing the best hope of attaining the national economic solvency that he had prayed for during the past dozen years. Washington believed in Hamilton, and like the Treasury secretary, the president identified the public well-being with the state of the economy. A few months after the funding plan was consummated, Washington declared that "our affairs assume a good aspect—Public credit is high, and stocks have risen amazingly." He added that "our public credit stands on that ground which three years ago it would have been considered a species of madness to have foretold."[38] For Washington—Unionist, Nationalist, entrepreneur—the Bank of the United States was crucial to the fulfillment of his aspirations.

The battle over the bank, Washington mused in an understated manner, had brought on a "line between the southern and eastern interests" that was "more strongly marked than could have been wished."[39] In fact, the creation of the bank opened the door to the emergence of formal political parties, ushering in one of the most tempestuous eras of partisan brawling in the history of American politics. In a sense, it was Madison, in newspaper essays, who fired the first shot in the partisan strife by purportedly giving an inside scoop on many of his former colleagues during the push for the Constitution. Some of the old Nationalist crowd were "antirepublican" in outlook, he reported, and for ten years or more they had been "attached to monarchy and aristocracy." A national government that was merely more efficacious than the Articles of Confederation would never satisfy them, he went on. They wanted a central "government without any limits at all." While Madison wrote his newspaper pieces, Jefferson provided seed money to lure Philip Freneau, a veteran journalist, into starting a newspaper to counter what he now was certain was the Hamilton-led counterrevolution. Seven months after Washington signed the bank bill, the first issue of Freneau's *National Gazette* was published. Jefferson's editor wasted no time baring his fangs. Hamilton, Freneau told his readers, "fancies himself the great pivot upon which the whole machine of government turns, throwing out of view . . . the president, the legislature, and the Constitution itself." Hamilton and the financiers would eventually reign supreme, he warned, and to this he added: The "accumulation of that power which is conferred by wealth in the hands of a few is the perpetual source of oppression and neglect to the rest of mankind." Although "the American Aristocrats have failed in their attempt to establish titles by distinction of law," he continued, "the destructive principles of aristocracy are too prevalent amongst us." The chief victims of their aggregation of power and influence, said Freneau, will be the "industrious mechanic, the laborious farmer, and generally the poor and middling class."[40]

In the spring of 1791, Jefferson and Madison traveled to New York and

New England on what they characterized as a "botanizing tour." They did study flora and fauna, but most of their trip was a study in politics. Visiting almost exclusively what had been backcountry Anti-Federalist strongholds, Jefferson and Madison were thinking in terms not so much of founding a political party in the modern sense of the word as of organizing resistance to the colossus of Hamiltonianism before it totally ruined their dreams for the American Revolution. Their hope was that an opposition would coalesce in Congress and in the state assemblies, which under the original Constitution chose United States senators. Their activities were redoubled when they witnessed the frenzy set off by the sale of stock in the bank on July 4, 1791. All twenty thousand shares were sold within an hour. It was bad enough that nearly every stockholder was a northerner, as Jefferson had feared would be the case, but he wrung his hands at what he saw happening to the United States. A delirium of "scrip-pomany" and a "rage of getting rich in a day" was turning the American landscape into a "gaming table," Jefferson moaned.[41]

Neither Jefferson nor Madison said anything untoward about Washington, in public or private, and they appear to have believed that the president sincerely occupied middle ground between their aspirations for the United States and Hamilton's. They misunderstood Washington, of course, and in May 1792, with the first round of congressional elections looming since the unveiling of Hamilton's plans, Jefferson revealed just how out of touch he was with regard to the president's thinking. First in a lengthy letter, then in a private meeting with the president, Jefferson expanded on Hamilton's malign influence, which he portrayed as spreading like a dark, iniquitous stain across the landscape. Jefferson urged Washington to remove Hamilton from his post. Describing in harrowing detail the frenzied spirit of avarice unleashed by funding and the bank, Jefferson told the president that Hamiltonianism had ruinously nourished "in our citizens habits of vice & idleness instead of industry & morality." It had also given birth to a "corrupt squadron" of stockjobbers that had taken control of Congress.

The principal argument that Jefferson made to Washington was that Hamilton's program had created political divisions that were potentially disastrous to the Union. Once ratification was achieved in 1788, he asserted, Americans had stood shoulder to shoulder behind the Constitution. But within three years Hamilton had divided the nation into factions of "Republican federalists" and "Monarchical federalists." The former wished to save the American Revolution. The latter, he contended, embraced Hamilton's affinity for all things British and saw each new installment of Hamiltonianism as "a stepping stone to monarchy."[42]

In their meeting at the President's House, Washington challenged Jefferson on most points. In his travels, the president said, he had found the citizenry to be "contented & happy." Those who resided in the North, Hamilton's region, were no less devoted to republicanism than were the residents of the South, he added. Washington saw no danger of monarchy taking hold in America. Anarchy might nourish the seeds of monarchy, he added, but he did not think that disorder loomed, unless partisanship created discontent where none had previously existed. Washington explicitly defended Hamilton's economic program. It had permitted indebtedness, but it was an "honest debt" that had done much to restore a sound economy. He believed that "sensible & moderate men" shared his outlook, and he doubtless told Jefferson what he had said to others: The "affairs of the United States still go on in a prosperous train . . . and the people are blessed with the enjoyment of those rights which can alone give security and happiness to a nation." Washington was convinced that the American people were more united than at any time since 1776. If Jefferson had harbored any doubts beforehand, he left the meeting with the president convinced as never before that Washington was "really approving [of] the treasury system."[43]

Fifteen months earlier, Jefferson had taken the first step to organize the opposition to Hamiltonianism, but after the summer of 1792, the smoldering partisanship burst into a raging conflagration that would burn for the remainder of the decade. Hamilton had not been fooled by Jefferson's and Madison's sudden interest in northern plant life. Guessing what they were up to on their supposed botanizing junket, Hamilton went on the attack. To this point, he had largely sought only to answer his critics. Now, Hamilton unsheathed his rapierlike pen. Writing often in the *Gazette of the United States,* the newspaper he had used successfully to promote his Treasury plans, Hamilton pillaged Jefferson with withering assaults. The Virginian affected the persona of a "retiring philosopher," Hamilton charged, but in reality he was a man of "profound ambition" whose quest for power had led him to establish a political party, the "Republican Party," as Madison had publicly called the opposition to Hamiltonianism. Madison had doubtless meant to identify a political faction, not a formal party in the sense that it would be known today, but Hamilton seized on the appellation as a term of opprobrium. Eighteenth-century Americans had been taught that political parties were an evil to be avoided, and Hamilton sought to exploit that prejudice—even as he covertly cobbled together a rival party, the Federalist Party.

But most of Hamilton's assault was intensely personal. He sketched Jefferson as a scoundrel, branding him "a cowardly assassin" for having covertly savaged the policies embraced by President Washington. A war hero himself, Hamilton pointed out that Jefferson not only had never borne arms, but had lived sumptuously at his mountaintop home in Virginia throughout most of the Revolutionary War. Jefferson, he charged, was the "Warrior of Monticelli." Hamilton also depicted Jefferson as a libertine, darkly hinting at sexual liaisons between master and a female slave at Monticello.[44]

Washington was fed up with the wrangling between his secretaries and the calumny they were publicly airing. Today, party battles are taken for granted. Partisanship was not unheard of in Washington's time, but never in peacetime had politics taken on such a harsh edge, nor had political attacks ever been so well orchestrated and so widely disseminated. Furthermore, the principal adversaries were members of Washington's administration. Churning with anxiety, Washington expressed his concern over what he called the tendentious and unsparingly "irritable charges" that had created "wounding suspicions." The remorseless harangues were "tearing [the] vitals" from the country, he said. In letters to Hamilton and Jefferson, Washington pleaded with them to cease their vilification of each other. Unless a more temperate tone prevailed, Washington warned, it would be impossible to "manage the Reins of Government or to keep the parts of it together."[45]

It may be that Washington took this position to make life easier for himself, but it is more likely that he genuinely feared for the well-being of the fragile nation. Given his inexperience with electoral politics—which from time to time he readily confessed to confidants—it is also possible that Washington overreacted to the dangers attending partisan warfare. Hamilton and Jefferson were no less eager than Washington to see the new nation survive, but both dismissed the president's exhortations and, without skipping a beat, continued to play hardball politics. They were veteran politicians who viewed partisanship as part and parcel of republican politics and as not necessarily unhealthy.

Something else conditioned Washington's response to the infighting. As his first term neared an end, Washington had obtained what he had sought. The strong national government was up and running, even exercising powers that many had not realized it possessed during the brawl to ratify the Constitution. Washington had made the presidency into a potent and magisterial office. Already, many of the seemingly intractable economic tribulations of the war years and immediate postwar period had been rectified, and a bright future beckoned. Washington was satisfied and foresaw no further government-produced domestic changes. Hamilton and Jefferson were truer revolutionaries than Washington, and for both much remained to be accomplished to fulfill their respective dreams. These two knew that years of political struggle lay ahead to achieve the America for which they longed. The forces unleashed by Hamilton's first economic report thirty months earlier had been merely the initial installment of an ongoing battle.

If Washington ever believed that his admonitions on behalf of harmony would do any good, he was disabused of those thoughts when Jefferson visited Mount Vernon early in October 1792. After strolling briefly outdoors, ignoring the early morning autumn chill, the president and his secretary of state came inside, possibly to Washington's cluttered study but more likely to a comfortable parlor. As always, their relationship was easy and convivial, but they had no more than taken their seats when the conversation turned to political matters, and the tenor of dialogue changed. Unburdened by doubt, Jefferson wasted no time in raising his all-too-familiar invidious allegations about Hamilton.

His colleague in the cabinet, Jefferson began, plotted to replace the Constitution with monarchy. The Treasury secretary had confided to him, Jefferson related, that "this constitution was a shilly shally thing of mere milk & water, which could not last, & was only good as a step to something better." The Treasury secretary had to have been thinking of monarchical government, Jefferson might have said, recalling for Washington what Hamilton had said at the Constitutional Convention about the wonders of the British governmental system. Through his economic program, Hamilton had fashioned a task force of "interested spirit[s] in the legislature." The behavior of Hamiltonian congressmen, Jefferson advised, was dictated by economic considerations. Someday, too, they would find it in their interest to see that the executive branch reduced the legislative branch to insignificance, as kings had once done to parliaments in Great Britain and France. Jefferson may have reminded the president that many Anti-Federalists had feared that the architects of the Constitution had plotted to lead America toward monarchy, and he also possibly raised the well-known warning of Patrick Henry that the Constitution "squints toward monarchy."

This was unpalatable to Washington and impossible to endure in silence. Struggling to keep his swiftly mounting emotions in check, Washington responded that there were not ten men in all the land who favored a king of America, and he probably pointed out what he had originally intended to say in his inaugural address: Hereditary monarchy would not start with him, as he had no children to whom to leave a throne. The president then launched into a defense of Hamilton, reiterating what he had told Jefferson in July. In two short years, he said, Hamilton's funding scheme had converted America from a "desperate" country without credit to a new nation on a sound footing. The president was correct. By late 1792, the market value of the new federal securities had climbed to six sevenths—85 percent—of their face value. Washington had just gathered a head of steam, transforming the atmosphere from amiable to sullen, when a servant appeared and announced that breakfast was served. The conversation about politics was at an end, and Washington saw to it that it was not renewed at the dining room table.[46]

HAMILTON AND JEFFERSON AGREED on only one thing. Both wished Washington to remain in the presidency for a second term, a step that appeared unlikely, as the president had spoken incessantly throughout 1792 of retiring. Some of what he said may have been a ploy aimed at temporizing the political battles, but for the most part Washington was sincere. When he had agreed to serve, he reminded those surrounding him, many who had beseeched his service had advised that "in 2 years all would be well in motion," leaving him free to step down sometime in 1791. Instead, he had stayed on, thinking "it was not worth while to disturb the course of things" throughout his elected term. But to accept another term would mean that he would remain in public life until age sixty-five, if he lived that long. Many of his wartime acquaintances were deceased by now, and during that very year, Washington had learned that his nephew and plantation manager, George Augustine, had one foot in the grave.

Tellingly, too, the president was aware of unmistakable signs that he was in decline. His hearing was failing, and so, too, was his memory. Washington feared, he said, that his memory loss might be worse than he realized, and he confided that he no longer trusted himself to remember things. He was plagued by diminished stamina as well, and from time to time since 1786 he had been riven with excruciating rheumatic pains, torments so severe that now and again he was unable to lift his arm and head or to turn over in bed. Washington had also experienced two frightening illnesses early in his presidency, both so serious that they were thought to have drawn him to death's doorstep. Two months after Inauguration Day, Washington came down with a high fever that was thought to be associated with a growth on his left thigh. It was diagnosed at the time as anthrax, or what contemporaries called "wool sorters disease," sometimes a fatal malady. A year later, he was felled with influenza, which turned into pneumonia, and his physicians did not think he would survive. He did, of course, but he admitted that he never fully recovered his strength, and some observers noted that he appeared to have aged considerably as a result of the ravages of that second illness. That said, the president's diminished capacity appears to have been exaggerated. In the year following his most serious illness, Washington undertook a tour of the South that spanned two thousand miles over several weeks—he plunged as far south as moss-draped Savannah—and he did so without harmful consequences.[47]

Over and above his concerns about health and longevity, and his hope to live out the time left to him in tranquillity at Mount Vernon, Washington told Madison that he simply did not enjoy being president. Though he had been spared personal attacks in the rough-and-tumble of partisanship, he felt, he said, as if he were "the indirect object" of Freneau's wicked assaults. To stay on might only invite criticism, as it would give some "room to say, that having tasted the sweets of office he could not do without them." But it was more than that. He did not enjoy politics. Public service inevitably invited distress, but politics at this level was like nothing he had ever experienced. To make matters worse, Washington often felt unfit for the presidency, as he lacked the legal training to judge issues that arose "out of the Constitution." In May 1792, Washington asked Madison to draft a farewell address for him.[48]

From the spring of 1792 onward, both Jefferson and Hamilton—and scores of essayists in the nation's newspapers—urged the president to accept a second term. Jefferson played on Washington's fears for the Union. "Your continuance at the head of affairs [is] of the last importance," he told the president. "The confidence of the whole union is centered in you. Your being at the helm" will prevent "the Monarchical federalists" under Hamilton from making "every argument which can be used to alarm & lead the people . . . into violence or secession. North & South will hang together, if they have you to hang on."[49] Hamilton also pleaded with Washington to stay on, but for him other matters were at stake. The continuation of Washington's presidency meant not only that the Treasury secretary and his allies would remain in power, but that Hamilton would exercise the utmost authority. He occupied the preeminent position in Washington's cabinet—the president, after all, had asked him to draft the State of the Union address that year—and Hamilton wanted to remain at his post in order to complete his agenda, which included further strengthening the powers of the executive. Since 1777, Washington had been Hamilton's "aegis," the word that Hamilton would one day use to describe how his association with Washington resulted in his elevation to ever bigger and better things. Washington's continuance in office was crucial for Hamilton's aspirations.[50] Equipped with a more exact sense than Jefferson for exploiting what made Washington tick, Hamilton reiterated to the president what he had counseled in 1788. Should the president retire, heedless to the calls of his countrymen to stay on for a second term, his reputation in history might suffer. If the United States did not survive, "your declining" to serve on "would be . . . deplored as the greatest evil" in having produced the catastrophe, a judgment that would be "critically hazardous to your own reputation."[51]

In the end, Washington agreed to "another tour of duty," as he put it, though it was not the forceful arguments of his cabinet secretaries alone that finally persuaded him. Progress on the new capital on the Potomac was dragging, leading Washington to wish to continue so that he might wield the leverage needed to push the work forward that would make the Federal City ready for occupancy by 1800.

But even that crucial matter was overshadowed by a gathering storm that Washington knew would buffet the United States, perhaps fatally. In the spring of 1792, France went to war with Austria and Prussia. Though the war was far away, Washington feared that in time its long tentacles would reach across the ocean and impinge on countless aspects of life in America, especially as the United States remained an ally of France. As 1793 approached, rumors swirled that Great Britain might soon join the coalition against France. Should that occur, Washington knew that a crisis would emerge that would make the political turbulence ignited by Hamilton's economic program a thing of child's play. The troubles caused by Europe's war could rip America asunder. More than any single factor, the ominous prospect of an Anglo-French war drove Washington to agree to a second term, turning his back on a retirement that he would have preferred.

10

Endless Crises: Washington's Second Term, 1793–1797

THE CONFLAGRATION THAT WAS TO RAVAGE EUROPE for a full generation was sired by the French Revolution, an epic train of events set in motion almost precisely as Washington was inaugurated in 1789. Most Americans cheered the earliest incidents in Paris and Versailles, seeing the French Revolution as akin to the American Revolution and even inspired by it. Hamilton said that he had not felt such exaltation since he heard the news of Lexington and Concord. When Lafayette sent Washington the key to the Bastille in the summer of 1790, the president proudly hung it in the central hall at Mount Vernon. Washington lauded the violent liberation of the prison that had symbolized tyrannical monarchy as a "Victory gained by Liberty over Despotism."[1]

For some time, Washington shrugged off the episodic violence that accompanied the French Revolution. "Disagreeable Things" were unavoidable if seminal reforms were to be achieved, he said with candor, but Washington also believed that his country would benefit from a revolutionary France that would be an ideological as well as an actual ally of the United States. As Washington's presidency entered its third year, his views had grown more mixed. Because "the tumultuous populace of large cities are ever to be dreaded," he exclaimed, Washington prayed for stability in France. At the same time, he rejoiced at the prospect of the French Revolution enhancing human liberty throughout Europe. But when violence increased dramatically in France in 1791, Washington for the first time spoke of those incidents as "outrages." He had begun to fear, too, that should revolution threaten to sweep across Europe, the monarchical nations would unite to destroy the French Revolution, setting off a continental war filled with danger for the United States.[2]

The European strife that Washington feared erupted early in 1792 when France declared war on Austria. As the year progressed, other nations joined with the Austrians in a coalition against France, an alliance bent on restoring the Old Regime. Most Americans continued to pray for the survival of the French Revolution, and when word reached the United States in December 1792 that an allied invasion of France had been repulsed at the frontier in the Battle of Valmy, spontaneous rejoicing swept the United States. Though in the grip of an icy winter, Americans expressed their euphoria with fireworks and parades. Yet the nearly unanimous jubilation did not last. War helped turn the French Revolution toward unbridled violence. Hard on the heels of word of Valmy, news arrived in America of the "September Massacres," a carnival of savagery in which over one thousand people perished, some of them clergymen. That was merely a prelude. In January 1793, Louis XVI and Marie Antoinette, the queen, were executed. In the months that followed, thousands more perished—twenty-six hundred in Paris alone—in the Reign of Terror.[3]

As Washington wrestled with the entreaties of Jefferson and Hamilton to accept a second term, American opinion toward the French Revolution and the European war began to divide along partisan lines. More conservative Federalists were alarmed by what they saw as the "democratical hurricane" blowing through France. Nothing troubled them more than the egalitarianism espoused by the most radical French revolutionaries. One Federalist spoke of the "contagion of levelism" that gripped France. Perhaps it was desirable that aristocratic titles had been abolished, some thought, but in homage to the tradition that separated and delineated social classes, they added that it was outrageous for the formal bow to be replaced with handshakes, for trousers to be substituted for knee britches and silk stockings, and for all class distinctions to be banished, so that all people were addressed as "Citizen" or "Citess." The French Revolution, one Federalist lamented, had reduced everyone in France to a status of equality with French barbers. No longer enthralled by affairs in France, Hamilton had taken to equating the French Revolution with a dreadful "volcano . . . spreading ruin and devastation." God forbid, it went without saying, that something similarly appalling might occur in the United States.[4]

But the French Revolution remained popular with many Americans— probably most—who likely would have applauded Jefferson's private defense of its excesses. The execution of the king was essential in order to prevent the "reestablishment of despotism," he said. It was regrettable that blood had been shed, but Jefferson equated it with the deplorable, though defensible, loss of lives in a just war. Better, he said, that a few lives were ruined than that all of France, and perhaps an entire continent, should groan under regal absolutism and privileged noblemen.[5]

Virtually no American wanted the United States to be involved in Europe's war. Less than a decade had passed since the end of the War of Independence, and the memory of that long, brutal war remained fresh. Furthermore, part of the appeal of independence in 1776 had been to escape a parent state that, as Thomas Paine put it in *Common Sense,* had repeatedly dragged the colonies into wars that were of no advantage to the American people. Yet many believed this war in Europe was not just another war. It was a pivotal struggle. With clarity, Washington captured that belief, remarking that the outcome of the war could determine the "fate of man" and the "happiness of posterity" for generations to come.[6] At the same time, Washington knew that the American public not only was divided over the French Revolution, his countrymen were set against one another with regard to how far their own American Revolution should go. One faction in American politics sought the preservation of much of pre-1776 Anglo-American social and political culture, and it feared that the triumph of radical French ideas would unlock the floodgates that held back the radicalism nourished by the American Revolution. The other faction feared that the defeat of the French Revolution by reactionary Europe would strengthen the hand of their counterparts in America. The annihilation of Parisian radicalism might snuff out all hope for the birthday of the new world that independence had seemed to offer in 1776. Thus, the French Revolution was not a faraway event remote to the lives of the American people. It was intertwined with the shape that the new American nation would assume. The success or failure of the French Revolution, many believed, would determine whether the American Revolution continued or was stopped in its tracks.

Many understood that the European war would take on even greater urgency should Great Britain join the coalition against France. By late that year, as Washington wrestled with the question of accepting a second term, he was convinced that Britain would soon be a belligerent. "For the sake of humanity I hope such an event will not take place," Washington said, as he knew that when Britain went to war, it would arouse American Anglophiles and Anglophobes alike, stretching partisan divisions to the breaking point and increasing the pressure for America to join the war. More than anything, Washington hoped that the United States would not be "forced into" the wars of the French Revolution. No one was more aware of the danger of going to war. For one thing, the new nation might not endure the strains of another war. For another, Washington, who knew just how miraculous America's victory had been in the Revolutionary War, worried about what might occur in another war, particularly in a conflict in which the population was even more badly divided than it had been in 1776. Washington also knew that if it came to it, the greatest pressure for going to war would come from those who hated Great Britain. Much residual goodwill existed toward France, the ally that had provided lifesaving assistance during the desperate days of the Revolutionary War, while enmity toward Britain burned in the hearts of many Americans. Washington did not want war with France, but above all he hoped to maintain peace with Great Britain. Roughly 90 percent of America's taxable imports arrived from Great Britain. War with Britain would, at the very least, shatter the mending American economy. With peace, Washington said, primarily meaning peace with Britain, the United States could in a few years attain "the great advantages which nature & circumstances have placed within our reach." Peace would also mean that in no time Americans would "be ranked not only among the most respectable, but among the happiest people on this globe."[7]

Four years earlier, Washington in part had accepted the presidency from a belief that his unique stature would be crucial to the launching of the American ship of state. Late in 1792, he consented to a second term because he understood that under his guidance the ship of state would stand its best chance of remaining afloat in a dangerous world at war. He rehearsed his customary disclaimers about remaining in power. He would prefer "those personal enjoyments" of Mount Vernon, but as always, he said, he felt that he must subordinate "private interest" to the "public desire." It was a familiar litany, but this time Washington meant what he said. In "no instance of my life have I ever been more sensible of the sacrifice" of accepting public service, he said, for "at my age, the love of retirement grows every day more & more powerful." But peace was imperative if the United States was to survive, and in the shape and form that Washington desired. Above all, it would be folly to join in the war, for "our weight could be but Small" and "the loss to ourselves would be certain."[8]

WASHINGTON NEVER ANNOUNCED HIS CANDIDACY in the election of 1792. He simply never said that he would not consider a second term, and by early 1793 it was clear that the electoral college had reelected him by another unanimous vote. Washington did not want a formal celebration for his second inaugural—he spoke of simply taking the oath in private at his residence—and to be sure, quite a few in the Republican Party hoped to avoid another extravaganza with all the trappings of a monarchical coronation. In the end, the cabinet persuaded the president to go through with a brief and simple ceremony. On Inauguration Day, March 4, Washington climbed aboard his carriage at the President's House and rode alone in the dappled sunshine of late winter. A large, happy throng overspilled onto the streets. The spectators cheered when the president alighted outside the Senate Chamber, watching with puzzled fascination as Washington was escorted inside by ushers who saluted him with white wands. The ceremony that followed was swift and without fanfare. Washington took the oath before the members of Congress and hurriedly read the shortest inaugural address on record, a mere two-paragraph, 133-word speech that was entirely forgettable. When he returned to his coach, the scrum of assembled well-wishers, and the curious, gave Washington three cheers. He bowed and returned to the President's House. It had been low-key in the extreme, but Washington, with his exquisitely deft feel for theater and public sentiment, had hit on something. As one of his biographers noted, this inauguration, in contrast with its predecessor, was "the greater and the more moving because of its simplicity."[9]

Perhaps even Washington had grown weary of the adulation. Already, he was widely referred to as "our Country's Father," and during the past decade numerous cities and towns and even churches had celebrated his birthday, singing reverential songs—"*Freeman!* attune the noble lay, / *George,* the Hero's born to day"—in his honor. More likely, Washington continued to feast on his acclaim, but he was vexed by the growing criticism of the public exaltation, which many thought out of place in a republic. He was uneasy, too, with the censure that his practices were arousing in the Republican press. Nothing that he did provoked greater disparagement than his weekly levees, leading him disingenuously to tell Jefferson that he had agreed to those regally styled undertakings only as a result of bad advice proffered by Hamilton and Adams.[10]

A few days after the low-key inaugural festivities, Washington departed the capital for Mount Vernon, his third trip home in a year. He had been away from Philadelphia for nearly five months in 1792, a radical departure from his stay-at-the-helm practices during his first three years in office. But if he expected a carefree vacation on this jaunt, he was rudely disappointed. Washington had been home for only a few days when word reached him that France and Great Britain were at war. He left the next morning for Philadelphia.[11]

From the moment he learned that Britain was a belligerent, Washington told the members of his cabinet that he favored American neutrality, a stance for which he has been widely and justly praised by scholars. But it was not as if Washington's leadership salvaged neutrality from a blindly warmongering citizenry. Neutrality was the nearly universal desire among Americans, though Washington lucidly saw that without an official policy the nation might be pulled unwillingly into hostilities. What perhaps most worried Washington was that unless forestalled, greedy entrepreneurs in the coastal areas would bankroll provocative privateering ventures. Thousands of American privateers had sailed the seas during the War of Independence— General Washington himself had invested in some of those ventures— hoping for a windfall should their ship succeed in taking a rich enemy prize. But if American privateering flourished in this European war, British ships would be almost the sole victims, as the British dominated America's import trade. Reprisals would inevitably follow. American property and lives would be lost, and the song of war would be quick to follow. The American craving for neutrality would yield to cries for vengeance against

Great Britain. Washington wished to head off the potential for such a mounting crisis, and his cabinet unanimously endorsed his position. He issued the Proclamation of Neutrality late in April.[12]

The proclamation did not—could not—stop every would-be privateer, though Washington's biggest initial headache came from an unexpected source. Citizen Edmond-Charles Genêt, revolutionary France's red-haired, thirty-year-old, ruinously intemperate minister to the United States, arrived that spring. He had hardly disembarked his ship, the *Embuscade,* before he sought to fan the smoldering fires of American nationalism, expansionism, and antipathy to Great Britain.

Prior to Genêt's arrival, Washington had bent over backward to placate France, the United States' lone ally. In February, when cash-strapped France asked the United States to make advance payments on its debt, Washington agreed despite Hamilton's objections. In March, when it was learned that the revolutionary French government that had recently executed Louis XVI was sending its first minister to the United States, Washington, once again contrary to Hamilton's wishes, decided to receive the diplomat. In April, Hamilton and Knox advocated the suspension of the Franco-American Treaty of Alliance, as the pact mandated American assistance should France go to war; for a third time in sixty days, Washington spurned Hamilton's recommendation and sided with Jefferson and Randolph, who had urged that the treaty remain in force but that the clause requiring American assistance be ignored.[13]

In one respect, Genêt eased Washington's cares. The French minister did not wish the United States to enter the war. It was more valuable to France as a neutral than as a belligerent. Genêt made that clear following his disembarkation in Charleston in April, but he was hardly ashore before he commissioned American privateers to prey on British shipping, established a French court to condemn captured British prizes taken at sea, purchased munitions for France, and sought to enlist volunteers in an expedition against Spanish Florida. No one had to tell Washington that Genêt's provocations were certain to precipitate a crisis, possibly even war, with Britain and Spain.[14]

When Genêt at last reached Philadelphia, about two weeks after the Proclamation of Neutrality was issued, Washington received him with icy coldness. Rarely in the annals of diplomacy has one ally greeted another with such unwelcoming formality. Washington, who had long since mastered the technique of silently conveying glacial displeasure, accentuated his feelings by receiving Genêt while standing beneath portraits of the French king and queen whom Genêt's revolutionary masters had recently executed.[15]

Intemperately, and very unwisely, Genêt made Washington's obvious displeasure into a test of wills. Challenging the head of state is seldom recommended for a diplomat. Defying an overwhelmingly popular chief executive such as Washington was the height of folly. Jefferson declared Genêt "a wreck" in July when the Frenchman provided arms for a privateer in Philadelphia and prattled on publicly about raising soldiers in Kentucky to march on Spanish Florida. A few days later, Washington demanded Genêt's recall.[16]

Genêt was gone quickly, but as Washington had feared since the final months of his first term, hostilities between France and Great Britain awakened harsh and potentially unmanageable feelings within the United States. Not even the deep vexation over the Articles of Confederation had posed as much danger to the Union as would the troubles with Britain that began to build in 1793. This crisis would present the greatest danger of sundering the United States that had existed since the dark days of wartime despair in 1780 and 1781.

Anti-British vehemence grew in 1793, rearing up from a stockpile of causes. The wellspring of Anglophobia could easily be traced to Britain's vexatious imperial policies after 1765. The bitterness sowed by British taxes and coercion was nourished and magnified a thousandfold by eight years of fighting during the War of Independence. Nor had Anglo-American relations returned to normal following the war. While London sped its wares to American shops, it refused to allow its former subjects to resume their prewar trade in British ports. American merchants lost fortunes, and thousands of laborers and artisans, who as colonists had found work through the export trade, faced years of austerity. London's activities in the trans-Appalachian West also poisoned Britain's standing with Americans and caused Washington, by far, his greatest concern. The Treaty of Paris stipulated that Britain was to remove its troops from the United States, but in 1793, on the tenth anniversary of that accord, the British army continued to occupy posts beyond the mountains. The redcoats' presence was not merely an affront to American sovereignty. The British army funneled arms from Canada to Native American tribes living west of the head of the Ohio. The British wanted to help the Indians, who had fought on their side during the Revolutionary War, but London also trafficked in arms for geopolitical reasons. Strengthening the Indians slowed the advance of Americans across the mountains, protecting British fur-trading interests in the region. What is more, if Washington in the course of his 1784 journey to Millers Run had come to understand that the western settlers might be turned away from the United States "with the touch of a feather," as he had said at the time, London had gleaned that as well.

What drew settlers beyond the mountains was abundant land and the prospect of commercial farming. Land was readily available, but profitable husbandry required access to America's east coast cities, as well as to European and Caribbean markets. Until the Potomac Canal Company, or some other canal company, succeeded in linking east and west, the only viable route to market was through New Orleans, the gateway to the Atlantic trade. Farmers living in the Northwest Territory could reach New Orleans only via the Ohio and Mississippi rivers. But New Orleans was part of Spanish Florida—Florida, everyone agreed, stretched west to the Mississippi River—and Madrid had never opened the river or the port of New Orleans to American shippers. With Britain and Spain at war with France, America's ally and republican cohort, an already volatile western situation seemed to be growing especially combustible. It might not take much to provoke America's western settlers to attack either the British or the Spanish, or both. By the same token, Spain and Britain might offer incentives to western farmers—opening the Mississippi River and New Orleans or restraining the Indians, for instance—to tempt them to separate from the United States.

The dangers and opportunities afforded by western territories had been recognized by Lawrence Washington and his generation in the 1740s, and they were a principal ingredient in driving George Washington, first, to embrace American independence, and second, to push for a strong American central government in the 1780s. After the Revolutionary War, Washington had recognized that only a powerful United States could deal with Britain and Spain. He also understood that a strong national government with ample economic resources was needed to assist those entrepreneurs whose projects might couple those Americans living on both sides of the mountains. Washington had his stronger national government when he became president. With Hamilton's economic program in place, the means of providing capital for business ventures had also been realized.

Between 1789 and 1793, President Washington followed the lead of his foreign policy predecessors under the Articles of Confederation. He, too, sought through diplomacy to normalize relations with Britain and Spain. It had not worked before, and it did not work for Washington. London was "high against America," as John Adams had reported while he was America's first minister to the Court of St. James after 1785, and it was not disposed to settle its differences with the United States. Above all, London made clear, there could be no settlement until the United States liquidated its prewar debts to British creditors, an obligation that the United States had agreed to in the Treaty of Paris. Spain, like Great Britain, was not keen to settle with the United States. It remained tied to what it had first offered the United States in 1786: a treaty that opened Spanish ports to American trade, but on condition that the United States renounced navigation on the Mississippi River for twenty years.[17]

WHILE PRESIDENT WASHINGTON BIDED his time with the European powers, he pursued a pugnacious course toward the Indians who lived in the Northwest. When Washington took office, the situation in present-day Ohio was urgent. The blood of western settlers was being shed in recurring clashes with the Indians, who were armed by the British and desperate to save their homeland from the never-ending waves of interlopers from the East. Washington thought the land-hungry settlers were mostly to blame for the carnage, and in private he acknowledged that there would never be peace until "we can restrain [their] tubulence and disorderly conduct." Yet his administration felt political pressure from several quarters to rapidly pacify the Indians. Flexing the muscles of the United States, Washington acknowledged in private, would mean that the "Western people would be endulged [and] Many Members of Congress gratified."[18] First and foremost, however, Washington hoped as well that pandering to the frontier inhabitants would wed them to the United States.

During 1790, Washington asked Congress to enlarge the frontier army, though his administration denied that it was bent on war. It claimed that the stronger army was designed to compel the northwestern tribes "to sue for peace before a blow is struck at them," leading to "just and liberal treaties" that would leave the Indians in numerous western reservations.[19] Taking the bait, Congress rapidly authorized the expansion of the army to one thousand men and the activation of fifteen hundred militiamen from Kentucky, Virginia, and Pennsylvania. This army was led by Colonel Josiah Harmar, a thirty-seven-year-old veteran soldier who had performed ably during the Revolutionary War and remained on duty afterward to serve as commander of the United States army on the frontier. Harmar was a protégé of Thomas Mifflin, Washington's sworn enemy, but with Hamilton's economic program on the front burner at the time, the president shied away from a divisive battle that would have ensued from changing commanders.

The plan, which Washington signed off on, called for Harmar's force to march nearly 150 miles through Indian territory, sowing terror along the way before it struck the principal towns of the Miami and Shawnee tribes. From the outset, the operation proceeded on a hope and a prayer. Strategically, it bore a close resemblance to the Sullivan Expedition, which Washington had unleashed in 1779, but Sullivan had possessed an infinitely larger force, including sizable numbers of Continental regulars. The army that Harmar led north in September from near present-day Cincinnati consisted of fourteen hundred men, 80 percent of whom were militiamen. In three weeks, the army had clambered through the lush green hills that splayed back from the Ohio River and onto the heat-rilled prairie in central Ohio. Autumn's chilly weather intruded by the time the army had plunged deep into the interior, but spirits remained high, as all was apparently going well. Forgoing resistance, the Indians had vanished. No warriors were to be seen as Harmar's men destroyed five Indian towns and torched thousands of bushels of corn. What the Americans did not know was that the Indians were waiting for them. Fearing an incident with the British army, Washington had notified the English of Harmar's expedition, assuring them the American objective was to pacify the Indian "banditti," not to assail the posts occupied by the British army. Unfortunately for Harmar, the British apprised the Indians, who organized their response and lay in wait.

On October 22, 1790, the Americans walked into an ambush in a wooded moraine heavy with the musty scent of fallen leaves. More than two hundred men were lost before the army could retreat to safety. The losses among Kentucky militiamen totaled nearly 30 percent, extinguishing their will to continue and stripping Harmar of the means of further campaigning. Ignominiously, Harmar fell back to his starting point on the Ohio. Washington responded as he nearly always did when his plans failed. He found a scapegoat. This time, as had been the case with General Stephen after Germantown, Washington passed along the tattle—which was entirely untrue—that Harmar had failed because he was a drunkard. Given Harmar's alleged yearning for the rum pot, Washington never explained why he had permitted such a supposedly undependable officer to remain in command of the army.[20]

The Harmar debacle had a silver lining, at least from Washington's perspective. Since just prior to the breakup of the Continental army in the final weeks of the Revolutionary War, Washington had recommended to Congress that it maintain a peacetime standing army consisting of twenty-six hundred men. No less important, Washington had urged the reorganization of the militia, with uniform regulations established by Congress and enforced by the inspector general of the United States army. In 1783, Congress's military committee had been chaired by Hamilton. Not surprisingly, it not only adopted Washington's recommendations, but went a step further and proposed that the standing army total more than three thousand men. But there was an ancient antipathy to standing armies in Anglo-America, and nowhere was that distrust stronger than in New England—which, not coincidentally, had no particular interest in opening the trans-Appalachian West. Yankee objections, together with the financial plight of the 1780s, shredded the hopes of Washington and his fellow Nationalists. Though military spending totaled 40 percent of the national budget, Congress approved only a small frontier force of seven hundred men, and during a considerable portion of the Articles of Confederation, America's army never reached the allotted number. It totaled six hundred men on Inauguration Day in 1789.[21]

Some Nationalists had expected Washington to push for a large army and a national militia system once he took office, but with the deft feel of an adroit politician, the president held back while Hamilton's economic program was under consideration. When the bank, the last indispensable element in the Treasury secretary's plan, was in place—a few short weeks after Harmar's defeat—Washington asked Congress to double the size of the army, bringing it to over two thousand men. The administration additionally pilloried the performance of the militiamen who had served under Harmar, which was easy enough to do, as Harmar himself had blamed the militia, calling its behavior a "damned farce."[22] Washington, of course, had been denigrating the militia since his days in command of the Virginia Regiment. He had little good to say of militiamen during the Revolutionary War, and in his postwar reflections on America's victory, he never acknowledged its important contributions. Around this time, Washington even publicly criticized General Nathanael Greene's judgment in the Battle of Guilford Courthouse, contending that Greene would have done better had he not put such a great reliance on his militiamen. Washington's remarks about Guilford Courthouse took considerable chutzpah, as Greene had achieved more in that engagement than had Washington in any pitched battle during the Revolutionary War.[23] Washington, of course, was not a dispassionate historian. He was a politician who was sowing the seeds for his long-cherished reform of the militia system. As that would take time, he opted to bypass the militia altogether when he put together the second expedition in Ohio. He proposed augmenting the larger army that he was seeking by raising fifteen hundred volunteers who would sign on for six months' service. Unlike militiamen, the volunteers would be subjected to regular army discipline.

Congress consented to the army's expansion and the recruiting of volunteers, and in March 1791, acting through Secretary of War Knox, the president appointed General Arthur St. Clair, governor of the Northwest Territory, to command the next expedition to pacify the Indians. St. Clair was a fifty-five-year-old Scotsman who had come to America as a subaltern in the British army during the French and Indian War. He left the army after the war but settled in the colonies. He had served in the Continental army, rising to the rank of major general, though his record had been undistinguished. That notwithstanding, Washington never considered giving Harmar a second chance, nor did he give any thought to elevating one of the officers who had gained experience under Harmar in the frontier army. Rejigging his strategy somewhat, the president directed St. Clair to construct a chain of forts—Washington was resurrecting Dinwiddie's

policy that had so angered him as a young Virginia colonel—and he furnished the expedition with more artillery than was given its predecessor.
As about three quarters of his men were to be volunteers, St. Clair was also
advised to impose a harsh disciplinary regimen. "Disciplined valor will triumph over the undisciplined Indians," Secretary of War Knox advised.

Ten months after Harmar's army had pushed off from Fort Washington
on the Ohio River, St. Clair's force of some two thousand men marched
out of the same site and into Ohio's forbidding interior. Tasked with building forts, St. Clair's army moved more slowly than its predecessor. Otherwise, St. Clair's advance was a repetition of Harmar's. By mid-autumn, as
harsh winds and swirling snow bedeviled the men, his army had seen few
Indians and met no resistance, though fear of a surprise attack hung heavy.
That was precisely what occurred early in November. St. Clair's army
walked into a trap. Miamis, Wyandots, Shawnees, Delawares, and braves
from the Six Nations Confederation had laid their plans well, organizing
an attack accented by a murderous crossfire. Before the Americans could
unlimber their artillery, the Indian warriors had raced past and behind
them, rendering the big guns useless. What followed was an unmitigated
disaster. Over nine hundred soldiers—and some fifty female camp
followers—were lost in the attack. Proportionately, St. Clair's losses almost
precisely duplicated the terrible casualties sustained by Braddock thirty-
six years before.[24]

According to his stepgrandson, who was residing at the President's House
in Philadelphia, Washington's hair-trigger temper snapped when he received
word of the disaster. "My last solemn warning" to St. Clair, he supposedly
roared, had been to "beware of a surprise! You know how the Indians fight
us." Instead, Washington raged, his voice straining with anger, St. Clair had
"suffer[ed] that army to be cut to pieces, hacked, butchered, tomahawked."[25]
Washington knew there would be questions and condemnations, and he was
correct. Criticism of the administration's Indian policies quickly surfaced in
the press and in Congress. Some thought a more diligent diplomatic campaign might have led to peace, making the use of military force unnecessary.
Others said straightaway that Washington's government had "unjustly undertaken" a bellicose policy from the outset. Still others scorned the administration for an unwise and unsuccessful military strategy. "Money by
millions" had been squandered in the Northwest Territory, said one

congressman, though "no one, except those who are in the secrets of the Cabinet, knows for what reason the war has been thus carried on for three years."[26]

Washington was in the uncomfortable position of explaining a failed policy and a military defeat. He knew that St. Clair could not be scapegoated. Doing so would compel him to explain how he had come to select a second incompetent general. Nor could militiamen be blamed for this misfortune. The administration responded by dropping its earlier pretense. Previously, the United States had pursued "pacific measures . . . for establishing peace" with the Indians, Jefferson told Congress with a straight face, but now it had to go to war with the northwest tribes. The "Community are called upon for considerable exertions to relieve a part which is suffering," Washington told Congress. Contending that St. Clair had failed because he had been given inadequate numbers and too few regulars, Washington asked for what he and his fellow Nationalists had always desired: a large standing army and an overhaul of the militia system. Knox went before Congress to request that the army be expanded to more than five thousand men, double what Washington in 1783 had said was needed and ten times the army that existed at the time of the Constitutional Convention. Not all Americans were happy with the prospect of a standing army, and some charged that there were those within the administration who secretly sought to obtain a huge national force that could be used to crush dissent and silence opposition voices. But in the wake of two humiliating frontier disasters, Congress, which conducted its deliberations in secret, consented.

Washington was less successful in reorganizing the militia. He asked Congress to bring the militia under national jurisdiction, but his request never stood a chance. The states simply would not relinquish control of their militias. In the end, Congress—in the Uniform Militia Act of 1792—merely decreed that all men between the ages of eighteen and forty-five were to serve in their state's militia and to provide their own arms.[27]

Washington gave considerable thought to selecting the commander of the new army, though in the end he failed to exert real leadership. Washington longed to appoint Light Horse Harry Lee, whom he thought the best of the available Revolutionary War officers. He shrank from that step, however, as Lee had never risen above the rank of colonel. To appoint Lee

over several surviving Continental army general officers was to risk a political firestorm. Washington feared, too, that "if any disaster should befal
the [army] it would instantly be ascribed to the inexperience" of the commander, "drawing a weight upon *my* shoulders too heavy to be borne."
Washington eventually settled on General Anthony Wayne, the best of a
bad lot, he seemed to say. Harmar and St. Clair had permitted themselves to
be surprised in battle, but so had Wayne, who at Paoli in Pennsylvania in
1777 had suffered an egregious defeat when surprised by the British.
Washington acknowledged that Wayne was "open to flattery—vain—
easily imposed upon—and liable to be drawn into scrapes," and he knew as
well that the general's record, at best, was one of sporadic accomplishments.[28] Washington chose him anyway.

Wayne took command of the remnants of St. Clair's army—fewer than
one hundred men—in the summer of 1792. A year later, when Washington demanded the recall of Genêt, Wayne was still recruiting and training
his army, though Washington did not pressure him to move before he was
ready. It was imperative that the third expedition into Ohio succeed. The
president merely exhorted Wayne not to relax "in the disciplining of the
troops and most especially in making them *perfect marksmen.*"[29] As Washington waited for Wayne to act, fresh intertwined crises sprang up.

GREAT BRITAIN'S WAR WITH FRANCE sparked the creation in 1793 of some
thirty Democratic-Republican Societies, the first of what would be a staple
of American politics: a pressure group that sought to shape public opinion.
This movement mined the democratic impulses that had stirred in the
coming of the Revolution. It neither wanted the bloody excesses of the
French Revolution to be exported to America nor called for radically new
departures. Instead, as historian Sean Wilentz has written, the paramount
objective of the societies was "to secure the [American] Revolution they
believed was already won," stanching the Federalist counterrevolution.[30]

A handful of these societies sprang up along the rim of settlement on
the frontier, though most chapters were in the eastern cities. Their members
were drawn overwhelmingly from the middle class—craftsmen, doctors,
lawyers, printers, teachers, innkeepers, and assorted small merchants. The
Philadelphia chapter, the largest and most important within the movement,
included some well-known members, such as Dr. Benjamin Rush, who

had been critical of General Washington during the desperate Valley Forge winter. On the whole, those active in the Democratic-Republican Societies passionately hated Great Britain and no less fervently defended the French Revolution as the great hope for European and American republicanism, democracy, and egalitarianism. They were just as ardently opposed to Hamiltonian finance and the royalist trappings of Federalism, both of which they deemed to be the antithesis of the glowing promise of 1776. Though circumspect about attacking President Washington, the societies were dismayed by what they saw as the reactionary tendencies in his presidency.

Above all, they were eager to have the United States do what it could to prevent Great Britain and the "combined tyrants" in Europe from crushing the French Revolution. If the forces of reaction succeeded in snuffing out the French Revolution, the societies warned, the royalists would then seek to "extinguish the fire of freedom in every part of the globe." Among Europe's counterrevolutionaries, Great Britain posed the greatest danger to America. It would seek to accomplish its ends in North America in one of two ways. With France brought to heel, Britain might again make war on the United States. The societies liked to point out that six thousand redcoats remained on American soil, or just inside Canada, and they frequently cited Benjamin Franklin's late-in-life warning that London, which had never "digested the loss of its dominion over us," harbored "flattering hopes of recovering" its former colonies. The societies' polemicists maintained that London might also subtly connive with the Federalist Party to assure that every vestige of the American Revolution was overcome. By virtue of Hamilton's economic program, they pointed out, London already pulled the strings that operated the American economy. The best hope for the preservation and advancement of the spirit of 1776, the societies contended, was through an indissoluble linkage of the American Revolution and the French Revolution. "If kings combine to support kings, why not republicans to support republicans?" they asked. Some urged the use of force to drive the British from the Northwest, even calling for an American invasion of Canada—that again, Washington must have muttered—and some wished to coerce Spain into opening the Mississippi River to American commerce.[31]

The most conservative Americans, including Washington, were horrified by the movement, which they denigrated as "self-created," a buzzword in that day for "democratic." (The societies answered the charge by pointing out that they had been preceded by the Society of Cincinnati, a self-created society of which General Washington was the president, and that the Constitutional Convention was a self-created conclave that had met in secret and ultimately proposed the overthrow of the Articles of Confederation.)[32] Conservatives understood that the Democratic-Republican groundswell was a bottom-up populist movement that threatened the existence of clearly delineated class divisions and the monopolization of national politics by the elite. What made the societies especially worrisome to conservatives was that they saw with clarity how the movement resembled the Sons of Liberty, the radical organization that had succeeded in mobilizing large chunks of the population in the coming of the American Revolution. An openly pro-British editor denigrated the clubs as confederations of "butchers, tinkers, broken hucksters, and trans-Atlantic traitors." In private, Washington said more or less the same thing. The societies, he wrote, were "absurd . . . arrogant . . . [and] pernicious" entities whose "*artful* and *designing*" members sought, "by destroying all confidence in the Administration," the overthrow of the government. Those who joined the Democratic-Republican Societies, he added harshly, were "traiters to their Country." Washington looked askance on the progressive political and social agenda that the Democratic-Republican Societies advocated, though he believed that the most immediate threat arose from their opposition to American neutrality. If the movement gained momentum, he said, it would become increasingly difficult to keep the United States from "the horrors of a disastrous War."[33]

What gave special urgency to Washington's worries was a new British policy invoked in the summer of 1793. In Orders-in-Council, London announced that it would not permit neutral shipments of wheat, corn, and flour to France, the very staples of American commerce with its ally. By early 1794, over four hundred American merchantmen had fallen victim to the Royal Navy, and American trade in the West Indies had been brought to a halt. With America's windswept docks idled, every city felt the hammer-blow impact of Britain's policy. Nor was it long before farmers, their wheat in storage rather than in the holds of ships, knew that they, too, were victims of London's new edict. (When Washington learned of the

Orders-in-Council, he wrote home with instructions not to sell Mount Vernon's wheat until prices spiked as a result of the British obstructions.)[34] As economic woes spread, so did the opposition to American neutrality. Britain was emboldened to issue the Orders-in-Council, it was said, because it saw neutrality as "a pusillanimous disposition on our part." Shrinking from criticizing Washington directly, the Democratic-Republican Societies portrayed him as the "grand Sultan of Constantinople, shut up in his apartment and unacquainted" with the sinister motives of the Federalists who surrounded him and supposedly manipulated him into issuing the Proclamation of Neutrality.[35]

For the first time since 1775, the fever to fight the British grew within the United States. The Democratic-Republican Societies fanned the flames, but the confrontational mood would have swelled even had the movement never existed. This was a bellicosity driven by nationalism and resentment of the economic malaise that Great Britain had provoked. Without a navy to speak of, America's only means of striking at the British was in the West. Calls grew for attacking the redcoats who remained on United States soil. Some implored the citizenry to demonstrate that, like their predecessors in 1776, they were capable of "brave and republican exertions." Others asserted that it was safe to attack the British, as London had its hands full with France. Some maintained that France would "stand by us until Canada is independent of Britain."[36] As if such truculence were not worrisome enough to Washington, the Republican members of Congress were calling for commercial discrimination against the British: America must not allow British imports until London permitted American ships to enter Britain's harbors.

In the twelve months since word of France's war with Britain had reached America, President Washington's troubles had grown by quantum leaps. Unless the volatile situation was controlled, war with Britain and the ruination of America's economy were entirely possible, twin evils that could threaten the very survival of the United States. Something had to be done. While the societies talked wildly and combatively, and the Republicans pushed for economic retaliation, Federalists from the northern mercantile states coalesced around the idea of a diplomatic initiative. In March, several Federalist congressmen met secretly with Washington and urged him to send an envoy to London. Never one to make a rapid decision, Washington considered the matter for more than a month, though during some of that time he was wrestling with his choice of whom to select for the mission. He rejected Hamilton, knowing that he was a "lightening rod for enmity." He also thought of naming Gouverneur Morris or Jefferson, though he decided against the former because he was widely seen as anti-French and against the latter as he was viewed as anti-British. Finally, in April 1794, Washington announced that John Jay, who had been the secretary of foreign affairs for a lengthy stretch in the 1780s, was being sent to England as an envoy extraordinary to seek "a friendly adjustment of our complaints" and to make clear the United States' "reluctance to hostility." Specifically, Jay was to seek to convince Britain to open its British ports to American goods, gain restitution for the property damages inflicted by the Royal Navy, persuade London to renounce its policy of impressment—the abduction of sailors from American ships—and derive compensation for the thousands of slaves who had sailed from America with the British army at the end of the Revolutionary War.[37] With Jay headed for London, something had to be done with the current envoy to the Court of St. James, Thomas Pinckney. Having received encouraging, though inconclusive, hints that Spain might be willing to resolve its differences with the United States, Washington dispatched Pinckney to Madrid to test the waters.

Washington's stab at a peaceful accommodation with London took the wind out of the sails of the movement to embargo British trade. The best that Madison and its other proponents could get was a thirty-day suspension of British imports, a step that Washington could live with, as it communicated to London what likely lay ahead should negotiations fail, and it did so without having a particularly deleterious impact on the collection of revenue from the impost. Yet if Washington thought that by naming an envoy he would solve his problems, he was mistaken. With the possible exception of Hamilton, Washington could hardly have selected a diplomat more likely than Jay to roil vast numbers of his countrymen.

While in charge of foreign policy in 1786, Jay, a New Yorker, had been willing to renounce America's right of navigation on the Mississippi River in exchange for a lucrative commercial pact with Spain. Northern ports would have flourished, while the South and West would have suffered from such a deal. Southerners and westerners had long memories. More recently, Jay had further antagonized many in those sections by openly denouncing Genêt and repeatedly urging the repayment of prewar debts—most of which was owed by southern planters—to British creditors. If all that was not enough, Jay was the chief justice of the Supreme Court. For him to take on the diplomatic assignment while he sat on the Court seemed to many to be not only a case of plural officeholding—one of the more hated facets of political life in the British colonies prior to the American Revolution—but a violation of separation of powers under the new Constitution.

Open criticism of Washington, virtually unheard of during the first five years of his presidency, swelled. Critics blasted the president for having violated the spirit of the Constitution and for having selected a New York aristocrat—a member of the "British party" within the United States, it was often said—who could not be trusted to safeguard the vital interests of all sections of his country. The Democratic-Republican Society in Washington County, Pennsylvania, near Millers Run, denounced Washington for habitually turning to the wealthiest men for government assignments. "The Revolution in France has sufficiently proved that generals may be taken from the ranks, and ministers of state from the obscurity of the most remote village." Why, that chapter wondered, could the president of the United States not find men of talent among ordinary republicans within the United States?[38]

Jay's appointment was not the sole provocation that ignited western fury. Anger and frustration had been growing in the backcountry. The bitterness of the westerners was not always rational, but it was quite real. The continued presence of the British army, and its largesse toward the Indians, was an obvious sore spot. So, too, was the Washington administration's utter lack of success—some, unfairly, said its lack of interest—in removing the British troops from United States soil. Nor had the settlers' dreams of becoming commercial farmers materialized. The Mississippi River and the port of New Orleans had not been opened. Genêt, who appeared to many to have been the official most interested in doing something to open the river, had been sent packing by Washington. Many in western Pennsylvania were additionally convinced that their standard of living had declined. Increasingly, lush bottomland was monopolized by the wealthy—often by absentee landlords like Washington. Unable to break out of the dirt-poor existence that went hand in glove with subsistence farming, many cash-strapped settlers had been compelled to sell portions of their farmsteads at rock-bottom prices, not infrequently seeing their property pass into the hands of affluent eastern speculators. The one commodity that the farmers could market was corn whiskey. The grain could be distilled cheaply, stored in barrels, and hauled by wagon over the mountains, where it fetched a decent price in eastern communities. But a considerable chunk of the profit that these hardscrabble yeomen hoped for from their spirits was siphoned off by the excise on whiskey that Washington and Hamilton had championed three years earlier. Those with a sense of political reality know that the tax system almost always reveals who truly is in control of government. No one likes to pay taxes, and more often than not those who have power impose the heaviest tax burdens on those who do not. Farmers in the American West knew full well by 1794 that in Federalist America they were at the bottom of the heap.[39]

It was clear in 1791, when the tax on whiskey was passed, that the levy would kindle fury on the frontier. Congress itself had been deeply divided by the legislation. The whiskey bill was defeated three times in the House of Representatives before it finally passed. Jefferson had warned Washington that to raise revenue from farmers for meeting the debts of society's most affluent members—the stockjobbers—would be "odious" to those who had to pay the duties, and it would create such a pernicious reservoir of discontent in the West that the tax would have to be collected by "arbitrary and vexatious means." If it came to that, Jefferson warned Washington, the administration would be seen as making "war on our own citizens." Pennsylvania's senator William Maclay advised that "war and bloodshed" would be the "most likely consequence" of the tax.[40]

Five state legislatures—those of Pennsylvania, North Carolina, Maryland, Virginia, and Georgia—condemned the proposed tax while it was under consideration (in part, they feared the federal tax would lay waste to their own tax base). Washington was advised that many in North Carolina, a state that had voted against ratification, were "declaiming furiously" against "the evil operations of such acts" as the excise on spirits. The president was also warned that some in North Carolina were engaged in "a premeditated attempt to draw" the state "into a contest" with the federal government. Some at the time were equally certain that Hamilton had opted for an excise on whiskey in the hope of provoking western resistance. If westerners reprised Shays' Rebellion, their speculation went, Hamilton would have a golden opportunity to demonstrate the mighty power of the new national government.

Alternatives had existed to the whiskey tax. Revenue could have been raised by selling western lands, or Hamilton might have urged a land tax, a levy on houses and commercial buildings, or a head tax. The Constitution authorized direct taxes, stipulating that they must be apportioned among the states according to population. Or Hamilton might simply have recommended an increase in the impost. But he stuck inflexibly to the whiskey tax, and Washington stuck with him.

While he never discussed the matter—at least on paper—it is also not likely that Washington, a great landowner who hoped to sell his western properties, would have favored a land tax. But there was something else. Though Washington acknowledged that "it was vehemently affirmed by many" that the whiskey tax "could never be executed in the Southern States," the president seemed to believe that his own colossal standing would be sufficient to curtail, even extinguish, whatever opposition might arise.[41]

In April 1791, soon after the whiskey tax passed Congress, Washington set out on a tour of the southern states. He had considered such a trip since his swing through New England in 1789, but that he undertook the arduous journey at this moment was due in part to his hope of demonstrating the power of his office and of strengthening the hand of those southerners who favored a strong national government. Over a period of more than sixty spring-soft southern days, he traveled through North Carolina, hugging roads near the coast, dropped into the low country, where he paused for a spell in both Charleston and Savannah, and returned home through the densely forested Carolina backcountry. Along the way, he followed a routine similar to that of his previous presidential trip. The president rode in a carriage until he approached a village, then he climbed aboard Prescott, his great white parade horse, whose hooves had been painted and polished for the occasion. At stops here and there, Washington spoke with numerous leaders and delivered a score of speeches. When it was done, Washington was convinced that the whiskey levy "will be carried into effect not only without opposition, but with very general approbation."[42]

He was wrong. The prescience of those who had predicted trouble was quickly borne out. The first tax collectors who entered western Pennsylvania in the fall of 1791, about three months after Washington completed his southern tour, were violently attacked. Some were tarred and feathered, while others were badly beaten, left tied to trees in the forest, and threatened with scalping. Still others were shot at or their homes were looted or burned. Protests and assaults were not limited to Pennsylvania. Spasms of bloody violence occurred in Kentucky and in every state south of the Potomac. Pennsylvania witnessed the largest and noisiest public gatherings demanding evasion of the federal tax, and the published statements by the Washington County Democratic-Republican Society were especially heated. That chapter not only portrayed the tax as a matter of the East making war on the West, but vowed not to submit to the excise. Eighteen months after the law took effect, not one cent in revenue had been collected in western Pennsylvania. A year after he had predicted western compliance with the law, Washington told Hamilton that most Virginians unwaveringly believed that western resistance against the whiskey levy could be broken only with a heavy hand and that such a dire step could have terrible consequences. Nevertheless, Washington would not back down. If it came to it, he told Hamilton, he would use force to break the resistance to the tax, "however disagreeable this would be to me."[43]

Nothing was more important to Washington than the retention of the West, but he faced a terrible quandary. Dealing stridently with the whiskey rebels not only risked fomenting the latent secessionist tendencies of the western settlers, but might prove fatal to the Nationalists' hopes of further strengthening the powers of the national government. But tolerating the dissidents' defiance was unpalatable. Doing nothing would exhibit personal weakness, betray the consolidationist movement, and deal a crumpling blow to Hamiltonian economics. Washington also had a personal stake in how things played out. Not only was his cherished reputation on the line, but he owned thousands of acres in the West that would remain worthless unless settlers moved in numbers to the region. He could hardly have forgotten, moreover, that the squatters on his Millers Run properties in western Pennsylvania had come to loathe him to such a degree that they abandoned the land they loved, and had assiduously developed, rather than rent from him. Washington's inextricable ties to the

West made him an intimately involved player in this crisis, and it may have led him to move slowly and cautiously, displaying incredible patience and statesmanship, even to try several peaceful approaches in an effort to placate the rebels.

During 1792, the administration revised flaws in the original law, lowered the duty on spirits, and dispatched emissaries to the Pennsylvania frontier both to reason with and to cajole the dissidents. The president also issued a stern but carefully worded proclamation "exhort[ing]"—he avoided the word *ordering*—the fractious westerners "to refrain and desist from all unlawful combinations and proceedings." Curiously, Washington was untroubled by the reality that other taxes were often evaded. (Customs agents smoothly enforced the tariff in the large port cities, but small shippers elsewhere—in Maine, for example—routinely dodged the federal tax collectors.)[44]

From the start, Washington had been under pressure to take a harsher line. Federalists—including Chief Justice Jay, who privately peddled advice to members of the executive branch during the western provocations—were clamoring for "Firmness," "strong measures," even the use of "requisite force." In September 1792, Hamilton advised the president that "Moderation enough has been shewn—'tis time to assume a different tone" lest "the authority of the Government" be rendered "prostrate." The Treasury secretary took it on himself that fall to elicit the chief justice's sanction for Washington to "repair in person to the scene of commotion" should the "application of force . . . be unavoidable." Washington was not moved by the combative recommendations of Hamilton and his friends. If force was used, Washington told Hamilton, the Republicans would exclaim: " 'The cat is let out. We now see for what purpose an Army was raised.' " Force must be "the dernier resort," Washington vowed, as he particularly feared that its use would tie his hands should it someday be necessary for him to ask Congress to raise a great army for America's defense against a foreign threat.[45]

Washington's velvet-glove approach seemed to have been the wisest course, as the frontier cooled down for nearly a year. Even though for the second straight year no revenue was collected in the troubled region, the president rejoiced during 1793 that western defiance "is not so universal" as it had been the previous year. But if Washington believed that the worst was behind him, his optimism was misplaced. Western anger and defiance grew once again and came to a rolling boil in 1794. Great Britain's entrance into the war, the polemical barrages of the Democratic-Republican Societies, Jay's appointment as the envoy to London, and the failure to pacify the Indians—though nearly three years had elapsed since St. Clair's debacle—were all factors in reigniting volatile passions along the frontier from Kentucky and Pennsylvania southward. Episodic attacks on tax collectors resumed, as did violent assaults on farmers who tried to pay the levy. Again, no revenue was collected in Kentucky or Pennsylvania's western counties in the 1793–1794 fiscal year.[46]

Oppressed with doubts, Washington did not immediately resort to the use of force, though the revenue shortfall occasioned by the stubborn western disobedience drove the administration to ask Congress for new taxes, including a sales tax on auctions, excise taxes on snuff, sugar, and carriages, a stamp tax on stock transfers, a license fee on retailers of imported spirits, and duties on manufacturing centered in the eastern cities. Urban businessmen fought being taxed, though they did so peacefully, arguing that the levy would be injurious to the economy and meeting, quietly and covertly, with congressmen with whom they had ready access. Congress did not tax the well-heeled businessmen.[47]

Washington's patience with the tax insurgency finally ran out in the summer of 1794. His private remarks suggest that nothing exasperated him more than the steady drumbeat of vitriol published by settlers around Mingo Creek and Millers Run and by the Washington County Democratic-Republican Society. While virtually every chapter condemned the actions of the tax insurgents as "unwarrantable and unconstitutional," the Washington County members charged that the western settlers were "kept in poverty" in large measure because of the folly and timidity—even indifference—of Washington's administration. Where, they asked, was "the strong-nerved government of America" that had been promised during the ratification battle? Why, they wondered, were westerners "subjected to all the burthens, and enjoy none of the benefits arising from government"? Washington's western policy was "preposterous," they charged. It consisted of "chasing Indians as you would fugitive wild beasts." Instead, they asserted, the president's armies should have been "attacking the source" of the Native Americans' strength, the British army. Denied British assistance, the

Indians, "like a serpent, without the heat of the sun, [would] become torpid and motionless." The western settlers, they went on, had believed that the American government was "lodged with the body of the people." That seemed not to be the case. Washington, who comported himself with "unapproachable splendor," had surrounded himself with a vestigial American aristocracy that was pro-British by choice. Toward the West, Washington's administration behaved with "supineness, lethargy, and sometimes a little toryism." The administration was lacking in the "integrity or spirit of republicanism." The country needed cleansing of the "degeneracy and corruption" that had taken hold of it since 1789. Only so much could be tolerated, they warned. "Patriotism . . . has its bounds."[48]

If one incident above all led Washington to unsheathe the sword, it was the July 16 attack on the home of General John Neville, the regional supervisor for collection of the federal excise in western Pennsylvania. The onslaught was sparked by the appearance of a federal marshal bearing warrants ordering sixty tax resisters into court in Philadelphia. Most of those who invaded Neville's property were Mingo Creek militiamen. Neville and members of his family, together with many of his eighteen slaves, fought back from inside his fortified house. Six of the attackers were wounded and two killed before they threw in the towel, ending the siege. No one inside Neville's house was injured.[49]

Washington was outraged when he learned of the attack, and not solely because the militiamen had assaulted a federal official. Neville was an old acquaintance whose life bore striking similarities to his own. The son of a Virginia planter, Neville had soldiered under Braddock and served in the Continental army, fighting at Trenton, Princeton, Germantown, and Monmouth and enduring the winter of misery at Valley Forge. Compounding matters, Washington, only thirty days before the attack, had retained Neville's son, Presley, to collect rents from his tenants in western Pennsylvania.[50]

Washington quickly summoned his cabinet and also invited several Pennsylvania officials to attend. The cabinet's composition had changed that year. Jefferson was gone. Having appealed to Washington to serve a second term, Jefferson announced his intention of resigning once Washington consented. Britain's entrance into the European war, and Washington's pleas that he stay on, led Jefferson to relent, but at the end of 1793 he quit and returned to Monticello to commence yet another "permanent" retirement, as Hamilton snidely remarked. Jefferson's successor, Edmund Randolph, was no Johnny-come-lately to politics or cabinet battles. A former governor of Virginia and delegate to the Constitutional Convention, Randolph had been Washington's attorney general for five years. But he was no match for Hamilton. Besides, Randolph's standing in Washington's eyes had plummeted earlier that year when he failed to enthusiastically support the Jay mission to London.[51]

Hamilton dominated the cabinet's deliberations. The Treasury secretary took the same line that he had taken two years earlier, advocating "an immediate resort to military force," and he urged that the force that was deployed must be "an imposing one." Nothing less than an army of twelve thousand men would do. The "very existence of Government demands this course," Hamilton avowed. The Pennsylvania authorities did not roll over. Thinking the Treasury secretary a provocateur, they contended that many reports of rebellion in the western counties were exaggerated. The judiciary could peaceably handle the matter, Governor Mifflin and his aides insisted.[52]

Washington listened to Hamilton, though it may have been a case of the Treasury secretary simply providing the resolve for steps that Washington already wished to take. Behaving more viscerally than rationally, Washington was convinced that the Democratic-Republican Societies were behind the insurgency, though they had not come into existence until nearly a year after the troubles began on the frontier. Pulsing with ferocity, Washington declared the Whiskey Rebellion was "the first *formidable* fruit" of the strident conduct of the societies. The calamity waiting to happen had occurred, he said, and demanded that the societies be brought into "disesteem" before they "shake the government to its foundations." Everything that Washington said indicated that he saw the societies as a greater problem than the antitax insurgents on the frontier. While he wanted to deal with the tax insurgents, Washington wished even more to wipe out what he called the "diabolical" Democratic-Republican movement.[53] He believed the Democratic-Republican Societies had overreached and were vulnerable. Aggressive action by his administration, he hoped, would shatter the movement, enervating all who stood for what he saw as unwelcome social and political change.

In August, Washington issued a proclamation couched in language that was remarkably similar to that used by George III in 1775 when he proclaimed that his American subjects were in rebellion. Decreeing that western Pennsylvania was in "open rebellion," Washington called 12,950 militiamen to service. The United States now had thirty times the number of men under arms that it had when Washington had taken office five years earlier.[54] He overcame his hesitancy to name Henry Lee, now the governor of Virginia, as commander of a United States military force and put him in charge of the expedition. As had been the case when Washington appeared threatened by Generals Conway and Gates, Hamilton was turned loose with his acid-laced pen. He wrote a series of newspaper essays that revealed to the nation that the upheaval west of the mountains was nothing less than a "dark conspiracy" to force the United States into another war with Great Britain. Hamilton additionally took pains to assert not only that Washington had in no way incited "violence by severe and irritating measures," but that the president had turned to the use of force as the only means of preserving "every thing . . . dear to a free, enlightened, and prudent people."[55]

ON SEPTEMBER 30, WASHINGTON, once again wearing his impeccably tailored buff-and-blue Continental army uniform and high black riding boots, rode out of Philadelphia to join with the army somewhere in Pennsylvania. While Colonel Lee would be in charge of the dirty work of actually repressing the western dissidents, Washington planned to stay with the army just long enough to see that it was properly organized.

In contrast with his dramatic departure for the front in 1775, this time there were few well-wishers on hand to bid Washington godspeed. Furthermore, as a concession to the aches and pains of age, Washington was seated in a carriage, not on horseback. With Hamilton at his side and also attired in full military regalia, the presidential carriage rolled through the nearly empty cobblestone streets of the city and onto the lonely, unpaved country roads that led west. Five days later, at Carlisle, the commander in chief met up with his army, a ragged collection of militiamen, some clad in makeshift uniforms, others in their day-to-day work clothes. Switching to a horse and strapping a sword to his side, Washington took command.

Riding at the head of this motley army—a force roughly as large as the armies that he had led into battle against the British regulars at places such as Brandywine and Yorktown—Washington and his dust-covered soldiers proceeded west across Pennsylvania's rolling green terrain. At night, in camp, the president managed army matters, brusquely barking out orders. One observer, who had never before seen Washington, was struck by his stern visage and "grave, distant, and austere" manner. About halfway to the scene of the tax insurgency, Governor Lee rendezvoused with the army, prompting Washington to announce that he would return to Philadelphia to tend to his other presidential duties. He wanted no part of killing American citizens, which must have appeared in the offing as he listened to Hamilton—a bitter stew of wrath, vengeance, maniacal energy, and lust for greater glory—loudly promise all within earshot that every whiskey rebel would be "skewered, shot, or hanged on the first tree." Nor did Washington wish to preside over a fiasco, should that be the outcome of this adventure. The commander in chief grandly delivered a "Farewell Address" to the army and rode eastward.[56]

Lee took charge and, with Hamilton in the saddle at his side, led the army toward battle. They did not find a fight. The disaffected westerners had availed themselves of an amnesty offered by the president or fled into hiding in the endless wilderness. Lee's army rounded up some 150 alleged rebels—many were dragged from their homes in the middle of the night— and with studied incivility confined them in squalor, often depriving them of adequate heat and food, until they could be interrogated. Ultimately, sufficient evidence could be found for prosecuting only 20 supposed insurgents—one dangerous rebel for every 600 soldiers. The score of captives were sent on a pitiless winter's march across the length of Pennsylvania. Just before Christmas in 1794, they were paraded, shackled and in rags, through the streets of Philadelphia. Only 2 of the prisoners were convicted. One was an imbecile, the other a madman. Washington pardoned both.[57]

Washington's use of force to suppress the Whiskey Rebellion won the approval of most citizens, the lion's share of whom not only deplored the violence of the tax resisters, but—in a country in which three fourths of the party-affiliated press consisted of Federalist newspapers—obtained most of their information about the affair from prejudicial sources.[58] But if the whiskey insurgents had erred with their ferocity, Washington, who normally had an excellent feel for the popular pulse, went too far in his

State of the Union address, delivered just prior to his government's show-casing of the captive rebels in downtown Philadelphia. Not content to pillory the western lawbreakers, Washington excoriated all the Democratic-Republican Societies. His hostile remarks were widely interpreted as noth-ing less than the condemnation of all who were committed to democracy and egalitarianism as public enemies. This was too much for Madison and Jefferson, who saw anew that Washington was lost to them. Madison pri-vately called the president's glowering speech "the greatest error of his po-litical life," while Jefferson, with ineffable sadness, lamented that where once Washington had been "the head of a nation," he had become just "the head of a party," the Federalists.[59]

The Federalists might have tried to soften the president's remarks, hop-ing to moderate the party's image. Instead, they embraced Washington's harsh rhetoric, as never before merging party and president. Some Feder-alists hoped to wheedle a third term out of Washington, but most simply wished to use the revered president to secure more of the party's goals be-fore his term expired. Washington's name could be of immeasurable help to the Federalists in stanching the growth of democracy and egalitarian-ism, further strengthening the powers of the national government, and as-sisting Great Britain as it faced the full fury of the French Revolution. At Valley Forge, Congress transformed General Washington into an icon as a means of holding together the American Union until Great Britain could be defeated. A dozen years later, the Federalists apotheosized President Washington in order to continue their dominance and, they hoped, assure Great Britain's survival.

In the aftermath of Washington's State of the Union speech, and in the face of the criticism it provoked, Federalist scribes endeavored to rally the base of the party around the president and the scornful spirit he had in-voked. Some urged that Independence Day be ignored and that the nation commemorate only two days, Columbus Day and Washington's Birthday. At some public gatherings, Federalists offered a toast: "Washington—loved as a father, as a god adored." Songs to the tune of "America" glorified Washing-ton, and poets praised his "dauntless" and "illustrious" deeds. There was open talk of the "god-like" character of Washington.

The Federalist idealization of Washington was eye-opening for some. The "idolatry for a popular citizen" was the antithesis of republicanism, some objected. Others questioned Washington's commitment to republicanism, inasmuch as he appeared to revel in the acclaim. Still others criticized the "notoriously base" manner in which Washington executed his duties. Like Jefferson, some who had seen Washington as above politics took another look. Many discovered a committed Federalist. Washington, said Massachusetts's Elbridge Gerry, a signer of the Declaration of Independence and delegate to the Constitutional Convention, had come to be the primary representative of "the union of the funded, bank, commercial, Cincinnati and anti-revolutionary or monarchical interest." Another Republican in Congress noted that the Hamiltonian faction used Washington's name as its "constant cover to every unconstitutional and irrepublican act."[60]

The most damaging assault on the president was that of Thomas Paine, who in 1796 published an open "Letter to George Washington." Paine, beloved and respected by many as the herald of the American Revolution, had once admired Washington, or at least thought him good for America. However, as Washington's presidency took on royal trappings, Paine grew suspicious. When Paine concluded that the administration's neutrality policy was merely a cover for aiding Great Britain to crush the French Revolution, his hostility toward Washington boiled over. He blasted Washington for "encouraging and swallowing the grossest adulation." But Paine's most scathing comments were reserved for Washington's policies. Presenting Washington as unfaithful to the ideals of the American Revolution, he asserted that the president and his "new fangled faction," the Federalist Party, were bent on transforming America into a land awash with "all the vices and corruptions of the British Government." Washington could never be believed, Paine charged, alleging that he had always been a "nondescribable, chameleon-colored thing." While appearing to stand for principle, Washington "easily slides" into deceit. In recent years, while pretending to be the ally of France, the president was in reality given to "a mean and servile submission" to Great Britain. Washington's public character and most of his supposed achievements were "fradulent," Paine charged. The great campaigns that had saved America in the Revolutionary War had been those conducted by Generals Gates and Greene or conceived by Rochambeau. Washington's prolonged inactivity after 1778—"you slept away your time in the field, till the finances of the country were completely exhausted," he charged—had nearly proven fatal to the cause. No thanks to Washington, the United States had been bailed out by France in 1781. The payback from Washington, "a hypocrite in public life," said Paine with his keen eye for cant, was his current betrayal of France, America's savior.[61]

Paine's blistering essay was uncommon. Most editors shrank from taking on Washington. Benjamin Franklin Bache, publisher of the Philadelphia *Aurora,* successor to the *National Gazette* as the most influential Republican newspaper, attacked the whiskey excise as Hamilton's "child" and depicted the decision to crush the foes of the tax as a "deep laid scheme" hatched by the Treasury secretary. Leaving Washington off the hook, Bache only obliquely criticized the chief executive for his excessive hostility toward the Democratic-Republican Societies. "Our aristocrats," said Bache, not daring to identify Washington by name, conspire to "discredit every establishment capable of keeping the people awake to their interests."[62]

Washington escaped greater criticism because most Americans— including Bache—opposed the western insurgents' use of illegal means to protest the whiskey tax. Washington's famous good luck held out as well. As Lee and Hamilton marched their army across Pennsylvania, serendipitous word arrived from farther to the west that General Wayne had accomplished what Harmar and St. Clair had been unable to achieve. Nearly two years had elapsed while Wayne raised and trained the Legion of the United States, as his army was grandly dubbed. As Washington had ordered, Wayne imposed an iron discipline on his men. During the initial ninety days of the legion's existence, three soldiers were executed, one was punished by branding, and innumerable men were flogged with up to one hundred lashes. Finally, about ten days after the attack on Neville's home, the legion—thirty-five hundred men strong—marched into Ohio's Indian country. A month later, a badly outnumbered band of Native Americans unwisely made a stand, selecting as a defensive site an area where a tornado had left tangles of uprooted trees. It was a mismatch, and within forty-five minutes the Battle of Fallen Timbers, as the engagement was known, was over. Routed, those Indians who could escape ran for their lives, their "moccasins trickl[ing] blood in the sand," as one brave who survived put it. It was a pivotal American victory. Indian resistance in Ohio was broken, a fact confirmed a year later when the Native American tribes in the region formally ceded two thirds of the present state of Ohio to the United States.[63]

WASHINGTON PROCLAIMED FEBRUARY 19, 1795, Thanksgiving Day to honor Wayne's victory and the suppression of the Whiskey Rebellion. Two weeks later, the Jay Treaty, the handicraft of the envoy who had sailed to London the previous spring, at last arrived at the President's House. Washington must have eagerly torn open the packet to read the treaty that he had so long awaited. What he read could hardly have been more disappointing. Jay had gotten next to nothing from his lengthy negotiations. There were "*no* reciprocal advantages in the treaty," and the "benefits are all on the side of G. Britain," Washington groaned. Jay, in a letter to the president, tried to put the best face on his work. "It breaks the ice," he said, depicting the accord as merely a first step in a long process of accommodation with the former parent state. The sad truth, borne out by what the archives subsequently revealed about what the British government was prepared to concede, was that Jay had not performed up to the mark. As critics had asserted at the time of Jay's appointment, Washington had selected too pliable an envoy.[64]

Britain's sole concession of substance was to agree to pay compensation for the damages inflicted by the Royal Navy since 1793. Nothing further! Washington's desperate hope that Britain would consent to receive American exports had not been realized. Although Article XII stated that Britain would open its West Indian ports to American ships under seventy tons—the smallest merchant vessels were generally six times that size—Washington knew that such laughably restrictive terms would be seen by all Americans as humiliating. The treaty was silent on the issues of impressment and compensation for the slaves carried away to freedom at the conclusion of the Revolutionary War. Otherwise, the accord repeated what the Treaty of Paris had stipulated a dozen years earlier: America was to pay its pre–Revolutionary War debts to British creditors, and the British army was to withdraw from United States territory.

As Congress had adjourned three days before the treaty arrived, Washington summoned it into a special session in June, some ninety days away, so that the Senate could consider ratification. In the meantime, the president sequestered the treaty, hoping to keep its contents out of the press. He believed that if the expected Republican uproar could be deferred until after the Senate met, the chances of ratification would be enhanced. Washington understood that the pact was flawed, but from the outset he favored ratification. His primary hope was to quiet the war fever that had been stirred in some sectors, but ringing in his ears was Hamilton's reminder that to spurn the treaty was to hazard Britain's commerce, which "would give a serious wound to our growth and prosperity." Washington additionally knew that nearly every Federalist wished that nothing be done to harm Great Britain as long as it waged its life-and-death struggle against the forces of radical change. Jefferson and Madison understood this, and privately, they viewed Jay's treaty as a purely partisan matter. Madison believed it "full of . . . party artifices," while Jefferson thought the treaty was designed to forestall Congress from ever retaliating against the commerce of the Federalists' "patron-nation." Seen through Jefferson's prism, the accord was a betrayal of America's neutrality.[65]

Washington's strategy of concealing the treaty's terms may have helped win ratification. The Senate quickly ratified the Jay Treaty by the absolute minimum majority, though, as expected, it repudiated Article XII. The final tally was along straight party and sectional lines. All twenty Federalists voted for ratification, all ten Republicans against; eighteen who voted for ratification were from northern states, while seven who opposed the treaty were from southern states. Once the Senate acted, Washington left Philadelphia and returned to Mount Vernon, a sojourn that has sometimes been portrayed as an attempt by an indecisive president to find the solitude to think through whether or not he should sign the treaty into law. Washington at times was given to indecision, but not in this instance. He knew from the outset that he would sign the treaty. He was artfully playing for time. Spreading the word that he was listening to "dispassionate" advisers about what to do, Washington in reality consulted only Hamilton, and he did not so much seek advice as encourage his trusted young helpmate to write newspaper essays defending the treaty.

Washington coached his young friend about how best to defend the accord: Contrast the good and bad of each article, but emphasize the positive; demonstrate how the treaty might have a positive impact on the ongoing negotiations with Spain; play up that America's exports to the

British West Indies consisted entirely of indispensable food and raw materials for manufacturing, providing a strong incentive for local royal officials to ignore London's prohibitive trade decrees; show that it was in France's interest to stir animosity between the United States and Great Britain; and accentuate that "good would flow" from ratification. Curiously, Washington never suggested that Hamilton play up the theme that the Jay Treaty would prevent war with Great Britain.[66] But then Washington knew that he would not be asking for a declaration of war against Great Britain, and should House Republicans advocate hostilities, their initiative could be headed off in the Senate, which was solidly in the control of the Federalist Party.

While time passed and Washington supposedly brooded over his decision, Hamilton took to his desk and began drafting a lengthy advocacy of the Jay Treaty. Ultimately, he penned twenty-eight newspaper essays collectively entitled *The Defence*. Hamilton also enlisted Rufus King to write ten additional essays in the series, which he edited carefully before permitting his New England friend to send them to the printer. Hamilton followed Washington's guidelines to the letter, but to them he added—and it was a principal point throughout his essays—the argument that to reject the treaty was to bring on war with Great Britain. Hostilities might be disastrous, he implied. The United States required another decade or more of peace in order to get its economic house in order. About thirty days after Hamilton's first tract was published, Washington signed the pact into law.[67]

Nothing since Hamilton's economic program in 1790–1791 had caused a stir to equal the Jay Treaty, and nothing did more to inflame the partisan warfare or, as historian Richard Buel noted, to fashion the "national political machinery" of the two warring factions. In a fevered manner, the party presses fought out the merits and drawbacks of the Jay Treaty. Both sides hovered at the sharp edge of hysteria, though Washington expressed dismay only at the attacks by Republican screeds, which he characterized as akin to the shrill "cry . . . of a mad-dog." Predicting that the pact would prompt French retaliation—it has "invited rather than avoided" war, Jefferson declared—the Republicans reserved most of their calumny for Jay. He was vilified alternately as too "courtier-like" to have secured more favorable terms and as a dolt who had been bamboozled by the lavish dinners and receptions that the British authorities had provided for him. When word was leaked to the press that Jay had kissed the hand of the queen at one reception, a Republican writer exclaimed that he prayed the envoy's lips had been "blistered to the bone." Jay remarked that he could have walked across the country at night in the illuminating glow of his burning effigies.[68]

If Jay bore the brunt of Republican outrage, Washington for a change was also sullied. No action that he had taken as a military commander or as chief executive produced such a torrent of invective as Washington endured following his signing of the treaty. He was reproached for his "superciliousness and arrogance." The president was advised to visit local taverns to discover what was on people's minds. Washington ruled like the "grand lama," according to one critic, like Nebuchadnezzar or the "omnipotent director of a seraglio," said others. Washington, a "usurper with dark schemes of ambition," ignored public opinion, treating it with "all the insolence of an Emperor of Rome," it was charged. No autocratic monarch had ever looked on the public with such disdain, and none had ever treated the appeals of his subjects "with as much insult" as did Washington. One writer called him a "tyrannical monster." From the start, said one Republican, Washington's objective had been to advance "the greatest good of the least number possessing the greatest wealth." He was portrayed as dishonest. Some limned him as demented, suggesting that his pronouncements were the "loathings of [a] sick mind." This terrible treaty, said one critic, was the nation's payback for its "servile adoration of one man." For too long, more than one Republican asserted, the people had been "duped" by Washington. The falsehood was circulated that Washington had called the British monarch "his great, good, and dear friend." One unabashed critic wished Washington a "speedy death." All the Federalists could say in defense of Washington's support of Jay's treaty, one Republican writer contended, was that it was necessary for the public to place "blind confidence" in the president, which, he added, had largely been their defense of the chief executive when he crushed the whiskey rebels.[69]

In fact, the Federalists had plenty of arguments in defense of Washington and Jay's treaty. Reminding the public of Washington's and Jay's wartime services, a Federalist broadside pointed out that it was preposterous to think that these two patriots had "become the tools of Great Britain and traitors to their country." Federalists portrayed the treaty's foes as demagogues who represented a tiny fraction of the public. The Republicans, they contended, merely hoped to gain political traction from the episode, and some Federalists claimed that the opposition to the treaty was part of a carefully contrived campaign to lay the groundwork for Jefferson's election to the presidency in 1796. They argued that the treaty, by leaving some British trade intact, had preserved American prosperity. They stressed, too, that the treaty not only would remove British troops from American soil, but would spare the blood-soaked Ohio frontier of further howls of the Indian "war whoop" and the haunting "shrieks of torture" by the unfortunate captives of the Native Americans. Above all, Federalists defended Washington's statesmanship. His courageous action in signing the treaty, they said in countless newspaper squibs, had prevented an inevitable war with Great Britain. "This Treaty, like a rainbow," said one Federalist congressman, "marked to our eyes the space where [war] was raging, and afforded . . . the sure pragmatic of fair weather."[70]

By year's end, this furious partisan war was burning itself out. Washington noted in December that "the general disposition of the people" had swung behind the treaty. Jefferson, at Monticello, agreed and acknowledged yet another Federalist success won because of Washington's extraordinary stature. The president, said Jefferson, was the "one man who outweighs them all in influence over the people." But Jefferson also knew that Washington alone was not responsible for getting the treaty through. Seeing Hamilton as the power behind the throne, Jefferson called his rival "a colossus to the anti-republican party. Without numbers, he is an host within himself."[71] Washington had won the battle, and adoring Federalists showered him with praise. In particular, they carved in stone the belief that Washington and his selfless action had saved the infant nation from a ruinous war with Great Britain. Not everyone saw it that way. Madison, for instance, believed that the public had been fooled into believing that another Anglo-American war was inevitable, a ploy undertaken so that the citizenry would listen to the Federalists' "summons 'to follow where Washington leads.' "[72]

Washington once said that the Jay Treaty had aroused a greater public fury than any event since the bloodshed at Lexington and Concord. Sadly, it also brought Washington's own passions, his darker side, to the surface. In the course of his long ascent to the pinnacle, Washington had been transformed. From his beginning as an observant youth who hugged the corners at Belvoir while seeking to learn from the actions of powerful men, Washington had become a chief executive who carried himself like an emperor. Like a grand monarch, President Washington had reached the point where he allowed only designated favorites to enter into his presence while, coldly, he banished from his court others who had fallen from favor. Washington always demanded the ultimate in loyalty, and in the heat of the Jay Treaty imbroglio, he concluded that Madison had been disloyal to him in opposing the pact. The president broke off all ties with the young man who once had been his confidant and trusted adviser. Several months later, artful Federalists, including Henry Lee, roused Washington to a rage with a mendacious tale that Jefferson had vilified him in private comments. There was no evidence for their allegations. Despite their political differences, Jefferson had never impugned Washington's character or motives. Washington should have seen that he was being manipulated. He did not. All too ready to believe in Jefferson's betrayal, he broke with his fellow Virginian who had served him so well. Never again in Washington's lifetime would either Madison or Jefferson be welcome at Mount Vernon.[73]

In terms of statecraft, there was a more salubrious side to the Jay Treaty imbroglio. On his birthday in February 1796, Washington received a packet bearing the Pinckney Treaty. If he tore it open with apprehension, he was pleasantly surprised by the contents. Unnerved by the knowledge of Jay's negotiations, and fearing that the former colonies and mother country would unite to grab Spanish territory in North America and the Caribbean, Madrid had caved in. Suddenly wishing to patch up its differences with the United States, Spain had agreed to a treaty that had to have exceeded Washington's wildest expectations. Spain opened the Mississippi River and New Orleans to the United States and agreed that Florida's northern border would be where the United States had always insisted it should be. The Battle of Fallen Timbers and the Pinckney Treaty, in conjunction with the withdrawal of the British army from the West, which occurred once the Jay Treaty took effect, dramatically changed the conditions facing western settlers. In a flash, the worry vanished that westerners would defect. As never before, it seemed certain that the West would remain within the sprawling American Union.[74]

BY EARLY 1796, WASHINGTON WAS WORN OUT, physically and emotionally. He was counting the days to the end of his presidency. For reasons that are not clear, he regarded age sixty-three as the "grand climacteric." Having reached age sixty-four, he believed that he had put one over on the grim reaper, but he suspected that he had little time left. A few years earlier, some observers had noted an uncharacteristic listlessness about him, and Washington himself acknowledged in 1796 "a gradual decline" in his endurance. He continued to be concerned about his memory and ability to concentrate, telling Jay that spring that the years had "worn away my mind more than my body."[75] He remained lithe and trim—standing six feet three inches tall and weighing 210 pounds—but some portraits made in his presidential years depict a man whose eyes had lost the sparkle of youth. Those Federalists who hoped that Washington might agree to a third term never had a chance of persuading him to stay on.

Washington's decision to lay down his burden was not solely a matter of age and infirmity. The waves of recrimination that he had endured during recent months added to his eagerness to be done with public office. He told correspondents that he shrugged off all calumny, but, unable to get the attacks out of his head, the president complained about them repeatedly. He feared that the abuse would only be ramped up during another term, possibly leaving an indelible stain on his historical reputation. The Republican rebukes, he said, were likely in the long run to sway the public's thinking, just as "drops of Water will Impress (in time) the hardest Marble," choosing words that could keep a psychologist busy for a long time.[76]

But there was something else to Washington's thinking. He had achieved everything that he had set out to accomplish. Indeed, no other president has been more successful. With him to rally around, the Union had survived eight years of incredible stress and strain. The economic torments that had persisted for nearly fifteen years in war and peace had been vanquished. As never before, American manufacturing faced a promising future, offering hope that the new nation would shortly overcome its dependence on foreign goods and be capable of equipping itself in time of war. Worries that the West might break away had been laid to rest. Peace with the European powers prevailed, and had throughout Washington's presidency. In truth, he said in his final State of the Union address, the survival of the new national government, an open question at the outset of his presidency, had been positively resolved. Most Americans believed the United States would endure.[77]

Once he made up his mind to retire, Washington decided to exit with a farewell address. It was his custom. When he had flirted with stepping down in 1792, Washington had asked Madison to draft his farewell remarks. In 1796, he turned to Hamilton. In May, Washington provided Hamilton with Madison's four-year-old draft and some thoughts of his own, especially on matters of foreign policy and the partisan press. Hamilton toned down the tenor of the latter and excised much that Madison had written. What emerged was an address that reflected the thinking of Washington and Hamilton, which in the broadest sense was indistinguishable.[78] Washington may have looked on his Farewell Address as a nonpartisan statement, and his Federalist backers certainly portrayed it in that light, but in reality his valedictory was carefully crafted to advance the interests of the Federalist Party and, he hoped, ensure its domination for years to come.

Many of the sentiments in the Address were shared by most Americans, especially Washington's ruminations on the importance of the Union—"a main Pillar in the Edifice of your real Independence"—and good citizenship, which he defined as including the "duty of every Individual to obey the established Government." However, his warnings about the evils of political parties stamped him as an anachronism. Washington labeled political parties a "danger" productive of "disorders & miseries," even "frightful despotism." His blast at those who questioned the decisions of those in authority—he spoke of dissenters as "cunning, ambitious and unprincipled men"—was rightly seen as directed toward the Democratic-Republican Societies and the Republican Party and its press. So, too, was his denunciation of those who sought to "impair the energy of the system" by raising needless constitutional issues.

Washington's admonitions on foreign policy were widely thought to be the heart of the document. He wisely cautioned against loyalty to any foreign power, reminding his fellow citizens that they were Americans first and that American national interests should be their primary concern. But in warning of the danger of foreign alliances and reminding his audience of the peril of becoming "the satellite" of a European superpower, Washington sounded very much like Federalist scribes and politicians who, for years, had denounced America's ties to France. His appeal to his country-men to overcome their "habitual hatred" of Great Britain also struck many as sounding very much like the mantra of the Federalist Party.[79]

If numerous historians over the years were fooled into seeing Washington's Farewell Address as nonpartisan, few contemporaries saw it in that manner. Madison concluded that the Address "shews that [Washington is] compleatly in the snares" of the Federalist Party, and many of his Republican colleagues saw it as the Federalists' opening salvo in the presidential election of 1796, which began the instant the document was published in a Philadelphia newspaper in September. Indeed, why other than to influence the election of 1796 would Washington have formally said good-bye six months before the end of his term?[80]

While Washington sat on the sidelines, the campaign of 1796—the nation's first contested presidential election—took place. Congressional members from each party caucused and selected their two nominees, as the Constitution yet mandated that electors were to vote for two persons for the presidency. The Federalists nominated Vice President Adams and Thomas Pinckney. The Republicans chose Jefferson and Aaron Burr, a United States senator from New York. Like Washington in 1789 and 1792, the candidates stayed off the hustings, leaving the politicking to others. The campaign was mercifully short. It began, as one congressman remarked, with the publication of Washington's Farewell Address, which served "as a signal, like the dropping of a hat, for the party races to start." It ended six weeks later on election day in November. The outcome revealed a flaw in the presidential election format stipulated in the Constitution. The Federalist Adams won the presidency; the Republican Jefferson received the second largest number of votes and, hence, was elected vice president.[81]

As with his final days in the army, Washington's last days as president were consumed with a bustling whirl of social events. One more time he soaked in the acclaim lavished on him at frequent public appearances, including a gala birthday parade in Philadelphia's cold winter streets. The festivities, for the most part, were the work of Federalists, eager to bask in the splendid rays of Washington's achievements. Many Republicans were simply happy to see Washington go, and at formal dinners some drank a telling toast: "George Washington—down to the year 1787, and no further."[82]

Washington's final act before riding home was to attend Adams's inauguration on March 4, 1797. The outgoing president drew louder cheers than the incoming chief executive, and many in the audience at Congress Hall wept openly at their impending loss of Washington. The Republicans, and Washington himself, were the happiest ones present. The observant Adams said that Washington's "countenance was . . . serene and unclouded," and the new president added: "Methought I heard him say, 'Ay! I am fairly out and your fairly in! See which of us will be happiest!' "[83]

11

THE SAND RUNS OUT

WASHINGTON WAS REJUVENATED by Mount Vernon as well as by his escape "from those cares [of] which public responsibility is never exempt." Plunging into what he called his "rural amusements," he kept careful watch on farm operations, erected a distillery that eventually produced over one thousand gallons of whiskey each month—distilling nearly six times more than a typical small farmer, the ex-president, like large eastern distillers, paid a lower flat fee on his whiskey than did the yeoman distiller in, say, Millers Run—and once again took up remodeling several rooms in the mansion. He contemplated constructing a separate building to house his voluminous collection of papers. Had he ever gotten around to that project, it might have become the first presidential library.[1]

Washington said that he worked from "the rising of the sun, to the setting of the same," and he may not have exaggerated. In addition to Mount Vernon, he stayed busy tending his numerous business interests. He succeeded in selling a substantial portion of his western land—some of which he had possessed for nearly forty years—although the Millers Run property dogged him to the end. He thought he had sold it, but the buyer ran into economic trouble. Thirty months after he returned home, Washington had received only a fraction of the agreed-on sales price. He also plunged back into the affairs of the Potomac Canal Company. He loaned it money, purchased additional stock, and served as an unofficial lobbyist in attempting to pry financial assistance from Maryland and Virginia. He succeeded with Maryland, and in one of the last letters he wrote, Washington mistakenly rejoiced that the company appeared to have turned the corner and, at last, was headed toward success.[2]

WASHINGTON REMAINED ALOOF from public affairs for fifteen months, though he eagerly kept abreast of what was occurring. He remained an avid newspaper reader, and he received inside information from Philadelphia provided by Timothy Pickering, James McHenry, and Oliver Wolcott, members of his cabinet whom President Adams unwisely kept on as part of his cabinet. Much of what they sent to Washington in 1797 pertained to simmering problems with France, an episode that would come to be known as "the Quasi-War Crisis." Late in his presidency, fearing that the Jay Treaty would prompt a hostile French response, Washington had dispatched to Paris Charles Cotesworth Pinckney, brother of the envoy who had succeeded beyond expectation in Madrid, in the hope that he might mollify the French. Pinckney's mission failed. Just days into his presidency, Adams learned that the French not only had refused to receive Pinckney, but had abrogated their 1778 commercial pact with the United States. To his credit, Washington refused to be drawn into what followed. While many urged a pugnacious American response, Adams, against the wishes of most of his cabinet, sent a three-member commission to France in the hope of gaining a peaceful resolution of differences. Many Federalists were beside themselves with fury. The president's initiative, they cried, would be seen in Paris as an act of weakness.

In March 1798, almost a year to the day since he had returned home, Washington learned what the rest of the country was discovering. Adams's three envoys had been treated with incivility in Paris. In what became known as "the XYZ Affair," French officials had demanded bribes and an American apology before negotiations could commence. France had, in effect, broken off diplomatic relations, insulting the United States in the process. War fever swept the country, some of it ginned up by the Federalist press, much as their counterparts had earlier stoked anger toward Great Britain. In the white hot mood that existed in the summer of 1798, the Federalist Congress passed the Alien and Sedition Acts, repressive measures that smacked less of an attempt to safeguard national security than of a means of intimidating and silencing Republican editors and politicians. Over

Adams's objections, Congress also created a Provisional army—sometimes called the New Army—of 12,500 men to guard America against a supposedly probable French invasion.[3]

In the run-up to these actions—depicted by the Federalists as defensive in nature, by the Republicans as warmongering—Hamilton, now a private citizen practicing law in Manhattan, wrote to Washington. During his first fifteen months at home, Washington had received only one letter from Hamilton, a brief note thanking him for a gift he had sent. Together with the present, Washington had told Hamilton of his "sincere regard and friendship." Later, Washington wrote again to express his "very high esteem and regard." Hamilton had not answered the second missive. Yet in May 1798, he evidently realized that the old general, whom he had nearly forgotten, could again be useful. Just before the legislation to create the Provisional army was introduced in Congress, Hamilton wrote Washington a warm letter, though its substance was political. Hamilton reported that the Republicans were under the thumb of the French and that they planned to "*new model* our constitution under the *coertion* of France." Neither statement was true. Either they were lies or the product of an inflamed mind that had lost touch with reality, or, more probably, this was another artful attempt on Hamilton's part to manipulate Washington, a task at which he usually succeeded. Hamilton additionally asked Washington to make a tour of Virginia and North Carolina—"under pretense of health"—to whip up sentiment for making defensive preparations for what he was to represent as a nearly certain French invasion.[4]

Washington concurred with Hamilton, but only to a point. While agreeing that the Republicans "aid & abet" France, Washington declined to make a speaking tour. Not only was he opposed to "*open War*," but he believed a French invasion was highly unlikely. Washington additionally intimated that should he publicly urge a hard line, he would inevitably be seen as blatantly partisan, which he declared was unacceptable.[5]

Hamilton had something else up his sleeve. Though a private citizen, he controlled the largest wing of the Federalist Party—in the political configuration of the time, Hamilton, not President Adams, was the dominant force within their party—and Hamilton knew that his faction was about to push in Congress for the creation of the Provisional army. In a second letter to Washington, Hamilton alerted the general that he might be called on to emerge from retirement to take command of the army. Hamilton also let it be known that he hoped to be named inspector general of the army, the second in command. Two months before the army's creation, Washington responded that he would agree to be its commander only on the condition that the public "unequivocally" called him from retirement. He did not comment on Hamilton's aspirations.[6]

Hamilton had still other plans that he did not share with Washington. Once the army was created, Hamilton envisioned using it whether or not France invaded the United States. As Spain was no longer a British ally, Hamilton wanted the army to seize Madrid's dominions from St. Augustine, on Florida's east coast, to New Orleans, on Florida's western border. New Orleans was the "Key to the Western Country," Hamilton told others, and its possession was "essential to the permanency of the Union."[7] Hamilton's plans replicated much that Genêt had advocated five years earlier.[8]

In the Newburgh episode in 1783, Hamilton had conspired to use the Continental army to gain what he desired, though his scheme had been a bluff, successfully carried through with Washington's tacit consent. Once again, in 1798, Hamilton badly needed Washington. Not close to Adams, Hamilton knew that Washington's support was crucial if he was to be appointed inspector general and become—as one of his satraps informed Washington, lest the general did not understand—"the *Second* to You— and *the Chief in your absence*."[9] Hamilton must have thought that Washington's appointment would be useful, too, in that it would unify public opinion, making possible the adventures of which he dreamed. The former president might not wish to invade Spanish Florida, but Hamilton had seldom failed to bring Washington around in support of his most grandiose projects.

NEARLY A MONTH AFTER LAST HEARING from Hamilton, Washington received a letter from President Adams asking that he take command of the Provisional army, if only in a titular sense. Beyond that, Adams confided, he had not decided "whether to call all the old Generals, or to appoint a young set." Adams had expected that Washington would rapidly consent to take command of the army, but the letter he received from Mount Vernon was difficult to decipher. It appeared to Adams that Washington had said he would accept command of the army only if he could select the general officers, men who must be of "sufficient activity, energy and health" to cope with "the *quick step*, long Marches, & severe conflicts" of battle.[10] Uncertain what was precisely on Washington's mind, Adams dispatched Secretary of War McHenry to Mount Vernon to find out.

McHenry's carriage rolled down Mount Vernon's gravel driveway in the shimmering heat of mid-July. Washington knew the secretary well. An Irish-born physician, McHenry had served as his aide during the war and, after the president's first four choices had turned him down, as Washington's final war secretary after 1795. Many thought McHenry incompetent, a view shared by Hamilton and Washington. Even so, Washington greeted his visitor warmly and spent the better part of three days conversing with him. Informed by McHenry that the Senate had approved his service, Washington consented to command the Provisional army, but on the condition that he would take the field only if France invaded the United States. So much for Washington's earlier insistence that there must be a public clamor for him to come out of retirement. Although only Adams, Hamilton, and the lopsidedly Federalist Senate had indicated a desire that he serve, Washington grandly announced that he would comply with "this New proof of public confidence." He also sent McHenry back to Philadelphia with a list of the generals he wanted in the newly created army. Hamilton topped his list.[11]

Adams was appalled by Washington's behavior, and rightly so. Washington, a private citizen, was dictating to the president of the United States. As commander in chief, it was Adams's responsibility to select the army's officers. In the absence of a chief executive, the Continental Congress had chosen the general officers throughout the Revolutionary War. During Washington's presidency, the chief executive had chosen the series of commanders who led the armies into the Northwest Territory. Adams not only was bitter that Washington was infringing on his authority, he also had pragmatic reasons for wishing to select the army's general officers. Adams believed that the Provisional army would be composed largely of New England men, as that had been the case in war after war throughout the century, including the War of Independence. In the latter conflict, New Englanders had refused to volunteer for service under General Schuyler, a New Yorker. If Washington had his way, and if he remained at home, the day-to-day commander of the Provisional army would be Hamilton, another New Yorker and Schuyler's son-in-law. Fearing that Hamilton's appointment would spell trouble with the Yankee recruits—if any could even be induced to enlist in an army commanded by Hamilton—Adams wanted General Knox, a native of Boston, to be second in command of the army, with South Carolina's General Charles Cotesworth Pinckney next in line. Adams wrote back to Washington proposing that the general officers be ranked according to the date of their commissions in the Continental army. There were to be seven general officers. Adams wished to name five Federalists and, to unite the country, two Republicans, one of whom would be Aaron Burr. Under the formula that Adams proposed, Hamilton would be fifth in line behind the four other Federalists, Knox, Pinckney, Henry Lee, and Edward Hand of Pennsylvania. Washington would not budge. Implicit in his guarded response to President Adams was the threat to resign as commander if he did not have his way. Adams buckled. Not even the president of the United States dared defy George Washington.[12]

Washington had spent the last five years of his presidency railing at the "Impudence" of the Republicans, who, he said, never ceased "endeavoring to embarrass every measure of the Executive." Washington's behavior regarding the Provisional army was cut from the same cloth. There can be little doubt that Washington was seeking to advance Hamilton's political fortunes and those of the Federalist Party. Through his ample appointment powers, Inspector General Hamilton would be able to name hundreds of junior officers, fashioning a potent Federalist base in every state and creating a solid phalanx of provincial leaders who would be personally indebted and loyal to him. That Hamilton was almost devoid of command experience—it consisted of having led four hundred men in a ten-minute assault on one of the Yorktown redoubts—appears not to have troubled Washington, perhaps because he thought hostilities unlikely. But if war came, Washington was bent on providing Hamilton with the opportunity to gain glory—to become, in fact, the next George Washington. In 1798, Hamilton was two years younger than Washington had been when he had taken command of the Continental army. Should Hamilton's command of the Provisional army lead to his being swathed in glory, he might influence American politics for another generation, as had Washington since the Treaty of Paris.

Washington was enamored of Hamilton's dazzling intellect, and he may never have met anyone who combined such extraordinary intelligence with almost superhuman industry and vigor. There was another side to Hamilton, which Washington either overlooked or thought useful. Not a few saw Hamilton as ruthless and dangerous. In time, Jefferson would refer to him as "our Buonaparte," and Abigail Adams called him "a second Buonaparty." The first lady, who had been in the company of innumerable powerful men in America and Europe, warned her husband about Hamilton: "O I have read his Heart in his wicked eyes many a time. the very devil is in them."[13]

President Adams viewed Hamilton as a man "in a delirium of ambition." Hamilton, he thought, had always "hated every man, young or old, who stood in his way or could in any manner eclipse his laurels or rival his pretensions." Hamilton feigned "disinterestedness as boldly as Washington," Adams said in private, but in reality the former Treasury secretary was an ideologue who would stop at nothing to achieve his ends. Adams even credited the spurious story making the rounds that Hamilton had blackmailed Washington—he had allegedly threatened to expose the shortcomings in Washington's generalship—in order to secure command of the attack on the British redoubt at Yorktown. Thinking Hamilton "the most restless, impatient, artful, indefatigable, and unprincipled intriguer in the United States, if not the world," Adams did not want to put him in charge of the nation's army.[14]

By 1798, when the Provisional army was created, Hamilton's stature had diminished as a result of scandals. While secretary of the Treasury, the public had learned that Hamilton had tolerated associates who benefited financially from insider information or used their positions to rig the markets. There was circumstantial evidence that Hamilton had personally manipulated the price of bank scrip. At the very least, many believed, as Ron Chernow, Hamilton's biographer, put it, that the Treasury secretary had "mingled too freely his public and private roles."[15] Many also thought that Hamilton had set up underlings to take falls for him once the revelations of misdeeds came out. Despite the suspicions of Hamilton, Washington kept him on. But after Hamilton resigned from the cabinet in February 1795, his reputation suffered a seemingly irrecoverable blow. Word leaked out to the public not only that he had been involved in a long, sordid extramarital affair, but that Hamilton had paid hush money to the husband of his lover to fend off exposure. Washington continued to stand by him. It was the revelation of his tryst and blackmail—and the anguish that he knew Hamilton must be suffering in his private life—that had prompted Washington, normally the most reserved of men, to send the gift to his former secretary in 1797.[16]

Washington believed in Hamilton—and he believed, too, that he could control him. No longer an elected official, Washington was also convinced that through Hamilton, and possibly through him alone, could his dreams of American power best be attained and the social and political order that he cherished best be preserved. Only if America grew sufficiently strong that it no longer was the sport of European powers, Washington once had said, would the American Revolution realize its potential for making generations yet unborn "completely free and happy."[17] Better than any other leader, Washington believed, Hamilton understood the need to make the United States truly strong. Hamilton was the best man to bring to fruition everything that Washington cherished. Washington acted to rehabilitate Hamilton, drawing him back into public life and positioning him to accomplish those ends that both longed to see achieved.

As a result of this bruising episode, Adams's attitude toward Washington was transformed. Raging that his predecessor had "puffed like an air balloon to raise Hamilton," Adams came to believe that Washington was but a puppet and Hamilton the puppeteer. Throughout the Nationalists' quest for consolidation, Adams concluded, Washington had been merely "a viceroy under Hamilton, and Hamilton was viceroy under the tories," who wished to salvage as much as possible of life and the political culture of pre-1776 Anglo-America.[18] It was as keen an appraisal of American history since 1783 as anyone ever offered, and to his dread, Adams now found Hamilton not only likely to be in command of a vast army, but perhaps capable of doing who knew what with it.

President Adams was not without powers of his own, and the scales having fallen from his eyes, he wielded his authority to stop Hamilton. His actions ensured, too, that Washington would never take the field. From the start of this crisis, Adams had sought a peaceful but honorable settlement of differences with France. At every step, the Hamilton-dominated wing of the Federalist Party had pushed for more truculent policies. Believing now that Hamilton's end game had always been the creation of the army and the triggering of war, Adams redoubled his efforts to reach a peaceful accord with Paris. He sent a new team of negotiators to France. From the moment the American envoys sailed in the summer of 1799, the bellicose mood in the country began to evaporate. Hamilton had an army, but there no longer was much hope that the public would support the adventures he had dreamed of launching.[19]

FOR FOUR MONTHS FOLLOWING HIS APPOINTMENT, Washington neither donned his uniform nor left Mount Vernon. All the while, he was kept in the dark about what was being done with the army he supposedly commanded. Unhappy, to put it mildly, Washington repeatedly wrote McHenry for information. Finally, he demanded to "know *at once* and *precisely*" what was being done with the army.[20] It may even have occurred to him that he had been used by Hamilton. Washington stewed until November 1798, when the War Department invited him to Philadelphia for a planning session.

The trip was Washington's last hurrah. Wearing his old buff-and-blue uniform, he was honored in every little village along the way. Once he reached Philadelphia, he found that the Federalists had arranged one final celebration to honor him. Astride his white charger, and escorted by militia units and a handful of soldiers from the embryonic Provisional army, Washington rode through streets festooned with flags and bunting and lined by cheering spectators. Those in the crowd hoped for a glimpse of the most famous man of their time and, possibly, a last chance to salute him.

Washington remained in Philadelphia for five weeks. He worked nearly every day, and in the evenings he enjoyed a mad whirl of dinners and parties. He reveled in the acclaim, though overall he was frustrated by his treatment. When Washington had left office, Jefferson had presciently predicted that the "bubble is bursting."[21] Power was passing to others. Washington now saw what Jefferson had foreseen nearly two years before. He was ignored or treated as an inconsequential figurehead. Aside from his thoughts on the design of uniforms, his views were for the most part brushed off. He knew it: "My opinions and inclinations are not consulted." Important decisions were made "not only without my recommendation, but even without my knowledge." Dispirited, Washington threatened to resign. That did no good. If Washington resigned, Hamilton would have no one above him. Hamilton's lackeys did not care much whether Washington stayed or left.[22] If he had not known so earlier, General Washington now understood not only that he had been used, but that the benefactor had been superseded by the legatee. Hamilton had supplanted Washington, at least within the Hamiltonian wing of the Federalist Party.

Nevertheless, the shabby treatment to which he was subjected did not alter Washington's belief in the necessity of the Provisional army. While he thought an invasion was unlikely as long as France remained at war with Great Britain, Washington continued to insist that it was imperative the United States maintain "a state of preparation" for the day when peace came to Europe. France had "ambitious plans," and once free of the European war and able to act, he predicted, it would attempt to gain Louisiana and Florida from Spain, "either by exchange or otherwise." Washington's mantra during the final year of his life was that his country must remain on a war footing. He thought Adams may have blundered in sending envoys to Paris in search of peace—"I see nothing in the *present* aspect of European Affairs" to warrant the mission, he declared—though he refused to say anything publicly.[23]

Even given his reservations about the president's diplomacy, Washington was far more restrained toward Adams than were the Hamiltonians. This coterie, a radical faction that historians have dubbed the "Ultra Federalists" or "High Federalists," wished to keep alive the war fever, either in hope of hostilities or from the knowledge that the party had flourished in the war crisis. Late in 1798, the Ultras had even introduced legislation, written secretly by Hamilton, that would have expanded the army to forty-five thousand men, another step in their aspiration of making this force a permanent standing army, and a huge one at that. Adams's peace mission stopped them in their tracks, however, leaving them "thunderstruck," as one Federalist put it. Feeling betrayed by their own party's president, the Ultras orchestrated a campaign to discredit and ruin Adams. Hoping to elect a Federalist president in 1800 whom they could control, the Ultras spread malicious allegations about Adams, claiming in the press that he ignored his advisers, acted capriciously, even that he might be insane. Adams was "unfit for the Office he now holds," several charged.[24] Some Ultras also launched a drive to persuade Washington to come out of retirement and take on a third term beginning in 1801.

"I have confidence . . . that . . . you will not disappoint the hopes & Desires of the Wise & Good . . . by refusing to come forward once more to the relief & support of your injured Country," a Federalist importuned Washington in the summer of 1799. Should he be a candidate in the election of 1800, Washington was advised, every Republican elector would vote for him, as would every Federalist. If he chose not to be a candidate, Jefferson would be the next president, for Adams was unelectable, Washington was told. Should that come to pass, he was warned, all that the Federalists had achieved would be imperiled. Even "the vast Treasure of your Fame [would] be committed to the Uncertainty of events," confided one clever Ultra. By leaving home and taking on the cares of public office in 1775, 1787, and 1789, Washington had won acclaim as his country's "Defender . . . Legislator . . . Statesman." Come back to power, said an Ultra who beseeched him to run again, and win "new and greater Glory."[25]

Washington was not swayed. He wished neither to leave Mount Vernon nor ever again to "become a mark for the shafts of envenomed malice and the basest calumny." Moreover, Washington said it would be "criminal" of him to hold an office that demanded energy and mental faculties that he no longer possessed. The Federalist Party must stand or fall on principles, not men, he declared, and he insisted that as the "true son[s] of Liberty" of their day, the Federalists should be capable of gaining victory in 1800, even with Adams as their candidate. Each reason that Washington ticked off was sufficient for declining the entreaties of the Ultras, but something else weighed on his mind. He was not convinced that every Republican elector would vote for him. He even thought it likely that nearly all would vote against him. Winning election by anything but a unanimous vote was intolerable. Losing the election was unthinkable. What guarantee was there, he asked one who had encouraged him to run, that he would not lose the election of 1800? It was Washington's wish that henceforth "no eye, no tongue, no thought, may be turned towards me" for again standing for the presidency.[26]

Washington understood that the country was changing and, above all, with the emergence of political parties and the spread of democracy, the nature of its politics was in transformation. The age that Washington had known and dominated was ending and a new epoch was beginning. George Washington's life in politics was at an end, and he knew it.

WASHINGTON NEVER AGAIN WANTED to hold public office, but one item of business that was both public and private in nature awaited his attention: slavery. The American Revolution's soaring rhetoric of freedom, as well as the Enlightenment that inspired many of the progressive ideas of Washington's age, served as the inspiration for the nation's first abolitionist movement in the immediate aftermath of the War of Independence. Washington had hardly returned home before Pennsylvania provided for the gradual end to slavery. Other northern states took similar steps during the next few years, and the much maligned Congress, under the Articles of Confederation, prohibited slavery in the vast Northwest Territory. Southern states outlawed the importation of slaves and made it easier for slave owners to emancipate their chattel, a step that some who owned slaves took.[27] Washington was not caught up in the antislavery fervor of the 1780s. He neither liberated his slaves nor, in the several pronouncements that he made to the nation during his final months as commander of the Continental army, addressed the issue of slavery.

Like most other political leaders of his time—including many, such as John Adams and Hamilton, who abhorred slavery—Washington wanted to keep the slavery question out of politics. In the 1780s, he had neither joined with Lafayette nor been swayed by Methodists or Quakers who wanted his help or urged him to set an example by liberating his slaves. As president, he had declined to side with Franklin on behalf of the Pennsylvania Abolition Society. Washington's first priority was to preserve the Union under a stronger national government. To interject slavery into the political arena was to introduce a volatile and divisive issue that would make his task inordinately more difficult.

Before the war, Washington had given little, if any, thought to slavery as a moral issue. Not only had he been raised in a society in which nearly every other person was enslaved, but he was a man on the make. Ascent to the elite in the Virginia of his day hinged on owning slave laborers, and lots of them. Washington's views may have changed during the war, though his actions were so contradictory that it is not clear what he thought. He first wanted blacks out of the army. Later, when on the brink of disaster, he was willing to have African Americans in the army. Still later, he refused to become involved in the campaign to raise black soldiers in the South. All the while, Washington was surrounded by bright young aides and officers, especially Hamilton, Lafayette, and John Laurens, who thought slavery not just ethically repugnant, but an unsound economic system. Washington's thinking may have been influenced by their ideas. Then again, it may not have been. Two years after he returned home from the Revolutionary War, Washington said privately that he regretted slavery's existence, and he added: "There is not a man living who wishes more sincerely than I do, to see a plan adopted for the abolition of it—but there is only one proper . . . mode by which it can be accomplished, & that is by Legislative authority."[28] But despite what he had said, Washington soon thereafter rebuffed the entreaties of those who urged him to throw his support behind abolitionist legislation in the Maryland assembly.

After 1786, Washington told visitors to Mount Vernon that he wanted to be rid of his slaves, and he fell into the habit of telling foes of slavery that he longed to lease most of his Potomac River property, freeing his slaves in the process and requiring the lessor to use only free labor.[29] But the conditions he set virtually guaranteed that his plan to lease the Mount Vernon properties was stillborn, which he must have known all along would be the case.

Washington continued to sell slaves after the war and to hunt down runaways. While president, he and his family were attended by slaves that he brought north from Mount Vernon, although he was careful that his slaves did not remain in Philadelphia for longer than six months, as under Pennsylvania law that would have made them free persons. Washington shuffled his slaves from the Potomac to the Delaware Valley, but he advised his aides to hide his practice from the public and to keep his chattel in the dark.[30]

During his eight years as president, Washington neither acted on nor responded to the antislavery petitions sent him, and he did not address slavery in any speech. In his final State of the Union address and his Farewell Address, when he turned his attention to major concerns that remained for the United States, Washington was silent concerning slavery. In addition, whatever moral concerns he may have come to harbor about slavery, Washington appeared above all to wish to continue to enjoy the sumptuous lifestyle made possible by those he owned.

Yet suddenly, in July 1799, Washington rewrote his will to provide for the emancipation of his slaves. Why he took the step and what led him to act when he did are mysteries. Washington certainly did not think that summer that his death was imminent, nor was he then, or ever, obsessed with death. He reflected on his demise, though not to an abnormal degree. A year earlier, he had said that his health "never was better," and there is no indication that it had deteriorated in the following months. He remained active, looking for ways to improve his income, even contemplating another demanding journey to the sites of his western properties. As far as is known, no dramatic incident occurred that led to his decision.[31]

In all likelihood, Washington acted that summer simply because he had at last resolved the conflict with which he had wrestled for years over what he had come to see as the iniquities of slavery versus the plainer way of life that he would face without slaves. He had a long memory when it came to criticism, and it is not likely that he had forgotten the harsh letter that Robert Pleasants had sent him fourteen years before, especially the Quaker's admonition that Washington's legacy would be adversely affected if he did not cut his ties to slavery. Already, Washington had been criticized as a slaveocrat by Anti-Federalists in the ratification battle and by Republican scribblers during his presidency.[32] Washington's growing awareness that the times were changing may have caused him to understand, as never before, that Pleasants was prescient. Having been a slave owner would sully his reputation with future generations. But he could not live without the comforts that his slaves provided. The will that he redrew in July 1799 sought to bridge the gap between his uneasy conscience and his yen for creature comforts. His new will stipulated that on his death or Martha's, whichever occurred last, the 123 Mount Vernon slaves that he owned outright were to be set free. The remaining 193 dower slaves—the chattel Martha had owned before their marriage and their descendants—were untouched by his will, "it not being in my power under the tenure by which the Dower Negroes are held, to manumit them," Washington wrote. Washington may not have been all that the abolitionists could have desired, but nonetheless he had taken a step that few contemporary slave owners in the South would take.[33]

IN HIS FINAL WEEKS, in the warm, golden days of the Potomac autumn, Washington remained busy running surveys, sending directions to McHenry about winter quarters for the army, wringing his hands over his dearth of liquid assets, and digesting the news of elections throughout 1799. His supple grasp of politics was slipping, causing him to misinterpret the outcome of the electoral contests. He viewed a handful of Federalist victories as evidence that the Republicans were on the skids. "The public has changed. . . . The people begin to see clearly. . . . We are progressing to a better state of things," he rejoiced, throwing off his cloak of nonpartisanship.[34] In fact, that year the Republicans took control of the New Jersey legislature for the first time, won the gubernatorial election in Pennsylvania, scored victories in three New England congressional districts that had previously been Federalist strongholds, and made significant gains in southern legislatures.[35] Far better than Washington, Jefferson understood what was occurring. "[A] wonderful & rapid change is taking place," he exulted. The dangers posed by the Ultras' repressive legislation and thirst for war were at last "becoming evident to the people and are dispelling the mist" brought on by their contrived foreign policy crisis.[36]

As NOVEMBER TURNED TO DECEMBER IN 1799, winter's approach was in the air. Mount Vernon's trees stood bare, and the once jewel green lawn that sloped gently from the piazza to the Potomac turned a gloomy shade of brown. Washington went outdoors less frequently. On December 7, he dined at the home of Bryan Fairfax, the grandnephew of Lord Fairfax, the patron who had been instrumental in starting Washington's ascent. Bryan Fairfax had been an officer under Washington in the Virginia Regiment, and later he had been ordained as an Episcopalian priest. He was the closest thing to a friend that Washington ever had. Four nights later, December 11, Fairfax, with two of his children, dined at Mount Vernon.[37] It was the last time that Washington entertained guests.

The end for Washington came swiftly and unexpectedly. He awakened on December 13 with what he described as a "very sore" throat, but it did not idle him. He worked briefly outdoors, though it was a numbingly cold day and a soft snow was falling, covering Mount Vernon with a three-inch white blanket. Back inside after a couple of hours, Washington wrote his last letter, an acrid directive to his farm manager, and penned his final entry in his diary. He probably thought he had come down with a bad cold, but his condition was far worse than he imagined. Almost certainly, as historian Peter Henriques has concluded, Washington had fallen prey to a bacterial infection that produced acute epiglottitis, a painful swelling of the tissue at the base of the tongue that can obstruct breathing. By the early morning hours of December 14, Washington's condition was perilous. Feverish and suffering, he sank steadily throughout the day. As he struggled to breathe, Washington knew that he was dying, but throughout his ordeal he evinced no sign of fear and stoically refused to complain. Late in the afternoon, Washington slowly faded into a semiconscious state. As darkness spread like a black stain over snow-swathed Mount Vernon, Washington's life ebbed away. With family and unavailing physicians surrounding him, the end came in his upstairs bedroom not long before midnight.[38]

"He died as he lived," said Tobias Lear, Washington's private secretary, who knew him well and had remained at his bedside throughout the ordeal.[39] Lear knew that Washington had died exhibiting the same courage he had displayed in countless battles, military and political.

RECKONING

PHENOMENAL LUCK IS REQUIRED to become a national hero. Being born at just the right time is the first essential element. Fortune smiled on George Washington. Had he been born twenty years earlier, he would have been seen as too old to command America's army in the Revolutionary War. Had he been born ten years later, he would have been too young to have held the highest post in either the Virginia Regiment or the Continental army. Washington was precisely the right age for every epic event in the second half of the eighteenth century—the French and Indian War, the American Revolution, the Constitutional Convention, and the founding of the American Republic.

Luck smiled on Washington in other ways as well. He grew to be large and imposing, so much beyond the norm of his day that it was impossible not to notice him. His half-brother Lawrence married into the most powerful family in the Northern Neck of Virginia, a step that, as it turned out, felicitously opened doors for young George. Despite an active life filled with adventure, Washington repeatedly dodged lethal hazards. He safely reached Fort Le Boeuf in 1753 and was treated kindly by the French once he was there. As a soldier for Virginia, and as commander of the Continental army, he was spared enemy bullets. Somehow, too, he escaped the camp diseases that killed untold numbers of soldiers. While residing at Mount Vernon, he dodged—or survived—the assorted fevers that proved fatal to innumerable inhabitants of the Chesapeake colonies.

Good fortune alone does not account for Washington's ascent. Indeed, he also had to overcome bad luck, including a modest inheritance and the lack of a formal education. But Washington was madly ambitious and obsessed with recognition and renown. He was driven to learn what led to success, and once he discovered the secrets of achievement, he endlessly attempted to improve himself, courted patrons, endured incredible hardships, unblinkingly faced danger, and took incalculable risks, both physically and financially. Furthermore, not only was he ever vigilant for enemies, he grew to be uncannily accomplished in dealing with them. No one was better at self-promotion than Washington, though he did it in such a quiet, understated manner that few were aware of what he was up to. Principally, Washington quietly accentuated his attributes and concealed what he believed were his weaknesses.

What is most remarkable about Washington's ascent is that he emerged an unsurpassed hero from two wars in which he committed dreadful— even spectacular—blunders and was personally responsible for only marginal successes. His monumental errors at Fort Necessity in 1754 would have ruined virtually any other commander. During the War of Independence, Generals Schuyler, Lee, and Gates must, in their private moments, have wondered why they suffered harshly for their failures—some quite pardonable—while Washington survived several blunders and disasters in the New York campaign, a striking lack of success at Brandywine and Germantown, and his long, nearly lethal hiatus from operations during the three years after 1778. In each war, Washington bitterly opposed the strategy that led to final success. General Forbes saw what was necessary to take Fort Duquesne in 1758, and Rochambeau conceived how to score a decisive victory in Virginia in 1781. Washington first resisted what they envisaged and then, in the case of Yorktown, miraculously was credited as the architect of the pivotal victory. After each war, he took steps either to absolve himself in the public mind for his failures or to ensure that the fiction of his having conceived the way to victory was embedded in the memory of his contemporaries.

Washington's advancement in both wars was facilitated by the realities of politics. Starting with the backing of powerful benefactors in the House of Burgesses in 1754, he cultivated other assemblymen until he had built a stout phalanx of supporters and protectors. In the Revolutionary

War, Congress came to understand that it was in the position of the proverbial man riding the back of a tiger. For better or worse, it had chosen Washington to head the army. Either it stuck with him or it faced potentially crippling political turmoil and possibly ruinous military upheaval following his dismissal.

That said, most congressmen never wished to replace Washington. Though a few would have preferred a different commander, most saw worthiness in Washington that stretched beyond his limitations as a tactician and strategist and his readily apparent inability to make a prompt decision.

Even most congressmen who questioned General Washington's abilities were aware of the difficulties with which he coped—poorly supplied armies, callow soldiers, unworthy officers, and a formidable adversary. Congress knew that it might have found another commander who was tactically or strategically superior to Washington—perhaps Benedict Arnold, Charles Lee, or Horatio Gates—but it understood that no other man would have brought all the virtues that Washington possessed to the post of commander in chief. Being a great leader of an army is not always the same as being the most brilliant general. General Ulysses S. Grant was not the most sparkling general in the Civil War, and during World War II, Dwight D. Eisenhower was probably a less gifted tactician than Field Marshal Bernard Law Montgomery. Like Grant and Eisenhower, Washington had his shortcomings, but like them, too, he succeeded. In the final analysis, as many in Congress understood throughout the War of Independence, Washington's character, judgment, circumspection, industry, meticulousness, example, and diplomatic and political skills set him apart from others, making him the proper choice to be the commander of the Continental army.

Throughout the war, but particularly in the face of the many crises of the Valley Forge winter, Congress shielded Washington by carefully managing the public's awareness of the commander and his army. After 1778, with sullen critics watching closely and morale sagging, Congress did what it could to make General Washington the symbol that fused America's disparate elements.

By the conclusion of the Revolutionary War, Washington was the great American icon. Jefferson never wavered in his belief that General Washington deserved the praise lavished on him. Hamilton, who saw Washington's generalship at close hand, came to think that Washington was unworthy of much of the acclaim that he received. John Adams's judgment of General Washington lay somewhere between that of Jefferson and Hamilton. It drove him crazy that Washington received more credit than he believed he was due, but Adams clung steadfastly to the belief that Washington was the best man for the job. What all three knew, however, was that the new republic needed a rudder. Indeed, that was the overwhelming consensus among the ruling elite. In the absence of a monarch who could serve as the glue that held things together, it was politically necessary that Washington be made the acclaimed symbol, the standard, around which all could rally.

Washington did little after the war to advance the movement to lionize him and nothing to deter it. His work was done by 1783. He had laid the cornerstone for his ascent to the status of demigod when he refused to accept a salary while commander of the army. He solidified his standing through years of unwavering dedication and sacrifice during the prolonged war, and especially through his remarkable leadership ability in keeping the dreadfully supplied and unpaid army intact. He completed the edifice when at the end of hostilities, in an act nearly without precedent, he relinquished power. After 1783, knowing that power would come to him without his having to chase after it, Washington convinced the nation that he was reluctant to hold public office. Yet twice he emerged from the tranquillity of Mount Vernon to play a public role. Genuinely conflicted, Washington was loath to take on further public responsibilities, though just as surely, retirement for this once powerful and always active man must at times have seemed stubbornly monotonous, especially as epochal events were unfolding in the public arena.

Washington's final curtain call was the presidency, and in that capacity he rose to the peak of power and the very heights of public adulation. Believing that most Americans wanted a kingly figure for their chief executive, President Washington, to the disgust of half of the politically active citizenry, behaved much like a monarch. If he misjudged on that score, it was nevertheless as president that Washington made his greatest contributions as a public servant. Merely by being there, as Jefferson and Hamilton told him, Washington enabled the new nation to hang together and survive its terribly difficult infancy. But he did far more than merely be there. He was a hands-on president. With the hidden skills of an illusionist, Washington combined discerning statesmanship with the partisanship of a chief executive with a political agenda. The country was extraordinarily fortunate to have had Washington as its first president. Through his support of Hamilton, Washington ushered America toward modernity, fashioning the economic system that sustained growth and gradually made the United States a truly independent and powerful nation capable of maintaining its security. Moreover, under any other president, the new nation might have slid into a ruinous war with Great Britain after 1793. Washington knew that another war so soon after the Revolutionary War was likely to end in catastrophe for the fragile American Union. No personal demons drove him to war. He had proven his manhood in two wars and was wreathed with military glory. Washington, perhaps uniquely so, was able to withstand the cacophonous din made by those who yearned for hostilities.

Yet while Washington was daring and forward looking on economic matters—so much so that the progressives of the day did not catch up with his thinking until sometime in the next century—he was constrained by social and political views that marked him as antiquated. Washington neither understood nor concurred with the egalitarian ideals that most of his countrymen believed to be at the very heart of the American Revolution. Nor was he favorably disposed toward democracy, an idea that gathered steam in the aftermath of the Revolutionary War. During his second term, Republican editors increasingly and accurately portrayed Washington as an antediluvian.

However fortunate the new nation was to have had Washington as its first president, it was also blessed to have had those who inspired, or were inspired by, the progressive spirit of the American Revolution. Had it not been for Jefferson and his political party, and the resistance they provided to the designs of the Hamiltonian wing of the Federalist Party to create a military state equipped with a standing army and seeded with monarchical elements—a program Washington acquiesced in and abetted—the history of the United States would have been vastly different.

Conservative though Washington may have been in many ways, he was indispensable in launching two great revolutions. He was among the first Americans to think in terms of breaking with Great Britain, and among the most vocal before Lexington and Concord in suggesting that the colonists might have to use force against the parent state. After 1775, he led the fight for American independence. In addition, under another first president, the new nation might have continued the more traditional and familiar economic system favored by Jefferson and Madison and their ad- herents. Washington, who always dreamed grandiose dreams and seldom feared taking risks, moved the nation down another path, one that led to the industrial and urban world with which we are familiar.

FOLLOWING WASHINGTON'S PRESIDENCY, John Adams sought to emulate his predecessor's style. It did not work. President Adams was ridiculed to such a degree that he rapidly abandoned his pretentious behavior. Jefferson, who was elected president in 1800, brought with him far fewer formal habits, famously greeting the British minister while wearing house slippers, hosting casual dinners at the White House, and riding about the capital on horseback rather than in a coach and six. Jefferson's way took hold in the democratizing and more egalitarian world of the nineteenth century. The stiff, near royal formality of Washington's presidency was gone forever, and so too for a century and a half were standing armies that Washington and the Federalists had sought to put in place. The "storm through which we have passed has been tremendous," Jefferson said upon taking office, but the ship of state "has stood the waves." Adding that he planned to put the United States "on her republican track," Jefferson in March 1801 advised Thomas Paine that the bright, promising future anticipated for humankind in *Common Sense* in 1776 was about to be realized.[1]

By then, Washington was gone. The world that he had been born into, much of which he relished and yearned to save, was rapidly vanishing as well, and no one had done more than Washington himself to hasten the end of the world that he had so loved.

MUCH OF THE AURA that surrounded Washington in life and death—in particular the perception of his masterful generalship, reluctance to hold power, and lofty disinterestedness on partisan issues—was mythological. But nation builders know that legendary heroes and mythical tales are es- sential for the creation and maintenance of their realm. Otherwise, the very idea of nationhood is likely to seem to many to be only a delusion. They also knew that the iconic Washington was as indispensable in death as he had been in life. Fusing myth and reality, George Washington was made the template for the virtues and character that supposedly were necessary for assuring national ascendancy.

SELECT BIBLIOGRAPHY

Few figures in American history have been the subject of as many books and articles as George Washington. What follows is a guide to some of the most important works on Washington, especially biographies. Readers who are interested in probing more deeply into Washington will find numerous additional works on him cited throughout the end notes in this book.

Two editions of Washington's papers have been, or are being, published. Both are indispensable to anyone interested in him. The modern work, which is packed with illuminating materials and documents provided by its editors, is *The Papers of George Washington,* published by the University of Virginia Press. It is divided into five series, the Colonial Series, Revolutionary War Series, Confederation Series, Presidential Series, and Retirement Series. Three of the series have been completed. At the time this book was completed, sixteen volumes of the Revolutionary War Series had been published, spanning the period through the late summer of 1778, while thirteen volumes of the Presidential Series had appeared, covering Washington's first term and six months of his second term. The *Papers* contains orders, documents, and letters written by Washington as well as letters written to him.

John C. Fitzpatrick edited an older edition of Washington papers, *The Writings of Washington from the Original Manuscript Sources, 1754–1799* (39 vols., Washington, D.C.: U.S. Government, 1931–1944). It is indispensable for periods not covered by the modern edition of Washington's papers. Unfortunately, the older edition does not contain letters to Washington.

Washington kept a diary off and on during his life, and those interested in pursuing him in depth will find it to be of considerable value. Readers should see Donald Jackson and Dorothy Twohig, eds., *The Diaries of George Washington* (6 vols., Charlottesville: University of Virginia Press, 1976–1979).

Among the biographies of Washington, the largest and most complete is that of Douglas Southall Freeman, *George Washington* (7 vols., New York: Charles Scribner's Sons, 1948–1957), a veritable treasure trove of information on Washington and his activities. Shorter, though also encompassing several volumes, is the extraordinarily well-written biography by James Thomas Flexner, *George Washington: The Forge of Experience, 1732–1775* (4 vols., Boston: Little, Brown & Co., 1965). Flexner's work was distilled into a less satisfactory single volume under the title *George Washington in the American Revolution* (Boston: Little, Brown & Co., 1967).

For other one-volume works, readers might consult John Ferling, *The First of Men: A Life of George Washington* (Knoxville: University of Tennessee Press, 1988); Joseph Ellis, *His Excellency: George Washington* (New York: Alfred Knopf, 2004); Willard Sterne Randall, *George Washington: A Life* (New York: Henry Holt & Co., 1997); Robert F. Jones, *George Washington: Ordinary Man, Extraordinary Leader* (New York: Fordham University Press, 2002); and John Alden, *George Washington: A Biography* (Baton Rouge: Louisiana State University Press, 1984).

Three analytical books on Washington are especially worth attention: Peter R. Henriques, *Realistic Visionary: A Portrait of George Washington* (Charlottesville: University of Virginia Press, 2006); Marcus Cunliffe, *George Washington: Man and Monument* (London: Collins, 1959); and Don Higginbotham, *George Washington: Uniting a Nation* (Lanham, Md.: Rowman & Littlefield, 2002).

For an excellent introduction to the great event of Washington's early life, the French and Indian War, see two books by Fred Anderson, the massive *Crucible of War: The Seven Years' War and the Fate of Empire in North America, 1754–1766* (New York: Vintage Books, 2001) and the more concise *The War That Made America: A Short History of the French and Indian War* (New York: Viking, 2005). The most valuable book among those devoted to Washington's life prior to the American Revolution is Bernhard Knollenberg, *George Washington: The Virginia Period, 1732–1775* (Durham, N.C.: Duke University Press, 1964).

Readers seeking an introduction to the Revolutionary War might turn to John Ferling, *Almost a Miracle: The American Victory in the War of Independence* (New York: Oxford University Press, 2007). Edward G. Lengel, *General George Washington* (New York: Random House, 2005), is the best one-volume treatment of Washington in the Revolutionary War. For useful essays on Washington as a soldier, see Don Higginbotham, *George Washington and the American Military Tradition* (Athens: University of Georgia Press, 1985). For a volume that contrasts Washington with Thomas Jefferson and John Adams during the American Revolution, see John Ferling, *Setting the World Ablaze: Washington, Adams, Jefferson, and the American Revolution* (New York: Oxford University Press, 2000).

Readers interested in an introduction to the political history of the era of Washington's presidency might turn to Stanley Elkins and Eric McKitrick, *The Age of Federalism* (New York: Oxford University Press, 1993), or John Ferling, *A Leap in the Dark: The Struggle to Create the American Republic* (New York: Oxford University Press, 2003). For a good volume specifically on his presidency, see Forrest McDonald, *The Presidency of George Washington* (New York: W. W. Norton, 1975).

On the shaping of Washington's image, see Paul K. Longmore, *The Invention of George Washington* (Berkeley, Calif.: University of California Press, 1988); Barry Schwartz, *The Making of an American Symbol* (New York: Free Press, 1987); and Gerald E. Kahler, *The Long Farewell: Americans Mourn the Death of George Washington* (Charlottesville: University Press of Virginia, 2008).

Abbreviations

The following abbreviations are used in the notes to designate frequently cited publications, libraries, and individuals.

AA   Abigail Adams.

AFC   L. H. Butterfield et al., eds. *Adams Family Correspondence.*
              4 vols. Cambridge, Mass.: Harvard University Press,
              1963–.

AH   Alexander Hamilton.

DAJA   L. H. Butterfield et al., eds. *The Diary and Autobiography
              of John Adams.* 4 vols. Cambridge, Mass.: Harvard
              University Press, 1961.

DAR   K. G. Davies, ed. *Documents of the American Revolution,
              1770–1783.* 21 vols. Dublin, Ireland: Irish University
              Press, 1972–1981.

DGW   Donald Jackson et al., eds. *The Diaries of George
              Washington.* 6 vols. Charlottesville: University Press of
              Virginia, 1976–1979.

Flexner, *GW* James T. Flexner. *George Washington.* 4 vols. Boston,
              Mass.: Little, Brown & Co., 1965–1972.

Freeman, *GW* Douglas Southall Freeman. *George Washington.* 7 vols.
              New York: Charles Scribner's Sons, 1948–1957.

GW   George Washington.

JA   John Adams.

JCC   Worthington C. Ford et al., eds. *The Journals of the Continental Congress.* 34 vols. Washington, D.C.: Library of Congress, 1904–1937.

JM   James Madison.

LDC   Paul H. Smith, ed. *Letters of Delegates to Congress, 1774–1789.* 26 vols. Washington, D.C.: Library of Congress, 1976–2000.

LP   [Charles Lee], *Lee Papers, Collections of the New-York Historical Society for the Year 1871 . . . 1872 . . . 1873 . . . 1874.* New York, 1871–1874.

LPL   Stanley J. Idzerda et al., eds. *Lafayette in the Age of the American Revolution: Selected Letters and Papers, 1776–1790.* 5 vols. Ithaca, N.Y.: Cornell University Press, 1976–1983.

PAH   Harold C. Syrett and Jacob E. Cooke, eds. *Papers of Alexander Hamilton.* 26 vols. New York: Columbia University Press, 1961–1979.

PC   President of Congress.

PGWC W. W. Abbot et al., eds. *The Papers of George Washington: Colonial Series.* 10 vols. Charlottesville: University Press of Virginia, 1983–1995.

PGWCF W. W. Abbot et al., eds. *The Papers of George Washington: Confederation Series.* 6 vols. Charlottesville: University Press of Virginia, 1992–1997.

PGWP Dorothy Twohig et al., eds. *The Papers of George Washington: Presidential Series.* Charlottesville: University Press of Virginia, 1987–.

PGWR Philander Chase et al., eds. *The Papers of George Washington: Revolutionary War Series.* Charlottesville: University Press of Virginia, 1985–.

PGWRT W. W. Abbot et al., eds. *The Papers of George Washington: Retirement Series.* 4 vols. Charlottesville: University Press of Virginia, 1998–1999.

PHL   Philip M. Hamer et al., eds. *The Papers of Henry Laurens.* Columbia, S.C.: University of South Carolina Press, 1968–.

PJA   Robert J. Taylor et al., eds. *Papers of John Adams.* Cambridge, Mass.: Harvard University Press, 1977–.

PJM   William T. Hutchinson et al., eds. *The Papers of James Madison.* Chicago and Charlottesville, Va.: University of Chicago Press and University Press of Virginia, 1962–.

PNG   Richard K. Showman, ed. *The Papers of Nathanael Greene.* 13 vols. Chapel Hill: University of North Carolina Press, 1976–2005.

PTJ   Julian P. Boyd et al., eds. *The Papers of Thomas Jefferson.* Princeton, N.J.: Princeton University Press, 1950–.

SP   Otis G. Hammond, ed. *Letters and Papers of Major-General John Sullivan, Continental Army.* 3 vols. Concord: New Hampshire, 1939.

TJ   Thomas Jefferson.

WMQ   *William and Mary Quarterly.*

WW   John C. Fitzpatrick, ed. *The Writings of Washington.* 39 vols. Washington, D.C.: United States Government Printing Office, 1931–1944.

NOTES

PREFACE

1. Flexner, *GW* 3:415.
2. Freeman, *GW* 6:383.
3. John C. Miller, *The Federalist Era, 1789–1801* (New York, 1960), 95–96.
4. Stanley Elkins and Eric McKitrick, *The Age of Federalism: The Early American Republic, 1788–1800* (New York, 1993), 289–292.
5. Joseph Charles, *The Origins of the American Party System: Three Essays* (Chapel Hill, N.C., 1956), 44.
6. Richard Hofstadter, *The Idea of a Party System: The Rise of Legitimate Opposition in the United States, 1780–1840* (Berkeley, Calif., 1970), 99–100.
7. Marcus Cunliffe, *George Washington: Man and Monument* (London, 1959), 108, 137, 139, 143, 144.
8. Michael Beschloss, *Presidential Courage: Brave Leaders and How They Changed America, 1789–1989* (New York, 2007), 30–31.
9. Peter R. Henriques. *Realistic Visionary: A Portrait of George Washington* (Charlottesville, Va., 2006), 51.
10. Jay Winik, *The Great Betrayal: America and the Birth of the Modern World, 1788–1800* (New York, 2007), 452.
11. Joseph Ellis, *His Excellency: George Washington* (New York, 2004), 194, 214.

INTRODUCTION: THE FOUNDING FATHER WHO WIELDED POWER
WITHOUT AMBITION

1. John Adams, Special Message: To Congress, December 15, 1799, and John Adams, Reply to the Senate, December 23, 1799, in James D. Richardson, ed., *A*

Compilation of Messages and Papers of the Presidents, 1789–1908 (New York, 1897–1917), 1:297–300; Page Smith, *John Adams* (New York, 1962), 2:1018.

2. On the state funeral in Philadelphia, see http://gwpapers.virginia.edu/project/exhibit/mourning/response.html. A detailed account can also be found in Gerald E. Kahler, *The Long Farewell: Americans Mourn the Death of George Washington* (Charlottesville, Va., 2008), 31–32.

3. François Furstenberg, *In the Name of the Father: Washington's Legacy, Slavery, and the Making of a Nation* (New York, 2006), 32.

4. Henry Lee, *Funeral Oration on the Death of Washington, Delivered December 26, 1799* (Philadelphia, 1800). The quotations are on pages 7, 10, 16, 17.

5. These two paragraphs draw on Barry Schwartz, *The Making of an American Symbol* (New York, 1987), 100–101.

6. Benjamin Whitwell, *An Eulogy on the Virtues of General George Washington . . . Delivered Before the Inhabitants of the Town of Augusta* (Boston, 1800), 6; Charles Caldwell, *Character of General Washington* (Philadelphia, 1801), 5, 7; George Blake, *A Masonic Eulogy on the Life of the Illustrious Brother George Washington, Pronounced Before the Brethren of St. John's Lodge* (Boston, 1800), 11; John Pierce, *A Eulogy on George Washington, the Great and the Good, Delivered . . . at Brookline* (Boston, 1800), 14; Asbury Dickens, *An Eulogium on General George Washington, Pronounced . . . Before the Hemathenian Society of Philadelphia* (Philadelphia, 1800), 25; Peter Lawrence Folsom, *An Eulogy on George Washington, Late Commander in Chief of the Armies of the United States of America* (Gilmanton, N.H., 1800), 6; Gouverneur Morris (New York, December 31, 1799), in *Eulogies and Orations on the Life and Death of George Washington* (Boston, 1800), 44; George Richards Minot (Boston, January 9, 1800), ibid., 22; Jonathan Mitchel Sewall, ibid., 38; George Blake (Boston, February 4, 1801), ibid., 104. The "sink unnerved" and "tremble" quotations are from a eulogy preached in a Baptist church in Savannah, Georgia, and can be found in Schwartz, *Making of an American Symbol,* 99. For an excellent survey of the national mourning and summation of the eulogies, see Furstenberg, *In the Name of the Father,* 25–70.

7. Folsom, *An Eulogy on George Washington,* 8–9; Ammi Ruhami Mitchell, *An Eulogy on General George Washington, Pronounced . . . in the First Meeting House in North-Yarmouth* (Portland, Mass., 1800), 12; Jacob McGaw, *An Eulogy on the Life of Gen. George Washington, Delivered at Merrimac* (Amherst, N.H., 1800), 11; Blake, *A Masonic Eulogy,* 14, 17, 19, 22; Caldwell, *Character of General Washington,* 9.

8. Whitwell, *An Eulogy on the Virtues of General George Washington,* 17.

CHAPTER 1: SOLDIER FOR VIRGINIA: AN INTRODUCTION TO POLITICS

1. Deed for Ferry Farm Land, July 7, 1748, *PGWC* 1:5n.

2. Joseph J. Ellis, *His Excellency: George Washington* (New York, 2004), 8.

3. *PGWC* 1:7n.

4. Charles Moore, ed., *George Washington's Rules of Civility, and Decent Behaviour in Company and Conversation* (Boston, 1926).

5. Richard Brookhiser, *Founding Father: Rediscovering George Washington* (New York,

1996), 122–125; Paul K. Longmore, *The Invention of George Washington* (Berkeley, Calif., 1988), 6–9, 173–174, 278n.

6. Robert Jackson to Lawrence Washington, September 18, 1746, *PGWC* 1:54n.

7. Dumas Malone, *Jefferson and His Time* (Boston, 1948–1981), 1:31.

8. *PGWC* 1:8–37n.

9. Lease of Mount Vernon, December 17, 1754, *PGWC* 1:232–234, 232n; GW to Governor Robert Dinwiddie, June 10, 1752, ibid. 1:50.

10. William S. Baker, *Early Sketches of George Washington* (Philadelphia, 1893), 13–14; John Ferling, "Soldiers for Virginia: Who Served in the French and Indian War?," *Virginia Magazine of History and Biography* 94 (1986): 312–313; Samuel E. Morison. "The Young Man Washington," in Samuel E. Morison, *By Land and by Sea: Essays and Addresses by Samuel Eliot Morison* (New York, 1953), 169; Brookhiser, *Founding Father.* 107–156. On the stature of males in eighteenth-century America, see Kenneth L. Sokoloff and George C. Villaflor, "The Early Achievement of Modern Stature in America," *Social Science History* 6 (1982): 435–481.

11. Edward G. Lengel, *General George Washington: A Military Life* (New York, 2005), 19–20.

12. Commission from Dinwiddie, October 30, 1753, *PGWC* 1:58, 56–58n, 59n; Instructions from Dinwiddie, October 30, 1753, ibid. 1:60–61; Passport from Dinwiddie, October 30, 1753, ibid. 1:62.

13. *PGWC* 1:157n.

14. For Christopher Gist's account, see *DGW* 1:157–158.

15. For GW's account of his expedition, see *The Journal of Major George Washington, Sent by the Hon. Robert Dinwiddie, Esq . . . to the Commandant of the French Forces on Ohio,* in *DGW* 1:130–161. The GW quotations are on pages 1:154, 156.

16. *DGW* 1:144, 152. The response of the French commander is in ibid. 1:151n.

17. *PGWC* 1:63–64n, 65n, 67n.

18. GW to Richard Corbin, [February–March 1754], *PGWC* 1:70.

19. GW to Horatio Sharpe, April 24, 1754, *PGWC* 1:85–86; GW to Dinwiddie, April 25, May 9, 1754, ibid. 1:87–88, 93–95; *DGW* 1:178, 180.

20. GW to Sharpe, April 24, 1754, *PGWC* 1:86; GW to James Hamilton, April 24, 1754, ibid. 1:83–84.

21. GW to Dinwiddie, May 18, 1754, *PGWC* 1:99–100; Dinwiddie to GW, May 25, 1754, ibid., 102–103.

22. GW to Dinwiddie, May 27, 1754, *PGWC* 1:105.

23. Dinwiddie, Instructions to GW, [January 1754], *PGWC* 1:65.

24. GW to Dinwiddie, May 29, 1754, *PGWC* 1:109–112; GW to Joshua Fry, May 29, 1754, ibid. 1:117; GW to John Augustine Washington, May 31, 1754, ibid. 1:118; *DGW* 1:191–196. For other accounts, see Flexner, *GW,* 78–91; Lengel, *General George Washington,* 30–39; John Ferling, *The First of Men: A Life of George Washington* (Knoxville, Tenn., 1988), 25–26; Fred Anderson, *Crucible of War: The Seven Years' War and the Fate of Empire in British North America, 1754–1763* (New York, 2000), 54–59. In GW's letters cited above, he says variously that ten, eleven, or even twelve French were killed.

25. GW to John A. Washington, May 31, 1754, *PGWC* 1:118.

26. GW to Dinwiddie, May 29, 1754, *PGWC* 1:116–117.

27. *PGWC* 1:77n.

28. GW to Dinwiddie, June 10, 1754, *PGWC* 1:130, 135.

29. Articles of Capitulation, July 3, 1754, *PGWC* 1:165–168; Account by GW and James Mackay of the Capitulation, July 19, 1754, ibid. 1:159–161; GW to ?, [c. 1757], ibid. 1:168–171; GW's Account of the Capitulation [1786], ibid. 1:172–173. See also ibid. 1:157–59n, 164n, and Harry Ward, *Major General Adam Stephen and the Cause of American Liberty* (Charlottesville, Va., 1989), 10, 12. For accounts of the battle and surrender, see Flexner, *GW* 1:100–106; Freeman, *GW* 1:377–411; Ferling, *First of Men*, 27–29; Anderson, *Crucible of War*, 62–64; Lengel, *General George Washington*, 42–45.

30. GW to ?, [c. 1757], *PGWC* 1:170. See also ibid. 1:80n, 171n; Lengel, *General George Washington*, 47.

31. *PGWC* 1:176–177.

32. Freeman, *GW* 1:415, 423–424; Flexner, *GW* 1:100.

33. The governor of Maryland told GW of "Stories & Representations" that were being bandied and of "some things inserted in the Publick papers" that were unfavorable. See Horatio Sharpe to GW, October 1, 1754, *PGWC* 1:215. The Half-King's comments can be found in Paul E. Kopperman, *Braddock at the Monongahela* (Pittsburgh, Pa., 1977), 103–104. See also Freeman, *GW* 1:415–417, 433.

34. Flexner, *GW* 1:110; Dinwiddie to GW, June 1, 25, August 3, 1754, *PGWC* 1:119, 148, 182; John Robinson to GW, September 15, 1754, ibid. 1:209.

35. *PGWC* 1:224n.

36. Sharpe to GW, October 1, 1754, *PGWC* 1:215; John Ridout to GW, October 14, 1754, ibid. 1:217, 217n; Flexner, *GW* 1:112; Freeman, *GW* 1:437–441. Sharpe, it turned out, bore no ill will toward GW and urged him to serve in the army he was raising.

37. Dinwiddie to GW, August 3, 1754, *PGWC* 1:182, 127n, 224n, 227n; *DGW* 1:187n; Lengel, *General George Washington*, 49; Flexner, *GW* 1:112–113.

38. GW to William Fitzhugh, November 15, 1754, *PGWC* 1:226; Freeman, *GW* 1:431–445.

39. GW to Robinson, October 23, 1754, *PGWC* 1:219; GW to Fitzhugh, November 15, 1754, ibid. 1:226.

40. Lease of Mount Vernon, *PGWC* 1:232–233; Division of Slaves, ibid. 1:227–231; Flexner, *GW* 1:114.

41. Robert Orme to GW, March 2, April 3, 1755, *PGWC* 1:241, 249; GW to Orme, March 15, April 2, 1755, ibid. 1:242–247; GW to Carter Burwell, April 20, 1755, ibid. 1:253; GW to Robinson, April 20, 1755, 1:255.

42. GW to Orme, July 28, 1755, *PGWC* 1:347–348; Robert Morris to GW, November 3, 1755, ibid. 2:155–156. I am indebted to both Arthur S. Lefkowitz and Philander Chase for pointing this out to me. See Arthur S. Leftkowitz, *George Washington's Indispensable Men: The 32 Aides-de-Camp Who Helped Win American Independence* (Mechanicsburg, Pa., 2003), 3.

43. Thomas A. Lewis, *For King and Country: The Maturing of George Washington, 1748–1760* (New York, 1993), 183.

44. Kopperman, *Braddock at the Monongahela*, a narrative as well as a compilation of original source materials, is indispensable for understanding the encounter. For other accounts of the disaster, see Stanley Pargellis. "Braddock's Defeat." *American Historical*

Review 40 (1936): 253–269; Flexner, *GW* 1:126–131; Freeman, *GW* 2:67–80; Ferling, *First of Men,* 37–39; Lengel, *General George Washington,* 57–60; and Anderson, *Crucible of War,* 86–107.

45. GW to Dinwiddie, July 18, 1755, *PGWC* 1:339–340; GW to John A. Washington, July 18, 1755, ibid. 1:343; GW to Warner Lewis, August 14, 1755, ibid. 1:360–363; GW to Mary Ball Washington, August 14, 1755, ibid. 1:359; GW to Andrew Lewis, September 6, 1755, ibid. 1:19; Dinwiddie to GW, July 26, 1755, ibid. 1:344; Philip Ludwell to GW, August 8, 1755, ibid. 1:356–357; Warner Lewis to GW, August 9, 1755, ibid. 1:358–359; Commission [to Command the Virginia Regiment], August 14, 1755, ibid. 2:3–4, 1–3n; Flexner, *GW* 1:138; Kopperman, *Braddock at the Monongahela,* 107, 130.

46. GW to Dinwiddie, July 18, 1755, *PGWC* 1:339.

47. Adam Stephen to GW, October 4, 1755, *PGWC* 2:72; GW to Stephen, December 28, 1755, ibid. 2:238–239; GW to Dinwiddie, January 14, 1756, ibid. 2:283; Dinwiddie to GW, January 22, 1756, ibid. 2:290–292; ibid. 2:293–295n, 304n; Lengel, *General George Washington,* 66–67; John Richard Alden, *Robert Dinwiddie: Servant of the Crown* (Williamsburg, Va., 1973), 98–99.

48. Stephen to GW, March 29, 1756, *PGWC* 2:324; Flexner, *GW* 1:145–148.

49. Lengel, *General George Washington,* 65; Stephen to GW, July 25, 1756, *PGWC* 3:294.

50. GW to Richard Washington [and Enclosure], December 6, 1755, *PGWC* 2:207–209; John Carlyle to GW, January 12, 1756, ibid. 2:276; ibid. 2:227–228n.

51. See John E. Ferling. "School for Command: Young George Washington and the Virginia Regiment," in Warren R. Hofstra, ed., *George Washington and the Virginia Backcountry* (Madison, Wis., 1998), 195–222.

52. Rosemarie Zagarri, ed., *David Humphrey's "Life of General Washington,"* with *George Washington's "Remarks"* (Athens, Ga., 1991), 19.

53. GW to Dinwiddie, October 11, 1755, *PGWC* 2:102.

54. GW to Dinwiddie, February 2, April 7, August 4, November 9, 1756, *PGWC* 2:314–315, 332–335; 3:312–318; 4:4; GW to John Robinson, November 9, 1756, ibid. 4:15; GW, Proposal for Frontier Forts, c. November 9, 1756, ibid. 4:10–11.

55. GW to Dinwiddie, November 9, 1756, March 10, 1757, *PGWC* 4:1, 3, 114; GW to John Campbell, Earl of Loudoun, January 10, 1757, ibid., 79, 87; GW to Richard Washington, April 15, 1757, ibid. 4:133.

56. GW to Dinwiddie, April 7, 16, 22, 24, 27, June 25, November 9, 1756, *PGWC* 2:333; 3:2, 33, 45–46, 60, 223; 4:3; GW to Richard Washington, April 15, 1757, ibid. 4:132–133; GW to Robinson, April 24, 1757, ibid. 4:48–49; GW to Loudoun, January 10, 1757, ibid. 4:80–90.

57. GW to Dinwiddie, August 4, November 9, 1756, September 24, 1757, *PGWC* 3:317; 4:4, 420; GW to Robinson, November 9, 1756, ibid. 4:14; GW to Loudoun, January 10, 1757, ibid. 4:82–83; GW to James Cuninghame, January 28, 1757, ibid. 4:106; GW to Richard Washington, April 15, 1757, ibid. 4:133; GW to John Stanwix, May 28, 1757, ibid. 4:169.

58. GW to Dinwiddie, May 3, September 28, 1756, *PGWC* 3:82, 420.

59. Dinwiddie to GW, August 19, 21, 1756, *PGWC* 3:358–359, 372–373.

60. *Virginia Gazette,* September 3, 1756, in *PGWC* 3:411–412n.

61. Dinwiddie to GW, November 16, 1756, August 27, September 2, 24, 1757, *PGWC* 4:25, 386, 397, 422; GW to Robinson, June 10, 1757, ibid. 4:199; William Peachy to GW, August 22, 1757, ibid. 4:382.

62. GW to Dinwiddie, September 17, October 5, 1757, *PGWC* 4:412; 5:3.

63. Augustine Washington to GW, October 16, 1756, *PGWC* 3:435–437.

64. Dinwiddie to GW, October 19, 1757, *PGWC* 5:21.

65. GW to John Campbell, Earl of Loudoun, January 10, 1757, *PGWC* 4:79–90. GW's plan for a colonial army to take the Ohio Country can be found in GW to James Cuninghame, January 28, 1757, ibid. 4:106.

66. GW presented Loudoun with a written statement. See GW, Memorial to John Campbell, Earl of Loudoun, March 23, 1757, *PGWC* 4:120–121. Dinwiddie's cautionary advice about making the trip to Philadelphia is in Dinwiddie to GW, February 2, 1757, ibid. 4:107. Loudoun's orders for GW and Virginia's army can be found in ibid. 4:127–128n. On Loudoun, see Anderson, *Crucible of War,* 142–144.

67. Anderson, *Crucible of War,* 176–179, 211–229, 232–236, 297–311.

68. GW to John Stanwix, April 10, 1758, *PGWC* 5:117–118; GW to Thomas Gage, April 12, 1758, ibid. 5:126; GW to John Forbes, June 19, 1758, ibid. 5:224–227; Freeman, *GW* 2:307, 314.

69. Henry Bouquet to GW, July 1, 1758, *PGWC* 5:252; GW to Robinson, September 1, 1758, ibid. 5:432.

70. Ferling, *First of Men,* 54–55; Lengel, *General George Washington,* 71.

71. Bouquet to GW, July 24, 1758, *PGWC* 5:320; GW to Bouquet, July 25, August 2, 13, 18, 28, ibid. 5:324, 353–360, 389, 397–398, 424–425; GW to Francis Fauquier, August 5, 1758, ibid. 5:370.

72. GW to Gabriel Jones, July 29, 1758 *PGWC* 5:350.

73. Dr. James Craik to GW, November 25, 1757, *PGWC* 5:64; Freeman, *GW* 2:264, 274–275; Ferling, *First of Men,* 50–51.

74. Freeman, *GW* 2:278–301; Bernhard Knollenberg, *George Washington: The Virginia Period, 1732–1775* (Durham, N.C., 1964), 26–28. On Martha Custis, see Patricia Brady, *Martha Washington* (New York, 2005), 1–64.

75. GW to Francis Halkett, August 2, 1758, *PGWC* 5:361; GW to Robinson, September 1, 1758, ibid. 5:432–433; GW to Francis Fauquier, August 5, 1758, ibid. 5:370; Freeman, *GW* 2:327–329, 332, 335; Knollenberg, *George Washington,* 64; Lengel, *General George Washington,* 74. For Forbes's changing views on GW, see *PGWC* 5:139n; ibid. 6:24n.

76. *PGWCS* 2:117–118n; 6:121–123n. GW's account can also be found in Zagarri, *David Humphreys' "Life of General Washington,"* xliii, 1–22, 105n.

77. GW to Forbes, November 15, 1758, *PGWC* 6:131.

78. Address from the Officers of the Virginia Regiment, December 31, 1758, ibid., 6:178–181.

CHAPTER 2: THE BURGESS: GEORGE WASHINGTON, VIRGINIA POLITICIAN

1. GW to the Officers of the Virginia Regiment, January 10, 1759, *PGWC* 6:187.

2. GW to J. A. Washington, May 28, 1755, *PGWC* 1:291–292, 293n.

3. The foregoing is based on Charles S. Sydnor, *Gentleman Freeholders: Political Practices in Washington's Virginia* (Chapel Hill, N.C., 1952), 11–59.

4. Stephen to GW, December 23, 1755, *PGWC* 2:226; Freeman, *GW* 2:146.

5. Robert Stewart to GW, November 24, 1757, *PGWC* 5:60 and 60n; Nathaniel Thompson to GW, February 20, 1755, ibid. 5:96; Freeman, *GW* 2:317.

6. Gabriel Jones to GW, July 6, 1758, *PGWC* 5:262; Sydnor, *Gentlemen Freeholders,* 41.

7. GW to Bouquet, July 19, 1758, *PGWC* 5:296.

8. Paul K. Longmore, *The Invention of George Washington* (Berkeley, Calif., 1988), 57–59. The quotations are from ibid., 58. See also *PGWC* 5:343n.

9. Robert Rutherford to GW, July 20, 1758, *PGWC* 5:305; ibid. 5:263n.

10. Freeman, *GW* 2:318–21; Charles Smith to GW, July 26, 1758, Enclosures I–IV, *PGWC* 5:331–334.

11. Resolution of the House of Burgesses, February 26, 1759, *PGWC* 6:192; Flexner, *GW* 1:227.

12. Thomas Jefferson, Sketch of GW, in Saul K. Padover, ed., *The Complete Jefferson: Containing His Major Writings, Published and Unpublished, Except His Letters* (Freeport, N.Y., 1969), 924–925.

13. TJ, Sketch of GW; Padover, *Complete Jefferson*, 925; GW to Bushrod Washington, November 9, 1787, *PGWCF* 5:424.

14. Sydnor, *Gentlemen Freeholders,* 98; Bernhard Knollenberg, *George Washington: The Virginia Period, 1732–1775* (Durham, N.C., 1964), 102–103; Harry M. Ward, *Major General Adam Stephen and the Cause of American Liberty* (Charlottesville, Va., 1989), 70; GW, Report to the House of Burgesses, November 10, 14, 1759, *PGWC* 6:371–372; GW, Cash Accounts, [1761], ibid. 7:1. For specifics on GW's committee assignments and private bills, see *PGWC* 7:20n; ibid. 8:53n, 158n, 271n; 9:453n; and William Ramsay, Robert Adam, and Carlyle & Dalton to GW and John West, May 16, 1774, ibid. 10:60–62, 62–64n.

15. Peter R. Henriques, *Realistic Visionary: A Portrait of George Washington* (Charlottesville, Va., 2006), 28.

16. Robert F. Dalzell and Lee Baldwin Dalzell, *George Washington's Mount Vernon: At Home in Revolutionary America* (New York, 1998), 47–53.

17. Joseph J. Ellis, *His Excellency: George Washington* (New York, 2004), 41.

18. *PGWC* 6:199n; 7:70n; GW to Richard Washington, October 20, 1761, ibid. 7:80; GW to Charles Green, August 26 [–30], 1761, ibid. 7:68; Henry Wiencek, *An Imperfect God: George Washington, His Slaves, and the Creation of America* (New York, 2003), 87–88.

19. Freeman, *GW* 3:341–42; John Ferling, *The First of Men: A Life of George Washington* (Knoxville, Tenn., 1988), 61–83; GW, Guardian Accounts, *PGWC* 9:370–374; GW to Robert Cary, November 10, 1773, ibid. 9:375; ibid. 9:379–380n.

20. Ferling, *First of Men,* 67–69, 123, 474–480.

21. GW to Loudoun, January 10, 1757, *PGWC* 4:79.

22. *PGWC* 1:65, 67n; Knollenberg, *George Washington,* 91. The text of Dinwiddie's Proclamation of 1754, as it came to be called, can be found in *PGWC* 7:117–118.

23. George Mercer to GW, September 16, 1759, *PGWC* 6:343; Robert Stewart to GW, September 28, 1759, ibid. 6:360–361; ibid. 6:345–346n; 7:44n.

24. *PGWC* 7:44n; Mercer to GW, February 17, 1760, ibid. 6:387–388.

25. Mercer to GW, February 17, 1760, *PGWC* 6:387–388; Charles Ambler, *George Washington and the West* (Chapel Hill, N.C., 1936), 135.

26. Stewart to GW, February 15, March 12, 1761, *PGWC* 7:12–13, 15.

27. GW to Van Swearingen, May 15, 1761, *PGWC* 7:42–43; Longmore, *Invention of George Washington,* 60; Ward, *Adam Stephen,* 69–71. The poll sheets for the 1758 election can be found in *PGWC* 5:334–343. GW kept those for the 1765 election as well, and they can be found in ibid. 7:377–383.

28. *PGWC* 7:119n; Proclamation of 1763, in Merrill Jensen, ed., *English Historical Documents: American Colonial Documents to 1776* (12 vols., London, 1953–1956), 9:640–643.

29. Mississippi Land Company Articles of Agreement, June 3, 1763, *PGWC* 7:219–223.

30. Mississippi Land Company's Petition to the King, December 1768, *PGWC* 8:149–152, 152n; GW to Baron de Botetourt, September 9, 1770, ibid. 8:379; ibid. 8:152–53n, 368n, 380n. See also Gordon S. Wood, *The Americanization of Benjamin Franklin* (New York, 2004), 135–136, and Carl Van Doren, *Benjamin Franklin* (New York, 1938), 394–398.

31. Petition to the King for the Virginia Regiment, [c. March 11–July 10, 1762], *PGWC* 7:117–119.

32. GW to William Crawford, September 17, 1767, *PGWC* 8:28; GW, Petition to Botetourt, [c. December 15,] 1769, ibid. 8:277–278; GW to Botetourt, December 8, 1769, ibid. 8:272–275.

33. GW to Crawford, September 17, 1767, *PGWC* 8:28–29.

34. GW, Advertisement, December 16, 1769, *PGWC* 8:280; ibid. 8:279n.

35. Memorial to Governor and Council, [c. November 1–4], 1771, *PGWC* 8:534–539; ibid. 533–534n; *DGW* 2:261. GW kept a diary during his lengthy trip to, and on, the Great Kanawha River. See *DGW* 2:277–328. The notes that he took while reconnoitering the Kanawha can be found in ibid. 2:307–308.

36. *PGWC* 8:533n.

37. Minutes of the Council, November 4 [and 6], 1771, *PGWC* 8:540–541.

38. Petition to Governor Dunmore and the Virginia Council, [c. November 4, 1772], *PGWC* 9:118–121; Knollenberg, *George Washington,* 94.

39. Crawford to GW, November 12, 1773, *PGWC* 9:380; Resolutions of the Officers of the Virginia Regiment of 1754, November 23, 1772, ibid. 9:128–130; GW to Presley Neville, June 16, 1794, *WW* 33:407.

40. GW, Memorandum List of Quitrents, [1769, 1770, 1771], *PGWC* 8:283, 421, 592.

41. GW to Robert Adam, November 22, 1771, *PGWC* 8:551; GW to Mercer, November 7, 1771, ibid. 8:541–544; GW to Charles Washington, January 31, 1770, ibid. 8:300; ibid. 8:552–53n; Ferling, *First of Men,* 73.

42. Jack P. Greene, "An Uneasy Connection: An Analysis of the Preconditions of the American Revolution," in Stephen G. Kurtz and James H. Hutson, eds., *Essays on the American Revolution* (Chapel Hill, N.C., 1973), 53–62.

43. *DGW* 1:338–340; GW to Francis Dandridge, September 20, 1765, *PGWC* 7:395–396; GW to Robert Cary & Co., September 20, 1765, ibid. 7:401–402.

44. GW to Capel and Osgood Hanbury, July 25, 1767, *PGWC* 8:15; *DGW* 2:51–52.

45. Woody Holton, *Forced Founders: Indians, Debtors, Slaves, and the Making of the American Revolution in Virginia* (Chapel Hill, N.C., 1999), 53n, 57.

46. GW to George Mason, April 5, 1769, *PGWC* 8:177–180; Arthur Lee to GW, June 15, 1777, *PGWR* 10:43.

47. GW to George William Fairfax, June 27, 1770, *PGWC* 8:353, 354n; GW to Jonathan Boucher, July 30, 1770, ibid. 8:361; Holton, *Forced Founders,* 77–91.

48. Hillsborough's Circular Letter, April 21, 1768, Jensen, *English Historical Documents* 9:716–717; GW to Thomas Lewis, February 17, 1774, *PGWC* 9:483; GW to James Wood, February 20, 1774, ibid. 9:490; John Ferling, *A Leap in the Dark: The Struggle to Create the American Republic* (New York, 2003), 67–68.

49. GW to Lewis, February 17, 1774, *PGWC* 9:483; ibid. 7:176–178n; *DGW* 3:65, 68, 153; Ferling, *First of Men,* 95.

50. *DGW* 3:108–109; GW to Jonathan Boucher, May 21, 1772, *PGWC* 9:49; Ferling, *First of Men,* 82.

51. GW to Boucher, May 23, 1772, *PGWC* 9:51.

52. GW to Thomas Lewis, February 17, 1774, *PGWC* 9:483; GW to James Wood, February 20, 1774, ibid. 9:490; GW to William Preston, February 28, 1774, ibid. 9:501; GW to Crawford, September 25, 1773, ibid. 9:329.

53. GW to Lord Dunmore, April 3, 1775, *PGWC* 10:320; Ferling, *First of Men,* 73; Holton, *Forced Founders,* 32–37. The Holton quotation is on page 36.

54. Fairfax County Resolves, July 18, 1774, *PGWC* 10:119–127; *DGW* 3:261.

55. GW to George William Fairfax, June 10 [–15], 1774, *PGWC* 10:96–97; Fairfax County Resolves, July 18, 1774, ibid. 10:122.

56. *DGW* 3:255.

57. Fairfax County Resolves, July 18, 1774, *PGWC* 10:122, 124; GW to George William Fairfax, June 10 [–15], 1774, ibid. 10:96–97; GW to Bryan Fairfax, July 4, 20, 1774, ibid. 10:109, 129–131.

58. GW to George William Fairfax, June 10 [–15], 1774, *PGWC* 10:96; GW to Bryan Fairfax, July 20, August 24, 1774, ibid. 10:129–131, 154–156; GW to Richard Henry Lee, August 9, 1774, ibid. 10:150–151.

59. Flexner, *GW* 1:322.

60. GW to George William Fairfax, June 10 [–15], 1774, *PGWC* 10:96–97.

61. *DGW* 3:271–272, 275.

62. *DGW* 3:276–287.

63. *DAJA* 2:117–119, 121; JA to AA, September 14, 1774, *AFC* 1:155; JA to William Tudor, September 29, 1774, *PJA* 2:177.

64. Silas Deane to Elizabeth Deane, September 10–11, 1774, *LDC* 1:61–62; John Ferling, *Setting the World Ablaze: Washington, Adams, Jefferson and the American Revolution* (New York, 2000), 94–95; John Ferling, *John Adams: A Life* (Knoxville, Tenn., 1992), 102–113.

65. GW to George William Fairfax, June 10 [–15], 1774, *PGWC* 10, 97; John Adams's Proposed Resolution, September 30, 1774, *LDC* 1:131; JA to Tudor, October 7, 1774, *PJA* 2:188; JA to William Cranch, September 18, 1774, *AFC* 1:160.

66. *DAJA* 2:120.

67. GW to John Connally, February 25, 1775, *PGWC* 10:273–274; *DGW* 3:304, 321, 323, 325; Freeman, *GW* 3:398–399.

68. GW to George William Fairfax, May 31, 1775, *PGWC* 10:368.

69. GW to Connally, February 25, 1775, *PGWC* 10:273.

70. GW to Mercer, April 5, 1775, *PGWC* 10:327; GW to Robert McKenzie, October 9, 1775, ibid. 10:172.

CHAPTER 3: THE CRUCIAL FIRST YEAR: BOSTON, 1775–1776

1. Richard Frothingham, *History of the Siege of Boston* (Boston, 1849), 101; Allen French, *The Siege of Boston* (New York, 1911), 217.

2. James Warren to JA, May 7, June 11, 1775, *PJA* 3:3–4, 24; ibid. 3:6n; DAJA 3:321; Jerrilyn Greene Marsten, *King and Congress: The Transfer of Political Legitimacy, 1774–1776* (Princeton, N.J., 1987), 144; Address from the Massachusetts Provincial Congress to GW, July 3, 1775, *PGWR* 1:52–53; Joseph Hawley to GW, July 5, 1775, ibid. 1:65.

3. *DAJA* 3:322–323; Peter R. Henriques, *Realistic Visionary: A Portrait of George Washington* (Charlottesville, Va., 2006), 37.

4. Thomas Cushing, June 21, 1775, *LDC* 1:530; Eliphalet Dyer to Joseph Trumbull, June 17, 1775, ibid. 1:499–500; Silas Deane to Elizabeth Deane, June 16, 1775, ibid. 1:494; Benjamin Rush to Thomas Rushton, October 29, 1775, in L. H. Butterfield, ed., *Letters of Benjamin Rush* (Princeton, N.J., 1951), 1:92; JA to AA, June 17, 1775, *AFC* 1:215–216; Henriques, *Realistic Visionary*, 37–38.

5. GW, Address to the Continental Congress, *PGWR* 1:1.

6. *PGWR* 1:3n.

7. GW, Address to the New York Provincial Congress, June 26, 1775, *PGWR* 1:41.

8. The literature on republicanism is enormous, but perhaps it is best to begin with Gordon S. Wood, *The Creation of the American Republic, 1776–1787* (Chapel Hill, N.C., 1969), 46–90; Gordon S. Wood, *The Radicalism of the American Revolution* (New York, 1992), 95–228; and Bernard Bailyn, *The Ideological Origins of the American Revolution* (Cambridge, Mass., 1967). For especially useful essays, see Robert E. Shalhope, "Toward a Republican Synthesis: The Emergence of an Understanding of Republicanism in Early American Historiography," *WMQ* 29 (1972): 49–80; Robert E. Shalhope, "Republicanism and Early American Historiography," *WMQ* 39 (1982): 334–356; Joyce Appleby, "Republicanism and Ideology," *American Quarterly* 37 (1985): 461–473; Joyce Appleby, "Republicanism in Old and New Context," *WMQ* 43 (1986): 20–34.

9. GW, Address to the Massachusetts Provincial Congress, July 4, 1775, *PGWR* 1:59–60.

10. GW to John Augustine Washington, June 20, 1775, *PGWR* 1:19; GW to Burwell Bassett, June 19, 1775, ibid. 1:12–13. See also the thoughtful analysis of Henriques, *Realistic Visionary*, 39–43.

11. GW to John Augustine Washington, June 20, 1775, *PGWR* 1:19; GW to Martha Washington, June 18, 1775, ibid. 1:3; GW to Burwell Bassett, June 19, 1775, ibid. 1:12; George W. Conner, ed., *The Autobiography of Benjamin Rush* (Princeton, N.J., 1948), 113.

12. Alan Valentine, *Lord North* (Norman, Okla., 1967), 1:314–318, 346–352.

13. Address from the Massachusetts Provincial Congress, July 3, 1775, *PGWR* 1:52; GW to the Massachusetts Provincial Congress, July 4, 1775, ibid., 59. Much of this paragraph draws on Don Higginbotham, *George Washington: Uniting a Nation* (Lanham, Md., 2002), 25–28. The quotation is taken from page 25.

14. JA to AA, June 23, 1775, *AFC* 1:226; Freeman, *GW* 3:458–459; Flexner, *GW* 2:23.

15. Commission from the Continental Congress, June 19, 1775, *PGWR* 1:6–7; Instructions from the Continental Congress, June 22, 1775, ibid. 1:21–22. On the Articles of War, see ibid. 1:8n, 64n.

16. GW to Lee, April 24 [–26], May 17, June 1, 1777, *PGWR* 9:256–257, 453, 580–581; GW to Joseph Jones, March 24, 1781, *WW* 21:372; GW to Gouverneur Morris, December 10, 1780, ibid. 20:458.

17. Hancock to GW, September 30, 1775, *PGWR* 2:71; GW to Hancock, August 4 [–5], September 21, 1775, ibid. 1:225, 227; 2:28–29.

18. Council of War, September 11, October 18, 1775, *PGWR* 1:450–451; Questions for the Committee, October 18, 1775, ibid. 2:185–188; Minutes of the Conference, [October 18–24, 1775], ibid. 2:190–203; Hancock to GW, December 22, 1775, ibid. 2:589–590, 590n.

19. Hancock to GW, June 28, 1775, *PGWR* 1:42–43, and 43n; Richard Henry Lee to GW, June 29, 1775, ibid. 1:45; Philip Schuyler to GW, July 1, 1775, ibid. 1:47–48; GW to Schuyler, July 28, 1775, ibid. 1:188; JA to Warren, June 7, 1775, *PJA* 3:17–18.

20. GW to Schuyler, August 20, 1775, *PGWR* 1:332.

21. On the Quebec campaign of 1775, see Hal T. Shelton, *General Richard Montgomery and the American Revolution* (New York, 1994); James Kirby Martin, *Benedict Arnold: Revolutionary Hero* (1997); Willard Sterne Randall, *Benedict Arnold, Patriot and Traitor* (New York, 1990); Arthur S. Lefkowitz, *Benedict Arnold's Army: The 1775 American Invasion of Canada During the Revolutionary War* (New York, 2008); and Thomas A. Desjardin, *Through a Howling Wilderness: Benedict Arnold's March to Quebec, 1775* (New York, 2006).

22. Council of War, July 9, 1775, *PGWR* 1:79–80, 81n.

23. JA to NG, March 9, April 13, May 9, 10, 1777, *PJA* 5: 106, 151, 185, 190; JA to William Tudor, ND, *DAJA* 3:439; JA to Daniel Hitchcock, October 1, 1776, ibid. 3:443, 444; JA to Samuel Parsons, October 2, 1776, ibid. 3:444.

24. Marsten, *King and Congress,* 144; James Warren to JA, May 7, June 11, 1775, *PJA* 3:3–4, 24; ibid. 3:6n; *DAJA* 3:321; GW to Richard Henry Lee, July 10, 1775, *PGWR* 1:99.

25. John Ferling, *Almost a Miracle: The American Victory in the War of Independence* (New York, 2007), 77; Robert Wright, *The Continental Army* (Washington, D.C., 1983), 45–50.

26. Council of War, July 9, October 8, 1775, *PGWR* 1:79–80; 2:125; GW, General Orders, November 12, 1775, ibid. 2:354–355; GW to Hancock, July 10 [–11], December 31, 1775, ibid. 1:90; 2:624; Henry Wiencek, *An Imperfect God: George Washington, His Slaves, and the Creation of America* (New York, 2003), 196–205.

27. GW to Joseph Reed, November 28, 1775, *PGWR* 2:449; GW to Hancock, February 9, 1775, ibid. 3:274–276.

28. The quotations of Samuel Adams and John Adams can be found, respectively, in Flexner, *GW* 2:67 and Don Higginbotham, *The War of American Independence: Military Attitudes, Policies, and Practice, 1763–1789* (New York, 1971), 390. See also Ferling, *Almost a Miracle,* 193–194.

29. Richard M. Ketchum, *Decisive Day: The Battle for Bunker Hill* (Boston, 1974), 135–180. The quotation is from Ferling, *Almost a Miracle,* 58.

30. GW, General Orders, October 26, 31, November 12, 14, 20, 1775, *PGWR* 2:235, 269, 354, 369, 443; GW, Address to the Massachusetts Provincial Congress, [c. July 4, 1775], ibid. 1:59.

31. GW to Reed, January 14, 1776, *PGWR* 3:87.

32. GW to Reed, December 15, 1775, *PGWR* 2:552.

33. Mercy Warren to JA, October [?], 1775, *PJA* 3:269; AA to JA, July 16, 1775, *AFC* 1:246–247.

34. General Howe to Earl of Dartmouth, November 26, 1775, *DAR* 11:193.

35. Council of War, January 16, February 16, 1776, *PGWR* 3:103–104, 320–322, 323–324n; GW to Reed, February 26 [–March 9], 1776, ibid. 3:373; Christopher Ward, *The War of the Revolution* (New York, 1952), 1:126–128; Edward G. Lengel, *General George Washington: A Military Life* (New York, 2005), 120; Ferling, *Almost a Miracle,* 104–107.

36. Address from the Boston Selectmen, [March 1776], *PGWR* 3:571–572. An illustration of the medal, together with an account of its convoluted history (it was not finally presented to GW until 1789), can be found in ibid. 4:2–4n.

37. GW to Hancock, March 19, 1776, *PGWR* 3:490.

CHAPTER 4: THE WAR IN 1776–1777: IN THE DEPTHS OF DESPAIR

1. GW to Reed, January 4, 1776, *PGWR* 3:24; GW to Hancock, January 4, 1776, ibid. 3:20.

2. Charles Lee to GW, January 5, 1776, *PGWR* 3:30; GW to John Augustine Washington, March 31, 1776, ibid. 3:570.

3. Lee to GW, February 5 [–6], 9, 29, 1776, *PGWR* 3:250–251, 291, 390–391; GW to Lee, January 8, 23, 30, February 10, 1776, ibid. 3:53–54, 170–171, 221–222, 282; Charles Lee, "Report on the Defenses of New York," March 1776, *LP* 1:354–357.

4. Hancock to GW, January 29, February 12, March 6, 1776, *PGWR* 3:211, 300, 415; Barnet Schecter, *The Battle for New York: The City at the Heart of the American Revolution* (New York, 2002), 76–77; John Ferling, *Almost a Miracle: The American Victory in the War of Independence* (New York, 2007), 120.

5. Schecter, *Battle for New York,* 90–91; Judith Livan Buskirk, *Generous Enemies: Patriots and Loyalists in Revolutionary New York* (Philadelphia, 2002), 16.

6. GW to Hancock, April 15, 1776, *PGWR* 4:69; GW to John Augustine Washington, April 29, 1776, ibid. 4:172–173; GW to Lee, May 9, 1776, ibid. 4:245; New York Convention to GW, July 16, 1776, ibid. 5:347–348; David Hackett Fischer, *Washington's Crossing* (New York, 2004), 83–84; Ferling, *Almost a Miracle,* 123.

7. GW to John Augustine Washington, March 31, 1776, *PGWR* 3:568.

8. GW to William Gordon, May 13, 1776, *PGWR* 4:286; GW to Benjamin Franklin, May 20, 1776, ibid. 4:345; GW to Hancock, June 17, 1776, ibid. 5:21.

9. Hancock to Certain Colonies, June 11, 1776, *LDC* 4:189; Hancock to GW, May 16, 1776, *PGWR* 4:312.

10. GW to John Augustine Washington, July 22, 1776, *PGWR* 5:428–429.

11. GW to Hancock, August 31, 1776, *PGWR* 6:177–178. For an extended discussion of the Long Island campaign, see Ferling, *Almost a Miracle,* 129–135; Christopher Ward, *The War of the Revolution* (New York, 1952), 1:211–237; Freeman, *GW* 4:153–175; Flexner, *GW* 107–115; John Gallagher, *The Battle of Brooklyn, 1776* (Edison, N.J., 2002), 101–134.

12. GW to Hancock, September 2, 4, 6, 8, 1776, *PGWR* 6:200, 216, 231–232, 249. See also General Greene's influential counsel in NG to GW, September 5, 1776, ibid. 6:222–224.

13. Certain general officers to GW, September 11, 1776, *PGWR* 6:279; Council of War, September 12, 1776, ibid. 6:288–289; GW to Hancock, September 8, 1776, ibid. 6:249; ibid. 6:252n, 273n.

14. Hancock to GW, September 3, 1776, *PGWR* 6:207; GW to Lund Washington, October 6, 1776, ibid. 6:494; GW to Hancock, September 22, 1776, ibid. 6:369; Hans Huth, "Letters from a Hessian Mercenary," *Pennsylvania Magazine of History and Biography* 62 (1938): 494–495; Governor William Tryon to Lord George Germain, September 24, 1776, *DAR* 12:230–231.

15. GW to Hancock, September 8, 19, 1776, *PGWR* 6:248, 341; GW to Lund Washington, October 6, 1776, ibid. 6:493; GW to Samuel Washington, October 5, 1776, ibid. 6:486; GW, General Orders, September 30, 1776, ibid. 6:432.

16. *PGWR* 6:273n, 443n; GW to Lund Washington, September 30, 1776, ibid. 6:442.

17. *LDC* 5:316n; William Williams to Joseph Trumbull, October 7, 1776, ibid. 6:316; JA to William Tudor, September 26, 1776, *DAJA* 3:439; JA to General Samuel Parsons, October 2, 1776, ibid. 3:444; JA to Samuel Cooper, September 4, 1776, *PJA* 5:11; JA to Warren, October 5, 1776, ibid. 5:46.

18. GW to Lund Washington, September 30, 1776, *PGWR* 6:441–442; GW to John Augustine Washington, September 22, 1776, ibid. 6:371–374; GW to Hancock, September 24, 25, 1776, ibid. 6:389, 396–397; GW to Samuel Washington, October 5, 1776, ibid. 6:486–487.

19. On the crucial period between Long Island and the evacuation of Manhattan, see Ferling, *Almost a Miracle,* 1–11, 135–146; Flexner, *GW* 3:116–127; Freeman, *GW* 4:176–203.

20. Ferling, *Almost a Miracle,* 151–154.

21. GW to Hancock, September 2, 25, 1776, *PGWR* 6:199–200, 394–400.

22. JA to Parsons, June 22, 1776, *PJA* 4:328; *DAJA* 3:434; Hancock to GW, September 24, 1776, *PGWR* 6:388–389; *JCC* 2:111–122; 3:331–334; 5:729, 747, 749, 751, 756–757, 762–763, 788–807.

23. The complete texts of the letters written by Lee and Reed can be found in *PGWR* 7:237–238n, 336n. Also see Lee to GW, November 19, 1776, ibid. 7:187.

24. GW to Hancock, September 2, November 16, 19 [–21], 1776, *PGWR* 6:199; 7:163, 183; GW to John Augustine Washington, November 6 [–19], 1776, ibid. 7:102.

Unfortunately, the letters that GW dispatched to Congress immediately following his escape from Manhattan Island have not survived.

25. *JCC* 6:1,024–1,027; GW to Hancock, December 20, 1776, *PGWR* 7:381–386; NG to Hancock, December 21, 1776, *PNG* 1:370–374; Edward G. Lengel, *General George Washington: A Military Life* (New York, 2005), 189; Board of War to Robert Morris, December 29, 1776, *LDC* 5:691. The Virginia delegate who is quoted was Benjamin Harrison.

26. On Trenton-Princeton, see Fischer, *Washington's Crossing,* 221–345.

27. GW to Hancock, December 27, 1776, January 1, 5, 1777, *PGWR* 7:454–456, 503–504, 519–523.

28. Geoffrey Perret, *Old Soldiers Never Die: The Life of Douglas MacArthur* (New York, 1996), 548.

29. Hancock to GW, January 1, 1777, *PGWR* 7:505–506.

30. GW to William Duer, January 14, 1777, *PGWR* 8:63; GW to Hancock, January 26, 1777, ibid. 8:160; Hancock to GW, January 18, 1777, ibid. 8:96.

31. GW to the Pennsylvania Council of Safety, January 12, 19, 29, 1777, *PGWR* 8:50, 108, 182–183; GW, General Orders, January 21, 1777, ibid. 8:119; Robert Morris to GW, February 27, 1777, ibid. 8:457.

32. GW to John Parke Custis, January 22, 1776, *PGWR* 8:123; GW to Morris, February 22, 1777, ibid. 8:416; Ferling, *Almost a Miracle,* 193–197. A smallpox epidemic additionally hampered recruiting early in 1777. See Elizabeth A. Fenn, *Pox Americana: The Great Smallpox Epidemic of 1775–1782* (New York, 2001).

33. GW to Custis, January 22, 1776, *PGWR* 8:123; GW to Samuel Washington, April 5, 1777, ibid. 9:72; GW to John Augustine Washington, February 24, April 12, 1777, ibid. 8:439; 9:144.

34. Morris to GW, February 27, 1777, *PGWR* 8:458; JA to Benjamin Rush, March 19, 1812, in John A. Schutz and Douglass Adair, eds., *The Spur of Fame: Dialogues of John Adams and Benjamin Rush, 1805–1813* (San Marino, Calif., 1966), 212; Barry Schwartz, *George Washington: The Making of an American Symbol* (New York, 1987), 22. I am indebted, too, to the wonderful essay on GW as a symbol and unifier in Don Higginbotham, *George Washington: Uniting a Nation* (Lanham, Md., 2002), 8–14.

35. A Committee of the Continental Congress to GW, April 10, 1777, *PGWR* 9:111; Richard Henry Lee to GW, April 10, 1777, ibid. 9:118; Hancock to GW, May 10, 1777, ibid. 375; Richard Peters to GW, May 11, 1777, ibid. 9:391; GW to Hancock, April 12 [–13], May 12, 1777, ibid. 9:128–129, 395.

36. For excellent accounts of Burgoyne's travail, see Richard M. Ketchum, *Saratoga: Turning Point of America's Revolutionary War* (New York, 1997), and Max Mintz, *The Generals of Saratoga* (New Haven, Conn., 1997). For a brief analysis, including the evolution of Howe's thinking, see Ferling, *Almost a Miracle,* 187–193, 211–241.

37. Flexner, *GW* 2:219.

38. Enoch Anderson, *Personal Recollections of Enoch Anderson* (New York, 1971), 38; JA to NG, April 13, 1777, *PJA* 5:151; *PGWR* 11:70n.

39. Schuyler to GW, July 26 [–27], 1777, *PGWR* 10:430; Paul David Nelson, *General Horatio Gates: A Biography* (Baton Rouge, La., 1976), 94–103; Jonathan G. Rossie, *The Politics of Command in the American Revolution* (Syracuse, N.Y., 1975), 159–165; Ferling, *Almost a Miracle,* 225–226.

40. GW to Putnam, July 31, August 22, 1777, *PGWR* 10:468; 11:46; GW to Schuyler, July 24, 1777, ibid. 10:397; Schuyler to GW, August 1, 1777, ibid. 10:483; GW to Jonathan Trumbull Sr., August 4, 1777, ibid. 10:507; GW to Gates, September 1, 1777, ibid. 11:107; Gates to GW, August 28, 1777, ibid. 11:84.

41. "Before and After the Battle of Brandywine: Extracts from the Journal of Sergeant Thomas Sullivan of H.M. Forty-ninth Regiment of Foot," *Pennsylvania Magazine of History and Biography* 31 (1907): 416. Useful accounts of the engagement can be found in Ward, *War of the Revolution,* 1:342–354; *PGWR* 11:187–193n; Lengel, *General George Washington,* 229–241; Stephen R. Taaffe, *The Philadelphia Campaign, 1777–1778* (Lawrence, Kans., 2003), 63–78.

42. GW to Samuel Washington, October 27, 1777, *PGWR* 12:35; Ferling, *Almost a Miracle,* 310; Lengel, *General George Washington,* 242.

43. GW to Hancock, September 11, 1775, *PGWR* 11:200.

44. GW to Hancock, September 13, 15, 1775, *PGWR* 11:213, 237.

45. GW to Hancock, September 17, 19, 23, 1775, *PGWR* 11:268, 301; Flexner, *GW* 2:227–230; Freeman, *GW* 4:490–499; Ferling, *Almost a Miracle,* 251–252.

46. GW to Hancock, September 18, 23, 1777, *PGWR* 11:262, 301; GW to Elbridge Gerry, September 27, 1777, ibid. 11:331. Gerry was a member of Congress.

47. "The Diary of Robert Morton," *Pennsylvania Magazine of History and Biography* 1 (1877): 3–4; Sarah Fisher, "'A Diary of Trifling Occurrences': Philadelphia, 1776–1778," *Pennsylvania Magazine of History and Biography* 82 (1958): 450.

48. GW to Henry, October 3, 1777, *PGWR* 11:383; GW to Hancock, September 15, 29, 1777, ibid. 11:237, 346.

49. Council of War, September 28, 1777, *PGWR* 11:338–339.

50. GW, General Orders for Attacking Germantown, October 3, 1777, *PGWR* 11:375–376. Good accounts of the Battle of Germantown can be found in Taaffe, *Philadelphia Campaign,* 93–107; Ward, *War of the Revolution,* 1:362–371; and Lengel, *General George Washington,* 249–259. See also *PGWR* 11:376–380n.

51. Benjamin Tallmadge, *Memoir of Colonel Benjamin Tallmadge* (New York, 1968), 23; Comment of General John Armstrong, October 9, 1777, in Henry Steele Commager and Richard B. Morris, eds., *The Spirit of '76: The Story of the American Revolution as Told by Participants* (Indianapolis, Ind., 1958), 1:628; Johann Ewald, *Diary of the American War: A Hessian Journal,* ed., by Joseph P. Tustin (New Haven, Conn., 1979), 93.

52. GW to Hancock, October 5, 1777, *PGWR* 11:393–395.

53. GW to Jonathan Trumbull Sr., October 7, 1777, *PGWR* 11:426–427.

54. Charles Carroll of Carrollton to GW, September 27, 1777, *PGWR* 11:330; Harry M. Ward, *Major General Adam Stephen and the Cause of American Liberty* (Charlottesville, Va., 1989), 135–196.

55. Quoted in Ward, *Major General Adam Stephen and the Cause of American Liberty,* 200–201.

56. GW to Richard Henry Lee, October 28, 1777, *PGWR* 12:41; William Heath to GW, October 22, 1777, ibid. 11:575; Jeremiah Dummer Powell to GW, October 25, 1777, ibid. 11:618; James Wilkinson to GW, October 24, 1777, ibid. 11:604; Nelson, *General Horatio Gates,* 143–145.

57. GW to Gates, October 30, 1777, *PGWR* 12:59–60; AH to GW, November 6, 1777, ibid. 12:141–142. See also Ron Chernow, *Alexander Hamilton* (New York,

2004), 102; Thomas Fleming, *Washington's Secret War: The Hidden History of Valley Forge* (New York, 2005), 116; and Nelson, *General Horatio Gates,* 146–147.

58. Lengel, *General George Washington,* 276; Benjamin Rush to JA, October 21, 1777, *PJA* 5:316–317.

CHAPTER 5: THE UNTOUCHABLE: GENERAL WASHINGTON'S GREAT CRISIS

1. John Ferling, *The Loyalist Mind: Joseph Galloway and the American Revolution* (University Park, Pa., 1977), 43; Wilbur Henry Siebert, *The Loyalists of Pennsylvania* (reprint, Boston, 1972), 42–52; Robert M. Calhoon, *The Loyalists in Revolutionary America, 1760–1781* (New York, 1973), 393–396; Thomas Fleming, *Washington's Secret War: The Hidden History of Valley Forge* (New York, 2005), 41.

2. NG to GW, January 1778, *PGWR* 13:424; *JADA* 2:263; JA to AA, October 26, 1777, *AFC* 2:361; John Ferling, *John Adams: A Life* (Knoxville, Tenn., 1992), 180–181; John Ferling, *Almost a Miracle: The American Victory in the War of Independence* (New York, 2007), 252; James Lovell to Samuel Adams, April 18, 1778, *LDC* 9:436; Lovell to Gates, October 5, 1777, ibid. 8:57; Fleming, *Washington's Secret War,* 79.

3. Elbridge Gerry to James Warren, October 6, 1777, *LDC* 8:66; Henry Laurens to John Lewis Gervais, December 30, 1777, ibid. 8:504; JA to AA, September 30, 1777, *AFC* 2:349–350; *JADA* 2:265.

4. John Ferling, *The First of Men: A Life of George Washington* (Knoxville, Tenn., 1988), 226–227; Theodore Thayer, "Nathanael Greene: Revolutionary War Strategist," in George A. Billias, *George Washington's Generals* (New York, 1964), 111; Rush to JA, February 12, 1812, in John A. Schutz and Douglass Adair, eds. *The Spur of Fame: Dialogues of John Adams and Benjamin Rush, 1805–1813* (San Marino, Calif., 1966), 210.

5. Rush to JA, October 1, 13, 21, 31, 1777, *PJA* 5:299–303, 315–316, 316–319, 323–325; Rush to William Duer, December 8, 1777, in Lyman H. Butterfield, ed., *Letters of Benjamin Rush* (Princeton, N.J., 1951), 1:172; Rush to Mrs. Rush, January 15, 1778, ibid., 1:186; Rush to Gates, April 9, 1778, ibid., 1:208–209; Rush to NG [?], February 1, 1778, ibid., 1:195.

6. James Lovell to Samuel Adams, December 20, 1777, *LDC* 8:451; Lovell to Gates, November 5, 27, 1777, ibid. 8:237, 329; Jonathan G. Rossie, *The Politics of Command in the American Revolution* (Syracuse, N.Y., 1975), 183.

7. Thomas Mifflin to Gates, November 17, 1777, *LDC* 8:314–315n.

8. Harry M. Ward, *George Washington's Enforcers: Policing the Continental Army* (Carbondale, Ill., 2006), 59–81. The quotation is on page 75.

9. The best source on Howe's campaign to open the Delaware River is Stephen R. Taaffe, *The Philadelphia Campaign, 1777–1778* (Lawrence, Kans., 2003), 108–144.

10. Quoted in Kenneth R. Rossman, *Thomas Mifflin and the Politics of the American Revolution* (Chapel Hill, N.C., 1952), 91.

11. John Penn to Richard Caswell, October 10, 1777, *LDC* 8:102; Lovell to John Langdon, October 14, 1777, ibid. 8:120; Thomas Burke to Caswell, November 4, 1777, ibid. 8:227; Elbridge Gerry to Thomas Gerry, October 21, 1777, ibid. 8:156; Christopher Ward, *The War of the Revolution* (New York, 1952), 1:372–378; GW to

NG, November 26, 1777, *PGWR* 12:407; GW to Thomas Nelson, November 8, 1777, ibid. 12:171.

12. Council of War, October 29, 1777, *PGWR* 12:46–48; John Cadwalader's Plan for Attacking Philadelphia, November 24, 1777, ibid. 12:371–373; NG to GW, November 24, 1777, ibid. 12:379–381; Sullivan to GW, November 24, 25, 1777, ibid. 12:382–383, 398–402; John Armstrong to GW, November 25, 1777, ibid. 12:383–384; Brigadier General Duportail to GW, November 25, 1777, ibid. 12:387–388; James Irvine to GW, November 25, 1777, ibid. 12:391–392; Johann Kalb to GW, November 25, 1777, ibid. 121:392–393; William Maxwell to GW, November 25, 1777, ibid. 12:393–394; John Patterson to GW, November 25, 1777, ibid. 12:394; Enoch Poor to GW, November 25, 1777, ibid. 12:394; Charles Scott to GW, November 25, 1777, ibid. 12:396; William Smallwood to GW, November 25, 1777, ibid. 12:397; William Stirling to GW, November 25, 1777, ibid. 12:397–398; Anthony Wayne to GW, November 25, 1777, ibid. 12:403; William Woodford to GW, November 25, 1777, ibid. 12:404.

13. David Hackett Fischer, *Washington's Crossing* (New York, 2004), 160–181, 192–195, 201–203; Ferling, *Almost a Miracle,* 165–166.

14. NG to GW, November 24, 1777, *PGWR* 12:377–378, 379–380. Greene's counsel is contained in two separate letters written on the same date.

15. GW to John Parke Custis, November 14, 1777, *PGWR* 12:250.

16. Ward, *War of the Revolution,* 1:379–382.

17. Lovell's "Fabiused" remark can be found in Rossie, *Politics of Command,* 184.

18. JA to Rush, March 19, 1812, Schutz and Adair, *Spur of Fame,* 213.

19. AH to Schuyler, February 18, 1781, *PAH* 2:565–567; AH to James McHenry, February 18, 1781, ibid. 2:569; Rush to JA, January 6, 1806, Schutz and Adair, *Spur of Fame,* 46; JA to Rush, January 25, 1806, November 11, 1807, ibid. 47–48, 98.

20. Rush to JA, February 12, 1812, Schutz and Adair, *Spur of Fame,* 207–208.

21. Quoted in Rossie, *Politics of Command,* 192.

22. GW to Thomas Conway, November 5, 1777, *PGWR* 12:129.

23. GW to Hancock, May 9, 1777, *PGWR* 9:370; ibid. 9:278–279n.

24. Bernhard Knollenberg, *Washington and the Revolution: A Reappraisal* (New York, 1941), 40–41.

25. NG to Jacob Greene,, January 3, 1778, *PNG* 2:243; Lord Stirling to GW, [August–September 1777], *PGWR* 11:105; GW to Richard Henry Lee, October 16, 1777, ibid. 11:529–530.

26. Lee to GW, October 20, 1777, *PGWR* 11:562–563.

27. GW to Conway, November 5, 16, 1777, *PGWR* 12:129, 277; Conway to GW, November 5, 1777, ibid. 12:130–131.

28. *PGWR* 12:470n; Elbridge Gerry to JA, December 3, 1777, *LDC* 8:373.

29. Continental Congress Camp Committee to GW, December 10, 1777, *PGWR* 12:588; GW to Henry Laurens, December 14 [–15], 22, 23, 1777, ibid. 12:606, 669, 685.

30. Knollenberg, *Washington and the Revolution,* 46; *LDC* 8:330n; *PGWR* 12:277n.

31. Knollenberg, *Washington and the Revolution,* 37, 48; Flexner, *GW* 2:258–259; Fleming, *Washington's Secret War,* 120–121; GW to Richard Henry Lee, October 28, 1777, *PGWR* 12:40, 42n; Henry Laurens to GW, November 30, 1777, ibid. 12:446; *JCC* 9:971, 975–976, 981; *LDC* 8:151n; Richard Peters to Robert Morris, January 21, 1778, ibid. 8:650–651n.

32. Henry Laurens to John Laurens, October 16, 1777, January 8, 1778, *PHL* 11:554–555; 12:275.

33. Edward G. Lengel, *General George Washington: A Military Life* (New York, 2005), 272–273, 279–280, 320–321; Elizabeth A. Fenn, *Pox Americana: The Great Smallpox Epidemic of 1775–1782* (New York, 2001), 14–79; Ferling, *Almost a Miracle,* 558–559; John Ferling, "Rethinking the Revolution," *American History* 42 (October 2007): 25–31.

34. GW to Colonel William Woodford, November 10, 1775, *PGWR* 2:346–347.

35. Eliphalet Dyer to William Williams, March 10, 1778, *LDC* 9:257; Robert Morris to Richard Peters, January 21, 1778, ibid. 8:649; Morris to Benjamin Harrison, February 19, 1778, ibid. 8:651n; Henry Laurens to John Lewis Gervais, September 5, 1777, *PHL* 11:498–499.

36. Conway to GW, December 29, 31, 1777, *PGWR* 13:40–41, 77–78; GW to Henry Laurens, January 2, 1778, ibid. 13:119.

37. John Laurens to Henry Laurens, January 3, 1778, *PHL* 12:246; Henry Laurens to John Laurens, January 8, 1778, ibid. 12:273; *PGWR* 13:78n; Clark to William Alexander, January 15, 1778, *LDC* 8:597; Knollenberg, *Washington and the Revolution,* 58; Henry Laurens to GW, April 28, 1778, PGWR 14:669.

38. GW to Gates, August 20, 1777, *PGWR* 11:12: Gates to GW, October 5, 1777, ibid. 11:392.

39. Joseph Jones to GW, January 22, 1778, *PGWR* 13:310.

40. *PGWR* 12:131; Gates to GW, December 8, 1777, January 23, February 19, 1778, ibid. 12:576–577; 13:319–321, 590.

41. GW to Gates, January 4, February 9, 24, 1778, *PGWR* 12:138–139, 484–487, 654–655; GW to Henry, March 28, 1778, ibid. 14:337. Emphasis was added by the author to GW's characterization of Mifflin as the "second part" of the cabal.

42. GW to Charles Lee, May 9, 1776, *PGWR* 4:245; Ferling, *First of Men,* 250–251.

43. Jones to GW, January 22, 1778, *PGWR* 13:310.

44. Fleming, *Washington's Secret War,* 108; Lund Washington to GW, February 18, 1778, *PGWR* 13:587.

45. Lund Washington to GW, February 18, 1778, *PGWR* 13:587.

46. GW to Henry, March 28, 1778, *PGWR* 14:336.

47. GW to Henry Laurens, January 31, 1778, *PGWR* 13:420.

48. John Laurens to Henry Laurens, January 1, 3, 12, 1778, *PHL* 12:231, 245, 286.

49. Hamilton to George Clinton, February 13, 1778, *PAH* 1:428.

50. NG to Jacob Greene, February 7, 1778, *PNG* 2:277.

51. Paul K. Longmore, *The Invention of George Washington* (Berkeley, Calif., 1988), 208.

52. GW to Lafayette, December 31, 1777, *PGWR* 13:83; Lafayette to GW, October 14, 1777, *LPL* 1:122; Lafayette to Henry Laurens, January 5, 26, 1778, *PHL* 12:256, 350–352.

53. [Thomas Paine], *The American Crisis* 5 (March 1778), in Philip S. Foner, ed., *The Complete Writings of Thomas Paine* (New York, 1945), 1:124, 129n.

54. Quoted in Ron Chernow, *Alexander Hamilton* (New York, 2004), 106.

55. Rossman, *Thomas Mifflin and the Politics of the American Revolution,* 138–139.

56. Lund Washington to GW, February 18, 1778, *PGWR* 13:587.

57. Knollenberg, *Washington and the Revolution,* 58.

58. William Duer to Francis Lightfoot Lee, February 14, 1778, *LDC* 9:96; Rossman, *Thomas Mifflin and the Politics of the American Revolution,* 140–164; *PHL* 14:154n. The quotation is from Rossman's study of Mifflin, page 144.

59. *DAJA* 4:5; Richard Peters to Robert Morris, January 21, 1778, *LDC* 9: 650–651n; Don Higginbotham, *Daniel Morgan, Revolutionary Rifleman* (Chapel Hill, N.C., 1961), 83.

60. Jones to GW, January 22, 1778, *PGWR* 13:310.

61. GW to Lafayette, December 31, 1777, *PGWR* 13:83; GW to William Gordon, January 23, 1778, ibid. 13:322: GW to Henry Laurens, January 31, 1778, ibid. 13:420.

62. Gordon to GW, January 12, 1778, *PGWR* 13:205; GW to Gordon, January 23, February 15, 1778, ibid. 13:322–323, 546.

63. GW, "Circular to the States," December 29, 1777, *PGWR* 13:36–37; GW to Henry Laurens, December 23, 1777, ibid. 12:683–687.

64. On conditions at Valley Forge and the army's supply crisis, the best starting places are Wayne K. Bodle, *Valley Forge Winter: Civilians and Soldiers in War* (University Park, Pa., 2002); E. Wayne Carp, *To Starve the Army at Pleasure: Continental Army Administration and American Political Culture, 1775–1783* (Chapel Hill, N.C., 1984), 43–47; and Taaffe, *Philadelphia Campaign,* 148–156.

65. Henry Laurens to Lafayette, January 12, 1778, *LDC* 8:572; GW to Laurens, December 22, 23, 1777, *PGWR* 12:667–670, 683–687; Elbridge Gerry to GW, January 13, 1778, ibid. 13:218–219.

66. The recommendations of the officers can be found in *PGWR* 13:54–57, 59–63, 90–92, 100–102, 128–130, 132–136, 151–157, 240–241, 262–266, 314–315. For the final draft, see GW to a Continental Congress Camp Committee, January 29, 1778, ibid. 13:376–404. See also ibid. 13:404–405n. The "state paper" quotation can be found in Fleming, *Washington's Secret War,* 178, while the "minor masterpiece" is in Lengel, *General George Washington,* 275.

67. Ferling, *Almost a Miracle,* 331–332. On the idea of republican sacrifice, see Gordon S. Wood, *The Creation of the American Republic, 1776–1787* (Chapel Hill, N.C., 1969), 46–124.

68. GW to a Continental Camp Committee, January 29, 1778, *PGWR* 13:376–404. The quotes are on pages 377, 379, 385, 389. For GW's comment on public assistance for the wives and children of enlisted men, see GW to John Stark, August 5, 1778, ibid. 16:256.

69. *PGWR* 13:695n; 14:551n; Gouverneur Morris to GW, May 15, 1778, ibid. 15:127–128; GW, General Orders, May 18, 1778, ibid. 15:149; Lengel, *General George Washington,* 276; Ferling, *Almost a Miracle,* 284–285.

70. Fleming, *Washington's Secret War,* 157; Lafayette to GW, January 20, 1778, *PGWR* 13:291–292.

71. Lafayette to GW, January 20, 1778, *PGWR* 13:291–292; Henry Laurens to John Rutledge, March 11, 1778, LDC 9:270; John Penn to Theodorick Bland, February 6, 1778, ibid. 9:42; James Lovell to JA, February 8, 1778, ibid. 9:54; Eliphalet Dyer to William Williams, February 17, 1778, ibid. 9:115; John Thaxton to JA, January 20, 1778, *AFC* 2:386; Sir Guy Carleton to Lord George Germain, June 10, 1778, *DAR* 15:137.

72. Paul David Nelson, *General Horatio Gates: A Biography* (Baton Rouge, La., 1976), 170–175; Instructions for the Marquis de Lafayette . . . Commanding an Expedition in Canada, January 31, 1778, *LPL* 1:263–267; *PGWR* 13:330–332n.

73. GW to Gates, January 27, 1778, *PGWR* 13:361.

74. GW to General Officers, April 20, 1778, *PGWR* 14:567; Washington's Thoughts upon a Plan of Operations for Campaign 1778 [April 26–29], ibid. 14:641–648; GW to Thomas Nelson, February 8, 1778, ibid. 13:481; Nelson, *General Horatio Gates,* 172.

75. *PGWR;* AH to George Clinton, February 13, 1778, *PAH* 1:428; NG to Knox, February 26, 1778, *PNG* 2:294; NG to Nicholas Cooke, February 5, 1778, ibid. 2:274; John Laurens to Henry Laurens, January 28, 1778, PHL 12:381–382; Henry Laurens to John Rutledge, January 30, 1778, ibid. 12:380.

76. Lafayette to Henry Laurens, January 26, 1778, *LPL* 1:253, 255.

77. Lafayette to GW, February 19, 23, 1778, *PGWR* 13:594–595, 649; ibid. 13:332n.

78. Henry Laurens to Isaac Motte, January 26, 1778, *PHL* 12:346.

79. Fleming, *Washington's Secret War,* 191–192.

80. Longmore, *Invention of George Washington,* 204–208.

81. Ibid., 207.

82. JA to Lovell, July 26, 1778, *PJA* 6:318–319.

83. Lafayette to Henry Laurens, January 5, 1778, *LPL* 1:216.

84. Henry Laurens to John Laurens, January 8, 1778, *PHL* 12:272; Henry Laurens to William Smith, September 12, 1778, ibid. 14:302.

85. Henry Laurens to Motte, January 26, 1778, *PHL* 12:348.

86. Rush to William Gordon, December 10, 1778, Butterfield, *Letters of Benjamin Rush,* 1:221; JA to Rush, March 19, 1812, *Spur of Fame,* 212; Barry Schwartz, *George Washington: The Making of an American Symbol* (New York, 1987), 23.

87. GW to Gouverneur Morris, May 18, 1778, *PGWR* 15:156.

88. John Alden, *Charles Lee: Traitor or Patriot?* (Baton Rouge, La., 1951), 190; Elias Boudinot, "Exchange of Major-General Charles Lee," *Pennsylvania Magazine of History and Biography* 15 (1891): 31–32; GW to Lee, April 22, 1778, *PGWR* 14:585.

89. Councils of War, June 17, 24, 1778, *PGWR* 15:414–417, 520–521; Cadwalader to GW, June 18, 1778, ibid. 15:435–436; Wayne to GW, June 18, 1778, ibid. 15:468–469; Lee to GW, June 18, 1778, ibid. 15:457–458. The written responses of the other generals who attended the initial council of war can be found in ibid. 15:431–470.

90. NG to GW, June 24, 1778, *PGWR* 15:525–526; Lafayette to GW, June 24, 1778, ibid. 15:528–529; Wayne to GW, June 24, 1778, ibid. 15:534–535.

91. GW to Lafayette, June 25, 26, 1778, *PGWR* 15:539, 552–553, 554, 555; GW to Lee, June 26, 1778, ibid. 15:556; GW to Philemon Dickinson, June 24, 25, 1778, ibid. 15:522–523, 536–537; GW to William Maxwell, June 24, 1778, ibid. 15:531; GW to Charles Scott, June 24, 1778, ibid. 15:534; GW to Daniel Morgan, June 24, 1778, ibid. 15:532; AH to Elias Boudinot, July 5, 1778, *PAH* 1:510. AH's quote about a "society of midwives" is in Chernow, *Alexander Hamilton,* 113.

92. Lee to GW, June 25, 1778, *PGWR* 15:541–542; GW to Lee, June 26, 1778, ibid. 15:556.

93. *PGWR* 15:573–575n.

94. Boudinot, "Exchange of Major-General Charles Lee," *Pennsylvania Magazine of History and Biography* 15 (1891): 32, 33; NG to Governor William Greene, May 25, 1778, *PNG* 2:408; NG to Griffin Greene, May 25, 1778, ibid. 2:406; Lee to Rush, June 4, 1778, *Lee Papers, Collections of the New-York Historical Society for the Year 1871, . . . 1872, . . . 1873, . . . 1874* (New York, 1872–1875), 2:398–399; Charles Lee, "Plan of an Army, &c.," ibid. 2:383–387; Alden, *Charles Lee,* 200.

95. Testimony of Colonel Richard Harrison, in Henry Steele Commager and Richard B. Morris, eds., *The Spirit of '76: The Story of the American Revolution as Told by Participants* (Indianapolis, Ind., 1958), 2:712; George Scheer and Hugh Rankin, *Rebels and Redcoats* (Cleveland, Ohio, 1957), 331; "Lafayette, Memoirs of 1779," *LPL* 2:11; Harry Ward, *Charles Scott and the "Spirit of '76"* (Charlottesville, Va., 1988), 50–51; Alden, *General Charles Lee,* 222; Theodore Thayer, *Washington and Lee: The Making of a Scapegoat* (Port Washington, N.Y., 1976), 52; GW to Henry Laurens, July 1, 1778, *PGWR* 16:4–6.

96. Good accounts of the Battle of Monmouth can be found in Ward, *War of the Revolution,* 2:576–580; Lengel, *General George Washington,* 297–306; Alden, *General Charles Lee,* 212–227; and Taafe, *Philadelphia Campaign,* 212–224.

97. GW to Lee, June 30, 1778, *PGWR* 15:595–596, 597; Lee to GW, June 29, 1778, ibid. 15:594–595, 596–597; Lee to Gouverneur Morris, July 3, 1778, *LP* 2:457; Lee to Reed, July 22, 1778, ibid. 2:479; Lee to President of Congress, April 22, 1780, ibid. 3:424; Lee to NG, September 12, 1782, ibid. 4:35; "General Lee's Vindication to the Public," *Pennsylvania Packet,* December 3, 1778, ibid. 3:255–265; [Charles Lee], "A Short History of the Treatment of Major General Conway . . . ," *Pennsylvania Packet,* December 3, 1778, ibid. 3:265–269; [Charles Lee], "Some Queries, Political and Military, Humbly Offered to the Consideration of the Public," *Maryland Journal and Baltimore Advertiser,* July 6, 1779, ibid. 3:341–345; Jared Sparks, *Life of Charles Lee* (Boston, 1846), in ibid. 4:330; Alden, *General Charles Lee,* 234, 260–275, 296–298; Thayer, *Washington and Lee,* 70–104; Rush to David Ramsay, November 5, 1778, Butterfield, *Letters of Benjamin Rush,* 1:219. The transcript of the court-martial proceeding can be found in *LP* 3:1–208.

CHAPTER 6: VICTORY AND GLORY

1. GW to Jonathan Trumbull Sr., July 22, 1778, *PGWR* 16:136–137; Flexner, *GW* 2:324.

2. GW to John Augustine Washington, September 23, 1778, *WW* 12:488.

3. NG to John Sullivan, July 23, 1778, *PNG* 2:466.

4. Paul F. Dearden, *The Rhode Island Campaign of 1778: Inauspicious Dawn of Alliance* (Providence, R.I., 1980), 93–126; GW to d'Estaing, September 11, 1778, *WW* 12:423.

5. GW to John Augustine Washington, November 26, 1778, *WW* 13:336.

6. John Ferling, *Almost a Miracle: The American Victory in the War of Independence* (New York, 2007), 327; James A. Huston, *Logistics of Liberty: American Services of Supply in the Revolutionary War and After* (Newark, Del., 1991), 121–123, 194.

7. Paul David Nelson, *General Horatio Gates: A Biography* (Baton Rouge, La., 1976), 197–198; Lafayette to Henry Laurens, June 4, 1778, *LPL* 2:67; Lafayette to Comte

d'Estaing, August 24, 1778, ibid. 2:145–146; Lafayette to Timothy Bedel, December 18, 1778, ibid. 2:211–212.

8. JA to Lafayette, February 21, 1779, *LPL* 2:235; Benjamin Franklin to Lafayette, August 19, 1779, ibid. 2:303; James Duane to Congress, October 18, 1778, *LDC* 11:83n; Governor Frederick Haldimand, Sketch of the Military State of the Province of Quebec, July 25, 1778, *DAR* 15:169–171; Haldimand to Lord Germain, October 15, 1778, ibid. 15:221. In March 1779, the Continental army consisted of 29,453 men. See Charles Lesser, ed., *The Sinews of Independence: Monthly Strength Reports of the Continental Army* (Chicago, 1976), 69–110.

9. Board of Officers to GW, September 10, 1778, *PGWR* 16:550–551; GW to the Board of War, August 3, 1778, ibid. 16:229; GW to Henry Laurens, September 12, 1778, ibid. 16:587; Laurens to GW, November 20, 1778, *PHL* 14:515.

10. *PNG* 3:28–29n; Nelson, *General Horatio Gates,* 201–202.

11. Freeman, *GW* 5:103.

12. GW to John Jay, April 14, 1779, *WW* 14:378, 382, 383; GW to Laurens, November 14, 1778, ibid. 13:254; GW to Conrad Alexandre Gérard, May 1, 1779, ibid. 14:470–473; GW to Henry Laurens, November 11, 1778, *PHL* 14:491n.

13. GW to Henry Laurens, November 14, 1778, *WW* 13:254–257.

14. TJ to Chevalier de Luzerne, April 12, 1781, *PTJ* 5:422.

15. *LDC* 12:287n.

16. Laurens to GW, November 20, 1778, *PHL* 14:514–515; Jay to Lafayette, January 3, 1779, *LDC* 11:409.

17. GW to PC, December 13, 1778, *WW* 13:389–390; John Jay to GW, December 18, 1778, *LDC* 11:355.

18. GW to Thomas Nelson, March 15, 1779, *WW* 14:246; GW to Mason, March 27, 1779, ibid. 14:300–301; GW to Benjamin Harrison, December 18 [–30], 1778, ibid. 13:467–468.

19. E. James Ferguson, *The Power of the Purse* (Chapel Hill, N.C., 1961), 25–47, 126; John Ferling, *Almost a Miracle: The American Victory in the War of Independence* (New York, 2007), 399–400.

20. John Ferling, *A Leap in the Dark: The Struggle to Create the American Republic* (New York, 2003), 222; Thomas Fleming, *The Perils of Peace: America's Struggle for Survival After Yorktown* (New York, 2007), 106.

21. GW to PC, July 9, 1779, *WW* 15:391–392; GW to John Armstrong, May 18, 1779, ibid. 15:98; GW to Lafayette, September 30, 1779, ibid. 16:372.

22. GW to Harrison, December 18 [–30], 1778, *WW* 13:467; Flexner, *GW* 2: 235–239; John C. Miller, *The Triumph of Freedom, 1775–1783* (Boston, 1948), 436, 474–476; Kate Haulman, "Fashion and Culture Wars of Revolutionary Philadelphia," *WMQ* 62 (2005): 625–662. The Samuel Adams quotation is in the Haulman essay, page 660.

23. GW to Mason, March 27, 1779, *WW* 14:299–300; GW to Burwell Bassett, April 22, 1779, ibid. 14:432; GW to Gouverneur Morris, May 8, 1779, ibid. 15:25; GW to John Augustine Washington, November 26, 1778, ibid. 13:335; GW to William Fitzhugh, April 10, 1779, ibid. 14:365; GW to Lund Washington, May 29, 1779, ibid. 15:180; GW to Reed, December 12, 1778, ibid. 13:383; GW to Harrison, December 18 [–30], 1778, ibid. 13:467–468.

24. Henry Laurens' Notes on South Carolina's Defense, [December 1778], *LDC* 11:392–393; James Duane to Mary Duane, January 23, 1779, ibid. 11:506; John Henry to Thomas Johnson, January 30, 1779, ibid. 11:538.

25. GW to Lafayette, March 8 [–10], 1779, *WW* 14:219; GW to Lachlan McIntosh, January 31, 1779, ibid. 14:62; Henry Laurens to Rawlins Lowndes, January 31, 1779, *LDC* 11:545.

26. See Joseph R. Fischer, *A Well-Executed Failure: The Sullivan Campaign Against the Iroquois, July–September 1779* (Columbia, S.C., 1997).

27. Jonathan Dull, *A Diplomatic History of the American Revolution* (New Haven, Conn., 1983), 108–110.

28. William B. Willcox, *Portrait of a General: Sir Henry Clinton in the War of Independence* (New York, 1964), 260–299; John Selby, *The Revolution in Virginia, 1775–1783* (Williamsburg, Va., 1988), 204–208.

29. Christopher Ward, *The War of the Revolution* (New York, 1952), 2:688–694; David K. Wilson, *The Southern Strategy: Britain's Conquest of South Carolina and Georgia, 1775–1780* (Columbia, S.C., 2005), 81–177; Alexander A. Lawrence, *Storm over Savannah: The Story of Count d'Estaing and the Siege of the Town in 1779* (Athens, Ga., 1951), 38–112.

30. GW to PC, April 3, 1780, *WW* 18:209; GW to Henry Champion, May 26, 1780, ibid. 18:424; GW to William Heath, December 21, 1779, ibid. 17:295; GW to William Livingston, December 21, 1779, ibid. 17:293; GW to Steuben, April 1, 1780, ibid. 18:203; Edward G. Lengel, *General George Washington: A Military Life* (New York, 2005), 320–321.

31. Germain to Clinton, January 23, June 25, September 27, 1779, *DAR* 17:44, 150, 214; Clinton to Germain, April 4, May 22, December 15, 1779, ibid. 17:97, 129, 259–260; Willcox, *Portrait of a General,* 272–273, 289–299. On Britain's southern strategy, see Ferling, *Almost a Miracle,* 263–271.

32. David B. Mattern, *Benjamin Lincoln and the American Revolution* (Columbia, S.C., 1995), 88–89; Samuel Huntington to Benjamin Lincoln, November 11, 1779, *LDC* 14:176; Huntington to John Rutledge, November 11, 1779, ibid. 14:177; Huntington to GW, December 4, 1779, March 9, 1780, ibid. 14:249, 482; William Sharpe to Richard Caswell, December 5, 1779, ibid. 14:250; John Mathews to Lincoln, December 9, 1779, ibid. 14:257; Mathews to Thomas Bee, January [?], 1780, ibid. 14:320–321; *JCC* 15: 1255–1256.

33. Committee at Headquarters to Congress, December 7, 1779, *LDC* 14:251.

34. Willcox, *Portrait of a General,* 301; Freeman, *GW* 5:147–148; Lesser, *Sinews of Independence,* 148–149.

35. Huntington to GW, March 9, 1780, *LDC* 14:482; John Mathews to GW, March 24, 1780, ibid. 14:542; GW to NG, March 26, 1780, *WW* 18:151–152; GW to PC, April 2, 1780, ibid. 18:197–200; *PNG* 5:480n. Emphasis added by the author.

36. Lesser, *Sinews of Independence,* 50.

37. Huntington to the States, February 10, 1780, *LDC* 14:406; ibid. 14:398n; GW to PC, April 3, 1780, *WW* 18:209–210; Lesser, *Sinews of Independence,* 101–158.

38. Rodney Atwood, *The Hessians: Mercenaries from Hessen-Kassel in the American Revolution* (Cambridge, U.K., 1980), 148–149; Freeman, *GW* 5:168–171; Freeman, *GW* 5:163–164, 164n; Lesser, *Sinews of Independence,* 168.

39. Benjamin Quarles, *The Negro in the American Revolution* (Chapel Hill, N.C., 1961), 52–57; Gregory D. Massey, *John Laurens and the American Revolution* (Columbia, S.C., 2000), 93–97, 130–131; Thomas Burke's Draft Committee Report [ante March 25, 1779], *LDC* 12:242–244, 244n; Henry Laurens's Draft Committee Report [ante March 25, 1779], ibid. 12:247; Burke to GW, March 24, 1779, ibid. 12:238–239; Henry Laurens to GW, March 16, 1779, ibid. 12:200; GW to Henry Laurens, March 20, 1779, *WW* 14:267; Henry Wiencek, *An Imperfect God: George Washington, His Slaves, and the Creation of America* (New York, 2003), 227–232. The quotation from Wiencek can be found on page 229.

40. Lee Kennett, *The French Forces in America, 1780–1783* (Westport, Conn., 1977), 3–13.

41. Conference at Hartford, September 22, 1780, *WW* 20:76–81; Summary of the Hartford Conference, September 22, 1780, *LPL* 3:175–178.

42. Kennett, *French Forces in America*, 30; W. J. Eccles, "The French Alliance and the American Victory," in John Ferling, ed., *The World Turned Upside Down: The American Victory in the War of Independence* (Westport, Conn., 1988), 161–162.

43. See Carl Van Doren, *Mutiny in January* (New York, 1947), 16–17.

44. JA to Gerry, June 24, 1780, *PJA* 9:470; JA to PC, April 18, December 14, 1780, June 23, 1781, ibid. 9:151; 10:10–11; 11:385; JA to Joseph Ward, April 15, 1809, *Adams Family Papers, 1639–1889*, microfilm edition, 608 reels (Boston, Massachusetts Historical Society, 1954–1959), reel 118; Richard B. Morris, *The Peacemakers: The Great Powers and American Independence* (New York, 1965), 179, 182; Jonathan Dull, *The French Navy and American Independence: A Study of Arms and Diplomacy, 1774–1787* (Princeton, N.J., 1975), 199–202; Edwin Corwin, *French Policy and the American Alliance of 1778* (New York, 1916), 285.

45. Vergennes to Lafayette, August 7, 1780, April 19, 1781, *LPL* 3:129; 4:47. See also Orville T. Murphy, "The View from Versailles: Charles Gravier Comte de Vergennes's Perceptions of the American Revolution," in Ronald Hoffman and Peter J. Albert, eds., *Diplomacy and Revolution: The Franco-American Alliance of 1778* (Charlottesville, Va., 1981), 140–141; William Stinchcombe, *The American Revolution and the French Alliance* (Syracuse, N.Y., 1969), 153–159; Stacy Schiff, *The Great Improvisation: Franklin, France, and the Birth of America* (New York, 2005), 264–274; Morris, *Peacemakers*, 180–181; Corwin, *French Policy and the American Alliance*, 284–295; Dull, *Diplomatic History of the American Revolution*, 123.

46. Freeman, *GW* 5:236–242; GW to Robert Howe, January 22, 1781, *WW* 21:128–129.

47. GW to John Laurens, January 15, 1781, *WW* 21:110.

48. Quoted in Carl P. Borick, *A Gallant Defense: The Siege of Charleston, 1780* (Columbia, S.C., 2003), 233.

49. John Mathews to Robert R. Livingston, April 24, 1780, *LDC* 15:66; GW to John Laurens, April 26, 1780, *WW* 18:300.

50. Paul David Nelson, *General Horatio Gates: A Biography* (Baton Rouge, La., 1976), 220–221; GW to Gates, August 8, 12, 1780, *WW* 19:340, 362; Freeman, *GW* 5:172.

51. The quotes are taken from James Haw, *John and Edward Rutledge of South Carolina* (Athens, Ga., 1997), 123–124.

52. TJ to Chevalier de Luzerne, April 12, 1781, *PTJ* 5:422.

53. Cornwallis to Clinton, August 6, 1780, in Charles Ross, ed., *Correspondence of Charles, First Marquis Cornwallis* (London, 1859), 1:54.

54. On the duel between Greene and Cornwallis and the latter's fateful choice in the spring of 1781, see Theodore Thayer, *Nathanael Greene: Strategist of the Revolution* (New York, 1960), 282–331; Terry Golway, *Washington's General: Nathanael Greene and the Triumph of the American Revolution* (New York, 2005), 231–262; Franklin and Mary Wickwire, *Cornwallis and the War of Independence* (London, 1971), 194–321.

55. Conference with Rochambeau, May 23, 1781, *WW* 22:105–107; GW to NG, June 1, 1781, ibid. 22:146; Flexner, *GW* 2:429, 430; Lengel, *General George Washington,* 329–330.

56. Lengel, *General George Washington,* 332; GW to Rochambeau, June 13, 1781, *WW* 22:208.

57. David Syrett, *The Royal Navy in American Waters, 1775–1783* (Aldershot, U.K., 1989), 178, 181, 191; Richard M. Ketchum, *Victory at Yorktown: The Campaign That Won the Revolution* (New York, 2004), 159; Freeman, *GW* 5:315.

58. William B. Willcox, "Arbuthnot, Gambier, and Graves: 'Old Women' of the Navy," in George Athan Billias, *George Washington's Opponents: British Generals and Admirals in the American Revolution* (New York, 1969), 280.

59. George Scheer, ed., *Private Yankee Doodle: Being a Narrative of Some of the Adventures, Dangers, and Sufferings of a Revolutionary Soldier* (Boston, 1962), 231–232.

60. Ferling, *Almost a Miracle,* 523–539.

61. GW to PC, October 19, 1781, *WW* 23:242.

62. See Comte de Rochambeau, *Memoirs of the Marshall Count de Rochambeau,* M. W. E. Wright, comp., reprint (New York, 1971).

63. Connecticut Delegates to Jonathan Trumbull Jr., October 25, 1781, *LDC* 18:165; George Partridge to Samuel Holten, October 30, 1781, ibid. 18:171.

64. Thomas McKean to GW, October 31, 1781, *LDC* 18:175.

65. JA to Jay, November 28, 1781, *PJA* 12:92–93; Elkanah Watson, *Men and Times of the Revolution; or, Memoirs of Elkanah Watson* (1855), in *PBF* 36:75; BF to JA, November 26, 1781, ibid. 36:115.

66. GW, Farewell Orders to the Armies of the United States, November 2, 1783, *WW* 27:223.

CHAPTER 7: WASHINGTON AND THE POLITICS OF INTRIGUE: TO THE END OF THE WAR

1. BF to GW, April 8, 1782, *PBF* 37:116.

2. GW to NG, July 9, 1782, *WW* 24:409.

3. GW to BF, October 18, 1782, *WW* 25:273; GW, "Circular to the States," May 4 [–8], 1782, ibid. 24:234; GW to James McHenry, September 12, 1782, ibid. 25:151; GW to William Gordon, October 23, 1782, ibid. 25:287; Substance of a Conference Between Comte de Rochambeau and General Washington, July 19, 1782, ibid. 24:434–435; GW, Memorandum, May 1, 1782, ibid. 24:197–199; John Ferling, *Almost a Miracle: The American Victory in the War of Independence* (New York, 2007), 541–549.

4. JM to Edmund Randolph, September 24, 1782, *LDC* 19:200; Elias Boudinot to

Lewis Pintard, October 22, 1782, ibid. 19:284; JM to JM Sr., February 12, 1783, ibid. 19:686–687; Virginia Delegates to Benjamin Harrison, February 18, 1783, ibid. 19:707; GW to NG, January 29, 1783, *WW* 26:77–78.

5. GW to William Heath, February 5, 1783, *WW* 26:97.

6. AH to Edward Stevens, November 11, 1769, *PAH* 1:4.

7. *PAH* 1:182n.

8. Alexander Hamilton, *The Continentalist,* in *PAH* 2:649–650, 664, 665; 3:103, 106; AH to James Duane, September 3, 1780, ibid. 2:400–418; AH to GW, March 17, 1783, ibid. 3:292. On Madison and Hamilton, see Lance Banning, *The Sacred Fire of Liberty: James Madison and the Founding of the Federal Republic* (Ithaca, N.Y., 1995); Jack Rakove, *James Madison and the Creation of the Federal Republic* (Glenview, Ill., 1990); Ron Chernow, *Alexander Hamilton* (New York, 2004); John Ferling, *A Leap in the Dark: The Struggle to Create the American Republic* (New York, 2003), 242–246, 266–268.

9. GW to Mason, March 27, 1779, *WW* 14:301. On the developing relationship between GW and Madison, see Stuart Leibiger, *Founding Friendship: George Washington, James Madison, and the Creation of the American Republic* (Charlottesville, Va., 1999), 11–27. GW's quotation about his activities in Philadelphia can be found in ibid., 23.

10. John Ferling, *The First of Men: A Life of George Washington* (Knoxville, Tenn., 1988), 258–259.

11. Ferling, *First of Men,* 258; Chernow, *Alexander Hamilton,* 155. See also Arthur Lefkowitz, *George Washington's Indispensable Men: The 32 Aides-de-Camp Who Helped Win American Independence* (Mechanicsburg, Pa., 2003).

12. Charles Royster, *A Revolutionary People at War: The Continental Army and the American Character, 1775–1783* (Chapel Hill, N.C., 1979), 312–314; E. Wayne Carp, "The Origins of the Nationalist Movement of 1780–1783: Congressional Administration and the Continental Army," *Pennsylvania Magazine of History and Biography* 107 (1983): 363–392; Ferling, *A Leap in the Dark,* 242. The Robert Morris quotation is from William Hogeland, "Inventing Alexander Hamilton," *Boston Review* (November/December 2007), http://bostonreview.net/BR32.6/hogeland.php, 4.

13. Robert Morris to GW, January 26, 1782, E. James Ferguson et al., eds., *The Papers of Robert Morris, 1781–1784* (Pittsburgh, Pa., 1973–), 4:120–121, 121n; GW to Morris, February 2, 1782, ibid., 4:153–154; E. James Ferguson, *The Power of the Purse: A History of American Public Finance, 1776–1790* (Chapel Hill, N.C., 1961), 134; Thomas Fleming, *The Perils of Peace: America's Struggle for Survival after Yorktown* (New York, 2007), 110–112; Ferling, *A Leap in the Dark,* 239.

14. GW to PC, October 11, 1780, *WW* 20:158; *LDC* 16:54, 235n; Samuel Huntington to GW, October 26, 1780, ibid. 16:265; Ferguson, *Power of the Purse,* 156.

15. *JCC* 24:291–293.

16. Quoted in Richard H. Kohn, "The Inside History of the Newburgh Conspiracy: America and the Coup d'État," *WMQ* 27 (1970): 194. On the three officers' discussions with Congress, see JM, "Notes on Debates," January 13, 1783, *PJM* 6:32.

17. Woody Holton, *Unruly Americans and the Origins of the Constitution* (New York, 2007), 67.

18. Quoted in Ferguson, *Power of the Purse,* 158.

19. Fleming, *The Perils of Peace,* 264.

20. Leibiger, *Founding Friendship,* 24–26.

21. Hogeland, "Inventing Alexander Hamilton," *Boston Review* (November/December 2007), http://bostonreview.net/BR32.6/hogeland.php, 4.

22. William Hogeland, *The Whiskey Rebellion: George Washington, Alexander Hamilton, and the Frontier Rebels Who Challenged America's Newfound Sovereignty* (New York, 2006), 38–39.

23. *JCC* 24:295–297.

24. AH to Philip Schuyler, February 18, 1781, *PAH* 2:566–567; AH to GW, February 13, 1783, ibid. 3:253–255.

25. GW, To the Officers of the Army, March 15, 1783, *WW* 26:222–227.

26. Joseph J. Ellis, *His Excellency: George Washington* (New York, 2004), 142.

27. JA to Rush, June 21, 1811, John A. Schutz and Douglass Adair, eds., *The Spur of Fame: Dialogues of John Adams and Benjamin Rush, 1805–1813* (San Marino, Calif., 1966), 181.

28. Josiah Quincy, ed., *The Journal of Major Samuel Shaw* (Boston, 1843), 101–105.

29. GW to PC, March 18, 1783, *WW* 26:229–232; GW to Joseph Jones, March 18, 1783, ibid. 26:232–234.

30. GW to Theodorick Bland, April 4, 1783, *WW* 26:286.

31. GW, "Circular to the States," June 8, 1783, *WW* 26:483–496.

32. Hogeland, *Whiskey Rebellion,* 46–47; Ferling, *Almost a Miracle,* 556–557; Holton, *Unruly Americans,* 69; George F. Scheer, ed., *Private Yankee Doodle: Being a Narrative of Some of the Adventures, Dangers and Sufferings of a Revolutionary Soldier. By Joseph Plumb Martin* (Boston, 1962), 281, 282, 287.

33. Charles H. Lesser, *The Sinews of Independence: Monthly Strength Reports of the Continental Army* (Chicago, 1976), 252–255.

34. Fleming, *The Perils of Peace,* 287–288.

35. GW, Farewell Orders to the Armies of the United States, November 2, 1783, *WW* 27:224.

36. GW to AH, March 4, 1783, *WW* 26:186.

37. Don Higginbotham, *George Washington: Uniting a Nation* (Lanham, Md., 2002), 37.

38. GW, "Sentiments on a Peace Establishment" (1783), *WW* 26:374–98.

39. GW, "Circular to the States," June 8, 1783, *WW* 483–496. The quotations are from pages 486, 487, and 488.

40. GW to AH, April 4, 1783, *WW* 26:293.

41. David Howell to Nicholas Brown, July 30, 1783, *LDC* 20:484; Howell to William Greene, September [9?], 1783, ibid. 20:647.

42. GW to PC, March 19, 1783, *WW* 26:237–238; GW to Arthur Lee, March 29, 1783, ibid. 26:265–266.

43. Ferling, *First of Men,* 314–317; Richard H. Kohn, *Eagle and Sword: The Federalists and the Creation of the Military Establishment in America, 1783–1802* (New York, 1975), 97.

44. GW, Farewell Orders to the Armies, November 2, 1783, *WW* 27:222–227.

45. Gerard H. Clarfield, *Timothy Pickering and the American Republic* (Pittsburgh, Pa., 1980), 82.

46. Fleming, *The Perils of Peace,* 308; Clarfield, *Timothy Pickering and the American Republic,* 82–84.

47. Freeman, *GW* 5:458–462; Edwin G. Burrows and Mike Wallace, *Gotham: A History of New York City to 1898* (New York, 1999), 260–261.

48. Fleming, *Perils of Peace*, 315–316; Ferling, *Almost a Miracle*, 560.

49. James Milligan to GW, January 13, March 9, 1784, *PGWCF* 1:36–38, 191–193; ibid. 1:38–39n, 193n. See also John C. Fitzpatrick, ed., *Account of Expenses while Commander in Chief* (Boston, 1917).

50. James Tilton to Gunning Bedford Jr., December 25, 1783, *LDC* 21:232; Howell to Greene, December 24, 1783, ibid. 21:228; GW, Address to Congress, *WW* 27:284–285.

CHAPTER 8: SOARING TO THE PINNACLE

1. William Pierce, "Character Sketches of Delegates to the Federal Convention," in Max Farrand, ed., *The Records of the Federal Convention of 1787* (Reprint, New Haven, Conn., 1966), 3:94. GW hunted frequently in 1784 but thereafter seldom indulged in the pastime.

2. *PGWCF* 1:113n; GW to Lafayette, February 1, 1784, ibid. 1:87–88.

3. GW to Lafayette, December 8, 1784, *PGWCF* 2:175; GW to Rochambeau, February 1, 1784, ibid. 1:102.

4. GW to John Francis Mercer, December 20, 1785, *PGWCF* 3:478; GW to Fielding Lewis Jr., February 27, 1784, ibid. 1:161; GW to George William Fairfax, June 30, 1786, ibid. 4:137; GW to Bushrod Washington, November 15, 1786, ibid. 4:369; Woody Holton, *Unruly Americans and the Origins of the Constitution* (New York, 2007), 59; John Ferling, *The First of Men: A Life of George Washington* (Knoxville, Tenn., 1988), 332–346; Robert F. Jones, *George Washington* (Boston, 1979), 78. On GW's postwar slave census, see *PGWCF* 3:389n.

5. GW to Lafayette, February 1, 1784, *PGWCF* 1:87–89.

6. GW to Hugh Williamson, March 31, 1784, *PGWCF* 1:245; *PGWRT* 4:522n; GW, Enclosure: Schedule of Property, July 9, 1799, ibid. 4:515–516; Freeman, *GW* 3:93–95, 101–103; 6:31–32; Charles Royster, *The Fabulous History of the Dismal Swamp Company: A Story of George Washington's Times* (New York, 1999), 420–421.

7. *PGWCF* 1:92–93n, 97–98n, 118n.

8. *DGW* 4:14–71. The story of Washington's trip to the West and his accompanying tribulations with the squatters is told in wonderful detail by Joel Achenbach, *The Grand Idea: George Washington's Potomac and the Race to the West* (New York, 2004), 47–150.

9. *PGWRT* 4:516, 524–525n.

10. *DGW* 4:52–68.

11. GW to TJ, March 29, 1784, *PGWCF* 1:237; ibid. 1:241n; *PGWP* 1:127n; GW, Enclosure: Schedule of Property, July 9, 1799, *PGWRT* 6:512–515; Robert J. Kapsch, *The Potomac Canal: George Washington and the Waterway West* (Morgantown, W.Va., 2007), 14, 28–29.

12. TJ to GW, March 15, 1784, *PGWCF* 1:216; GW to TJ, March 29, 1784, ibid. 1:237–239; TJ to JM, February 20, 1784, *PTJ* 6:348.

13. Stuart Leibiger, *Founding Friendship: George Washington, James Madison and the*

Creation of the American Republic (Charlottesville, Va., 1999), 33, 39–42. Leibiger was the first to point out that GW misspelled JM's name.

14. Gates to GW, December 24, 1784, *PGWCF* 2:229–230; GW to Madison, December 28, 1784, ibid. 2:233; GW to TJ, March 29, 1784, ibid. 1:238–239; GW to Lafayette, December 23, 1784, ibid. 2:229; GW to Knox, January 5, 1785, ibid. 2:253–255; GW and Horatio Gates to the Virginia legislature, with Enclosures I, II, and III, December 28, 1784, ibid. 2:235–246; Thomas Stone to GW, January 28, 1785, ibid. 2:297; Leibiger, *Founding Friendship,* 43–44.

15. Thomas Stone to GW, January 28, 1785, *PGWCF* 2:297; Leibiger, *Founding Friendship,* 49–50.

16. GW to Patrick Henry, October 29, 1785, *PGWCF* 3:326, 327n; GW to Edmund Randolph, July 30, 1785, ibid. 3:164; TJ to GW, July 10, 1785, ibid. 3:113; Leibiger, *Founding Friendship,* 45, 56–57; Flexner, *GW* 3:76.

17. GW to Knox, January 5, 1785, *PGWCF* 2:254; GW to Greene, May 20, 1785, ibid. 3:5; GW to William Grayson, June 22, 1785, ibid. 3:69; GW to Samuel Holden Parsons, July 15, 1788, ibid. 6:379; ibid. 6:418–419n.

18. Achenbach, *The Grand Idea,* 121–137, 213–266; Kapsch, *Potomac Canal,* 68–69, 209, 211, 213, 223, 236, 238.

19. GW to Adrienne de Lafayette, April 4, 1784, *PGWCF* 1:257; GW to Knox, February 20, 1784, ibid. 1:137; GW to George William Fairfax, June 30, 1785, ibid. 3:90; GW to Jonathan Trumbull Jr., October 1, 1785, ibid. 3:290; GW to Lafayette, February 1, 1784, ibid. 1:87–89.

20. Lafayette to GW, January 10, 1784, *PGWCF* 1:27; Henry Pendleton to GW, January 10, 1784, ibid. 1:31; Elias Boudinot to GW, January 11, 1784, ibid. 1:33–34; South Carolina legislature to GW, February 10, 1784, ibid. 1:111; Thomas Lewis to GW, February 24, 1784, ibid. 1:155; Duportail to GW, March 3, 1784, ibid. 1:168; Chastellux to GW, March 6, 1784, ibid. 1:174; Nicholas Simon van Winter and Lucretia van Winter, April 10, 1784, ibid. 1:279; Marquise de La Rouërie, January 12, 1784, ibid. 1:395; Catherine Macaulay Graham, July 13, 1784, ibid. 1:185; BF to GW, September 20, 1785, ibid. 3:266.

21. Ferling, *First of Men,* 339; *DGW* 4:115, 137, 142, 147, 201.

22. GW to William Goddard, June 11, 1785, *PGWCF* 3:50.

23. GW to William Gordon, March 8, 1785, *PGWCF* 2:412; GW to Noah Webster, July 31, 1788, ibid. 6:413–415. On Gordon, see ibid. 1:177–178n.

24. *PGWCF* 1:2–4n.

25. David Humphreys to GW, September 30, 1784, January 15, 1785, *PGWCF* 2:80–82, 268–269; GW to Humphreys, July 25, 1785, ibid. 3:90.

26. Rosemarie Zagarri, ed., *David Humphreys' "Life of General Washington," with George Washington's "Remarks"* (Athens, Ga., 1991), xviii–xxi, xxvii. GW's corrections and emendations to Humphreys's rough draft can be found in GW, "Remarks" [1787–1788], *PGWCF* 5:515–526.

27. *PGWCF* 1:143–144n, 329–330n; GW to Knox, February 21, 1784, ibid. 1:229; GW to William Barton, September 7, 1788, ibid. 6:502–503; TJ to GW, April 16, 1784, November 14, 1786, ibid. 1:288–290; 4:365; Humphreys to GW, September 24, 1786, ibid. 4:264–265.

28. GW to TJ, March 29, 1784, *PGWCF* 1:237, 239; GW to Benjamin Harrison, January 18, October 10, 1784, ibid. 1:56; 2:92.

29. GW to Knox, December 5, 1784, *PGWCF* 2:171–172.

30. The quotations in the two foregoing paragraphs are from GW to George Clinton, November 25, 1784, *PGWCF* 2:145–146; GW to Knox, January 2, December 5, 1784, ibid. 1:419; 2:171–172.

31. GW to Edward Newenham, June 10, 1784, *PGWCF* 1:439; GW to Lafayette, May 10, 1786, ibid. 4:42.

32. On Great Britain's discriminatory trade policies, see John Ferling, *A Leap in the Dark: The Struggle to Create the American Republic* (New York, 2003), 257–258, 262–264.

33. Holton, *Unruly Americans*, 31–45, 66, 69, 101–102.

34. [Thomas Paine,] *Common Sense* (1776), in Philip Foner, ed., *The Complete Writings of Thomas Paine* (New York, 1945), 1:17, 45.

35. GW to JM, November 5, 1786, *PGWCF* 4:330–331. On the changes unleashed by the American Revolution, see Gordon Wood, *The Radicalism of the American Revolution* (New York, 1992).

36. GW to Grayson, July 26, 1786, *PGWCF* 4:169; GW to JM, November 5, 1786, ibid. 4:330–331.

37. GW to Henry Lee, October 31, 1786, *PGWCF* 4:318; GW to JM, November 5, 1786, ibid. 4:331.

38. *PGWCF* 3:467n.

39. Address of the Annapolis Convention [September 14, 1786], *PAH* 3:686–690.

40. GW to Humphreys, December 26, 1786, March 8, 1787, *PGWCF* 4:479; 5:72–73; GW to Jay, March 10, 1787, ibid. 5:79–80; GW to Knox, March 8, 1787, ibid. 5:74–75; Jay to GW, January 7, 1787, ibid. 4:503; Ferling, *First of Men,* 354.

41. JM to GW, February 21, March 18, 1787, *PJM* 9:285–286, 315; Leibiger, *Founding Friendship,* 63.

42. Knox to GW, October 23, 1786, *PGWCF* 4:300; GW to Knox, December 26, 1786, ibid. 4:481; GW to Humphreys, December 26, 1786, ibid. 4:478; GW to Benjamin Lincoln, February 24, 1787, ibid. 5:51–52; GW to Lafayette, March 25, 1787, ibid. 5:106.

43. Walter A. McDougall, *Freedom Just Around the Corner: A New American History, 1585–1828* (New York, 2004), 296.

44. Holton, *Unruly Americans,* 9, 10, 187, 188, 203–204; [James Madison], *The Federalist,* No. 10. The Holton quotations are on pages 187 and 188 of *Unruly Americans.*

45. Alfred F. Young, "The Framers of the Constitution and the 'Genius' of the People," *Radical History Review* 42 (1988):8–9; Gordon S. Wood, "The Localization of Authority in the 17th-Century English Colonies," *Historically Speaking* (July–August 2007): 3–5; Gordon Wood, "What America Started," *New York Review of Books* (November 8, 2007): 34, 35. For an elaboration on the movement for the Constitutional Convention and the convention itself, see Ferling, *A Leap in the Dark,* 252–308.

46. *DGW* 5:185.

47. GW to Lafayette, September 15, 1787, *PGWCF* 5:334; GW to PC, September 17, 1787, ibid. 5:330; GW to Harrison, September 24, 1787, ibid. 5:339; GW to Knox, October 15, 1787, ibid. 5:375; GW to Humphreys, October 10, 1787, ibid. 5:365.

48. Leibiger, *Founding Friendship,* 91, 93; *PGWCF* 5:340n; GW to Lincoln, February 11, 1788, ibid. 6:107; GW to JM, January 10, February 5, June 8, 1788, ibid. 6:32, 89–90, 320; GW to John Armstrong, April 25, 1788, ibid. 6:224–226; GW to Thomas Johnson, April 20, August 31, 1788, ibid. 6:217–218, 495–496; GW to James McHenry, April 27, 1788, ibid. 6:234–235; GW to Samuel Powel, January 18, 1788, ibid. 6:45–46; GW to Jay, January 20, 1788, ibid. 6:49–50; Freeman, *GW* 6:134–135.

49. Colleen A. Sheehan and Gary L. McDowell, eds., *Friends of the Constitution: Writings of the "Other" Federalists, 1787–1788* (Indianapolis, Ind., 1998), 12; Pennsylvania Packet, October 12, 1787, in John B. McMaster and Frederick D. Stone, eds., *Pennsylvania and the Federal Constitution, 1787–1788* (reprint, New York, 1970), 1:111, 117; Pennsylvania Packet, September 27, 1787, ibid. 1:135. On ratification, see Ferling, *A Leap in the Dark,* 297–312.

50. [Philadelphia] *Independent Gazeteer,* October 8, 1787, McMaster and Stone, *Pennsylvania and the Federal Constitution,* 1:159–160; Candidus, *Boston Independent Chronicle,* December 6, 1787, in Herbert J. Storing, ed., *The Complete Anti-Federalist* (Chicago, 1981), 4:128–129; *Massachusetts Gazette,* January 25, 1788, ibid. 4:224; Letters of Centinel, ibid. 2:144; *Hamshire Gazette,* April 16, 1788, ibid. 4:264; *New York Journal,* February, 14, 1788, ibid. 6:66–67.

51. GW to Lafayette, April 28 [–May 1], 1788, *PGWCF* 6:245.

52. GW to Trumbull, December 4, 1788, *PGWP* 1:158; GW to Benjamin Fishbourn, December 23, 1788, ibid. 1:198.

53. AH to GW, September [?], 1788, *PGWP* 1:23.

54. *DGW* 5:445.

55. John P. Kaminski and Jill Adair McCaughan, eds., *A Great and Good Man: George Washington in the Eyes of His Contemporaries* (Madison, Wis., 1989), 117–121.

56. Ferling, *First of Men,* 371–372; GW, First Inaugural Address, April 30, 1789, *PGWP* 2:173–177. See also the editorial note in ibid. 2:152–158. On the ceremony and Federal Hall, see Edwin G. Burrows and Mike Wallace, *Gotham: A History of New York City to 1898* (New York, 1999), 296, and Alvin M. Josephy Jr., *The American Heritage History of the Congress of the United States* (New York, 1975), 7–8, 47.

57. Burrows and Wallace, *Gotham,* 297–298.

58. GW to Lafayette, June 18, 1788, *PGWCF* 6:338.

CHAPTER 9: PRESIDENT OF THE UNITED STATES: THE FIRST TERM, 1789–1792

1. GW to JA, May 10, 1789, *PGWP* 2:247.

2. AH to GW, May 5, 1789, *PGWP* 2:211–214; JA to GW, May 17, 1789, ibid. 2:312–314.

3. Kenneth R. Bowling and Helen E. Veit, eds., *The Diary of William Maclay and Other Notes on Senate Debates* (Baltimore, Md., 1988), 342, 349; Worthington C. Ford, *The True George Washington* (Philadelphia, 1896), 174.

4. AH to GW, May 5, 1789, *PGWP* 2:212. For GW's coat of arms see Freeman, *GW* 6:77–78.

5. Forrest McDonald, *The Presidency of George Washington* (Lawrence, Kans., 1974), 28–30; John C. Miller, *The Federalist Era, 1789–1801* (New York, 1960), 5–10; Stanley

Elkins and Eric McKitrick, *The Age of Federalism* (New York, 1993), 49; John Ferling, *The First of Men: A Life of George Washington* (Knoxville, Tenn., 1988), 377. The McHenry quotation can be found in Gordon Wood, "What America Started," *New York Review of Books* (November 8, 2007): 34.

6. Ron Chernow, *Alexander Hamilton* (New York, 2004), 277; David McCullough, *John Adams* (New York, 2001), 413. The Theodorick Bland quotations can be found in Barry Schwartz, *George Washington: The Making of a Symbol* (New York, 1987), 59, 62.

7. Joseph J. Ellis, *His Excellency: George Washington* (New York, 2004), 200; GW, First Inaugural Address, April 30, 1789, *PGWP* 2:176; ibid. 2:359n.

8. HZ to GW, March 24, 1789, *PGWP* 1:441–442; Chernow, *Hamilton,* 287.

9. GW to Charles Lee, April 4, 1788, *PGWCF* 6:198.

10. Ellis, *His Excellency,* 199, 205.

11. Gary B. Nash, *The Forgotten Fifth: African-Americans in the Age of the Revolution* (Cambridge, Mass., 2006), 69–122. Nash argues that the possibility existed that slavery might have been abolished before 1800. Franklin's endorsement of the Pennsylvania Abolition Society's petition to Congress in 1790 can be found in Gary B. Nash, *Race and Revolution* (Madison, Wis., 1990), 144–145.

12. Lafayette to GW, February 5, 1783, *PGWCF* 3:121n.

13. Quoted in Nash, *Forgotten Fifth,* 103.

14. Nash, *Forgotten Fifth,* 99–100; *PGWCF* 3:357n.

15. Robert Pleasants to GW, December 11, 1785, *PGWCF* 3:449–451.

16. On GW and slavery, and the Quaker petition battle in 1790, see Joseph J. Ellis, *Founding Brothers: The Revolutionary Generation* (New York, 2000), 81–119; Ellis, *His Excellency,* 160–167, 201–202; Ferling, *First of Men,* 330–331, 474–480; Henry Wiencek, *An Imperfect God: George Washington, His Slaves, and the Creation of America* (New York, 2003), 275–278.

17. JA to GW, May 17, 1789, *PGWP* 2:313; *DGW* 5:452–453, 454, 456.

18. *DGW* 5:468.

19. Hancock to GW, October 26, 1789, *PGWP* 4:228; GW to Hancock, October 26, 1789, ibid. 4:229; Flexner, *GW* 3:230. On the tour, see *DGW* 5:460–497 and the scattered letters and notes in *PGWP* 4:198–282.

20. Five Framers at the Philadelphia Convention took notes on AH's lengthy speech. The various versions can be found in *PAH* 4:178–211. The quotations can be found in ibid. 4:186, 192.

21. Chernow, *Hamilton,* 71, 295–296. For a succinct view of what lurked in the shadows of Hamilton's thinking and in that of some of his Federalist Party followers, see Richard H. Kohn, *Eagle and Sword: The Federalists and the Creation of the Military Establishment in America, 1783–1802* (New York, 1975), 284–286.

22. For the complete report and useful editorial materials, see [Alexander Hamilton], *Report Relative to a Provision for the Support of Public Credit,* January 9, 1790, *PAH* 6:51–168. These two paragraphs draw on Max M. Edling, "'So Immense a Power in the Affairs of War': Alexander Hamilton and the Restoration of Public Credit," *WMQ* 64 (2007): 287–301. The quotation is from Edling, page 299.

23. Hamilton, *Report Relative to a Provision for the Support of Public Credit, PAH* 6:106.

24. GW, First Inaugural Address, April 30, 1789, *PGWP* 2:175.

25. Stuart Leibiger, *Founding Friendship: George Washington, James Madison and the Creation of the American Republic* (Charlottesville, Va., 1999), 97–123.

26. James Roger Sharp, *American Politics in the Early Republic: The New Nation in Crisis* (New York, 1993), 36; Leibiger, *Founding Friendship,* 124–133; John Ferling, *A Leap in the Dark: The Struggle to Create the American Republic* (New York, 2003), 321–323; Elkins and McKitrick, *Age of Federalism,* 147–151; Ellis, *His Excellency,* 207. For a thoughtful piece on the split between JM and AH, one that sees it coming earlier than in 1790, see Michael Schwarz, "The Great Divergence Reconsidered: Hamilton, Madison, and U.S. British Relations, 1783–1789," *Journal of the Early Republic* (2007): 407–436.

27. For good starting places on TJ, see Dumas Malone, *Jefferson and His Time* (Boston, 1948–1981), volumes 1 and 2. See also Merrill Peterson, *Thomas Jefferson and the New Nation* (New York, 1971); Fawn Brodie, *Thomas Jefferson: An Intimate History* (New York, 1974); Noble Cunningham, *In Pursuit of Reason: The Life of Thomas Jefferson* (Baton Rouge, La., 1987); Joseph Ellis, *American Sphinx: The Character of Thomas Jefferson* (New York, 1997); and Richard Bernstein, *Thomas Jefferson* (New York, 2003).

28. Ellis, *His Excellency,* 207.

29. Ferling, *First of Men,* 393–394.

30. William Hogeland, *The Whiskey Rebellion: George Washington, Alexander Hamilton, and the Frontier Rebels Who Challenged America's Newfound Sovereignty* (New York, 2006), 66–69.

31. Chernow, *Hamilton,* 342; [Alexander Hamilton], *First Report on the Further Provision Necessary for Establishing Public Credit,* December 13, 1790, *PAH* 7:210–236; [Alexander Hamilton], *Second Report on the Further Provision Necessary for Establishing Public Credit (Report on a National Bank),* December 13, 1790, ibid. 7:236–342. *PAH* accompanies each report with lengthy and useful editorial comments.

32. Paul Gilje, "The Rise of Capitalism in the Early Republic," *Journal of the Early Republic* 16 (1996): 162, 171.

33. Chernow, *Hamilton,* 345, 347.

34. Ibid., 349–350, 346; Ferling, *A Leap in the Dark,* 332–336.

35. Malone, *Jefferson,* 2:256–268; Ferling, *A Leap in the Dark,* 331–334.

36. TJ to GW, February 15, 1791, *PGWP* 7:348–353; Edmund Randolph to GW, February 12, 1791, ibid. 7:330–331; Edmund Randolph, Enclosure on the Constitutionality of the Bank, February 12, 1791, ibid. 7:331–340; AH, Enclosures Opinion on the Constitutionality of an Act to Establish a Bank, February 23, 1791, ibid. 7:425–452; Leibiger, *Founding Friendship,* 134–135; Ellis, *His Excellency,* 205.

37. Leibiger, *Founding Friendship,* 136.

38. GW to Gouverneur Morris, December 17, 1790, *PGWP* 7:94; GW to Humphreys, July 20, 1791, ibid. 8:359.

39. GW to Humphreys, March 16, 1791, *PGWP* 7:583.

40. The Freneau quotations can be found in Chernow, *Hamilton,* 425, and Lewis Leary, *That Rascal Freneau: A Study in Literary Failure* (reprint, New York, 1961), 199.

41. James Madison, "A Candid State of Politics," *PJM* 14:370–372; TJ to GW, May 23, 1792, *PGWP* 10:410; GW to Humphreys, July 20, 1791, ibid. 8:359; TJ to Edward Rutledge, August 25, 1791, *PTJ* 19:241–242; TJ to Henry Innes, March 13, 1791, ibid. 19:542–543.

42. TJ to GW, May 23, 1792, *PGWP* 10:408–414; Chernow, *Hamilton,* 400.

43. GW to AH, July 29, 1792, *PGWP* 10:588–592; GW to Lafayette, June 10, 1792, ibid. 10:447–448; GW to JM, May 20, 1792, ibid. 10:401; Jefferson's Conversation with Washington, July 10, 1792, ibid. 10:537.

44. *PAH* 12:163–164, 381, 383–385, 393–401, 499, 504; Elkins and McKitrick, *Age of Federalism,* 286–288; Chernow, *Hamilton,* 407.

45. GW to TJ, August 23, 1792, *PGWP* 11:30; GW to AH, August 26, 1792, ibid. 11:38–39.

46. Jefferson's Conversation with Washington, October 1, 1792, *PGWP* 11:182–185; Woody Holton, "Abigail Adams, Bond Speculator," *WMQ* 64 (2007): 837–838; Ellis, *His Excellency,* 184. Patrick Henry's quote was certainly known to GW already, having been passed on to him by the husband of a relative. See David Stuart to GW, July 14, 1789, *PGWP* 3:198–204.

47. Thomas Jefferson's Memorandum of Conversations with Washington, March 1, 1792, *PGWP* 10:6–7; Madison's Conversations with Washington, May 5 [–25], 1792, ibid. 10:351; Jefferson's Conversation with Washington, July 10, 1792, ibid. 10:535; Flexner, *GW* 3:100, 108, 414; Ferling, *First of Men,* 378, 389–390.

48. Jefferson's Memorandum of Conversations with Washington, March 1, 1792, *PGWP* 10:6; Jefferson's Conversation with Washington, July 10, 1792, ibid. 10:535; Madison's Conversation with Washington, May 5 [–25], 1792, ibid. 10:349–354; GW to JM, May 20, 1792, ibid. 10:400–401.

49. TJ to GW, May 23, 1792, *PGWP* 10:411–412.

50. Chernow, *Hamilton,* 419; AH to Tobias Lear, January 2, 1800, *PAH* 24:155.

51. AH to GW, July 30 [–August 3,] 1792, *PGWP* 10:594–596.

CHAPTER 10: ENDLESS CRISES: WASHINGTON'S SECOND TERM, 1793–1797

1. John Ferling, *The First of Men: A Life of George Washington* (Knoxville, Tenn., 1988), 424; Lafayette to GW, March 17, 1790, *PGWP* 5:243; GW to Lafayette, August 11, 1790, ibid. 6:233.

2. GW to Rochambeau, August 10, 1790, *PGWP* 6:231; GW to Humphreys, March 16, July 20, 1791, ibid. 7:584; 8:360; GW to Catherine Macaulay Graham, July 19, 1791, ibid. 8:357; GW to Lafayette, July 28, 1791, June 10, 1792, ibid. 8:378; 10:447; GW to Marquis de Ségur, May 4, 1792, ibid. 10:348; Philipp Ziesche, "Exporting American Revolutions: Gouverneur Morris, Thomas Jefferson, and the National Struggle for Universal Rights in Revolutionary France," *Journal of the Early Republic* (2006): 427.

3. Simon Schama, *Citizens: A Chronicle of the French Revolution* (New York, 1989), 514–792.

4. John Howe, *The Changing Political Thought of John Adams* (Princeton, N.J., 1966), 171; David Waldstreicher, "Federalism, The Style of Politics, and the Politics of Style," in Doran Ben-Atar and Barbara B. Oberg, eds., *Federalists Reconsidered* (Charlottesville, Va., 1998), 115–116; Chauncey Goodrich to Oliver Wolcott, February 1793, in George Gibbs, ed., *Memoirs of the Administrations of Washington and Adams, Edited from the Papers*

of Oliver Wolcott (New York, 1946), 1:88; Alexander Hamilton, "French Revolution," *PAH* 17:586–587.

5. TJ to William Short, January 3, 1793, *PTJ* 25:14; TJ to Thomas M. Randolph Jr., January 7, 1793, ibid. 25:30.

6. GW to Lafayette, June 10, 1792, *PGWP* 10:447.

7. GW to Humphreys, March 23, 1793, *PGWP* 12:362–363; Samuel Flagg Bemis, *The Jay Treaty: A Study in Commerce and Diplomacy* (New Haven, Conn., 1926), 28–50.

8. *PGWP* 12:363; GW to G. Morris, March 25, 1793, ibid. 12:380.

9. *PGWP* 12:265n; Thomas Jefferson's Notes on a Conversation with Washington, February 7, 1793, ibid. 12:107; Freeman, *GW* 7:8–9.

10. Mary Endress to GW, March 27, 1793, *PGWP* 12:384; George Wehrs to GW, January 25, 1793, ibid. 12:47–48; GW, Second Inaugural Address, March 4, 1793, ibid. 12:264–265; Thomas Jefferson's Notes on a Conversation with Washington, February 7, 1793, ibid. 12:107; Cabinet Opinion on the Administration of the Presidential Oath, February 28, March 1, 1793, ibid. 12:231–232, 242–243.

11. TJ to GW, April 7, 1793, *PGWP* 12:419–420; Tobias Lear to GW, April 8, 1793, ibid. 12:435.

12. GW to AH, April 12, 1793, *PGWP* 12:447; GW to TJ, April 12, 1793, ibid. 12:448; GW, Neutrality Proclamation, April 22, 1793, ibid. 12:472–473.

13. Freeman, *GW* 7:27–29, 33, 35; Jacob E. Cooke, *Alexander Hamilton: A Profile* (New York, 1967), 127; Thomas Jefferson, "Anas," in Paul L. Ford, ed., *Writings of Thomas Jefferson* (New York, 1892–1899), 1:224, 226–227; Alexander Hamilton and Henry Knox, Answer to Question Proposed by the President of the United States, April 18, 1793, *PAH* 14:367–408; Thomas Jefferson, Opinion on the Treaties with France, April 28, 1793, *PTJ* 25:607–618.

14. Robert E. Tucker and Daniel C. Hendrickson, *Empire of Liberty: The Statecraft of Thomas Jefferson* (New York, 1990), 53–54; Stanley Elkins and Eric McKitrick, *The Age of Federalism* (New York, 1993), 330–336.

15. Freeman, *GW* 7:44–51; TJ to JM, April 28, 1793, *PTJ* 25:619; Harry Ammon, *The Genet Mission* (New York, 1975), 54–59.

16. Genêt to TJ, June 22, 1793, *PTJ* 26:339–341; TJ to JM, August 11, 1793, ibid. 25:652.

17. John Ferling, *John Adams: A Life* (Knoxville, Tenn., 1992), 274–282.

18. GW to Lear, April 3, 1791, *PGWP* 8:49; GW to Knox, December 26, 1791, ibid. 9:324.

19. GW to Humphreys, July 20, 1791, *PGWP* 8:360; Knox to Arthur St. Clair, December 19, 1789, ibid. 5:376n; Joseph J. Ellis, *His Excellency: George Washington* (New York, 2004), 212.

20. GW to Lear, April 3, 1791, *PGWP* 8:49; GW to Knox, November 19, 1790, ibid. 6:668; Wiley Sword, *President Washington's Indian War: The Struggle for the Old Northwest, 1790–1795* (Norman, Okla., 1985), 89–130; Howard Peckham, "Josiah Harmer and His Indian Expedition," *Ohio State Archives and Historical Quarterly* 55 (1946): 227–241; Francis Paul Prucha, *The Sword of the Republic: The United States Army on the Frontier, 1783–1846* (Bloomington, Ind., 1977), 3–21; Richard H. Kohn, *Eagle*

and Sword: The Federalists and the Creation of the Military Establishment in America, 1783–1802 (New York, 1975), 97–107.

21. GW, Observations on an Intended Report, September 8, 1783, *WW* 27:140–144; GW, Sentiments on a Peace Establishment [May 1783], ibid. 26:374–398; Kohn, *Eagle and Sword,* 60–62, 73–88.

22. Quoted in Kohn, *Eagle and Sword,* 106.

23. TJ, Notes on Conversations with John Beckley and George Washington, June 7, 1783, *PTJ* 26:219–220.

24. Sword, *President Washington's Indian War,* 145–200.

25. Quoted in Sword, *President Washington's Indian War,* 201. See also *PGWP* 9:275n.

26. *PGWP* 9:425–426n, 505n.

27. *PGWP* 9:289–290n, 425n; GW, Preface to Henry Knox's Statement on the Causes of the Indian War, ca. January 25, 1792, ibid. 9:507; Kohn, *Eagle and Sword,* 107–135.

28. GW, Memorandum on General Officers, March 9, 1792, *PGWP* 10:74–78; GW to Henry Lee, June 30, 1792, ibid. 507–508. Emphasis added by the author.

29. Knox to Wayne, March 5, 1793, *PGWP* 268–69n.

30. Sean Wilentz, *The Rise of American Democracy: Jefferson to Lincoln* (New York, 2005), 40–41, 53–62. The quotation is from page 56.

31. Eugene Link, *Democratic-Republican Societies, 1790–1800* (New York, 1942), 53–69, 72; Philip S. Foner, ed., *The Democratic-Republican Societies, 1790–1800: A Documentary Sourcebook* (Westport, Conn., 1976), 19, 22.

32. Foner, *Democratic-Republican Societies,* 33–34.

33. Wilentz, *Rise of American Democracy,* 61; GW to Burgess Bell, September 25, 1794, *WW* 33:506; GW to Henry Lee, October 16, 1793, August 26, 1794, ibid. 33:133, 475–476.

34. GW to William Peace, April 6, 1794, *WW* 33:315.

35. Foner, *Democratic-Republican Societies,* 75, 134.

36. Ibid., 404, 132.

37. Freeman, *GW* 7:155–160; AH to GW, April [14], 1794, *PAH* 16:266; GW to the Senate, April 16, 1794, *WW* 33:332.

38. GW to the Senate and House of Representatives, March 28, 1794, *WW* 33:306; Wilentz, *Rise of American Democracy,* 66–67; Link, *Democratic-Republican Societies,* 130–131; Walter Stahr, *John Jay: Founding Father* (New York, 2005), 212–217, 313–319. The "Revolution in France" quotation is from Link, page 131.

39. Thomas P. Slaughter, *The Whiskey Rebellion: Frontier Epilogue to the American Revolution* (New York, 1986), 67, 88, 106–107; Elkins and McKitrick, *Age of Federalism,* 471.

40. TJ to GW, May 23, 1792, *PGWP* 10:409–410; Slaughter, *Whiskey Rebellion,* 98.

41. John Steele to GW, January 4, 1791, *PGWP* 7:181, 182n; GW to Humphreys, July 20, 1791, ibid. 8:359; TJ, "Notes of Agenda to Reduce the Government to True Principles," [ca. July 11, 1792], *PTJ* 24:215; Slaughter, *Whiskey Rebellion,* 95–105, 113–114; Robin L. Einhorn, *American Taxation, American Slavery* (Chicago, 2006), 158, 174, 187.

42. *PGWP* 8:23n; GW to Humphreys, July 20, 1791, ibid. 8:359; Ellis, *His Excellency,* 196. On the southern tour, see *DGW* 6:107–163.

43. Slaughter, *Whiskey Rebellion,* 109–124, 156, 163–164; John R. Alden, *George Washington: A Biography* (Baton Rouge, La., 1984), 261–262; GW to AH, July 29, August 5, September 7, 1792, *PGWP* 10:589, 612; 11:75–76; ibid. 11:60–61n.

44. GW, Proclamation, September 15, 1792, *PGWP* 11:122–123; Einhorn, *American Taxation, American Slavery,* 188–189.

45. Jay to AH, September 8, 1792, *PAH* 12:334–335; Rufus King to AH, September 27, 1792, ibid. 12:493; AH to Jay, September 3, 1792, ibid. 12:317; AH to GW, September 1, 1792, *PGWP* 11:59–60; GW to AH, September 17, 1792, ibid. 11:126.

46. GW, To the Ministers and Members of the Methodist and Episcopal Church in Fayette County, Pennsylvania, January 30, 1793, *PGWP* 11:63.

47. Slaughter, *Whiskey Rebellion,* 160–161; Einhorn, *American Taxation, American Slavery,* 188.

48. Foner, *Democratic-Republican Societies,* 94, 127–128, 132, 133, 135, 136; Link, *Democratic-Republican Societies,* 131, 133; Wilentz, *Rise of American Democracy,* 63.

49. Elkins and McKitrick, *Age of Federalism,* 463; Slaughter, *Whiskey Rebellion,* 179; Wilentz, *Rise of American Democracy,* 63.

50. GW to Presley Neville, June 16, 1794, *WW* 33:405–409.

51. John Ferling, *A Leap in the Dark: The Struggle to Create the American Republic* (New York, 2003), 366; Forrest McDonald, *The Presidency of George Washington* (New York, 1974), 141–142.

52. AH to GW, August 2, 5, 1794, *PAH* 17:15–17, 24–58; Slaughter, *Whiskey Rebellion,* 193.

53. GW to Henry Lee, August 26, 1794, *WW* 33:475–476; GW to Daniel Morgan, October 8, 1794, ibid. 33:542.

54. GW, Proclamation, August 7, 1794, *WW* 33:457–461.

55. AH's "Tully" essays can be found in *PAH* 17:132–135, 148–150, 159–161, 178–180. The quotations can be found on pages 134 and 160.

56. Chernow, *Alexander Hamilton,* 475.

57. Slaughter, *Whiskey Rebellion,* 217–220.

58. Jeffrey L. Pasley, *"The Tyranny of Printers": Newspaper Politics in the Early American Republic* (Charlottesville, Va., 2001), 106.

59. GW, Sixth State of the Union Address, November 19, 1794, *WW* 34:29–35; JM to TJ, November 30, 1794, *PJM* 15:396–397; TJ to JM, December 28, 1794, ibid. 15:426–428; JM to James Monroe, December 4, 1794, ibid. 15:406.

60. These two paragraphs draw on Link, *Democratic-Republican Societies,* 192–195.

61. Thomas Paine, "Letter to George Washington," in Philip S. Foner, ed., *The Complete Writings of Thomas Paine* (New York, 1945), 2:691–723. The quotations can be found on pages 693, 695, 700, 710, and 723.

62. James Tagg, *Benjamin Franklin Bache and the Philadelphia* Aurora (Philadelphia, 1991), 216–217, 219.

63. Sword, *President Washington's Indian War,* 249–311; Prucha, *Sword of the Republic,* 30–38; Paul David Nelson, *Anthony Wayne: Soldier of the Early Republic* (Bloomington, Ind., 1985), 228–283.

64. GW to Edmund Randolph, July 31, 1795, *WW* 34:266; Elkins and McKitrick, *Age of Federalism,* 403–407, 410–414. The Jay quotation is in ibid., page 413. For a more charitable evaluation of Jay's diplomacy, see Stahr, *John Jay,* 319–332.

65. AH to GW, July 9–11, 1795, *PAH* 18:452; Stuart Leibiger, *Founding Friendship: George Washington, James Madison, and the Creation of the American Republic* (Charlottesville, Va., 1999), 198; Dumas Malone, *Jefferson and His Time* (Boston, 1948–1981), 3:247.

66. GW to AH, July 3, 13, 29, October 29, 1795, *WW* 34:226–228, 237–240, 262–264, 350. AH responded with thoughts of his own in AH to GW, July 9–11, 1775, *PAH* 18:411–453. For an excellent appraisal of Washington and the Federalists in the run-up to the Senate's consideration of Jay's treaty, see Todd Estes, "Shaping the Politics of Public Opinion: Federalists and the Jay Treaty Debate," *Journal of the Early Republic* 20 (2000): 393–422; Todd Estes, "The Art of Presidential Leadership: George Washington and the Jay Treaty," *Virginia Magazine of History and Biography* 109 (2001): 127–158.

67. *PAH* 18:475–479n. The essays that AH penned under the name of "Camillus" can be found scattered through volumes 18 and 19 of ibid.

68. GW to AH, July 29, 1795, *WW* 34:262; Richard Buel, *Securing the Revolution: Ideology in American Politics* (Ithaca, N.Y., 1972), 52; TJ to James Monroe, March 2, 1796, *PTJ* 29:4; John C. Miller, *The Federalist Era, 1789–1801* (New York, 1960), 168; Elkins and McKitrick, *Era of Federalism*, 416; Donald Stewart, *The Opposition Press of the Federalist Period* (Albany, N.Y., 1969), 230; Stahr, *John Jay*, 334–338.

69. Tagg, *Benjamin Franklin Bache*, 252–253; James Roger Sharp, *American Politics in the Early Republic: The New Nation in Crisis* (New Haven, Conn., 1993), 126; Jay Winik, *The Great Upheaval: America and the Birth of the Modern World, 1788–1800* (New York, 2007), 492, 495; David Waldstreicher, "Federalism, The Styles of Politics, and the Politics of Style," in Ben-Atar and Oberg, eds., *Federalists Reconsidered*, 106.

70. Fisher Ames, Speech of April 26, 1796, in W. B. Allen, ed., *Works of Fisher Ames, as Published by Seth Ames* (Indianapolis, Ind., 1983), 2:1143–1182; Ferling, *A Leap in the Dark*, 387–388.

71. GW to Jay, December 21, 1795, *WW* 34:397; Barry Schwartz, *George Washington: The Making of an American Symbol* (New York, 1987), 67; TJ to JM, September 21, 1796, *PTJ* 28:475; Chernow, *Alexander Hamilton*, 499.

72. Quoted in Estes, "Art of Presidential Leadership," *Virginia Magazine of History and Biography* 109 (2001):155.

73. GW to Thomas Pinckney, May 22, 1796, *WW* 35:62; Liebiger, *Founding Friendship*, 209; Ellis, *His Excellency*, 232; Malone, *Jefferson and His Time*, 3:308–311.

74. Samuel Flagg Bemis, *Pinckney's Treaty: America's Advantage from Europe's Distress, 1783–1800* (Baltimore, 1926).

75. TJ, "Anas," in Paul L. Ford, ed., *Writings of Thomas Jefferson* (New York, 1988), 1:68; GW to Edmund Pendleton, January 22, 1795, *WW* 34:98; GW to Jay, May 8, 1796, ibid. 35:37; Ferling, *First of Men*, 411, 421, 445–447, 491, 504.

76. GW to Oliver Wolcott, July 6, 1796, *WW* 35:126. On GW's response to criticism, see GW to Edmund Randolph, July 29, 1795, ibid. 34:256; GW to Wolcott, February 1, July 6, 1796, ibid. 34:447; 35:126; GW to Humphreys, June 26, 1796, ibid. 35:102; GW to TJ, July 6, 1796, ibid. 35:119, 120.

77. GW, Eighth Annual Address to Congress, December 7, 1796, *WW* 35:310–320.

78. GW to AH, May 15, August 25, September 2, 6, 1796, *WW* 35:48–51, 190–192,

199–201, 204–220; AH, Draft of GW's Farewell Address, *PAH* 20:265–288; "Introductory [Editor's] Note," ibid. 20:169–173; Chernow, *Alexander Hamilton,* 505–506.

79. GW, Farewell Address, September 19, 1796, *WW* 35:214–238.

80. JM to James Monroe, September 29, 1796, *PJM* 17:403.

81. For a brief history of the election of 1796, see John Ferling, *Adams vs. Jefferson: The Tumultuous Election of 1800* (New York, 2004), 83–94. The quotation can be found on page 85.

82. Bernard Mayo, *Myths and Men: Patrick Henry, George Washington, Thomas Jefferson* (Athens, Ga., 1959), 36.

83. Ferling, *John Adams,* 338.

CHAPTER 11: THE SAND RUNS OUT

1. GW to Wolcott, May 15, 1797, *PGWRT* 1:142; GW to James McHenry, April 3, 1797, ibid. 1:71; GW to Sarah Cary Fairfax, May 16, 1798, ibid. 2:272; GW to Tobias Lear, March 25, 1797, ibid. 1:50; GW to Robert Lewis, January 26, 1798, ibid. 2:47–48; Editor's Note, ibid. 2:127n; William Hogeland, *The Whiskey Rebellion: George Washington, Alexander Hamilton, and the Frontier Rebels Who Challenged America's Newfound Sovereignty* (New York, 2006), 68–70.

2. GW to James Anderson, February 6–7, 1798, October 1, December 13, 1799, *PGWRT* 2:74–75; 4:331–333, 455; GW to Wolcott, June 7, July 3, 1797, ibid. 1:172–173, 234–235; GW to Israel Shreve, September 1, 1797, 1799, ibid. 1:334–335; GW to Alexander Addison, November 24, 1799, ibid. 4:423; Editor's Note, ibid. 4:112–113n; GW to John Mason, January 2, 1798, December 8, 1799, ibid. 2:1–2; 4:447; GW to Clement Biddle, May 28, 1798, ibid. 2:301.

3. See John Ferling: *A Leap in the Dark: The Struggle to Create the American Republic* (New York, 2003), 405–435.

4. GW to AH, August 21, October 8, 1797, *PGWRT* 1:313, 388; AH to GW, August 28, 1797, May 19, 1789, ibid. 1:322–323; 2:279–281.

5. GW to AH, May 27, 1798, *PGWRT* 2:297–299.

6. AH to GW, May 19, June 2, 1798, *PGWRT* 2:280–281, 310; GW to AH, May 27, 1798, ibid. 2:297–299.

7. AH to King, August 22, 1798, *PAH* 22:154; AH to Harrison Gray Otis, January 26, 1799, ibid. 22:441; AH to Francisco de Miranda, August 22, 1798, ibid. 22:156.

8. For a different view of Hamilton during this episode, see Aaron N. Coleman, "'A Second Bounaparty?': A Reexamination of Alexander Hamilton During the Franco-American Crisis, 1796–1801," *Journal of the Early Republic* 28 (2008): 183–214.

9. Timothy Pickering to GW, July 6, 1798, *PGWRT* 2:387.

10. JA to GW, June 22, 1798, *PGWRT* 2:351–352; GW to JA, July 4, 1798, ibid. 2:368–371.

11. AH to GW, August 1, 1798, *PGWRT* 2:467; GW to AH, August 9, 1798, ibid. 2:501; GW to JA, July 13, 1798, ibid. 2:402–404.

12. JA to McHenry, August 29, September 30, 1798, *PAH* 22:8n, 16n; GW to JA, September 25, 1798, *PGWRT* 3:36–43.

13. TJ to Thomas M. Randolph, February 2, 1800, *PTJ* 31:358; Alexander DeConde, *The Quasi-War: The Politics and Diplomacy of the Undeclared War with France, 1797–1801* (New York, 1966), 97; AA to JA, January 28, 1797, *Adams Papers, 1639–1889,* microfilm edition, 608 reels (Boston: Massachusetts Historical Society, 1954–1959), reel 383.

14. JA to Benjamin Rush, January 25, 1806, September [?], 1807, December 4, 1805, in John A. Schutz and Douglass Adair, eds., *The Spur of Fame: Dialogues of John Adams and Benjamin Rush, 1805–1813* (San Marino, Calif., 1966), 48, 92, 45; James Parton, *The Life and Times of Aaron Burr* (reprint, New York, 1967), 235.

15. Ron Chernow, *Alexander Hamilton* (New York, 2004), 385.

16. Ibid., 293, 360, 362, 364–370, 409–418, 425–429, 529–546.

17. GW, "Circular to the States," June 8, 1783, *WW* 26:485, 486.

18. JA to Rush, September 30, 1805, Schutz and Adair, *Spur of Fame,* 42; John Ferling, *John Adams: A Life* (Knoxville, Tenn., 1992), 424.

19. For expanded accounts of Adams's role in the crisis, see Ferling, *A Leap in the Dark,* 437–449, and Ferling, *John Adams,* 348–395.

20. GW to James McHenry, August 10, September 14, 16, October 23, 1798, *PGWRT* 2:509–510, 610–612; 3:4–5, 132; GW to Timothy Pickering, September 9, 1798, ibid. 2:596–599.

21. TJ to JM, January 8, 1797, *PTJ* 29:255.

22. GW to McHenry, October 1, 1798, January 27, February 10, March 25, May 13, July 7, 1799, *PGWRT* 3:65, 342–343, 364–365, 438–443; 4:70–72, 177–179; GW to James McAlpin, May 12, 1799, ibid. 4:67.

23. GW to Timothy Pickering, October 18, 1798, November 3, 1799, *PGWRT* 3:108–109; 4:384; GW to John Trumbull, June 25, August 30, 1799, ibid. 4:157, 275.

24. Gouverneur Morris to JA, December 9, 1799, *PGWRT* 4:452; Ferling, *A Leap in the Dark,* 443, 445–446; Joseph J. Ellis, *His Excellency, George Washington* (New York, 2004), 250.

25. Trumbull to GW, June 22, August 10, 1799, *PGWRT* 4:144, 236; G. Morris to GW, December 9, 1799, ibid. 4:452–453. GW never read Morris's letter. He died before it reached Mount Vernon.

26. GW to Trumbull, July 21, August 30, 1799, *PGWRT* 4:202–203, 275–276.

27. Peter Kolchin, *American Slavery, 1619–1877* (New York, 1993), 63–92.

28. GW to John Francis Mercer, September 9, 1786, *PGWCF* 4:243.

29. GW to Arthur Young, November 9, 1794, *WW* 34:21; Flexner, *GW* 4:432–434.

30. GW to Lear, April 12, 1791, *PGWP* 8:84–86; Henry Wiencek, *An Imperfect God: George Washington, His Slaves, and the Creation of America* (New York, 2003), 311–317.

31. GW to AH, May 27, 1798, *PGWRT* 2:297; GW to Anderson, September 16, 1798, ibid. 3:1–3; John Ferling, *The First of Men: A Life of George Washington* (Knoxville, Tenn., 1988), 505.

32. Letter from the Yeomanry of Massachusetts, (January 25, 1788), in Herbert J. Storing, ed., *The Complete Anti-Federalist* (Chicago, 1981), 4:224; James Tagg, *Benjamin Franklin Bache and the Philadelphia* Aurora (Philadelphia, 1991), 277.

33. George Washington's Last Will and Testament [July 9, 1799], *PGWRT* 4:479–492. The quotation can be found on page 480. For an excellent brief survey

of Washington and slavery, see Peter Henriques, *Realistic Visionary: A Portrait of George Washington* (Charlottesville, Va., 2006), 145–165.

34. *DGW* 6:374; GW to McHenry, November 5, 1799, *PGWRT* 4:392; GW to Addison, November 24, 1799, ibid. 4:423; GW to Trumbull, June 25, 1799, ibid. 4:158.

35. John Ferling, *Adams vs. Jefferson: The Tumultuous Election of 1800* (New York, 2004), 127; Stanley Elkins and Eric McKitrick, *The Age of Federalism* (New York, 1993), 727.

36. TJ to Archibald Stuart, February 13, 1799, *PTJ* 31:35; TJ to Edmund Pendleton, February 14, 1799, ibid. 31:36.

37. *DGW* 6:378.

38. See Tobias Lear, Narrative Accounts of George Washington, December 14, 15, 1799, *PGWRT* 4:542–552. The best narrative and analysis of GW's demise is Peter Henriques, *The Death of George Washington: He Died as He Lived* (Mount Vernon, Va., 2000), and Henriques, *Realistic Visionary,* 187–204.

39. Quoted in Henriques, *Realistic Visionary,* 197.

RECKONING

1. TJ to John Dickinson, March 6, 1801, *PTJ* 33:196; TJ to Paine, March 18, 1801, ibid. 33:358–359.

INDEX

Washington, Augustine (father), 9, 10
Washington, Augustine (half-brother),
  36–37
Washington, D.C.:
  construction of, 294, 306
  location of, 294–95, 298
Washington, George:
  as "above politics," xviii, xx, 5, 65, 87,
    163–64
  achievements of, 44–45, 171–72, 303, 347
  adolescence of, 10–13
  aging, 246, 273, 347, 364
  ambition of, 6, 9, 12, 14, 21, 27, 30, 37–39,
    41, 50, 56, 70, 75, 108, 368
  biographers of, xix–xxi, 257
  birthday celebrated, 4, 172–73, 313, 346, 349
  and canal project, 250–55, 258, 261
  "Circular to the States" by, 238–39, 272
  and the Constitution, 266, 267–73
  courage under fire, 29, 30, 44, 89, 155
  critics of, 25, 35–36, 43, 89, 119, 120,
    131–32, 135, 139, 141–44, 146, 148–49,
    153–56, 161–64, 176, 178, 180, 207–8,
    229, 272–73, 324, 326, 328, 333–34,
    338–40, 344, 347, 364, 371
  damage control by, 22, 24–25
  death of, xviii, 1, 365–66
  debts of, 55–57, 69
  depressions of, 115–16, 117
  early adulthood of, 13–14, 27
  eulogies for, 3–5
  as Father of His Country, 173, 312–13, 338
  finances of, 242, 243, 247–48, 260, 370
  first taste of combat, 22, 30
  at Fort Necessity, 23–24, 26, 28, 59; *see also*
    French and Indian War
  as gambler, 31, 38, 72, 129, 247
  health problems of, 41–42, 56, 305
  historians' views of, xix–xx, 143
  and House of Burgesses, 47–54, 59, 60, 66,
    67–69, 260, 368
  inaugural addresses of, 276–77
  land interests of, 32, 42, 57–66, 71, 73–74,
    76, 79, 88, 240, 248–51, 260, 329, 330,
    331–32, 351
  as land surveyor, 12–13, 14, 15, 65
  leadership skills of, 6, 32, 44, 85, 124, 148,
    155–56, 235, 284–85, 369, 370
  lifestyle of, 56, 87, 144, 193, 245, 280, 363,
    364
  luck of, 367–68
  memorial services for, 1–6
  military lessons learned by, 27, 28, 123

  military skills of, 52, 123, 142, 154, 171–72,
    284, 371
  mission to Ohio Country, 15–18
  mythology of, xvii, 6, 125, 143, 156, 174,
    216, 338, 372–73
  and Newburgh Affair, 232–35, 238, 239, 283,
    354
  papers of, 256–57, 261–62, 351
  personal traits of, 4–6, 13, 14, 30, 33, 44,
    52–53, 57, 79, 86, 100, 154–56, 278,
    280–81, 345–46, 369
  physical appearance of, 13–14, 79, 280
  as planter, 32, 43, 55–57, 67, 69, 260, 286; *see
    also* Mount Vernon
  political appointments of, 12–13, 282–84,
    334–35, 352
  political connections of, 13, 32, 40, 47,
    48–49, 50–51, 60, 368
  political lessons learned by, 26, 32–33,
    35–37, 45, 60
  political skills of, xxi, 30, 66, 93, 98–103,
    107, 123–26, 166, 171, 234–35, 251–52,
    260, 342–43, 345, 371–72
  politics as distressing to, 305–6, 361–62,
    371
  portraits of, 72–73, 88, 256
  as president, *see* President, U.S.
  properties of, 9, 13, 32
  public image of, xviii–xix, xx, 5, 29, 32–33,
    49, 73, 77, 87, 88–89, 125, 148, 157, 164,
    171–74, 182, 239, 255, 268, 306, 368,
    370
  radical transformation of, 68–71, 75, 87–89,
    237–39, 265, 270, 346
  and retirement, 255–58, 311–12, 351–54,
    361–62, 370
  scapegoats of, 25, 34, 43, 66, 119–20, 132,
    135–37, 319, 368
  schooling of, 9, 98
  self-serving reports by, 29, 37–38, 121–23,
    256
  self-study by, 11–12
  "Sentiments on a Peace Establishment" by,
    238
  slaves of, 9, 27, 30, 32, 55, 57, 201–2, 272,
    286, 362–64
  social activities of, 38, 72, 76, 225, 243–44,
    349–50
  strong central government sought by,
    258–67, 272, 316–17
  as untouchable, 163, 180–81, 182, 273
  and Virginia Regiment, *see* Virginia
    Regiment

A Note on the Author

John Ferling is professor emeritus of history at the University of West Georgia. A leading authority on American Revolutionary history, he is the author of nine books, including *Adams vs. Jefferson: The Tumultuous Election of 1800; The First of Men: A Life of George Washington;* and the award-winning *A Leap in the Dark: The Struggle to Create the American Republic.* His most recent work, *Almost a Miracle: The American Victory in the War of Independence,* was an award winner and history bestseller. He and his wife, Carol, live in metropolitan Atlanta.